William J. Lowenberg

The registers of the parish church of Bury in the County of Lancasrter.

Christenings, burials, & weddings - Vol. 2

William J. Lowenberg

The registers of the parish church of Bury in the County of Lancasrter.
Christenings, burials, & weddings - Vol. 2

ISBN/EAN: 9783337724320

Printed in Europe, USA, Canada, Australia, Japan

Cover: Foto ©ninafisch / pixelio.de

More available books at **www.hansebooks.com**

Lancashire Parish Register Society.

The Registers
OF THE
Parish Church of Bury.

The Registers

OF THE

Parish Church of Bury

IN THE

County of Lancaster

Christenings, Burials, and Weddings
1617—1646

Transcribed and Edited by the late
REV. W. J. LÖWENBERG
Vicar of St. Peter's, Bury,
and
HENRY BRIERLEY
Registrar of the County Court, Wigan.

Printed by permission of the Rev. Foster Grey Blackburne, Rector of Bury and Hon. Canon of Manchester.

Rochdale:
Printed for the Lancashire Parish Register Society,
by James Clegg, at the Aldine Press

1901

Preface.

There is nothing to add by way of General Preface to that which precedes the first portion of the Bury Registers already issued as Vol. I. of the Lancashire Parish Register Society's publications. We have now in print the whole of the first original volume of the Bury Registers.

It has been a melancholy pleasure to see the first Secretary's manuscript gradually come into print and one would gladly—remembering Mr. Löwenberg's splendid accuracy—have issued a volume absolutely free from error of every kind. Human nature is however always fallible and it is sad to discover that in a few instances wrong contraction forms have crept into the printing. Perhaps, however, the infinite pains which our members, Mr. Arrowsmith and Mr. Taberner, have taken with the Index—which it will be noted is an Index to both Parts I. and II. of "Bury" issue—will help to condone any typographical errors. In future, too, it will be well to incorporate the Episcopal Transcripts in the body of the volume. As in this volume this has not been done a separate Index of any variations and additions supplied by these Transcripts is appended, and it is hoped that the table of Errata covers any mistakes made.

Nothing now remains but to express sincere gratitude to Canon Blackburne of Bury, who has furnished every facility for access to the original Register, with which every scrap of proof has been carefully collated, and to hope that any shortcoming in this volume may be charged solely against the surviving Editor.

Table of Contents.

	PAGES.
PREFACE . . .	v.—vi.
CHRISTENINGS	205—280
BURIALS	281—350
WEDDINGS . .	351—372
INDEX OF SURNAMES AND CHRISTIAN NAMES	373—440
,, PLACES . . .	441—450
., TRADES, ETC. . .	451—453
EPISCOPAL TRANSCRIPTS .	454—462
INDEX TO EPISCOPAL TRANSCRIPTS .	463—466
ERRATA .	467

The Registers of the Parish of Bury.

CHRISTENINGS.
1617.

Alice dau. of James Aynsworth of Holcom ...	28 March
Katherine dau. of Will Romsbothome de Holc.	30 ,,
Mary dau. of Lawrence Allanes de Cockey ...	
Josua son of Larence Nabbe	
Alice daughr of Robte Holte de fowle	
Michaal son of Gabriell Wolsenholme de Hasl.	6 Aprilis
Margaret dau. of George Holte de tott.	
Mary dau. of Will Haworth de Woodgate hill...	23 ,,
Mary dau. of Jeffrey Lomax de Heape	
Mary dau. of James Brearley	
John son of John Sharphous of Aynsw.	27 ,,
James son of John Brook de Tott.	
Isabell dau. of Rich' Leach de Wham ...	
Mary dau. of Edmond Kaye de Shuttl	
John son of Joseph Ored de Bury	4 Maij
Isabell dau. of Thomas Whitehead de B. ...	
Anne dau. of Edmond Holte de B.	8 ,,
Roger son of Thomas Cockshead	
Priscilla dau. of James Lomax	
Richard son of Edmond Smethurst	12 ,,
Elizabeth dau. of Frauncis Wood	
Susan dau. of John Kaye de B.	16 ,,
Alice dau. of Robte Leach de Bury	18 ,,
Anne dau. of Lawrence Bury	25 ,,
Elizabeth dau. of Richard Crosley of B.	8 Junij
Mary dau. of Samuell Makyn of Hey	
Nicholas son of Richard Rasthorne de Hol. ...	15 ,,
Mary dau. of John Grenehalgh de B.	
Sara dau. of Richard Toothill of Elt. ...	
Henry son of Mathew Jackson	
John son of Thomas Booth	
Richard son & Mary dau. of Bartholomew Smethurst	
John son of Thomas Birch de Cockey	
Mary dau. of James Holte de B.	22 ,,
John son of Edward Lomax de Heywood ...	
Katherine dau. of Wm Rasthorne de Somp	26 ,,
Elizabeth dau. of John Booth de Holc.	

B

Ralphe son of Wm Rushton de Elton	4	Julij
Ann dau. of Richard Booth de Elton	6	,,
Roger son of Thomas Fletcher de Reds.	20	,,
Caleb son of Robte Benson de B.		
Elizabeth dau. of Richard Haslome de Reds....	23	,,
Anne dau. of Robte Butterworth de Bamf. ...		
Mary dau. of John Whitehead de Ratcl.		
Katherine dau. of Ralph Nuttall de Tott. ...		
Richard son of James Barlowe of Heape ...	31	,,
Mary dau. of Edmond Kaye of Bury		
Elizabeth dau. of Abraham Bridge	7	Augusti
Sara dau. of James Hunt of Tott	10	,,
John son of John Byrom of Heywood		
Mary dau. of James Grenehalgh of Bury ...		
Emar son of John Roydes [of] Holc'	14	,,
Robte son of Tho. Barlow of Redds.		
Thomas son of Peter Seddon of Holc.	18	,,
Mary dau. of Roger Fletcher of Elton		
Elizabeth dau. of Richard Rasthorne of Holc....		
b Alice dau. of John Morrice of Bolton & Mary Holte of Lomax		
John son of Robte Hardman of Holc.	24	,,
Abraham son of Mich. Bentley		
b Anne dau. of Alice Sharphouse		
John son of John Wormald of Heyw.	30	,,
James son of Rich' Sydall of B.		
Alice dau. of Roger Booth of B.		
John son of Robte Smethurst of Walmᵒ ...		
Mathew son of Oliuᵒ Booth of Elton		
John son of John Hilton	7	Septembris
Mary dau. of Jeremy Aynsworth	14	,,
Mary dau. of James Kirshaw	21	,,
Roger son of Ralph Vnsworth		
John son of George Nuttall	28	,,
Dorathie & Jane filiae Riči Rothwell		
Sara dau. of James Milles of Hey.		
Richard son of James Lomax of Bolt.		
Elizabeth dau. of Edmond Leach of Shuttl. ...	5	Octobris
James son of Samuell Kay of Elton		
Thomas son of Frauncis Warburton of Stubb ...	12	,,
Peter son of Rich. Brooke of Bury*	19	,,
Mary dau. of Richard Booth of Holc.		
John son of John Hardman of Heyw.	26	,,
James son of Rich. Grenehalgh of Tott.		
Alice dau. of John Nuttall of Holc.	9	Novembris
Elizabeth dau. of Robte Fletcher of Redd. ...		
Robte & Tho' twins of Jo. Grenehalgh of Brand. Esqr.	16	,,

* "Bury" in a later hand, apparently over an earlier "B"

CHRISTENINGS.

Mary dau. of Lawrence Lorte señ of Bury	...	Novembris
John son of Peter Clough of Bury	...	
Elizab. dau. of Edmond Booth of Redds.	...	
John son of Thomas Haworth	...	
Grace dau. of George Heaton of Hey.	...	
John son of John Bridge of Holc.	...	30 ,,
James son of Jeremy Barlow de Croych	...	7 Decembris
Susan dau. of John Wrigley of Heyw.	...	
Thomas son of Robte Livesey	...	14 ,,
Wiħm son of Wiħm Morrice	...	21 ,,
Margaret dau. of John Lomax of Elton	...	21 ,,
Rich' and Jane twines of John Fletcher	...	
Ellen dau. of Ralphe Nuttall of Tott.	...	28 ,,
Anne dau. of Richard Romsbothome of B.	...	
John son of Richard Duckworth of Elt.	...	
Roger son of Roger Kaye de Brodecarre	...	1 Januarij
James son of Charles Leach of Bamford	...	4 ,,
Alice dau. of Abrah: Kaye of Bury	...	11 ,,
b Elizabeth dau. of Ric. Rosco & Elizab Gee	...	15 ,,
Roger son of Josuah Holte	...	18 ,,
Ellen dau. of James Eccarsell	...	
Robte son of John Haworth of Birk.	...	
b Charles son of Charls Butterworth and Alice Holte of Bury	...	20 ,,
Alexand⁹ son of Thomas Heyward	...	25 ,,
Elleno⁹ dau. of John Allens	...	
Ellen dau. of Wiħm Yate of Bu:	...	
Jeremy son of Wm̃ Stott of Heyw.	...	1 Februarij
Thomas son of Abell Woolsenholme...	...	
Katherine dau. of Frauncis Medoweroft	...	eod. die
Samuell son of James Scholefeild	...	
Edmond son of James Wood of Heape	...	8 ,,
Ellen dau. of Oliu⁹ Chadwicke	...	15 ,,
Elleno' dau. of Robte Booth of Bu:	...	
Elizab dau. of Roger Nuttall of Fear	...	
b James son of James Haworth & Susan Livesey		16 ,,
Richard son of John Vnsworth of Holc.	...	18 ,,
Anne dau. of Zachary Bridge	...	22 ,,
Isabell dau. of Tho. Anderton of Wal.	...	
Elizabeth dau. of Peter Fletcher of Bu.	...	
Richard son of Rich. Grime of Walm⁹	...	
b Thurstan son of Wm̃ Rastorne of Elt.	...	
John son of Miles Holme of Walm⁹	...	1 Marche
Ralph son of Robte Crompton	...	
Edmond son of Abrah. Kaye of Elton	...	
b John son of Richard Holte & Jane Aynsworth		
Richard son of John Heywood eodem die.		
Richard son of John Wood of Birk.	...	8 ,,
James son of Thomas Smyth of Bury	...	

Roger son of Richard Heald of Redds. ...	15	Marche
John son of John Jenkinson		
Francis son of Rich' Booth of Totting. ...	22	,,
Edward son of Thomas Brooke of Tott. ...		
John son of Thomas Buckley		
Alice dau. of Edmond Seddon of Heape		
Susan dau. of Richard Tayler of Birk. ...		

1618.

Thomas son of Thomas Fletcher of Heathy ...	30	Marche
b Elizabeth dau. of Richard Howorth of Holcom̄		
Elizabeth dau. of Richard Anderton and Anne Holte of Bury		
John son of Michaell Sale	5	Aprilis
Alice dau. of James Grenehalghe		
John son of Richard Hey collier		
Roger son of Roger Grenehalghe		
Mary dau. of Roger Booth of Redd.	6	,,
Anne dau. of Giles Rothwell		
b Alice dau. of James Milnes and Alice Scolefeld	23	,,
Alice dau. of John Wiggan	19	,,
Alice & Isabell gemini Geo. Emerson	26	,,
Hughe son of Hughe Seddon	3	Maij
John son of Richard Lomax wynd		
Peter son of John Walworke		
Fo. 59 Richard son of Willm Hargraves of Bury ...	10	,,
Alice dau. of James Holte of Bury		
b Marie dau. of Elizabeth Hunt of Bury* ...		
Isabell dau. of Thomas Nuttall of Bury † ...	23	,,
James son of John Hardman	24	,,
James son of Tho. Kaye of Hole.		
Richard son of John Kirkman		
James son of Symon Barlowe of Croch: ...	31	,,
Willm son of John Isherwood of Tott.		
Elizabeth dau. of Ellis Haworth of Edenf. ...	7	Junij
Edmond son of Lawrence Lorte		
Mary dau. of Henry Dunstier iunior	14	,,
Mary dau. of John Hynde of Tott.		
Frauncis son of Frauncis Pilkington		
Margarett dau. of Roger Lomas of Pils. ...		
Susan dau. of Richard Tayler of Hey.	27	,,
Tho. son of Willm Dickenson of Birkle ...		
Richard son of Richard Duckworth of B. ...	5	Julij
Robte son of John Hunte of Walmᵒ		
Robert son of Robte Lomax of Bury	12	,,
Mary dau. of James Lomax		
Elizabeth dau. of Robte Anderton of B.		

* In a different handwriting. † Inserted after the following entries.

1618 CHRISTENINGS.

Mary dau. of Thomas Hamer of W:	Julij
John son of Arthure Scolefeld iunior	19 ,,
Dyonis son of Edmond Kaye of Sh:	
James son of Thomas Pacocke of Hole.	23 ,,
Edward son of Rich: Rasthorne of Shutt.	26 ,,
Willm son of Rich. Shippobothome of Hole.	2 Augusti
Susan dau. of Arthure Kay de Houghe	
James son of James Openshawe de B.	
Elizab dau. of Thomas Pilkington	
Susan dau. of John Kaye de Woodr.	9 ,,
Robte son of James Hardman de Redds.	
Thomas son of Willm Haslome de Redds.	
Mary dau. of Jeffery Feildinge	
Willm son of Robte Kenian	16 ,,
Elizabeth dau. of Richard Shawe de Bamf.	23 ,,
Anne dau. of James Kaye de Bawds.	30 ,,
Ellis son of Richard Fletcher de Elton	6 Septembris
Elizab dau. of Alexander Clegge	
John son of Edmond Fenton	13 ,,
Anne dau. of Richard Crosley	
Mary dau. of John Aynsworth of Ch:	20 ,,
Elizabeth dau. of Robte Kay de Bent.	23 ,,
Ellen dau. of Rich. Kaye de Hawsh	
Judeth dau. of John Warburton	5 Octobris
Ellen dau. of Robte Farneworth	
Anne dau. of Robte Kaye of Bentlum	
Mary dau. of Richard Overall	
Elizabeth dau. of Ralph Bridge	
Robte son of James Fogge	15 ,,
Anne dau. of Rich. Wood of Tott.	25 ,,
Susan dau. of John Aspinall	1 Novembris
Anne dau. of Rich. Leach of Shutl.	4 ,,
Richard son of Thomas Walker	8 ,,
James son of Peter Toothill de B.	15 ,,
Tho. & Anne gemini Tho. Rigby	
Mary dau. of Daniell Allens	22 ,,
Alice dau. of Tho. Nuttall of Hole.	
Ellen dau. of Richard Booth de Booth*	
John son of Richard Grenehalghe de Fearnes	13 Decembris
Susan dau. of Robte Crossley de Heyw.	
Edward son of Tho. Hynde of Elton	
Mary dau. of Tho. Nuttall of Hole.	
Edward son of John Croston	26 ,,
Thomas son of John Whitehead	
Mary dau. of Jefferey Lomax	
Richard son of Charles Nuttall of Hole.	6 Januarij

* In the right hand margin, in different handwriting, but apparently contemporary, is this entry, "Bartholomew Stones nat November yᵉ xviij, 1618."

Jane dau. of James Scholefeild	17	Januarij
Margarett dau. of Richard Duckworth ...		
Mary dau. of Owen Bury		
Roger son of Richard Kaye de Widdell	24	,,
John son of John Fenton		
Ric. son of Ric. Banister Bury eodem.*		
Richard son of John Bridge fil. Ralp. ...		
Anne dau. of George Haworth		
John son of Richard Kaye		
Mary dau. of Roger Kaye de Birdh : ...		
Thomas son of James Haworth & Anne Bexwicke a Bast.	26	,,
Richear † son of Richard Banister	31	,,
Mary dau. of Henry Pilkinton		
Joseph son of Abraham Cowpe	2	Februarij
Elizabeth dau. of Peter Lomax	7	,,
Mary dau. of Henry Nuttall de Hole. ...	14	,,
Isabell dau. of Robte Nabbe of Bury ...		
Thomas son of Thomas Turner	18	,,
Susan dau. of Roger Smethurst	21	,,
Ralph. son of John Barlowe of Wal. ...		
Richard son of Richard Nuttall of Tott :...	28	,,
Thomas son of Ralph Sheppard		
Sarah dau. of Richard Fildes		
Oliuer son of Oliver Lomax	7	Martij
Anne dau. of John Alton of Redds. ...		
Edmond son of Rich. Haslome of Elton ...		
Thomas son of Rich. Nuttall of Tott. ...		
John son of Samuell Grene		
Willm son of Willm Rasthorne		
Elizabeth dau. of Emar Aynsworth	14	,,
Elizabeth dau. of Joh : Heywood		
Alice dau. of John Medowcrofte of Bamf :	21	,,
Eliz : dau. of John Tayler of Walm⁹sley		
Tho : son of John Wood of Tott :		
James son of Edmond Benson		
Francis son of James Toothill		
Ellen dau. of Lawrence Horrocks ...		
Mary dau. of Joh : Wardle of Birk. ...		

‡ Hu : Watmoughe
George Nuttall
Richard Rosthorne
Edmund Ashworth
Richard Houlden
Peter Lomas
Robert Shepert

* Written in the margin, in another handwriting, but apparently contemporary.
† "Mary d." crossed out and "Richear" written below.
‡ The names of the churchwardens seem to be in the same handwriting.

1619.

	Jane dau. of John Medowcrofte of Bamford ...	29	Martij
	John son of Roḃte Duckworth of Heape		
	Ellyn dau. of Frauncis Haworth of Bury ...		
	Francis son of Willm Whitakers of Walmᵒ ..	4	Aprilis
	Alice dau. of John Romsbothome butcher ...		
b	Nathaniell son of James Haworth & Burton wife	5	,,
	Hamlett son of Willm Lawe of Holcome	11	,,
	James son of Robert Sheppard of Ches. ...		
	Mary dau. of Thomas Smyth of Elton ...		
61	Thomas son of Richard Seddon of Heape	18	,,
	Thomas son of Richard Whitehead of Bury ...		
	Anne dau. of John Hoyle	23	,,
	Awdry* dau. of Peter Romsbothome of Elton		
	Elizabeth dau. of Henry Dunstier senᵒ	26	,,
	Sara dau. of Edmond Seddon		
	Mary dau. of John Booth of Walmᵒsley		
	John son of John Brooke		
	Thomas son of James Smethurst		
	Elizabeth dau. of Ellis Haslome of Wal:		
	John son of George Bradshawe of Tott. ...	2	Maij
	Peter son of James Lomax of Castlehill	9	,,
	Thomas son of Thomas Goddard of Elton	16	,,
	Elizabeth dau. of John Kaye de Banklam		
	Alice dau. of Edmond Holte of Lees ...		
	Mary dau. of John Booth of Walmᵒsley	23	,,
	Sara dau. of Isaacke Royde of Holcome		
	Roger son of Edward Halliwell of Bury ...	30	,,
	Roḃte son of James Kaye of Croshall		
	Jane dau. of Roḃte Leach		
	Richard son of Richard Rastorne de Lum̃e	6	Julij
	James son of Richard Kaye de Sheephey		
	Willm son of Richard Heyward of Bury ...		
	Frauncis son of James Grenehalgh of Bury	13	,,
	Katherine dau. of Richard Jones of Heape		
	Anne dau. of James Kaye of Holcome ...	20	,,
	John son of Ruben Haworth ...		
	John son of Thomas Worsley		
	Mary dau. of James Sheppard of Chessome	27	,,
	Anne dau. of Francis Grenehalgh of Heape ...	27	,,
	George son of Thomas Brooke of Aynsworth ...		
	Mary dau. of John Rastorne of Holcome	4	Julij
	Elizabeth dau. of John Hinde of Elton ...	11	,,
	John son of John Allens of Aynsworth		
	James son of John Stott of Heywood ...	18	,,
	John son of Richard Leach of Ashworth		
	Alice dau. of David Naden	25	,,

* "Alice" is crossed out and "Awdry" written over it.

Edward son of Andrew Holte		Julij
Alice and Dorothie daus. of Thomas Buckley		
b Richard son of Thomas Wilkinson of Walm^ssley and Alice Vnsworth	30	,,
Elizabeth dau. of Peter Cowpe	1	Augusti
John son of Miles Holme of Walm^s		
Debarah dau. of Lawrence Allens		
b Edmond spurious	7	,,
Mary dau. of Francis Wood of Bury	13	,,
Mary dau. of Leonard Ashworth		
Roger son of Robte Hardman of Holcome ...	21	,,
b John son of Willm Booth of Blackholt		
George son of James Livesay	5	Septembris
Arthure son of Bartholomew Smethurst		
Ellen dau. of Richard Kaye de Redds. ...		
Sara dau. of Henry Fildes		
Roger son of Henry Haworth of B :		
Charles son of Ralph Nuttall of Tottingt : ...	7	,,
b Susan dau. of Samuel Taylor of Ashton-vnder-line & Eliz : Cowp of Heywood	8	,,
Abell son of Mr. Rathbone	12	,,
Alice dau. of John Holte of Bury		
Lawrence son of Lawrence Bury		
Richard son of James Fletcher of Elton ...		
Anne dau. of Ralph Nuttall of Tot :	19	,,
Elizab dau. of Wm Rostorne		
b Ellen dau. of Thomas Smethurst & Alice Heywood	26	,,

Fo. 62

Elizabeth dau. of John Turner collier	30	,,
John Anne & Mary twines of Thomas Heyward	2	Octobris
Anne dau. of Edmond Seddon		
Susan dau. of James Eccarsall	7	,,
Ellen dau. of Richard Booth of Totting. ...		
Jane dau. of Thomas Livesay of Birk. ...		
James son of James Aynsworth of Holc. ...	24	,,
b William son of Wm Bancroft & Jane Leach ...	29	,,
Thomas son of Thomas Holte of Heywood ...		
Richard son of Richard Wiggan of Tott. ...		
Easter dau. of Gilbte Lawe	5	Novembris
Anonimus son. or dau. of James Crossley ...		
Thomas son of Henry Wood	7	,,
Susan dau. of Thomas Allens		
Mary dau. of Edmond Holte de Lees ...		
Edmond son of John Grenhalghe		
Sarah dau. of James Fenton of Heywood ...		
b Richard son of . . Laycocke & . . Watson		
Alice dau. of Willm Booth of Bury	14	,,
Anna dau. of Henry Crosley de Birkle	21	,,
Edmond son of Symon Lomax of Tott : ...	28	,,

1619 CHRISTENINGS. 213

John son of John Jenkinson	Novembris
Anne dau. of Martin Hopwood of Birkle	
Mary dau. of John Walker de Bamford ...	5 Decembris
Ellyn dau. of George Holte de Tott. ...	
Thomas son of George Nuttall de Gollinr⁹	12 ,,
Wiłłm son of John Grenehalgh	14 ,,
Roɓte son of Wiłłm Kaye de Cobbas ...	19 ,,
Lawrence son of John Broughton de Hole.	
Abell son of Martin Kaye	25 ,,
John son of Zachary Bridge	26 ,,
John son of Tho: Wood de Birch	
Nathan son of Xp̄ofer Cunliff de Heape ...	
Margaret dau. of Richard Damport	27 ,,
Edward son of Abell Woolsenholme	
Abraham son of Charles Leach de Deanebancke	2 Januarij
John son of Stephen Sagar	
John son of John Whitehead of Bury	6 ,,
Oliver son of Wiłłm Haworth of Walm⁹sley ...	9 ,,
James son of Richard Fletcher of Bury	
James son of Richard Romsbothome of Bury	15 ,,
Josua son of Wiłłm Hargreaves	16 ,,
Ralph son of Henry Nuttall of Edenfeld ...	
Mary dau. of Roɓte Smethurst of Redds. ...	
b John son of Edmond Fenton & Ellen Brindle	
Mary dau. of James Rothwell	23 ,,
Anne dau. of Wiłłm Bancrofte	
Alice dau. of Thom⁹ Hawoorth de Tott. ...	30 ,,
Anne dau. of George Emerson	
Lawrence son of John Buckley	
Henry son of Richard Bury	
John son of Roger Booth de Bury	6 Februarij
Edward son of Edmond Pilkinton de Tott. ...	
Elizaɓ dau. of Rich. Booth de Tott.	
b Elizaɓ dau. of John Hopwood & Eliz: Heald	17 ,,
Jane dau. of John Hames of Bury	20 ,,
Thom⁹ son of Rich: Allens of Bury	
James son of Thomas . . of Heape	27 ,,
Richard son of George Battersby	
Rich. son of John Medowcrofte of Elton ..	5 Martij
George son of George Anderton of Elton ...	
Anne dau. of Rich: Heald of Bury	
Thomas son of Thomas Wood of Tott:	
Anna dau. of Thom⁹ Booth of Tott.	
James son of Lawrence Haslome of Walm⁹ ...	12 ,,
Alice dau. of Roger Grenehalgh of Bury ..	
Thomas son of Thomas Haworth of B.	
John son of Edmond Kaye de Bury	19 ,,
Arthure son of Arthure Scholefeld	

1620.

Fo. 63	Thomas son of Jeremy Barlowe	26 Martij
	John son of John Lomax of Elton	
	Elizabeth dau. of Richard Grenehalgh of Bury	
	Martha dau. of Edmond Wrigley	9 Aprilis
	Martha dau. of Robert Whitehead	15 ,,
	Roger son of Robte Fletcher of Redds.	23 ,,
	Michaell son of Michaell Woolstenholme of Elton	
	John son of Jeffrey Lomax	30 ,,
	Richard son of Ric. Hopwood	
	Mary dau. of Peter Lomax of Elton ...	
	Anne dau. of John Wiggan of Tott.	8 Maij
	Willm son of Ric. Grenhalghe of Elton	
	Susan dau. of Henry Rastorne	
	John son of Richard Horrocks de Midd[9] p: ...	14 ,,
	Wm son of Rich. Armeworth de Birch	
	Bartin son of James Kaye de Tuch.	21 ,,
	Giles son of Giles Rothwell of Walmesl. ...	
	Dorothie dau. of Jeremy Ainsworth	
	Richard son of Ralph Vnsworth	4 Junij
	Elizab dau. of Thomas Wood of Tott.	
	Richard son of Richard Crosley of Bury	14 ,,
	James son of Hughe Seddon of B.	
b	James son of Richard Nuttall of Tott:	
	Grace dau. of Thomas Kaye	19 ,,
	John son of Lawrence Haslome of Haslomehey	
	Richard son of Rich: Haslome	25 ,,
	Robte son of Robte Kaye of Bent:	
	Jonathan son of Samuell Machon	
	Ellen dau. of Ralph Battersby of Aynsw: ...	
	Peter son of Richard Bury of Hey:	2 Julij
	Isabell dau. of John Birome of Hey:	
	Mary dau. of James Barlowe of Heap.	9 ,,
b	John son of John Kaye of Elton	
	Mary dau. of Will Grenehalgh de p: Midl	
	Richard son of Richard Rastorne of Elton	17 ,,
	Mary dau. of John Hilton of Heape	
	Richard son of John Romsbothome of Wal ...	23 ,,
	Willm son of Thomas Booth of Hole.	25 ,,
	John son of John Smyth of Bury	27 ,,
	Peter son of James Kershawe of He:	30 ,,
	Willm son of Joseph Oredd of Bury	
	Richard son of James Smethurst	
	Roger son of Robte Smethurst de Redds ...	11 Augusti
	Susan dau. of Roger Smethurst de Bu:	
b	Jennett dau. of Margarett Bate and Edmond Fenton	

1620 CHRISTENINGS.

Margarett dau. of Ric: Hunt of Bur:	Augusti
Charles son of Richard Nuttall de Hole. ...	16 ,,
Mary dau. of Abraham Shruyde	
Elizabeth dau. of Peter Lomax of Tott: ...	20 ,,
Anne dau. of John Wood of Birkhill ...	
Robte son of James Fogge	27 ,,
John son of Edmond Lowe	
Henry son of Henry Aynsworth	8 Septemb
b Edmond son of Joseph Livesay of Middleton pish	
Dorothie dau. of Francis Medowcrofte ...	11 ,,
Thomas son of Jeremy Hinde of Tott.	
James son of Edward Symond festo Bartholmei	
Jenett dau. of John Fenton of Bury...	27 ,,
Elizabeth dau. of Edward Hinde	
Robte son of Robert Whitakers of Wal: ...	
Jane dau. of John Shawe	1 Octobris
Susan dau. of Thomas Cockshutt	
Richard son of Willm Romsbothome of Hole⁹	8 ,,
James son of Thomas Birch of Bamford	
Ellen dau. of Lawrence Lorte of Bury	
Richard son of Tho: Fletcher of Heathy hill ...	
John son of Ralph Nuttall of Tott.	15 ,,
Samuell son of Arthure Smethurst	
Robte son of Robte Livesay of Heape ...	22 ,,
Robte son of James Kaye of Crossehall ...	
John son of John Kirkman de poch Middl ...	27 ,.
George son of George Holme of Rade.	30 ,,
Charles & Richard gemini Johis Nuttall	9 Novembris
John son of Ellis Haworth	12 ,,
Margaret dau. of Thomas Willms	
Katherine dau. of Thomas Heald	
Margarett dau. of Rich: Rastorne	
Henry son of Henry Dunster	29 ,,
John son of John . . of Hole.	
Anne dau. of John Brooke of Hole. ...	3 Decembris
James son of James Scholefeld of Edf.	
b Anne dau. of Alice Holte and George Emerson	
Anne dau. of John Horredge	7 ,,
Henry son of Thomas Nuttall of Bu:	17 ,,
John son of Rich. Romsbothome of Bury	
Margarett dau. of James Holte of B. ...	
Katherine dau. of Roger Lomax of Cath:	26 ,,
Martha dau. of John Robinson	7 Januarij
John son of John Whitehad de Rate. ...	
Tho: son of Tho: Anderton de Wal ...	
Elizabeth dau. of Zachary Bridge	14 ,,
Rich: son of Thomas Smethurst	
Sarah dau. of John Heaton de Reds. ...	

Roger son of Roger Booth de Redds.	20	Januarij
James son of John Walworke		
Richard son of James Grenhalgh de Tott.		
Richard son of Thomas Livesaye de Birk:	25	,,
Mary dau. of Wiłłm Dickonson of Birk.	29	,,
Wiłłm & Frauncis gemini Edri Hamar de Buck.	30	,,
James son of Richard Heald of Bury	4	Februarij
Wiłłm son of Rich: Duckworth de B.		
Richard son of Edward Rastorne de Tott:		
Anne dau. of Thomas Lomax de Croychl:	11	,,
Peter son of Peter Rothwell de Walm⁹sl:		
b Anne dau. of Thomas Bury and Susan Lomax of Walmersley		
Richard son of Mathew Bury of Elton	18	,,
John son of Peter Toothill of Bury	25	,,
b Susan dau. of Eliz. Hunte & John Grenehalghe of Bury		
Peter son of Rich: Leach of Shutt.		
Anne dau. of John Lomax de Tott:		
David son of David Naden of B.		
Jane dau. of John Alton of Bu:		
James son of Oliu⁹ Lomax of Wal		
Jane dau. of Jervas Grenhalgh of El:		
Lawrence son of Rich: Banaster of B.		
John son of John Warburton of Holc.	4	Martij
John & Elizab gemini Jacob Warburton		
Richard son of James Kaye of Hartlee		
Jane dau. of Arthure Kaye de Hough	11	,,

Fo. 65

1621.

Jeremy son of John Croston	25	Martij
Richard son of Richard Davenport		
Abraham son of Joseph Holte de Hay:		
John son of Edmond Turner de Tott.		
John son of Richard Fletcher of Bury	1	April
James son of James Lomax of Bury		
Dorothie dau. of Tho. Rushton		
Jane dau. of Edmond Wilde of Hey.		
Peter son of Peter Cloughe	2	,,
b Edmond son of James Haworth & Anne Bexwicke	3	,,
b Richard son of John Baguley & Isabell Heald of Redds.	7	,,
Anne dau. of Josuah Holte of Bury	8	,,
James son of Robte Nabs of Elton		
Alice dau. of Richard Nuttall		
Alice dau. of Richard Allens of Bur:	15	,,
Henry son of James Holte of B.		
Anne dau. of Wiłłm Heald of Mide:		

CHRISTENINGS.

Frauncis son of Roger Pilkinton		April
James son of Richard Smyth of Mide:	18	,,
Henry son of Richard Rothwell of Hole. ...	21	,,
Mary dau. of John Hopwood of Midl:		
Mathew son of Richard Wood of Grenes		
Edmond son of Richard Finch de Heape ...	24	,,
Anne dau. of Francis Grenehalgh de B.		
Edw. son of James Scholefeld de Tot.		
Anne dau. of John Heywood of Midl:	5	May
Ellen dau. of Roger Kaye de Burss.		
Ralph son of Thomas Pilkinton	10	,,
Ellen dau. of John Bridge of Hole.	13	,,
Margaret dau. of James Rothwell de Hole. ...		
Rich: son of Rich: Nuttall of Holcome ...		
b Anne dau. of Francis Medowcroft & Anne Tayler of Haslo hey		
Anne dau. of John Hardman of Hey:		
John son of John Warburton of Hole.	16	,,
John son of Ralph Blakley of Midl:		
John son of John Crompton of Heath		
Tho. son of James Openshawe of Bold		
b Anne dau. of Robte Bradley & Hannah Smethurst		
b Mary dau. of Adam Holte & Anne Bates of Bury		
Susan dau. of Robte Kitchin of Elton	3	June
Edmond son of Mathew Jackson		
John son of Thomas Walker of Bury		
Richard son of Richard Kaye of Widd.		
John son of Robte Shepard of Chess.	16	,,
John son of Tho. Wood of Hole.		
George son of Charles Nuttall		
Thurstan son of Will Brook	17	,,
Alice dau. of George Heaton		
James son of Richard Hamar	24	,,
Anne dau. of Thomas Hynde	29	,,
Elizabeth dau. of John Barlowe	1	Julij
Katherine dau. of Roger Grenehalgh		
Elizabeth dau. of Tho. Hamar de bamf.	8	,,
Richard son of John Warburton of Hole. ...	15	,,
John son of Thomas Turner		
Mary dau. of James Brearley of Hey.	18	,,
Jane dau. of Robte Crosley of Heyw.	29	,,
Ellen dau. of Willm Aspinall of Scout		
Alice dau. of John Asmall of B.		
Sarah dau. of John Kaye de woodr.		
Mary dau. of Thomas Buckley	5	Augusti
Elizabeth dau. of Ellis Haslom of Wal:		
Elizabeth dau. of George Haworth of Leeye ...	12	,,
Mary dau. of James Hardman of Reds.		
Richard son of Charles Nuttall of Hole.		

Thomas son of John Kaye de Bank l. ... ... 20 Augusti
Ellino⁹ dau. of Richard Heyward ... ... 27 ,,
Dorothie dau. of James Fenton of Heyw. ... 3 Septembris
Mary dau. of Robte Ridings ... ...
Thomas son of Willm Haworth ... ...
Sarah dau. of James Lomax ... ...
Margaret dau. of James Eccersall ... ... 10 ,,
Richard son of John Kaye of Bury ... ...
Katherine dau. of John Birch ... ...
John son of Daniell Allens ... ...
Mary dau. of John Wiggan ... ... 11 ,,
Richard son of Lawrence Bury ... ... 18 ,,
Roger son of Peter Holte of Bridge ... ... 20 ,,
Katherine dau. of John Medowcrofte ... ... 9 Octobris
Ellen dau. of Richard Grenehalgh de B.... ...
Anne dau. of Reuben Haworth... ... ... 14 ,,
b Dorothie dau. of Abrah: Taylor & Margaret
   Kay ... ...
Ralph son of Ralph Sheppd ... ... 20 ,,
Susan dau. of Symon Barlow ... ...
Katherine dau. of John Grenehalgh Esqʳ ...
James son of Willm Whitakers ... ... 28 ,,
Alice dau. of James Grenehalgh ... ...
Thurstan son of John Smethurst ... ... 4 Novembris
Edward son of Richard Booth of Tott. ... ...
Henry son of Henry Wood of Tott. ... ... 21 ,,
Francis son of Abell Woolstenholme ... ... 25 ,,
Elizabeth dau. of Martin Kaye... ... ...
Alice dau. of Richard Toothill ... ...
Nathan son of Gilbte Lawe ... ...
Elizabeth dau. of John Booth of Bury ... ... 2 Decembris
Frauncis son of Francis Pendlebury ... ...
Mary dau. of Edmond Lowe ... ... 6 ,,
Richard son of Isaacke Royde of Hol. ... ... 9 ,,
James son of Edward Helliwell ... ... 20 ,,
George son of George Vnsworth of B. ... ...
Elizabeth dau. of George Bradshawe ... ...
Dorothy dau. of Robte Kaye of Wal. ... ...
Mary dau. of Edmond Pilkinton ... ...
Robte son of Robte Anderton ... ...
Sarah dau. of John Aynsworth ... ...
Robte son of John Poole of Bury ... ... 21 ,,
James son of John Medowcrofte ... ...
Ellen dau. of Richard Heald ... ... 2 Januarij
b Richard son of Richard Nuttall ... ... 6 ,,
George son of George Nuttall ... ...
Ellen dau. of Richard Overall ... ...
Elizabeth dau. of John Marcrofte ... ... 13 ,,
Fo. 67 James son of Robte Scholefeld ... ... 16 ,,

CHRISTENINGS.

Richard son of Richard Grenehalge of Bury	20 Januarij
Elizabeth dau. of Ric. Kaye of Middle : ...	
James son of Richard Kaye of B. ...	
Richard son of Wiłm Rasthorne ...	21 ,,
Alice dau. of Jo. Bridge of Hole. ...	27 ,,
Roger son of Roger Seddon of B. ...	
Anne dau. of Roger Fletcher	
James son of Abraham Kaye	3 Februarij
James son of Ric. Siddall	
Zachary son of Zachary Bridge ...	
Thomas son of Francis Haworth	10 ,,
Isabell dau. of Barthol. Smethurst ...	
Ellen dau. of Richard Haslome ...	
Mary dau. of James Scholefeld	
Richard son of Charles Nuttall	
Margaret dau. of Will Kay of Cobb. ...	17 ,,
Tho. son of Hugh Diggle of Bur :... ...	
Mary dau. of Roger Grenehalgh ...	
Margaret dau. of James Fowler... ...	
Margaret dau. of Jo. Whitehead ...	
Anne dau. of Edw. Hind of B.... ...	
John son of Joh. Hinde of Elt. ...	
Margaret dau. of John Rastorne ...	24 ,,
Rich. son of John Kaye of Bury ...	
Edmond son of Edm. Bridge	
Elizabeth dau. of Mathew Wood	
James son of James Kaye	28 ,,
Roger son of Roger Bromeley	
Mary dau. of Rich. Brearley of Hey. ...	
Anne dau. of John Turner of Hole. ...	3 Martij
Fancis son of Francis Scholefeld	
Daniell son of Robte Dunster	10 ,,
Mary dau. of James Wrigley	
Peter son of Richard Grenehalgh	17 ,,
Dorothy dau. of Ric. Haworth	
Rich' son of John Whitehead	24 ,,
Margarett dau. of Thomas Kaye	
Jonathan son of John Wardle	8 ,,
Samuell son of Arther Skolefeld ...	
James son of Robert Smithersté	20 ,,
Thomas son of William Bothe	
Elizabeth dau. of Richard Kay	
Elizabeth dau. of John Jenkinson	
John son of Ric. Romsebothō of Bu : ...	
John son of Peter Totell	23 ,,
John son of James Kay of Wal.	
James son of Richarde Whitheade	
Thomas son of Roger Kay of Elton... ...	

1622.

Richard son of Thomas Buckley of Burie	21 Aprill
Grace dau. of Edmund Houlte of Burie	
Samuell son of Edmund Kaie of Borows	
Ann dau. of Richard Bouthe of Tott.	
John son of Francis Medowcrofte of Wal.	
Imn* . . James Woolsenham of Wal.	
Richard son of James Kaie of Wal.	
Margreate dau. of John Hunte of Wal.	28 Aprill
Peter son of Thomas Smethurste of Burie	
Alice dau. of Abraham Stringer of Burie	
John son of Henrie Nuttall of Tottingtō	

Fo. 68

[On this occasion the year is made to end at the close of April.]

John son of John Cropper of Bamford	5 Maij
Alice dau. of Thomas Heald of Burie	
John son of Ollyvyer Gryme of Scoute	
Grace dau. of Richard Crosse of Burie	12 ,,
Isabell dau. of John Crompton of Etenfeild	
Ann dau. of Richard Johnns of Heape	
Richard son of Josephe Livsey of Birckle	19 ,,
Alice dau. of James Livsey of Heape	
Ann dau. of Richard Horobin of Tott.	30 ,,
Alice dau. of Roberte Kaie of Walmersley	
Marie dau. of Edward Symon of Elton	2 Juñ
Alice dau. of Thomas Livsey of Birckle	
Alice dau. of John Taylor of Walmersley	
Alice dau. of James Houlte of Holcome	9 ,,
Thomas son of Roberte Duckworthe of Heape	16 ,,
Sara dau. of Francis Barlowe of Prestwiche	
Elizabethe dau. of Richard Heald of Burie	27 ,,
Marie dau. of James Schofeild of Buri hamell	
Elsabethe dau. of Roger Houlte of Walmersley	
Roberte son of Robert Farworthe of Holcome	14 Julij
John son of William Grinhalghe of Tottingtō	21 ,,
Roberte son of Roberte Duckworthe of Heape	25 ,,
Ann dau. of Richard Allence of Burie	
Mary dau. of George Anderton of Birchey	28 ,,
Susanna dau. of Mr. Hugh Watmoughe of Burie	11 August
Joab son of William Rawborne of Tottington	
Ann dau. of Myles Houlme of Midlton	
Margreate dau. of Richard Rosthorne of Elton	
Thomas son of Roger Bouthe of Tenters	23 ,,
John son of Arthure Kaij of Walmersley	
Margreate dau. of Omffrey Broume of Ratcliffe	2 September
Peter son of John Fenton of Burie	15 ,,

* Sometimes Imyn—Imin—Emanen. In Rochdale Registers used both for male and female.

CHRISTENINGS.

Ellen dau. of John Rosthorne of Holcome ...	3	October
Alice dau. of Richard Nuttall of Holcome ...	6	,,
Marie dau. of Roberte Howorthe of Bamford ...		
Elsabeth dau. of Thomas Bouthe of Holcoṁ ...	13	,,
Edward son of Roger Hamer of Buckden ...		
Josua son of Henrie Crosley of Heywood ...	20	,,
Thomas son of Lawrance Haslome of Wal. ...		
John son of John Hamer of Chesam ...		
Alice dau. of Jervis Grinhalghe of Tott. ...		
Alice dau. of Richard Smethurste of Heape ...	27	,,
Ellen dau. of Thomas Nuttall of Buriha ...		
Elsabethe dau. of Leonard Asheworthe of Midlt.	3	Nouember
John son of Martyne Hopwood of Midleton ...	10	,,
b Elsabeth dau. of John Broughton & Marie Chadwick of Burie	29	,,
John son of William Heald of Midlton	12	Deceb̄er
Jeremy son of Jeremy Ainsworthe of Tott. ...	15	,,
John son of Thomas Woolner of Midlto. ...	22	,,
John son of Francis Woode of Burie	27	,,
Thomas son of Roger Kaij of Elton...	1	Januarij
James & Roberte sons of James Fletcher of Elton		
Marie dau. of Mr. Smythe of Heywood	12	,,
Susan dau. of George Houlte of Tott.	19	,,
Marie dau. of Mr. John Croston of Elton... ...	26	,,
Ric̄ son of John Bouthe & Katrin Jackson of Burie	2	February
John son of Jermy Barlowe of Holcome	19	,,
Marie dau. of Roger Grinhalghe of Buriha ...	23	,,
Jane dau. of Francis Pendleburie of Midlton ...	26	,,
Marie dau. of William Broucke of Wal.	26	,,
Thomas son of Mathewe Woolsenham of Elton	2	Marche
Marie dau. of John Wylde of Heape...		
b Alice dau. of Ric. Battersbie & Isabell Kaij of Berie	13	,,
Richard son of Gyles Rothwell of Wal.		
b Ric. son of Ric. Houlte & Jane Ainsworthe of Tott.	23	,,
James son of George Vnsworthe of Burie ...		
Isabell dau. of Arthure Partington of Wal. ...		

1623.

Ellen dau. of Henrie Ainsworthe of Holcome...	30	Marche
Richard son of Roberte Livsey of Heape ...		
John son of Roberte Anderton of Holcome ...	6	Aprill
Margreate dau. of Thomas Smythe of Eltonn ...		
Josephe & Benginn sons of Zackerie Bridge of Holco.	16	,,

George son of George Emerson of Burie	April
Ann dau. of Raphe Clarkson of Heape	20 ,,
Elsabeth dau. of James Grinhalghe of Elton ...	
Ollyver son of Abraham Nabbe of Wal.	
Elsabeth dau. of William Lowe of Holcom ...	
Jane dau. of Richard Houlte of Tott.	27 ,,
Jane dau. of Richard Nuttall of Elton	
John son of Henry Dunster of Elton	4 Maij
John son of Giberte Lowe of Rediuals	11 ,,
John son of Peter Lomax of Tott.	18 ,,
Thomas son of James Barlowe of Heape... ...	
Isabell dau. of Edmund Seddon of Heape ...	
Doritie dau. of Richard Barlowe of Elton ...	25 ,,
John son of James Hardman of Rediuals... ...	
Marie dau. of George Bradshawe of Tott. ...	
Margreate dau. of Geffray Lomax of Heape ...	1 Jun
Ann dau. of Emer Ainsworthe of Holcom ...	
Marie dau. of Richard Duckworth of Elton ...	
Richard son of Peter Cloughe of Elton	15 ,,
Henry son of Richard Lomax of Buriha... ...	
Roberte son of Roberte Howorthe of Wal. ...	23 ,,
Thomas son of Thomas Smethurste of Midlto.	
James son of James Houlte of Buriha	30 ,,
Susa dau. of James Houlte of Buriha	
Elizabethe dau. of James Chadwicke of Bamford	6 Julij
Thomas son of Hughe Seddon of Burie	13 ,,
Marie dau. of Dauid Nadden of Buriha	20 ,,
Marie dau. of James Kaij of Hartlie	27 ,,
Lawrance son of Mathewe Berie of Tott. ...	3 August
Alice dau. of John Lomax of Holcom	10 ,,

Fo. 70 b

John son of John Hill & Doritie Wood of Elton	
Katrin dau. of John Lomax of Elton	24 ,,
Peter son of Peter Houlte of Bridge...	8 September
William son of William Kaij of Wal.	12 ,,
Alice dau. of Roger Grinhalghe of Midlton ...	15 ,,
Richard son of Thomas Nuttall of Burie	28 ,,
Roberte son of Thomas Kaie of Mosse	
Isabell dau. of Roger Lomax of Midlton	12 October
Isabell dau. of James Houlte of Holcom	15 ,,
Margreate dau. of John Barlowe of Burie... ...	8 November
James son of James Eckersall of Burie ...	
Elizabethe dau. of John Atton of Rediuals ...	9 ,,
Marie dau. of Richard Banester of Burie ...	20 ,,
Richard son of Frauncis Grinhalghe of Burie ...	
Arthure son of Arthure Smethurste of Ratcliffe	
Marie dau. of Thomas Pilkington of Elton ...	
Isabell dau. of Ellis Howorthe of Etenfeild ...	7 December
Ellen dau. of John Shawe of Burie	21 ,,
Elsabell dau. of Mathewe Bouthe of Rediuals...	21 ,,

CHRISTENINGS.

James son of James Kaij of Wal.	December
Richard son of Richard Overall of Burie... ...	4 January
Raphe son of Roberte Magnals of Tott.	
Marie dau. of Martyne Kaij of Burih	11 ,,
John son of Francis Bouthe of Tott.	18 ,,
Alice dau. of Peter Lomax of Tott.	21 ,,
John son of Edmund Lowe of Holcom̃	24 ,,
James son of John Fenton of Burie	
John son of Roger Seddon of Buriha.	
Marie dau. of Richard Heald of Rediuals ...	1 Februarij
Elsabeth dau. of Charles Broucke of Burie ...	
James son of James Kaic of Wal.	8 ,,
Elsabethe dau. of Richard Rosthorne of Elton	
Richard son of Richard Berie of Heywood ...	
Anne dau. of Thomas Birche of Bamford... ...	
Marie dau. of Richard Kaie of Widdell	15 ,.
Sara dau. of John Walworke of Buriha.	
Diana dau. of Henry Bridge of Holcom̃	
Richard son of Roberte Duckworth of Heape	
John son of John Heywood of Midleton	22 ,,
John son of Peter Tuttall of Burie	
Henry son of Abell Woolsenham of Elton ...	29 ,,
John son of Richard Nuttall of Tott.	7 Marche
Elsabell dau. of Richard Taylor of Wal.	
Thomas son of Richard Haslome of Rediuals ...	14 ,,
Marie dau. of George Nuttall of Golinroad ...	21 ,.
Richard son of & Sara son *(sic)* of Ric. Nuttall of Holcō	
James son of James Howorthe of Midlete & Elsabethe Howorthe of this pishe	
Elsabethe dau. of James Wilson of Holcon ...	23 ,,

1624.

Sara dau. of Edmund Bridge of Holcome ...	12 Aprill
Ann dau. of John Marcrofte of Midltone... ...	
Alice dau. of Henrie Burie of Tottington ...	
Doritie dau. of Jeremy Barlowe of Houlcom̃ ...	15 ,,
Isabell dau. of Edward Rothwell of Holcom̃ ...	
Alice dau. of Andrewe Berie of Heywood ...	25 ,,
James son of John Kaie of Road Elt.	
Elsabeth dau. of John Whithead of Burie ...	2 Maij
Willm son of William Romsbothom of Holco.	6 ,,
John son of Edmund Hopwood of Heywood ...	9 ,,
Thomas son of John Marcrofte of Midlton ...	23 ,,
John son of Peter Cowpe of Elton	27 ,,
Thomas son of Roberte Scofeild of Bamford ...	6 Jun
John son of John Smethurst of Rediuals	26 ,,
Katrin dau. of Richard Romsbothom of Holcom̃	18 July

BURY PARISH REGISTERS. 1624

Margreate dau. of Henrie Wood of Tottington	22	July
Roger son of Roger Kaij of Tott.	29	,,
Grace dau. of Mr. John Grenehalghe of Brandlsō Esquire		
Raph son of John Rothwell of Holcome* ...	7	August
Ester dau. of John Croston of Eltonn †	8	,,
John son of John Stotte of Heywood		
Marie dau. of Richard Wood of Elton	12	September
John son of John Battersbie of Sutlworthe ...		
Richard son of Thomas Hynd of Elton	19	,,
James son of James Jacksonn of Burie	26	,,
Elizabeth dau. of Richard Asheworthe of Wal.	3	October
Alice dau. of Richard Bouthe of Tott.		
James son of Mathewe Wood of Wal.		
Jonathan son of Bartholomewe Smethurste of Heape	10	,,
Thomas son of James Kaie of Elton	17	,,
Alice dau. of Raphe Bridge of Holcome		
Marie dau. of Roger Vnsworthe of Buri hamell		
Roberte son of Andrewe Knowles of Sutlworth	24	,,
Elsabeth dau. of Edward Hynde of Burie ...		
Zackerie son of Zackerie Bridge of Holcome ...	30	,,
Josua son of James Lomax of Midletonne ...		
Isabell dau. of Thomas Burie of Tottingtō ...		
Edmund son of Willm Berie of Tottingtonn ...	14	Nouember
Alice dau. of Roberte Hamer of Tottingtonn ...		
Willm son of Richard Romsbothome of Burie	28	,,
Elizabeth dau. of Willm Kaij of Cobhowse ...		
Roberte son of Willm Asley of Holcome	5	December
Ester dau. of James Scofeild of Etenfeild ...		
Peter son of John Rombinson of Heywood ...		
Katrin dau. of Thomas Kaie of Walmersley ...	12	,,
Elizabethe dau. of Thomas Bouthe of Burie ...		
Elizabethe dau. of Symond Barlowe of Tott. ...		
Isabell dau. of James Kaie of Hartlie	1	Januarij
Martha & Maria daus. of Arthure Furnis of Burie		
John son of Lawrance Berie of Elton		
Alice dau. of Roger Kaie of Walmersley		
Elizabeth dau. of Mr. George Murrey pson of Burie	2	,,
John son of Edward Lomax of Heywood ...		
Elizabethe dau. of Hamlet Lowe of Walmersley	9	,,
John son of John Whithead of Elton	16	,,
John son of Richard Kaij of Widdell	23	,,
Alice dau. of Ellis Haslome of Boulton		
Peter son of Roberte Crosley of Heywood ...	30	,,

Fo. 72

* Baptised on the 7th appears to have been added at a later date.

† This in the register is before that on the 7th.

CHRISTENINGS.

Roger son of Roger Kaie of Elton ...	6	Februarie
James son of James Kershawe of Burie		
Marie dau. of Peter Houlte of Bridghale	13	,,
Zara dau. of George Bromelie of Buri hamell ...		
Ester dau. of Richard Nuttall of Holcome	20	,,
John son of David Nadden of Buri ha. ...		
Raphe son of Abraham Lorte of Burihamell ...	6	Marche
George son of Rubin Howorthe of Eltonn		
James son of Edward Roshorne of Tottington...		
James son of James Scofeild of Burihamell		
Thomas son of Thomas Nuttall of Holcome ...		
Tho. & Marie children of Edward Rothwell of Elton		
Roger son of Thomas Risheton of Burihamell		
Elsabethe dau. of Roberte Hopwood of Midltonn		
Marie dau. of Arthurie Scofeild of Bamford ...	13	,,
Marie dau. of Richard Kaie of Gosforthe ...		
Ann dau. of Richard Hadocke of Burihamell ...		
Alice dau. of George Houlte of Elton ...	20	,,
John son of John Barlowe of Burie ...	27	,,
Marie dau. of Thomas Woolner of Rediualls ...		
Thomas son of Thomas Wood of Birchey ...		
Elsabethe dau. of John Howorthe of Burie ...		

1625.

John son of Jeremy Ainsworthe of Holcom̃ ...	3	April
James son of Roger Fletcher of Burie ...		
Richard son of Richard Ouerall of Burie ...		
Elsabethe dau. of Thomas Nabbe of Holcome	11	,,
Jonothan son of Henry Crossley of Midltonn ...		
Doritie dau. of John Barlowe of Holcome ...		
Elsabeth dau. of Raphe Vnsworthe of Burie ...		
Susan dau. of Henry Nuttall of Tottingtō ...		
Richard son of James Lorte of Heywood ...	17	,,
Katrin dau. of Raphe Nuttall of Tott. ...	24	,,
John son of Omphrey Broomle of Heape ...		
Marie dau. of Edmund Bouthe of Rediualls ...	1	May
Margreate dau. of Abraham Mackcon of Tott.		
John son of Edmund Barlowe of Tottington ...		
John son of John Scole of Rediuals ...		
John son of Richard Crosse of Burie ...		
John son of John Houlte of Bamford ...	8	,,
Judithe dau. of Roberte Hopw' of Birckle ..		
Margreate dau. of Richard Kaie of Gosforthe...		
Elizabeth dau. of George Howorthe of Buriha.		
Ann dau. of Richard Wigan of Tott. ...	15	,,
William son of John Bridge of Holcome ...	18	,,
Alice dau. of Roberte Taylor of Burie ...	22	,,

	Alice dau. of James Ainsworthe of Tottington	26	May
	Marie dau. of Thomas Nuttall of Burie	29	,,
	Francis son of Roberte Rydinge of Heape ...		
	Robert son of Ollyver Lomax of Wal.		
	Richard son of Thomas Bouthe of Tott.		
Fo. 73	Margreate dau. of Roger Bromley of Burie ...	5	Juñ
	Alice dau. of John Kaie of Burie		
	James son of Richard Fletcher of Burie	9	,,
	Richard son of Roger Sedon of Burie	12	,,
	Edmund son of Wiłłm Lomax of Holcome		
	Elsabethe dau. of John Fletcher of Holcome...		
	Edmund son of Wiłłm Lomax of Elton		
	Renold son of Ellis Howorthe of Etenfeld ...	16	,,
	Doritie dau. of Thomas Barlowe of Holcome ...	23	,,
	Susan dau. of Ollyver Lomax of Wal.		
	John son of John Taylor of Walmersley		
	Grace dau. of Roberte Howorthe of Bamford ...		
	Peter son of James Grinhalghe of Burie		
	Thomas son of Thomas Knowles of Holcome...		
	Elizabeth dau. of Lawrance Haslome of Wal. ...		
	Doritie dau. of Roberte Kaie of Walmersley ...		
	Marie dau. of Thomas Fletcher of Redivalls ...	3	Julij
	Marie dau. of Abraham Strenger of Burie ...		
	John son of John Lomax of Holcome	17	,,
	Alice dau. of John Bouthe of Blackhoulte ...	23	,,
	Jane dau. of Ellis Howorthe of Facid		
	Marie dau. of Jarvis Grinall of Elton	8	August
	Marie dau. of John Hamer of Burihamell ...		
	Daniell son of Henry Dunster of Eltonn		
	Edward son of Edward Ratcliffe of Ratcliffe ...	14	,,
	Alice dau. of Isacke Roide of Holcome		
	Ann dau. of Edward Hamer of Burihamell ...	21	,,
	Alice dau. of Raphe Houlte of Walmersley ...		
	Jonathan son of James Brearley of Hewood ...	28	,,
	Grace dau. of Richard Hunte of Burie		
	Elizabethe dau. of Richard Bouthe of Burie ...		
	Ellen dau. of Lawrance Howorthe of Burie ...	4	September
	John son of Mathewe Berie of Tottington ...		
	Margreate dau. of Edward Pilkington of Wal. ...		
	Susan dau. of Roberte Magnals of Tottingto. ...		
	Henrie son of Henrie Berie of Tottington ...	11	,,
* x	Isabell dau. of Abell Wolsenham of Elton ...	14	,,
x	Ann dau. of John Buckley of Tottington ...	18	,,
x	John son of Abraham Kaie of Burie		
x	Edward son of George Vnsworthe of Burie ...	25	,,
	Richard son of Thomas Livsey of Mideltonn ...		
	Marie dau. of Francis Scofeild of Bamford ...	9	October
x	Ann dau. of Roger Grinhalghe of Mildltonn ...		
x	Alice dau. of John Kaie of Litlewood	16	,,

* Henceforth Crosses opposite entries become frequent.

1625 CHRISTENINGS.

Raphe son of Roberte Sheaphard of Chesham	23 October
Alice dau. of James Giliam of Manchester ...	26 ,,
b Peter son of Peter Heald & Jane Grinall of Buriha:	30 ,,
Ann dau. of John Hynd of Tottington	
Richard son of John Heape of Rediuals ...	6 November
Ann & Ellen daus. of Richard Smethurste of Broadocke	
Alice dau. of John Fenton of Burie	27 ,,
b Marie dau. of John Taylor & Marie Asheworthe of Bamford	
Marie dau. of Martyne Hopwood of Midlto. ...	30 ,,
Elsabethe dau. of Richard Duckworthe of Burie	
Raphe son of Raphe Fyles of Heape	4 December
James son of James Fogge of Elton	
Henry son of Thomas Rothwell of Holcome ...	15 ,,
Willm son of Willm Overall of Burie	18 ,,
John son of Richard Bouthe of Tott.	18 ,,
Ann dau. of James Smethurste of Buriha: ...	25 ,,
Peter son of Willm Rosthorne of Elton	27 ,,
John son of Richard Romsbothom of Holcome	1 Januarij
James son of Roberte Lyvseye of Heape ...	
Symon son of Richard Medowcrofte of Smithurst gent	6 ,,
John son of Richard Berie of Heywood	8 ,,
Alice dau. of William Houlte of Holcome ...	22 ,,
Alice dau. of James Kaie of Tuchroad	
Ann dau. of Cristopher Smethurste of Rediuals	
Ann dau. of Thomas Smethurste of Burie ...	
Ann dau. of Francis Pendleburie of Midletone	
Henry son of Mr. John Croston of Elton ...	29 ,,
Alice dau. of Edmund Duckworthe of Buriha	
Alice dau. of Symond Barlowe of Holcome ...	
Margreate dau. of Edmond Houlte of Buriham el	
John son of Lawrance Chadwicke of Bamford	5 Feb.
Ann dau. of James Hardman of Rediuals ...	
Edmund son of Richard Haslome of Rediuals	
Ann dau. of Mr. George Murrey pson of Burie	12 ,,
James son of Omphrey Barlowe of Burie ...	
Elsabeth dau. of Roger Lomax of Midlton ...	
Francis son of James Kaie of Hartlie	19 ,,
Marie dau. of John Hatton of Rediuall	
John son of Adam Kaie of Walmersley	
Alice dau. of Ellis Lomax of Tott.	
Thomas son of Thomas Bouthe of Burie ...	26 ,,
Marie dau. of James Lomax of Buriha:	5 Marche
Thomas son of Thomas Buckley of Holcome	
Jeremy son of John Barlowe of Tott.	
Ann dau. of Thomas Smethurste of Midlto. ...	

x	Susan dau. of Cristopher Cunliffe of Redi. ...	Marche
x	James son of James Houlte of Burihamell ...	
x	Elizabethe dau. of James Lomax Gosforthe ...	12 ,,
	Elizabethe dau. of John Marcrofte of Midlton	
	James son of John Whorockes of Birchey ...	
x	Abraham son of Thomas Wilkingson of Wal.	
x	Elizabeth dau. of George Battersbie of Wal. ...	
x	Katrin dau. of Mathewe Wolsenhame of Tott.	19 ,,
x	Francis son of Francis Nuttall of Wal.	
	Jeremy son of Henry Ainsworthe of Holcome	
	George son of Thomas Kaie of Suttlworthe ...	

1626.

x	William son of John Yate of this hamell ...	26 Marche
x	George son of Roger Bouthe of Tenters ...	
	Marie dau. of John Grinhalghe of Midlton ...	
x	Alice dau. of John Holcome of Holcome ...	
x	Roberte son of William Kaie of Wal.	
x	Ann dau. of John Byrome of Heywood	
x	Ann dau. of John Wylde of Heape	
x	Ann & Alice daus. of Tho. Pilkington of Elton	
x	Marie dau. of Richard Barlowe of Elton ...	2 Aprill
Fo. 75 x	Isabell dau. of Roberte Fenton of Holcome ...	
x	Thomas son of Thomas Wood of Tottington ...	9 ,,
x	John son of Peter Houlte of Bridge Hall ...	
x	Richard son of Richard Hopwood of Buryha. & Ann Hamer	
x	Edward son of Roberte Scofeild of Bamford ...	16 ,,
x	Sara dau. of Martyne Kaie of Litlwood	19 ,,
x	James son of James Kershawe of Buriha. ...	23 ,,
x	Edward son of Arthure Partington of Wal. ...	1 Maij
x	Daniell son of Gilberte Lowe of Buriham. ...	
x	Richard son of Richard Heald of Rediualls ...	7 ,,
x	Marie dau. of Roberte Duckworthe of Heape	
x	James & Willm sons of John Walmersley of Birchey	
x	John son of Edmund Wrigley of Holcome ...	
	Elsabethe dau. of John Crompton of Holcom	
x	Jane dau. of Thomas Grinhalghe of Chamber	21 ,,
x	Thomas son of Peter Tutell of Burie	
x	John son of Ollyuell* Nabbe of Wal.	7 June
x	Judithe dau. of John Warbartonn of Holcome	11 ,,
x	Richard son of Francis Howorthe of Burie ...	
x	Alice dau. of John Howorthe of Burie	
x	Ann dau. of Roberte Leache of Burie	18 ,,
x	Roberte & Alice children of Roberte Nabbe of Elton	

* Ottynell.

	John son of James Hartley of Holcome ...	21 June
x	Thomas son of Thomas Nuttall of Burie ...	25 ,,
	Charles son of William Romsbothom of Holcome	Julij
	James son of Richard Baron of Etenfeild ...	
x	Richard son of John Mulenex of Tottington ...	9 ,,
x	James son of James Leach of Burie ha: ...	16 ,,
x	Richard son of Edward Rothewell of Holcome	23 ,,
x	John son of Richard Houlte of Tottington ...	
b	Jane dau. of John Wolfenden & Isabell Houlte of Bamford ...	25 ,,
x	Elsabeth dau. of John Medcrofte of Eltonn ...	30 ,,
	Ellen dau. of John Heywood of Midlton ...	6 Auguste
b	John son of John Overall & Isabell Heald of Burie ...	
x	Ann dau. of Edmund Whiticar of Heape ...	
x b	John son of John Fletcher & Ellen Aspinall of Buriha. ...	13 ,,
x	John son of Thomas Hamand of Buriha. ...	16 ,,
x	Marie dau. of Steeuen Sager of Buriha. ...	
x	Richard son of Arthure Smethurste of little bridge* ...	20 ,,
x	George son of Richard Kaie of Widell ...	
x	Alice dau. of Richard † Bouth of Bouthall ...	
	Katrin dau. of Thomas Kaie of Holcom̃ ...	
x	Isabell dau. of John Kaie of Woodroade ...	27 ,,
	Josua son of Zacarie Bridge of Holcome ...	
x	Abraham son of Abraham Nabbe of Wal. ...	10 September
b	Alice dau. of Edward Haulte & Jane Nabbe of Walmersley ...	
x	Ann dau. of Thomas Nabbe of Holcome ...	17 ,,
	Katrin dau. of Edmund Lowe of Holcome ...	
	Marie dau. of Francis Mackon of Heywood ...	8 October
	Grace dau. of Roberte Howorth of Bamford ...	
x	Edward son of George Houlte of Eltonn ...	15 ,,
	Alice dau. of Willm ‡ Aspinall of Scoute ...	
x	Doritie dau. of Richard Kaie of Widell ...	22 ,,
x	Willm son of Roberte Duckworthe of Burihamell	
x	Susan dau. of Roberte Sheaphard of Buriha ...	1 November
x	James son of George Nuttall of Gollinroad ...	
	Anne dau. of Thomas Turnor of Holcome ...	5 ,,
x	Richard son of Abraham Stringer of Burie ...	12 ,,
x	Marie dau. of Ellis Leache of Etenfeild ...	19 ,,
x	Willm son of Francis Grinhalghe of Burie ...	
b	Margreate dau. of Lawrance Fletcher & Elizabeth Chadwicke of Wal. ...	

* "Buriha" crossed through and "little bridge" written over it.
† "John" crossed through and "Richard" written over it.
‡ There has been an erasure at "Willm."

x	Thomas son of Edward Hynde of Burie	26 November	
x	Edmund son of Thomas Smethurste of Lomax		
	John son of Josephe Leache of Bamford ...		
x	Anna dau. of James Kaie of Gosforthe	3 December	
	Martha Marie, & Margreate, daughters of John Walworke of Burihamell	9	,,
x	Marie dau. of Arthure Furnis of Burie	10	,,
	Katrin dau. of Edmund Bridge of Holcome ...		
x	Richard son of Roger Grinhalghe of Midlton...	17	,,
x	Susan dau. of Thomas Walker of Burie		
x	Theophilus son of Bartholomewe Smethurst of Midlto.		
x	Marie dau. of John Longworthe of Burie ...	24	,,
	Richard son of Richard Bouthe of Holcome ...	31	,,
x	Marie dau. of James Jacksonn of Burie	7 Januarij	
x	Ann dau. of Richard Medowcrofte of Lomas...		
	Raphe son of Raphe Battersbie of Midlton ...		
	Alexander son of Ellis Howorthe of Facid ...	14	,,
	Elizabethe dau. of Raphe Bridge of Holcome...		
x	James son of James Buckley of Burihamell ...		
	Raphe son of William Bridge of Holcome ...	21	,,
x	John son of Roberte Grinhalghe of Tottingtō	28	,,
	Lydia dau. of Charles Nuttall of Holcome ...		
	Charles son of Richard Pilkington of Holcome		
x b	Roberte son of Roberte Knowles of Holcome & Margreate Bouthe of Burihamell		
b	Peter son of Thurstan Rawshorne of Elton & Elizabeth Grinhalghe of Holcome		
x	Thomas son of Mathewe Berie of Tottington ...	4 Februarij	
x	Alice dau. of William Berie of Tottington ...		
x	James son of Henry Crosley of Birkhill		
x	Elsabeth dau. of George Howorthe of Burie ...	11	,,
	John son of Mr. Henry Byrome of Byrome (sic) of Gristhurste	18	,,
x	Thomas son of Thomas Fletcher of Rediualls		
x	Richard son of John Fenton of Burie		
x	Roberte son of James Grinhalghe of Tottington		
x	Roger son of Lawance (sic) Berie of Tottington		
x	Edmund son of Ompffrey Browne of Burihamell		
	Alice dau. of Francis Hamer of Holcome ...		
x	James son of James Grinhalghe of Burihamell		
b	Marie dau. of John Mulenex & Clemence Grinall of Tott.		
x	Thomas son of Jeremy Ainsworthe of Holcom̃	25	,,
x	Richard son of John Barlowe of Burie		
x	Marie dau. of James Lorte of Heywood		
x	Susan dau. of John Bouthe of Burie		
	Ann dau. of Jeremy Barlowe of Holcome ...	4 Marche	
Fo. 77 x	Sara dau. of Thomas Birche of Midlton		

x	Richard son of Richard Smethurste of Broadocke	Marche
x	Ann dau. of Thomas Brige of Holcome … …	
x	James son of Roberte Houlte of Birchey …	
	James son of James Scofeild of Etenfeild …	
	Ellis son of Thomas Howorthe of Walmersley	
	Elsabeth dau. of Richard Nuttall of Holcome…	8 ,,
x	Margreate dau. of George Heaton of Lomax …	11 ,,
x	Adam son of Mathewe Suttcliffe of Wal. …	
	Francis son of Mr. Murrey parson of Burie …	18 ,,
x	Andrewe son of Peter Romsbothom of Elton..	
	Thomas son of John Barlowe of Boulton ..	
x	Roger son of Roberte Hamer of Tottington …	
x	Doritie dau. of Edmund Houlte of Elton …	
	Richard son of Henry Bridge of Holcome …	

1627.

x	Jane dau. of Richard Hadocke of Burie …	1 Aprill
b	Marie dau. of Mathewe Nuttall & Ann Busicke of Burie … … … …	
x	Doritie dau. of Thomas Wood of Tottington …	8 ,,
	Margreate dau. of Thomas Rothwell of Birchey	
x	Marie dau. of Thomas Kaie of Eltonn … …	
x	Marie dau. of John Smethurste of Rediualls…	15 ,,
x	Bengamyn son of John Devis of Manchester…	22 ,,
	Abraham son of Roberte Asheworthe of Midlto.	
x	Susana dau. of Thomas Woolner of Burihamell	24 ,,
	Doritie dau. of William Hoult of Holcome ..	29 ,,
	Doritie dau. of Arthure Scofeild of Heywood	
x	Ann dau. of Lawrance Horockes of Midleton…	
x b	Elizabeth dau. of James Milnes & Elizabethe Hardman of Buriha. … … … …	
x	Elizabethe dau. of Richard Nuttall of Elton …	6 Maij
	John son of Roberte Howorthe of Suttleworthe	10 ,,
x	Sara dau. of John Broughtonn of Burie … …	13 ,,
x	Margreate dau. of George Battersbie of Wal. …	
	Alice dau. of Thomas Warbartonn of Holcome	
x	John son of James Houlte of Burihamell …	
x	John son of Thomas Stotte of Heywood	20 ,,
x	Ann dau. of John Lomax of Elton … … …	24 ,,
x	Roger son of Thomas Rishton of Buri hamell…	3 Jun
x	Marie dau. of Thomas Bouthe of Burie … …	
x	Henrie son of Richard Taylor of Walmersley ..	10 ,,
x	John son of Roberte Hopwood of Midltonn …	
x	Roberte & Susana children of Thomas Gothrope of Elton … … … … … … …	17 ,,
x	John son of James Chadwicke of Midlton …	
x	James son of Roger Fletcher of Burie hamell …	
x	Katrin dau. of Mathewe Woolsenham of Elton	24 ,,

x	Elizabeth dau. of John Whithead of Burie	...	Juñ
x	Cristopher son* of Roger Kaie of Bridhole	...	
x	Marie dau. of Dauid Nadden of Buriha. ...	...	
x	Roberte son of Thomas Lomax of Holcome	...	1 Julij
x	Raphe son of Thomas Wood of Burie	...	
x	Ann dau. of Richard Wood of Elton	...	
	Ann dau. of Richard Wood of Midleton		
x	Doritie dau. of Abraham Mackon of Tott.	...	8 ,,
x	Richard son of Humfrey Barlowe of Burie	...	15 ,,
Fo. 78 x	Alice dau. of James Barlowe of Heape	...	29 ,,
x	Lawrance son of John Lomax of Holcome	...	5 Auguste
x	Thomas son of John Hamer of Burihamell	...	
x	Alice dau. of Arthure Partington of Wal:	...	
	John son of John Wofenden of Bamford ...	...	
x	Marie dau. of Henrie Pilkington of Holcome...		12 ,,
x	James son of Laeonard Leache of Midlton	...	
x	Doritie dau. of John Kaie of Tuchroad ...	...	
x	Raphe son of Raphe Houlte of Walmersley ...		
x	John son of Richard Romsbothom of Holcoñ		19 ,,
x	Thomas son of Roger Seddon of Burie	...	
x	Alice dau. of Edmund Seddon of Heape		
x	Alice dau. of Roberte Fenton of Holcome	...	2 September
x	Jeremy son of Richard Howorth of Holcome		
x	Alice dau. of Jarvis Grinhalghe of Tottingtō	...	
x	Arthure son of William Whiticar of Tottington		9 ,,
x	Ann dau. of Roberte Heald of Redivalls	...	
b	Alice dau. of Thomas Wood & Marie Howorth of Tott.		
	Jane dau. of Abraham Taylor of Holcome	...	16 ,,
x	Marie dau. of George Vnsworthe of Burie	...	24 ,,
	Ester dau. of Francis Scofeild of Bamford	...	
b	George son of George Howorth of Midlton & Marie Oswood (sic) of Walmersley...	...	
	Richard son of Richard Houlte of Haugh shawe		30 ,,
b	Francis son of Edward Barlowe & Alice Houlte of Burie		
	Alice dau. of William Hitchinson of Holcome		7 October
x	Jane dau. of James Rothwell of Burihamell	...	
	Richard son of John Pates of Burihamell	...	
	Susan dau. of John Berie of Heywood	...	...
x	Elizabeth dau. of James Lomax of Midlton	...	14 ,,
	James son of James Taylor of Burihamell	...	
x	Ellen dau. of Thomas Kaie of Sutleworthe	...	
	Andrewe son of Andrewe Berie of Heywood	...	
	John son of Thomas Bouthe of Midlton ...	...	17 ,,
x	Marie dau. of Peter Smythe of Burihamell	...	
x	Richard son of Hamelete Lowe of Walmersley		28 ,,
x	Richard son of Mylles Holme of Midlton	...	

* Marked "d" of Roger Kaie.

1627 CHRISTENINGS

x	Roberte son of Roberte Kaie of Wal.	October
x	Martha dau. of James Brearley of Heywood ...	4 November
x	Richard son of William Overall of Burie	11 ,,
x	Gyles son of Gyles Vnsworthe of Rediuals ...	
x	Ann dau. of John Isherworthe of Holcome ...	
b	Jane dau. of James Byrome & Marie Hoppwood of Heywood	
x	Roberte son of Roberte Crosley of Heywood ...	24 ,,
x	John son of John Fletcher of Burie	
	Elizab dau. of Geo. Wood*	27 ,,
x	Alice dau. of Richard Heald of Rediuals ...	9 December
x	John son of Roberte Whiticar of Wal.	
x	Ann dau. of James Scofeild of Buriha.	16 ,,
x	Katrin dau. of Thomas Nabbe of Holcom ...	
x	Alice dau. of Henrie Dunster of Elton	
x	John son of James Kaie of Wal.	27 ,,
x	Roger son of Richard Houlte of Holcome ...	6 Januarij
	John son of John Grinhalghe of Midlton ...	
x	Ellen dau. of Thurstan Rawshorne of Elton ...	
	William son of William Rothwell of Midlton ...	13 ,,
	Margreate dau. of Isacke Royd of Holcome ...	
b	Marie dau. of James Scofeild & Marie Grinall of Buriha:	
b	Marie dau. of John Whiticar & Katrin Sale of Burie	
79 x	Richard son of Raphe Vnsworthe of Buriha:...	26 ,,
x	Alice dau. of Raphe Fylds of Burihamell ...	
x	John son of Henry Berie of Tottingtonn ...	3 Februarij
x	Elsabeth dau. of Ellis Lomax of Tott.	
	Margreate dau. of James Kaie of Hartlie ...	
	Thomas son of Robert Wood of Burie	
b	Katrin dau. of Henry Bouthe & Ellen Kaie of Burie	
x	Arthure son of James Kaie of Walmersley ...	10 ,,
x	Marie dau. of Francis Stotte of Heywood... ...	
x	Richard son of Richard Wigan of Tottingto ...	17 ,,
x	Alice dau. of Henry Nuttall of Tott:	
x	Margreat dau. of Thomas Fletcher of Buriha:	
x	Roger son of Richard Fletcher of Burihamell...	24 ,,
x	Jane dau. of Roger Grinhalghe of Midltonn ...	
x	Susan dau. of Robert Lyvsey of Heape	2 March
x	Richard son of Roger Kaie of Elton	
x	Marie dau. of James Fletcher of Tottingten ...	
x	Roberte son of Roger Kaie of Walmersley ...	
	Alice dau. of Richard Duckworthe of Burihamell	
x	Marie dau. of Richard Haslome of Rediuals ...	
x	Elsabethe dau. of Edmund Barlowe of Holcome	

* Written on right hand margin.

x	b	John son of John Butterfield & Alice Grinhalghe of Burie	6 March
		Thomas & Robert sons of James Warbarton of Holcome	
x		Jeffrey son of John Fenton of Burie	16 ,,
x		Jonathan son of William Stotte of Heywood ...	
x		Marie dau. of George Howorthe of Burie ...	23 ,,
x		Martha dau. of Samuell Sale of Buriha.	
x		John son of Richard Rosthorne of Tottington	
x		James son of Thomas Whithead of Burie ...	
x		John son of John Howorthe of Burie	

1628.

x		Peter son of Peter Lomax of Tottington ...	30 Marche
x		Margreate dau. of Roberte Dunster of Tottington	
		Raphe son of William Bouthe of Walmersley ...	6 Aprill
		John son of Francis Mackon of Heywood ...	
x		James son of Roberte Taylor of Burie	
x		Elizabethe dau. of Richard Banester of Burie...	
		Doritie dau. of Mr. George Murrey Rector of Burie	11 ,,
x		Henry son of James Hardman of Rediualls ...	13 ,,
x		John son of John Yate of Burichamell	
	b	Elsabethe dau. of George Livsey & Jane Duckworth of Midlton	
x		Jane dau. of Francis Wood of Burihamell ...	20 ,,
x		Thomas son of John Atton of Ratcliffe	
		James son of Ellis Gryme of Satleworthe ...	
x		Alice dau. of Thomas Bouthe of Holcome ...	23 ,,
x		Thomas son of Zackerie Bridge of Holcome ...	27 ,,
x		James son of Richard Overall of Burie	
Fo. 80 x		William son of Peter Houlte of Bridghall ...	4 Maij
x		Dorathie dau. of William Kaie of Cobhouse ...	
x		John son of Roger Bromeley of Burie	
x		John son of John Marcrofte of Midlton	
x		Roger son of Richard Bouthe of Burie	11 ,,
		Ann dau. of James Fogge of Elton	
x		Ollyver son of James Lomax of Gosforthe ...	
x		Marie dau. of James Openshawe of Burihamell	
x		Ellen dau. of Raphe Nuttall of Tottington ...	22 ,,
x		Thomas son of George Howorthe of Tottington	
x		James son of James Houlte of Holcome	1 Juñ
x		Thomas son of Thomas Kenion of Midlton ...	8 ,,
x		Doritie dau. of Mathewe Nuttall of Burie ...	15 ,,
x		Richard son of Richard Lyvesey of Heape ...	22 ,,
x		Joan dau. of Abell Wolsenham of Elton	29 ,,
x		Jonas son of Mr. John Croston of Elton ...	1 Julij
x		Richard son of Lawrance Burie of Tottington	6 ,,

1628 CHRISTENINGS.

	John son of Richard Pilkington of Holcome...	Julij
x	Marie dau. of Christopher Smethurste of Rediualls	
b	Genet dau. of George Platt of Prestwiche parishe & Ann Anderton of this parish	13 ,,
x	Doritie dau. of Richard Bouthe of Bouth Hall	16 ,,
x	Ann dau. of Richard Houlte of Burie	
x	Marie dau. of Thomas Lomax of Holcome ...	27 ,,
x	Alice dau. of John Taylor of Tottington ...	
x	Marie dau. of Thomas Lomax of Croslowe ...	
	James son of Edward Lomax of Heywood ...	3 Auguste
	Elizabethe dau. of James Crompton of Heywood	10 ,,
x	Katrin dau. of Lawrance Haslom of Wal: . .	
x	Michaill son of Michaill Wolsenham of Elton. .	
x	Thomas son of James Jacksonn of Burie ...	10 ,,
x	Ollyver son of Richard Hunte of Burie	
	Thomas son of Theophilus Houlte, Brandlesorne gent	17 ,,
x	Richard son of John Lomax of Holcome ...	24 ,,
	Katrin dau. of Richard Nuttall of Holcome ...	
	Ann dau. of John Houlte of Holcome	
x b	James son of Francis Berie of Heywood ...	
x	Marie dau. of Thomas Fletcher of Rediuals ...	
x	George son of George Houlte of Tottington ...	31 ,,
x	Thomas son of Roberte Scofeild of Bamford ...	7 September
x	Marie dau. of John Kaie of Burie	
	Samuell son of Samuell Mackon of Heywood ...	
x	Deboura dau. of Roberte Duckworthe of Heape	14 ,,
x	Richard son of Gilberte Lowe of Buriha: ...	
x	Elizabethe dau. of Ollyver Lomax of Wal. ...	28 ,,
b	Richard son of Raphe Barlowe & Marie Houlte of Burie	5 October
	James son of Edward Rothwell of Holcome ...	
	Gilian son of James Hartley of Holcome ...	
b	Edward son of Edward Leache & Elsãthe Hunte of Bury	
	Elizabethe dau. of Martyne Hopwood of Midlton	26 ,,
x	Richard son of Roger Lomax of Midleton ...	2 Nouember
x	William son of Ollyver Nabbe of Wal.	
x	Rubin son of Rubin Howorthe of Elton ...	
	Lawrance son of Thomas Smethurste of Heape	9 ,,
x	Arthure son of Roger Kaie of Elton ...	16 ,,
x	Sara dau. of Edmund Duckworth of Buriha. ...	
x	Jonathan son of Roberte Shephard of Buriha.	23 ,,
	Jane dau. of Roberte Asheworth of Midlton ...	
	John son of Charles Houlte of Tottington ...	30 ,,
x	Edmund son of John Hunte of Tott.	7 December
x	Elizabethe dau. of William Kaie of Wal. ...	14 ,,
	Roberte son of Roberte Howorth of Bamford...	

	Richard son of Sher Roger Taylor of Buriha. ...	21	December
x	Immyn dau. of Francis Pendlton of Midlton ...		
x	Edward son of Arthur Furnas of Burie	28	,,
x	Francis son of Richard Medowcrofte of Heape	4	Jañ
x	Mary dau. of Samuell Townsend of Heywood		
x	Abraham son of John Whitehead of Bury ...		
	Richard son of Frauncis Emerson of Tottingtō	18	,,
x	Andrew son of Robt Shepheard of Chesham...		
	Anne dau. of Roger Holt of Walmersley ...	25	,,
x	James son of Tho. Hamond of Bury		
	Alice dau. of Edmund Rothwell of Holcome ...		
x	William son of John Warberton of Holcome ...	29	,,
	Elizabeth dau. of Tho. Howarth of Shuttleworth	1	Feb
	Mary dau. of John Street of Midleton		
x	Susanna dau. of Geoffry Lomax of Heape ...		
b	Thomas son of Thomas* & Mary Howorth of Holcome		
x	Margret dau. of William Dutton of Holcome ...	8	,,
x	Raph son of Robt Duckworth of Woodgate Hill		
x	Richard son of John Fletcher of Bury		
x	Mary dau. of Tho. Mather of Walmersley ...		
x	James son of James Chadwicke of Holcome ...	15	,,
x b	Elizabeth dau. of Tho. Gotherope & Elizabeth Parsivall		
x	Jane dau. of George Nuttall of Walmersley ...	22	,,
	Thomas son of Richard Booth of Holcome ...		
	Ellen dau. of William Lummas of Birch hey...		
	Catherine dau. of Francis Medowcroft of Haslam hey		
x	Grace dau. of Ric. Seddon of Bury		
	Hesther dau. of Ric. Livesay of Middleton ...	1	Mar.
x	Elizabeth dau. of Ric. Hoult of Birch hey ...		
x	Richard son of John Kay of Walmersley	1	,,
x	William son of Willm Bury of Tottington ...	8	,,
x	James son of James Lort of Heywood		
	Catherine dau. of William Romsbothō of Holcome		
b	George son of Geo. Hulls & Eliz. Pens of Bury		
x	John son of John Booth of Bury	15	,,
x	Mary dau. of John Hind of Washy-lane		
x	Edmund son of Edward Pilkington of Walmersley		
	Alice dau. of John Wardleworth of Manchester	18	,,
x	Edward son of Arthur Partington of Walmersley	26	,,
x	John son of Roger Fletcher of Bury		
x	Elizabeth dau. of Richard Kay of Widdell ...		

By mee Willm Alte Curat

* Father's name not inserted.

1629.

o. 28	Edmund son of Ellis Howorth of Walmersley...	29 March
	Richard son of John Heywood of Middleton ...	
x	James son of William Heald of Bury	5 Aprill
x	James son of John Kay of Chatterton	
x	William son of Abraham Nabbe of Walmersley	12 ,,
x	Elizabeth dau. of James Greenhalgh of Walmersley	
	Jane dau. of Robt Hopwood of Middleton ...	
	Elizabeth dau. of Edmund Whittaker of Bury Hamell	
	William son of Thomas Fletcher of Bamford ...	
x	Margrett dau. of Richard Bridge of Tottington	
	James son of Jeremy Ainsworth of Tottington	
x	William son of Robt Kay of Walmersley	
x	Margrett dau. of Edmund Holt of Heape ...	
	Richard son of Edmund Low of Walmersley...	
	Abraham son of Ellis Fletcher of Birch hey ...	15 ,,
	Richard son of Edmund Holt of Tottington ...	19 ,,
	Elizabeth dau. of Edmund Bridge of Tottington	
	Thomas son of Thomas Bridgman of Holcome	23 ,,
x	Margrett dau. of Henry Nuttall of Birch hey ...	25 ,,
x	Ellizabeth dau. of John Byrom of Heywood ...	26 ,,
x	Sara dau. of John Buckley of Holcome	
x	Alice dau. of John Barlowe of Bury	3 May
x	Mary dau. of John Booth of Bury	
x	John son of Edward Hind of Bury	
x	John son of Peeter Smith of Bury hamell ...	
x	Edward son of Giles Vnsworth of Redivalls ...	
	Dorothy dau. of Richard Romsbotham of Holcom	
b	Abraham son of Abraha Taylor of Middleton & Anne Holt of Heywood	10 ,,
x	Alice dau. of Thomas Kay of Walmersley ...	
x	John son of Steven Sagar of Redivalls	
x	Anne dau. of Edmund Pilkington of Elton ...	17 ,,
x	Thomas son of Francis Haymer	24 ,,
x	Thomas son of James Livesay of Bury hamell	
x	George son of Robt Marcroft of Bury hamell ...	
x	Anne dau. of Richard Smethurst of Broad-cke	
	Mary dau. of Tho. Warberton of Holcome ...	
x	Elizabeth dau. of John Kay of Walmersley ...	31 ,,
x	Bartholomew son of Barthol. Smethurst of Midleto	
x	Dorothy dau. of John Hill of Tottington	
	Robert son of Peter Clough of Bury	
	Deborah dau. of Tho. Walmer of Heape ...	
	Ellen dau. of Tho. Kenion of Midleton	7 June
	Martin son of Richard Nuttall of Elton	14 ,,
	Richard son of John Kay of Banke Lane ...	

D

x	Henry son of Thomas Wood of Holcome	17	June
x	Jonathan son of John Fenton of Bury	28	,,
x	Anne dau. of Thomas Pilkington of Elton		
x	Mary dau. of Humphrey Broome of Bury hamell	5	July
x	John son of Gideon Coupe of Holcome		
x	Richard son of Jeffrey Brooke of Bury		
x	Anne dau. of John Aspinwall of Middleton		
x	James son of Tho. Turner of Birch hey		
	James son of Robert Walworke of Walmersley	12	,,
x	Alice dau. of William Greenleafe of Bury	19	,,
Fo. 83 x	Anne dau. of John Kay of Little-wood	26	,,
x	Robert son of Robert Greenhalgh of Elton		
	Mary dau. of Raph Nuttall of Holcome		
x	Mary dau. of Phillip Martindale of Bury	2	August
x	Thomas son of Raph Holt of Walmersley	16	,,
x	Ellis son of Ellis Leach of Walmersley		
x	Francis son of Richard Prescott of Bury	23	,,
x	Anne dau. of Humphrey Barlowe of Bury		
x	Anne dau. of Robert Nabbe		
x	Josiah son of Richard Booth of Tottington	6	September
	Rachell dau. of Mr. George Murrey Rector of Bury	13	,,
x	Sarah dau. of John Croston of Elton		
x	Alice dau. of Robert Marcroft of Tottington		
x	Susanna dau. of John Lomax of Elton		
b	Thomas son of Henry Allens & Margery Bromely of Bury		
x	James son of Henry Bury of Tottington	20	,,
x	John son of Thomas Rushton of Middleton		
x	James son of Richard Buckley of Bury hamell		
x	James son of John Ainsworth of Bury hamell	4	October
x	Elizabeth dau. of Edmund Haworth of Shuttleworth	11	,,
x	Richard son of John Greenhalgh of Tottington		
	Martha dau. of Richard Bury of Heywood	18	,,
	Mary dau. of Willm Bridge of Holcome		
x	Alice dau. of Richard Hadocke of Bury		
	George son of John Smith of Midleton	25	,,
x	Mary dau. of Henry Dunster of Elton		
x	Thomas son of Robt Haymer of Tottington	1	Novem
	Thomas son of Richard Wood of Middleton	8	,,
x	Abraham son of John Longworth of Bury		
x	Thomas son of Thomas Whitehead of Bury	15	,,
x	Roger son of Roger Seddon of Bury	18	,,
b	Raph son of Raph Digle & Eliz. Hull of Bury	22	,,
x	Thomas son of Raph Bridge of Birch hey	29	,,
	Mary dau. of James Stott of Heywood		
x	Jane dau. of Richard Wood of Elton	6	Decem
x	Jane dau. of Thomas Wilkinson of Walmersley	20	,,

1629-1630   CHRISTENINGS.

x	Mary dau. of Richard Kay of Elton	25	Decem̃
x	Mary dau. of Thomas Wood of Tottington ...	27	,,
	Alice dau. of William Holt of Tottington ...	1	January
x	Anne dau. of Thomas Wood of Bury hamell ...	3	,,
	Mary dau. of Richard Kay of Walmersley ...	10	,,
x	Anne dau. of Richard Romsbotham of Tottingtõ		
x	Susanna dau. of Richard Howorth of Holcome	17	,,
x	Jane dau. of Richard Duckworth of Middleton		
x	Elizabeth dau. of Rob̃t Heald of Redivalls ...	24	,,
x	Peter son of Mathew Wolsenhā of Haslom hey		
	Catherine dau. of James Leach Bury hamell ...		
x	William son of William Hitchinson of Tottington	31	,,
x	Arthur son of Rob̃t Whitaker of Elton ...		
x	Mary dau. of Ellis Vnsworth of Bury hamell ...		
	Elizabeth dau. of Roger Kay of Walmersley ...		
x	Alice dau. of Edmund Seddon of Bury		
x	Richard son of Richard Booth of Booth... ...	7	Feb̃
x	Richard son of Peter Holt of ye Bridge		
x	Elizabeth dau. of Roger Greenhalgh of Midletõ		
b	Edmund son of Edmund Holt & Jane Nabbe ...		
x	Mary dau. of John Holt of Holcome	14	,,
x	Peter son of Thomas Smethurst of Heape ...		
x	Anne dau. of John Whitehead of Bury		
84 x	Hannah dau. of Abraham Makin of Tottington	21	,,
x	Elizabeth dau. of Henry Booth of Bury		
b	John son of John Haymer & Anne Kay		
	Thomas son of James Wilson of Holcome ...		
x	Elizabeth dau. of Thomas Lomax of Tottingtõ	28	,,
x	William son of John Smethurst of Redivalls ...		
b	Alice dau. of John Singleton of Prestwich & Alice Barlowe of Middleton		
x	Alice dau. of Thomas Nabbe of Tottington ...	7	March
	Anne dau. of Francis Makin of Heywood ...		
	Thomas son of Henry Bridge of Tottington ...		
	Anne dau. of William Johnson of Birch hey ...		
	William son of Rob̃t Diggle of Middleton ...		
	Mary dau. of Robert Kay of Walmersley ...	14	,,
	Thomas son of Thomas Taylor of Tottingtõ ...	14	,,
	Alice & Jennet daus. of George Howorth of Elton		
	Anne dau. of James Crompton of Heywood ...	17	,,
	John son of Mathew Sutliffe of Elton		
	William Alte Curate		

* Anno Domini 1630.

x	Ruthe dau. of John Buttrworth of Hasselingden	28	March
	Jane dau. of James Shuttllworth of Houlkorn ...	4	Aprill
x	John son of George Vnsworth of Bury		

* " Anno Domini " written over and crossed out " Ano Domeny."

x	Keathernn dau. of George Hoult of Hassellom heay		April
x	Jane dau. of Richard Hasselam of Rediuells ...	11	,,
x	Margrertt dau. of Richard Hollt of Bury ...		
x	James son of William Asselay of Houlkom ...		
x	Ellen dau. of Symond Barllowe of Tottington...	18	,,
x	Ellen dau. of Franches Nuttall of Tottington...		
x	Mary dau. of Raphe Fylles of Heape	25	,,
	John son of John Wriglay of Midelton	2	May
	Suzana dau. of Richard Taylio' of Heape ...		
	Franches son of James Fentton of Heawood ...		
x	Keatheren dau. of Charlls Vnsworth of Houlkom		
	Arthur son of Robertt Smethrst of Ellton ...	9	,,
	Henery son of Thomas Berche of Midelton ...		
x	John son of Richard Tealio' of Whamerslaye...	16	,,
x	Allis dau. of Thomas Kay of Ellton		
x	James son of James Ainsworth of Houlkom ...	28	,,
x	Thomos son of Arthur Smethrst of Heape ...		
x	Ellen dau. of Pettr Lomax of Tottington ...	30	,,
	Mary dau. of Roger Flecho' of Bury hamell ...		
x	Franches son of Franches Sttott of Heawood...	6	June
	Allies dau. of Thomos Smethrst of Bury		
	Thomos son of John Howorth of Tottington ...	13	,,
	Elizabeth dau. of John Chadwick of Heawood		
x	Robertt son of Robertt Wood of Berch heay ...	20	,,
x	James son of David Naden of Bury hamell ...	27	,,
x	Ann dau. of Edmond Hoult of		
Fo. 85	Edward & Josua sons of Richard Crosse of Bury	18	July
x	Richard son of Richard Holt of Bury		
	John son of Henry Nuttall of Tottington ...		
	Anne dau. of Richard Rosthorne of Tottington	25	,,
x	Richard son of Thomas Wood of Tottington ...	1	August
x	Mary dau. of John Hunt of Tottington		
x	Laurence son of Abraham Nabbe of Walmersley	8	,,
x	Abraham son of James Kay of Walmersley ...		
	Thomas son of Frauncis Emerson of Holcome	22	,,
	James son of Robert Crosley of Heywood ...		
x	Elizabeth dau. of Robt Greenhalgh of Middleton		
	Thomas son of John Bury of Holcome		
x	Mary dau. of Samuell Sale of Bury hamell ...		
x	Edward son of John Fenton of Bury	5	Sep^t
x	Thomas son of John Bridge of Holcome	12	,,
x	Richard son of James Lomax of Middleton ...		
x	Alice dau. of Thomas Rothwell of Holcome ...		
x	Richard son of Francis Pens of Middleton ...	19	,,
x	William son of Richard Bannister of Bury ...		
x	Peter son of Robert Livesay of Heape		
x	Roger son of Richard Isherwood of Bury ...	2	October
x	Alice dau. of James Hardman of Chesham ...	3	,,

1630 CHRISTENINGS.

x	John son of Edmund Greenhalgh of Bury lane		October
	Isabell dau. of John Kay of Walmersley		
x	Richard son of Robert Horabin of Birch hey...	24	,,
x	Daniell son of Gilbert Lowe of Bury hamell ...		
x	James son of James Jenkinson of Heape ...		
x	Thomas son of Thomas Nuttall of Bruckshawe		
x	Mary dau. of George Wood of Bury	31	,,
x	Alice dau. of Gideon Coupe of Holcome ...		
x	Anne dau. of Raph Vnsworth of Bury hamell ...	5	Novem̃
x	John son of John Greenhalgh of Tottington ...		
x	Mathewe son of Mathew Booth of Redivalls		
x	John son of John Atton of Ratcliffe		
x	Ellen dau. of Robt Shepheard of Chesha jun:r		
x	Anne dau. of James Shepheard of Chesha ...	14	,,
x	James son of Miles Holme of Walmersley ...	21	,,
x	Henry son of James Hartly of Holcome		
	John son of Roger Taylor of Middleton		
x	Mary dau. of Thomas Booth of Holcome ...	28	,,
	Daniell son of Josua Leach of Heywood		
x	Mary dau. of Robt Dunster of Tottington ...	5	Decem̃
x	Arthur son of Arthur Furnes of Bury	9	,,
x	Robert son of Robert Kay of Sheepe-hey ...	12	,,
x	Abraham, Isaac, Jacob, sons of George Nuttall of Golinrode	13	,,
x	Ellis son of Ellis Lomax of Walshaw lane ...	19	,,
x	Dorothy dau. of James Kay of Gooseford ...		
	John son of Peter Seddon of Holcome	26	,,
x	Edmund son of Ellis Fletcher of Birch hey ...		
x	Arthur son of William Kay of Cobbas	1	Jañ
86 x	Robert son of Abell Woolsenham of Haslom hey		
x	Susanna dau. of John Haworth of Bury	2	,,
x	Elizabeth dau. of Roger Smethurst of Bury ...		
x	William son of William Overall of Bury	6	,,
x	Peter son of Richard Livesay of Middleton ...	9	,,
x	Thomas son of Edmund Pilkington of Walmersley	16	,,
x	Elizabeth dau. of John Yate of this hamell ...		
x	Francis son of James Jackson of Bury		
	Mary dau. of Richard Booth of Bury		
x	Mary dau. of Raph Nuttall of Tottington ...	19	,,
x	Mary dau. of Richard Bridge of Walshaw lane	23	,,
x	Thomas son of John Warberton of Elton ...	30	,,
x	Elizabeth dau. of Arthur Partington of Burrowes	6	Feb
x	George son of Richard Booth of Booth	13	,,
	Anne dau. of Thomas Kay		
	Richard son of Charles Holt of Tottington ...		
x	Rachell dau. of Richard Prescott of Bury... ...	20	,,
b	Margrett dau. of Thomas Rothwell & Elizabeth Nabbe of Walmersley		
	Alice dau. of Jerimy Barlow of Tottington ...	27	,,

x	Richard son of John Booth of Bury...	Feb	
x	Richard son of Raph Holt of Walmersley ...		
x	Ellen dau. of Richard Livesay		
b	William son of John Overall & Isabell Heald of Bury		
	Elizabeth dau. of Richard Romsbothā of Romsbothā	6 March	
x	Jennett dau. of John Robinson		
	Thomas son of Thomas Whitehead of ye feilds, bapt: at Middleton*		
	James son of Henry Dawson	20	,,
x	Thomas son of Thomas Dawson of Midleton...		
x	James son of James Hoult of Holcome		
x	Anne dau. of James Kershawe		

William Alte, Curat:

1631.

	Mary dau. of William Bamford of Bamford ...	27 March	
x b	John son of Roger Kay of Elton		
x	Anne dau. of Edward Rothwell of Elton ...		
	Anne dau. of Thomas Howorth of Walmersley		
x	John son of Robert Livesay of Middleton ...		
	Susanna dau. of George Hull of Bury		
x	Arthur son of Arthur Kay of Bass lone	10 Aprill	
x	Alice dau. of Roger Lomax of Cathole		
x	Margrett dau. of Laurence Fletcher of Renford feild		
x	Thomas son of Thomas Wharmby of Redivalls		
x	Ellen dau. of Thomas Hamond of Littlewood...		
x	Jeremy son of John Barlowe of Bury	11	,,
x	Arthur son of Arthur Holt of Bury hamell ...	17	,,
x	Anne dau. of William Heald of Bury hamell ...		
	Anne †	20	,,
x	Jane dau. of Richard Haslom of Redivalls ...	23	,,
x	Peter son of Robert Shepheard Sen' of Chesham	24	,,
	Elizabeth dau. of Mr. William Alte, Curaᵗ of Bury	1 May	
Fo.87 x	Anne dau. of John Ransom of Bury	8	,,
x	John son of John Fletcher of Bury		
x	Elizabeth dau. of Robert Marcroft of this hamell		
	Martha dau. of Robert Ridings of Heape ...		
x	Anne dau. of Roger Bromeley of Bury	15	,,
x	Alexander son of Edmund Howorth of Greenhill	19	,,
	John son of William Holt of Hollingreave ...	22	,,
x	John son of Hamlett Lowe of Walmersley ...		
x	Anne dau. of Richard Kay of Widdell	29	,,

* Inserted at a little later date, by a later hand.
† The rest is blank.

1631 CHRISTENINGS.

	Katherine dau. of George Howorth of Bury ...	12 June
x	Isabell dau. of John Croston of Elton	19 ,,
	Roger son of John Kay of Banke lane	
	Robert son of James Livesay of Heape	26 ,,
x	Robert son of Robert Scofeild of Bamford ...	
x	Anne dau. of Edmund Kay of Burrowes	
x	Jane dau. of Richard Barlow of Elton	
	John son of Thomas Nabbe of Tottington ...	3 July
x	. . . daughter of George Heaton of Heape	
x	Ellen dau. of Mathew Woolsenham of Haslom hey	10 ,,
x	Deborah dau. of James Chadwicke of Bury hamell	
x	John son of Michaell Bentley of Haslom hey ...	24 ,,
x	Ellen dau. of Richard Nuttall of Elton	
	John son of Raphe Buckley of Houlcome ...	27 ,,
	Alice dau. of John Brooke of Houlcome	7 August
b	Mary dau. of Francis Nuttall and Jane Booth of this parish	
x	John son of Richarde Rey of Widdall	14 ,,
	Añe dau. of Thomas Booth of Bury	
	Dorethy dau. of James Lortt of Heywood ...	
x	Olliuer son of Olliuer Nabbe of Walmersley ...	28 ,,
	Añ dau. of Henery Hoult of Shutelworth ...	
x b	William son of William Crompton of Boulton parish and Alice Holt of Bury parish ...	
x	Añ dau. of John Barlow of Heape	4 September
b	Robert son of Robert Langley of Midelton parish and Katherine Kary of Haywood	11 ,,
x	Richard son of Samuell Makin of Heywood ...	18 ,,
x	William son of Richard Heald of Reddiuls ...	
x	Alice dau. of Richard Ouerall of Bury	
	Mary dau. of Arthur Hoult of Lomax	
x	Elizabeth dau. of William Bury of Elton... ...	2 October
x	Sisely dau. of Henery Nuttall of Houlcome . .	
x	Isabell dau. of John Taylor of Houlcome ...	9 ,,
x	Thomas son of John Fenton of Bury	16 ,,
	Arthur son of Robert Taylor of Bury	23 ,,
x	Mary dau. of John Kay of Wamersley	
	Jane dau. of Roger Booth of Redduols ...	
	John son of Elize Howoorth of Shuttelworth ...	
	Elizabeth dau. of Richard Leach of Houlcome	30 ,,
	John son of Thomas Fletcher of Rediuols ...	
	Bartholomew son of John Hamer of Chesham	
	Edward son of Edward Hynde of Bury	
	William son of William Bury of Tottington ...	
38 x	John son of Edward Leach of Tottington ...	7 Nouember
x	Alice dau. of Robert Nabb of Elton	
x	Mary dau. of John Hoult of this hamell	21 ,,

x	Richard son of Jefferv Brooke of Bury	Nouember
	Richard son of Thomas Kenyon of Mydelton parish	28 ,,
x	Rodger son of Richard Isherwood of Bury ...	4 December
x	Richard son of John Key of Rediuells	
x	Añ dau. of Gyles Vnsewoorth of Rediuells ...	11 ,,
x	Dorithy dau. of Richard Ramsbothome of Wamersley	
	Elizabeth dau. of Thomas Warburton of Houlcome	23 ,,
x	Thomas son of George Hoult of Haslome hey...	1 January
	Añe dau. of John Key of Wamersley	
	Mary dau. of Henery Nuttall of Birch hey ...	
x	Richard son of Richard Seddon of Bury hamell	8 ,,
x	James son of Robert Greenhalgh	
	Arthur and Grace twins of Peter Hoult of the bridg.	18 ,
x	James son of James Key of Bury	
	Richard son of Raph Seddon of Heape	22 ,,
	Gyles son of George Vnsworth of Bury	29 ,,
	Mary* dau. of Richard Booth of Booth	
x	Thomas son of Thomas Smetheurst of this hamell	5 February
	James son of Richard Bury of Heywood	
x	Susan dau. of Thomas Milner of Wamersley ...	12 ,,
x	Richard son of William Hopewood of Midelton	
	Marie dau. of James Cramptō of Heywood ...	19 ,,
	Thomas son of Thomas Fletcher of this hamill	
x	Mary dau. of Robert Kenion of Rediuels ...	26 ,,
	Sara dau. of Arthur Fourness of Bury	
x	Elizab dau. of Richard Rey of Wamersley ...	
	Richard son of John Hopwood of Ashwood ...	4 March
x	Alice dau. of Richard Wood of Eltō	
x	Dorathy dau. of Williā Key of Wamersley ...	
x	Mary dau. of Francis Nuttall of Wamersley ...	
x	Elizab. dau. of Robt Shipherd of Cheshā ...	11 ,,
	Esther dau. of Thomas Wolmer of this h. ...	
x	Henry son of Robt Dunster of Tottingtō ...	18 ,,

Baptizats Ao. Dom. 1632.

x	John son of Roger Sedden of Bury	25 ,,
	Jane dau. of Francis Hamer	
x	Roger son of John Booth of Bury	8 April
	Ann dau. of Henry Both of Bury	
	James son of Richard Wiggin of Holcom̄ ...	15 ,,
x	Jane dau. of James Lummax of Wamersley ...	
x	Ann dau. of Robt Marcroft of Midletō	

* Originally "Grace" but crossed through with a pen, "Mary" being written over it.

1632 CHRISTENINGS.

89 x	Mary dau. of Francis Key of this hamel	22 April	
	Anne dau. of Jonas Haworth of Howlcoṁ		
	Hellen dau. of Rich. Hadach of Bury ...		
	Rich. son of James Key of Gyndles		
x	Dorathy dau. of James Howlt of this hamel ...	29	,,
	Isabel dau. of Mr. Byram of Byrā	6 May	
	Henry son of Jeremy Answorth of Holcoṁ ..	13	,,
x	Sarah dau. of Robt Duckworth of Heape ...	20	,,
	Edward son of Edward Rosthorne of the Lume	23	,,
x	Richard son of Jephray Lumas of Heape ...	27	,,
x	Arthure son of Richard Smethurst of Broadoke	3 June	
	Gyles son of James Rothwell of Holcoṁ		
x	George son of George Howorth of Shutleworth	10	,,
	Elizabeth dau. of Francis Emersome of Holcome		
x	Richard son of Rich. Holt of Haslom hey ...	17	,,
x	Thom. son of Thomas Wood of Bury		
x	George son of Williā Greenhalgh of Bury ...	1 July	
	Alice dau. of William Holt of Holcoṁ	8	,,
x	Elizab dau. of Henry Dunster of Elton	15	,,
x	Thomas son of Thom. Key of Elton	18	,,
x	Thomas son of George Battersby of Wamersley	29	,,
	Francis son of Robt Fletcher of Ashworth ...		
	Anne dau. of Gideon Coupe of Holcome ...		
x	Anne dau. of Roger Greame of Tottington ...	4 August	
x	John son of Robert Greenall of Ensworth ...	12	,,
	James son of James Tayler		
	Samuell son of Frances Macken of Hewed ...	26	,,
	James son of Rapth Vnsworth of this hamell ...		
x	Elise son of Richard Flecher of this towne ...	9 September	
	Marie dau. of Thomas Beirch		
x	John son of James Fenton of Bamfort		
x	Elizabeth dau. of John Kay of Widdill	16	,,
x	Marie dau. of Roberte Hamer of Tottington ...	30	,,
	Isabell dau. of Thomas Warberton of Tottington	7 October	
x	Marie dau. of John Holt of Ballderstone ...		
x	Elizabeth dau. of Abram Nabbe of Wamersle...		
x	Elizabeth dau. of Robert Smethurst of Tottington	14	,,
	Thomas son of Richard Nuttall of Hollcome ...	21	,,
x	Richard son of George Wood of Burie		
x	Marie dau. of John Kay of Redivalls ...	28	,,
x	John son of John Bate of Burie	4 November	
x	Ralfe son of George Nuttall of Gallenrode ...		
x	James son of Gilberte Lowe of this hamell ...	18	,,
	Richard son of Richard Romsbothom of Holcome		
x	Dorithie dau. of Roger Kay of Woollfould ...		
90 x	George son of Richard Prescott of Burie	25	,,
	Edmond son of John Haywood of Berkle		
x	Alis dau. of John Hamer of Tottington ...		
x	Marie dau. of Roberte Heald of Redivalls	2 December	

	John son of Roger Kay of Bridhole		December
	Elizabeth dau. of Richard Pacocke of Hollcome	9	,,
x	Ellen dau. of Raplh Holte of Wamersle	16	,,
x	Richard son of John Yate of this hamell		
	Martha dau. of Robert Digle of Berkle		
	John son of John Birde of Ashworth	23	,,
	Mary dau. of Thomas Warburton of Houlcom̃		
x	Abraham, Isack, & Rebecca, twins of Edmund Law of	...26	,,
x	Jaccob son of James Jackson of Bury	29	,,
x	Tho. son of John Smethurst of Rediwels... ...	1	Januarie
	Robert son of Richard Barlow of Ellton ...	6	,,
x	Sarah dau. of John Grenehalghe of Holcome...		
x	Mary dau. of Francis Dawson of Walm^{9}sley ...	13	,,
x	George son of James Buckley of Bury	20	,,
	Ellen dau. of Thomas Blakelow of Burkle ...	28	,,
x	Francis son of Thomas Rothowell of Holcom̃		
x	John son of James Gee of Bury		
b	Daurothie dau. of Henry Allens & Margeris Bromille of Bury		
x	Samuell son of Peeter Smith of Bury	3	February
x	Robert son of James Sheppard of Chesham ...		
	John son of James Stock of Heywood		
x	Robert son of Thomas Ham^9 of Chesom ...	10	,,
x	Elizebeth dau. of Oliu^9 Nabb of Walm^{9}sley ...		
x b	Abrahã son of Thomas Woolner and Jennett Wild of Heape		
x b	Daurothie dau. of John Lomax of Birkle and Ann Lomax of this pish		
x	Daurothie dau. of John Haworth of Bury ...	17	,,
x	Ann dau. of John Barlow of Bury		
	Arthur son of Arthur Partington of Wall ...		
	Jonathan son of Willm Makon of Heywood ...		
x	James son of Willm Lomax of Birch hey ...	24	,,
x	John son of Charles Romsbothome of Holcō...		
b	Sussan dau. of Francis Medowcrofte and Sussan Cowp of Bury		
x	Gennett dau. of Georg Ashworth of Bury ...	3	March
	Richard son of Rich. Romsbothome of Holcom̃		
	Mary dau. of John Whithead of Bury	10	,,
x	Thomas son of Willm Bury of Woodroad ...		
x	James son of Robert Makon of Heywood ...		
	Willm son of John Bury of Hclcom̃	17	,,
x	John son of Martin Kaye of Bury		
x	Richard son of Ellis Vnsworth	24	,,
x	Mar. dau. of James Hardman of Chesham ...		
	Abigall son of Edmund Holte		

Anno Domin. 1633.

)1 x	Elen dau. of James Kay, Wamersle	31	March
x	Susan dau. of James Kay, Burie		
x	Thomas son of George Hawworth, Faside ...	7	Aprill
x	Ann dau. of Richard Haslome		
x	Elizabeth dau. of Elis Lech, Wamersle	14	,,
	Alice dau. of Mr. Morry pson of Burie	21	,,
x	Debera dau. of John Warberton		
x	John son of John Greenalgh	28	,,
x	Edward son of Edward Rothell		
x	Jane dau. of Edmond Greenalgh		
	Thomas son of Richard Greenall of Brandlesome*	16	,,
x	Caterin dau. of Rodger Flecher	5	May
x	Henry son of Mihill Farer †		
x	Elis son of Lawrance Flecher of Redivals ...	12	,,
x	Susan dau. of John Croston of Elton		
x	Esther dau. of Thomas Hamon of Litlewood...		
x	Frances son of John Wofenden of Hewed ...		
x	Elizabeth dau. of Richard Bridge of Holcome	19	,,
x	Henery son of John Ridgle		
x	James son of James Willsonne	26	,,
x	John son of Robert Crosle of Hewed	2	June
x	Richard son of Richard Medocroft	9	,,
x	John son of John Rowsone		
	Will son of Thomas Rushton		
x	Henery son of Ralfe Woasencroft	16	,,
x	Jane dau. of Rodger Taylor		
b	Alice dau. of John Ouerall		
	Athur son of Peter Holt of Bridge	23	,,
	Will son of Richard Rushtonn		
x	Thomas son of John Flecher of Burie	30	,,
x	Elen dau. of Thomas Wharmbie		
x	Jane dau. of Edmond Hawworth	7	July
x	Marie dau. of Samuell Nuttall		
x	Jonie dau. of John Hawworth of Burie	14	,,
	John & Elen twinles of John Nabbe	21	,,
	Thomas son of Thomas Lifsie	28	,,
x	Ann dau. of Edmond Withiteker		
x	Elizabeth dau. of Robert Kay		
x	Jonie dau. of Robert Shepert		
x	Ann dau. of Will Bamforte of Bamforte	4	August
	Peter son of George Hall of Burie		
x	John son of Peter Lomax	11	,,
	Peter son of Elis Lomax		
x	Ann dau. of Thomas Whithead of Feilds ...	18	,,
x	Elizabeth dau. of Henery Lort of Burie		

* S q. written in the margin on the left hand side.
† Or "Faver."

Fo. 92 Rodger* son of Richard Banister of Burie ... 25 August
Cester son of Thomas Nuttall & Jane Rushton   1 September
Ralfe son of Ralfe Nutall of Tottington ... ... 8 ,,
Henery son of Peter Seddon ... ...
Henery son of Jerimie Ensworth ... ... 15 ,,
Martha dau. of Philip [?] Martindele † ...
Richard son of Ralfe Bridge of Holcome ...
Elizabeth dau. of Richard Vnsworth ... ... 22 ‡ ,,
Añ dau. of Samuell Makeon of Hewwood ...
John son of Richard Hoult of this towne ...
Añ dau. of John Longworth of this towne ...
Thomas son of John Warberton of Holcome...
William son of Rapth Bridge of Berch hey ...
Ginit dau. of Gerimie Ensworth of Holcome ...
Eliz. dau. of William Kay of Wamersley ...
Mary dau. of John Stotte of Hewwood ... ...
Arthur son of John Greenhalgh of Holcome ...
Mary dau. of Robert Scōfilld of Bamfort ...
Isabell dau. of John Kay of Redivalls ... ...
George son of Peter Digle of Midleton ... ...
John son of John Barlow of Heape ... ... 16 January 1633 §
George son of Thomas Turner of Holcoñ ...
Eliza dau. of Roger Seddon of this towne ...
Jane dau. of William Brooke of Holcoñ ... ...
Bartholō son of Bartholomew Smethurst ...
John son of William Warberton of Holcome ...
Ann dau. of Frances Stotte of Hewwood ...
Peter son of Robert Scowfild of Bamfort ...
Mihill son of John Buckley of Tottington ...
George son of John Lomas of Berchey ... ...
Caterin dau. of Roger Greenhalgh of Midleſ ...
Thomas son of George Holt of Haslome hey ...
b John son of John Greenahalgh & Caterin
     Flecher of this pish ... ...
Grace dau. of Henery Romsbothom of Holcoñ
Richard son of Richard Romsbothom of Romsb.
Henery son of James Fenton of Bamforte ...
Robert son of Robert Kay ... ...
Edward son of Mihill Bentley of Haslom hey ...
Arthur son of Richard Kay of Widdell ... ...
Alice dau. of William Makeon of Hewwood ...
Mary dau. of James Lifsi ... ...
Eliz. dau. of Thomas Burie of Woodrod ...
Elen dau. of John Wofendine of Hewwood ...
Dorathie dau. of John Lomax of Berch hey ...

* In the margin, "xiijs. 4d. paied," "all paied Before."
† Inserted afterwards.
‡ No dates from this time to March 29th, 1634.
§ Date added at a later period.

1633-1634   CHRISTENINGS.

Arthur son of Rich. Romsbothom ... ...
Johnie dau. of George Holt ... ...
fo. 93 Peter son of John Rosthorne ... ...
Thomas son of Flecher of Redivalls ... ...
Mary dau. of Frances Nuttall ... ...
Eliz. dau. of Rapth Seddon of Heape ... ...
James son of Henery Dawson of . . . ...
Frances son of Henery Dowson ... ...
Elen dau. of Mathew . . . .
Mary dau. of John Ashworth of Hewwood ...
Peter son of Robert Shepeard of Chesam ...
Jerimie son of Elis Howworth of Etenfild ... ˙
John son of Rodger Grime of Holcome ... ...
Eliz. dau. of Elis Flecher of Holcome ... ...
Thomas son of Rapth Seddon of Heape ... ...
John son of Edward Mills ... ...

1634.

Sara dau. of Richard Burie of Heyw. ... ... 29 March
Robte son of Arthur Scofeild of Bamf. ... ...
Jane dau. of Willm Hichenson of Tott. ...
John son of Robte Howarth of Shutt. ... ...
John son of Robte Howorth of Shutt. ... ...
Marie dau. of Willm Holt... ... ... 6 April
Peter son of Peter Lomax ... ... 13 ,,
Elizabeth dau. of Jeremie Ainsworth ... ...
Kathrin dau. of Willm Booth de Tott. ... ...
John son of Francis Burie of Heyw. ... ...
Mary dau. of John Asheworth ... ...
James son of John Wrigley of Heywo. ... ... 20 ,,
Susan dau. of John Howorth of Burie ... ...
Elizabeth dau. of Edm Lomax of Heaw. ...
Thomas son of Tho. Smethurst of Tott. ... ... 22 ,,
Rogr son of James Fenton of Hea. ... ...
Jonathan son of Thomas . . . . 14 May
James son of Gilbert Lowe of Burie ... ... 18 ,,
Dorithie dau. of Rogr Kay of Tot. ... ...
John son of Robte Greenhalgh of Ainsw. ...
Marie dau. of Robte Doson of Bamf. ... ...
Jonathan son of Willm Rostron ... ... 25 ,,
Jeffrey son of Ellis Howorth of Edenf. ... ...
Tho. son of Francis Scott of Heaw. ... ...
Jane dau. of Ric. Holt of Tott. ... ...
Mary dau. of Tho. Bridge of Holcom ... ... 1 June
George son of Ric. Millington of Holc. ... ...
An dau. of Ric. Lomax of Tott. ... ...
Grace dau. of Ric. Booth of Tott. ... ...
Jonathan son of Joseph Leach of Bamfo. ... 14 ,,

Fo. 94 Ann dau. of Roger Gryme of Shuttleworth		June
Robte son of Georg Howorth of Fac.		
Kathrin dau. of Michaell Bentlie		
Tho. son of George Holt		
Jane dau. of Ryc. Prescott of Burie		6 Julie
Ann dau. of Willm Greenhalgh of Bur.		
John son of John Smethurst of Redivals		13 ,,
Marie dau. of Robt Shepard of Chesam		
Willm son of Tho. Warberton of Tott.		
Marie dau. of Edm Schofeld of Hea.		20 ,,
Jane dau. of Francis Hamer		
Ann dau. of Edm Millnes		27 ,,
Ann dau. of Arthur Smethurst de Heap		3 August
Thomas son of Francis Stott of Hea.		
John son of Arthur Smethurst		
Ellin dau. of John Booth of Tott.		10 ,,
John son of Ric. Johnes		
Edm son of Edm		
Elizabeth dau. of Willm		17 ,,
Elizabeth dau. of Franc Scofeld of Bam.		
Isabell dau. of . . . . of Houl.		
Arthur son of Ric. Kay of Elt.		24 ,,
Dorithie dau. of Rogr Kay of Woolf		
Sara dau. of Robt Macon of Hea.		31 ,,
James son of Robt Greenhalghe		
An dau. of Robte Shepard of Ches.		
Tho. son of Tho. Smethurst		
Tho. son of Tho. Whithead of Burie		
Rogr son of George Unsworth of Burie		14 September
James son of Robte Reade of Rediso		
Susan dau. of Tho. Mather		28 ,,
Ric. son of Willm Hopwood		
Elizabeth dau. of Ric. Kay of Walm.		
Elizabeth dau. of Francis Empsō of Holc.		
Ann dau. of Samuell Makin of Hea.		7 October
John son of Ric. Holt of Burie		
Ann dau. of John Longworth of Burie		13 ,,
Tho. son of Thom. Warberton of Holc.		
Willm son of Ra. Bridge of Birch he.		
Ann dau. of Gyles Unsworth of Rediu.		
Fo. 95 Mary dau. of William Greenhalgh*		19 ,,
Marie dau. of Jo. Holt de Burie		
Ann dau. of Tho. Stott of Burie		2 November
Richard son of Jeffrey Brook		
Marie dau. of Tho. Fletcher of Rediu.		16 ,,
Ric. son of John Hopwood		
Alice dau. of Ric. Wood of Elton		30 ,,
Dorithie dau. of Willm Kay of Walm.		

* Added at later date.

1634-1635 CHRISTENINGS. 251

Henerie son of Robte Dunstier	November
Jane dau. of Francis Ham⁹ of Tott.	
Susan dau. of Francis Medowcroft	14 December
Thomas son of Tho. Greenhalgh of Heap.	28 ,,
Elizabeth dau. of Olyuer Nabb of Wal.	
Marie dau. of John Whithead of Burie	4 Januarie
Willm son of Richard Burie of Woodr.	28 ,,
Margerie dau. of Willm Lomax of Birch	
Abraham son of Thomas Woolner of Burie	25 ,,
Willm son of John Burie of Holcom̃	8 Februarie
Jeffrey son of Georg Marcroft of Midle.	22 ,,
John & Willm sons of John Ramsbothom Holcome	
Sara dau. of Henrie Ainsworth	1 March
James son of James Wilson	
Edmund son of Edm̃ Rothell of Holcom̃	15 ,,
Ellin dau. of James Kaie of Walm.	
Ric. son of Ric. Kaie of Widdell	18 ,,
Jane dau. of Henerie Holt of Shutlew.	22 ,,
James son of James Kay of Burie	
John son of Ellis Kaie of Elton	

[Here follows about four inches of erasures apparently not entries of baptisms].

Richard son of Arthur Smethurst de Wham.	7 March

1635.

Fo. 96	Susan dau. of Robert Makon of Heywood	29 March
	Richard son of Richard Haddok of Bury	4 April
	James son of Richard Haddok of Bury	5 ,,
	Thomas son of James Breerley de Bury	
	Thomas son of Edmund Howorth de Walm.	
	Ester Nuttall, dau. of Henry Nuttall de Holcome	12 ,,
	Susan dau. of Richard Overall de Bury	
	Ratcliffe son of George Nuttall de Walm.	23 ,,
	John son of Robert Smethurst de Heape	
	Aemar son of Aemar Ainsworth de Holcom̃	26 ,,
	James son of Henry Dunster de Elton	
	John son of James Greenhalgh de Tottington	
	Dorathy dau. of John Walworks	1 May
	John son of John Greenhalgh de Elton	3 ,,
	Thomas son of Richard Pilkinton de Walm.	7 ,,
	John son of George Holt de Elton	10 ,,
b	Susan dau. of John Couper & Alice Whitehead	
	Humfrey son of Richard Booth of Booth	17 ,,
	Joan dau. of Robert Duckworth of Heap	
	Thomas son of Edmund Smoolt of Bury	20 ,,
	Mathew & John sons of Richard Wigan	24 ,,
	Anne dau. of Dennice Kay of . . .	31 ,,
	Katherin dau. of Gideon Coupe	

	Henry son of Thomas Whitehead	7 June
	Abraham spurius...	8 ,,
	Henry son of Henry Bridge	14 ,,
	Richard son of Richard Fenton	
	Mary dau. of Thomas Nabb	21 ,,
	Mary dau. of Robert Greenhalgh	
	Robert son of John Warberton of Holcom ...	
	Richard son of Robert Smethurst	28 ,,
	Mary dau. of Thomas Fletcher of Bury	5 July
	Alice dau. of Thomas Smethurst of Tacklee ...	
	Anne dau. of Richard Nuttall	12 ,,
	Ellin dau. of James Hardman	
	Ellin dau. of John Walkden	
	Mary dau. of Jarvice Lowe	2 August
	James son of William Makon	
	Isaak son of Thomas Birch	
b	Elisabeth dau. of Henry Allens	9 ,,
	Richard son of Robert Horrobin	11 ,,
	Roger son of Richard Lomax	23 ,,
	Thomas son of Henry Wood	
	Alice dau. of Edmund Holt of Tott.	30 ,,
	Elizabeth dau. of Tho. Wharmbie	6 September
	Elizabeth dau. of James Kay of Walm.	
x	John son of James Howorth	13 ,,
	Richard son of John Whitehead	
x	Richard son of John Smethurst	
	Richard son of Tho. Wood	
	Dorathy dau. of Robert Liusey...	
x	Jane dau. of Oliver Nabbe	
b	James son of James Milnes	
x	Henry son of John Bury*	
x	Alice dau. of Richard Haslom of Rediv. ...	16 ,,
	Abraham son of Tho. Jackson	20 ,,
x	John son of Martin Kay	
	Dorathy dau. of Robert Crosly	27 ,,
b	Jane dau. of Mathew Burie	
x	Arthur son of Edmund Beacom	
x	Andrew son of Will. Bury of Chamber	4 October
Fo. 97	Alexander son of Hugh Bradshaw	11 ,,
x	Mary dau. of Richard Bridge	
	Alice dau. of Ralph Vnsworth	
x	Abraham son of Abrahā Wood	18 ,,
x	Richard son of Thomas Holt	
	Henry son of Henry Kay	18 ,,
x	Sarah dau. of James Kay of Burrows	21 ,,
	Mary dau. of William Greenall	
x	Emmine dau. of Francis Penns	8 November
	Peter son of Francis Emerson	

* " James son of Richard Bury," has been crossed through.

CHRISTENINGS.

x	Elizabeth dau. of Edmund Halliwell	November
x	Dorathy dau. of Matthew Sutcliffe	
	Edmund son of George Howorth	12 ,,
	Rodger son of Margret Bromeley	
x	John son of John Warberton	15 ,,
	Josias son of Henry Lort	22 ,,
x	Richard son of Martin Kay	
	Mary dau. of Mr. James Greenhalgh	4 December
x	Henry son of Rodger Kay of Woof:	6 ,,
	John son of Robert Butterworth of Moorehole	
x	Susan dau. of John Fletcher	
x	Anne dau. of John Roiley	13 ,,
b	Elizabeth dau. of John Hardis & . . (sic)	28 ,,
x	Susan dau. of James Holt of Middl psh	1 January
x	Ellis son of Thomas Fletcher of Rediv.	3 ,,
	John son of John Hunt of Totting	
x	Thomas son of Geofray Brooke of Bury	
	Mary dau. of Richard Rosthorne	17 ,,
	James son of Richard Romsbotham	
	Sarah dau. of Richard Bury of Heywood	24 ,,
	Jane dau. of John Brid of Ashworth	
x	John son of Raphe Seddon of Heape	31 ,,
	John son of Adam Liuecey of Mid. pish	
x	Mary dau. of Samuell Holt of Bury	
x	Richard son of Richard Lomax of Bury	7 February
x	Alice dau. of Peter Heald	
	Katherin dau. of Richard Lomax	
	John son of Francis Nuttall	14 ,,
x	Jane dau. of John Holt of Bury	
x	Thomas son of Robert Heald	
	George son of William Howorth	21 ,,
	Richard son of John Hopwood	28 ,,
	Jonathan son of James Chadwick	
	James son of Richard Romsbothom	
x	Sarah dau. of John Whitehead	
x	Thomas son of Jonas Hoileley	
	Dorathy dau. of Richard Howorth	6 March
	Dorathy dau. of John Chadwicke	
	Ann dau. of Mr. Heywood	8 ,,
x	Susan dau. of Samuell Sayle	13 ,,
x	Martha dau. of Edward Holt	
x	Katharin dau. of Mr. Raustorne	16 ,,
x	Robert son of Robert Hitchinson	
x	Dorathy dau. of Peter Smith	20 ,,
x	Robert son of Reuben Howorth	
x	William son of Richard Battersby	
	Henry son of Francis Nuttall	23 ,,

William Rothwell, Curat

1636.

Fo. 98	Thomas son of Robert Standfeild ...	3 Aprill
x	John son of Edward Seddon	
x	Margret dau. of Richard Booth ⎫	10 ,,
x	Susan dau. of Henry Booth ⎬ of Bury	
x	Mary dau. of Edmund Pilkinton ⎭	
	John son of Jeremy Kay	17 ,,
	John son of John Bury	
x	James son of James Brooke	24 ,,
x	James son of Thomas Nuttall	
x	Susan dau. of John Yate	
x	Sarah dau. of Thomas Hamond	1 May
	Robert son of George Howorth	
x	Sarah dau. of Michaell Bentley	8 ,,
x	Elizabeth dau. of John Greenhalgh	
x	Bartholemew son of Thomas Butler	
x	Richard son of Richard Fletcher	15 ,,
	Thomas son of William Hitchenson	22 ,,
	James son of Peter Holt of Bircle	
x	Anne dau. of Edmund Barlow	
	Richard son of John Bridge de Nooke	29 ,,
x	Henry son of Charles Romsbotham	5 June
	Katharin dau. of William Howorth of dry gap...	9 ,,
x	Mary dau. of Rodger Seddon of Bury	15 ,,
x	Mary dau. of Richard Kay de Hough	26 ,,
x	Abraha son of Thomas Wood	
x	John & George sons of James Openshaw ...	
x	Susan dau. of John Longworth	3 July
x	John son of William Bowker	10 ,,
x	Thomas son of Thomas Nuttall	
	Alexander son of Mr. Bamford	17 ,,
x	John son of Edmund Seddon	
x	Lawrance son of Lawrance Nabbe	
	Dorathy dau. of Richard Wignall	31 ,,
x	Mary dau. of George Hull	
	Richard son of Edmund Lort	7 August
x	Anne dau. of Thomas Liuesay	
x	Anne dau. of John Greenhalgh	
	William son of John Holt...	14 ,,
x	Thomas on of Richard Kay	21 ,,
x	William son of Michaell Holme	
b	Elizabeth dau. of Anne Lomax of Walm. ...	24 ,,
	Anne dau. of Francis Hamar	28 ,,
	John son of Thomas Warberton of Holcomhey	4 September
x	Mathew son of William Bury of Woodrode ...	
	Richard son of Richard Taylor	
x	Elizabeth dau. of John Coupe	16 ,,
x	Alice dau. of John Barlow of Water	18 ,,

1636 CHRISTENINGS.

x	Alice dau. of James Jenkinson		September
x	Richard son of Thomas Johnson		2 October
x	Jane dau. of Richard Haddoke		
x	Mary dau. of Robert Martincroft		
x	Francis child of Francis Booth		9 ,,
x	John son of Thomas Topping		
	Peter son of Peter Sayle		
	James & Thomas sons of John Battersby		
x	Mary dau. of James Holt		
x	Anne dau. of John Kay		
x	Margret dau. of John Hamar		
	Mary dau. of Thomas Kay		16 ,,
x	Anne dau. of Robert Read		19 ,,
x	Francis son of Thomas Medowcroft		23 ,,
	Thomas son of Francis Booth		
	Henry son of Henry		30 ,,
x	James son of James Isherwood		
99 x	Jane dau. of Thomas Wood of Mosse		6 November
x	Isabell dau. of John Bently of Haslomhey		
x	Elizabeth dau. of Thomas Pilkinton jun^9		13 ,,
x	Edward son of Edward Hind		
x	Thomas son of John Ashton of Heywood		27 ,,
	John son of Richard Romsbothā gentl.		30 ,,
x	Thomas son of Peter Holt of Bridge		4 December
x	Thomas son of Ellis Kay		
x	John son of John Barlow		
	James son of James Gabbet		
x	John son of James Buckley		11 ,,
x	Anne dau. of Robert Sheaphard		
	Frances son of Richard Bury		14 ,,
x	Elizabeth dau. of James Kay of Gindlee		25 ,,
	Anne dau. of Francis Emerson		27 ,,
x	Robert son of Henry Lort		28 ,,
x	Anne dau. of Peter Lomax		1 January
	John son of Henry Holt of Hollingreave		8 ,,
x	Jane dau. of John Matorcroft		
	Jane dau. of Thomas Warberton		
	Daniell son of Daniell Lort		
x	James son of Edward Leach		
	Mary dau. of James Howorth		15 ,,
	Anne dau. of Edward Rothwell		
x	Anne dau. of James Gee		
x	John son of John Ranson		
	John son of John Mullinex		
x	Sarah dau. of Thomas Kay of Elton		
x	John son of John Shippobotham		22 ,,
x	Nathaniell son of Mr. William Romsbothā minister		26 ,,
x	James son of James Howorth of Shuttl.		29 ,,

	Mary dau. of Thomas Mallocke		January
x	John son of Martin Kay of Littlewood		
	Elizabeth dau. of James Romsbotham		
	Anne dau. of Richard Pilkinton		
x b	Thomas son of Thomas Bury	3	February
x	Edmund son of Edmund Greenhalgh	5	,,
x	George son of Henry Holt		
	Mary dau. of Edward Milnes		
	Anne dau. of Henry Tattersall		
	Richard son of Rodger Grime	12	,,
	Ellin dau. of Aemar Ainsworth		
x	James son of Thomas Eckersall of Bury ...	19	,,
x	Elizabeth dau. of Lawrance Fletcher of Rediv.		
	Anne dau. of Lawrance Carter of Prestwich* ...		
x	Jane & Mary daus. of John Kay of Bauderstone		
x	Thomas son of James Whitaker	26	,,
b	Elizabeth dau. of Oliuer Brendwood		
x	Alice dau. of Edward Hunt		
x	Richard son of Richard Holt of Bury		
	Jonathan son of Rodger Taylor	5	March
	Thomas son of Thomas Kenian		
b	Ellin dau. of Rodger Hamar		
	Margret dau. of Martin Hopwood	12	,,
	Abrahā son of Edward Lomas of Heyw. ...		
x	John son of Thomas Wharneby		
	Edward son of Thomas Leach of Bamf. ...		
x	John son of Robert Duckworth	19	,,
x	Sarah dau. of John Hill		

William Rothwell, Curaᵗ

1637.

Fo. 100	x	Margery dau. of Thomas Whittle	26	March
	x	Margret and Raphe children of Raphe Bridge...		
	x	Henry son of William Asmall		
	x	Anne dau. of Edmund Howorth		
		Edward †		
	x	Margret dau. of George Holt	2	April
	x	Thomas son of Richard Battersby		
	x	Rodger son of Francis Woofenden		
		Deborah dau. of Robert Greenhalgh		
	x	James son of William Kay of Kobbas		
		Alice dau. of Edmund Holt		
		Edward son of Mr. Edward Rausthorne	3	,,
		Dorathy dau. of James Fenton of Bamf. ...	9	,,
		George son of John Fenton of Bury	16	,,
	x	Jeremy son of Jeffry Lomax	19	,,
	x	Ellin dau. of Richard Siddall	23	,,

* This entry is struck through in the original.
† This probably relates to the "Edward" christened on April 3rd.

1637 CHRISTENINGS.

x	Anne dau. of Lawrance Bradshaw	25	April
	Joan dau. of Rodger Vnsworth	30	,,
x	Richard son of William Kay		
x	Jane dau. of Francis Dawson		
x	John son of William Greenhalgh		
x	William son of Richard Isherwood of Bury	7	May
x	Jeffry son of Jeffry Hardman	11	,,
x	John son of Ellis Lomax	14	,,
x	Susan dau. of James Kay		
x	Susan dau. of Robert Liuesay	21	,,
	John son of Ellis Fletcher	8	June
x	Robert son of Raphe Holt	11	,,
x	Alice dau. of George Eckersley of Bury	18	,,
	Mary dau. of Raphe Bridge		
	Edward son of Edward Hamar	29	,,
x	Jarnice son of Jarnice Greenhalgh	2	July
x	Thomas son of Richard Smeythurst	9	,,
	Mary dau. of John Hopwood		
x	Jone dau. of John Shaw	23	,,
x	Thomas son of Richard Haslom	30	,,
	Alice dau. of Thomas Walker		
	Richard son of James Hartley	6	August
	Raphe son of Thomas Blakley		
x	Ellen dau. of Robert Maiorcroft		
x	Richard son of Martin Kay	13	,,
x	Ellis son of Robert Holt		
x	Thomas son of Thomas Kay	20	,,
x	Anne dau. of Richard Fenton		
	William son of Mr. Rothwell Curat	27	,,
x	Elizabeth dau. of Thomas Halliwell	3	September
	Richard son of William Holt		
	James son of James Gorton	10	,,
x	Ellin dau. of William Coleson		
	Katharin dau. of Richard Kay	17	,,
	Margret dau. of Francis Nuttall	24	,,
x	John son of Robert Hamar		
	Alice dau. of William Lomax	1	October
x	Henry son of Edmund Breerley		
x	John son of Raphe Clarkson		
x	James son of William Diggle		
x	Anne dau. of Edmund Holt		
x	Grace dau. of Humphrey Broome		
x	Kathrin dau. of Richard Booth	8	,,
x	John son of Richard Croston		
	Robert son of Robert Warberton	15	,,
x	John son of James Openshaw		
	William son of William Kay		
	Elizabeth dau. of John Romsbotham	22	,,
	John son of Rodger Greenhalgh		

Fo. 101	Elizabeth dau. of Richard Rausthorne	29	October
x	Elizabeth dau. of Thomas Tilsley		
	Anne dau. of Edward Scofield		
x	Richard son of James Kay		
x	Peter son of Peter Heward		
	William son of William Greenhalgh	5	Nouember
x	Robert son of Henry Dunster of Lane		
	James son of Richard Lomax		
x	Mary dau. of George Hull		
x	James son of John Lomax		
x	William son of Richard Nutttall	12	,,
x	Richard son of Bartholemew Stones		
	Elizabeth dau. of George Croston	17	,,
	Thomas son of Thomas Nabbe	19	,,
	Richard son of Richard Fletcher		
	Richard son of Robert Heald	26	,,
x	Robert son of Hamlet Low		
	Susan dau. of Edward Johnson		
x	Ellin dau. of Arthur Smeythurst		
x	Richard son of Richard Jones		
	Oliuer son of Edward Taylor	30	,,
	Richard son of Thomas Fletcher	4	December
	Richard son of Edmund Booth		
	Mary dau. of James Kay	10	,,
x	George son of Raphe Seddon		
x	Alice dau. of Edmund Smoult	17	,,
x	Elizabeth dau. of Robert Sheaphard		
x	John son of Francis* Booth	24	,,
x	Elizabeth dau. of William Bury		
	Henry son of James Holt	26	,,
x	Ester dau. of Thomas Warberton	31	,,
x	Richard son of John Greenhalgh	6	January
	Alice dau. of James Ashworth		
x	Elizabeth dau. of Edward Vnsworth	7	,,
	William son of Francis Makon	14	,,
	Thomas son of Thomas Greenhalgh		
	Susan dau. of Robert Hopwood	21	,,
	William son of Richard Rausthorne		
	Anne dau. of Richard Bridge		
	Henry son of Richard Banester		
	Elizabeth dau. of William Booth	28	,,
	Mary dau. of James Reade		
	Katharin dau. of Francis Nuttall	4	February
	James son of Thomas Smeythurst		
	Edmund son of Richard Barlow		
	Grace dau. of Thomas Wood		

William Rothwell, Curat
[There are no christenings for March.]

* " Roger " struck through and " Francis " written over it.

1638.

Thomas son of Thomas Howorth	1 April
Anne dau. of James Howorth	
Elizab dau. of Edward Rausthorne	8 ,,
Raphe son of Martin Kay	
Thomas son of Robert Leach	
Grace dau. of James Chadwicke	
Elizab dau. of John Wood	15 ,,
Alice dau. of Henry Nuttall	
Mary dau. of Giles Vnsworth	
William son of Peter Heald	22 ,,
Elizab dau. of George Liuesay	
Henry son of Jeffry Brooke de Bury	
John son of Thomas Mather	
Jane dau. of Robert Liuesay	6 May
Mary dau. of John Rausthorne	
Margret dau. of Richard Lomax of Bury	13 ,,
James son of John Fletcher	
Anne dau. of James Wilson	20 ,,
Robert son of Andrew Knowles	24 ,,
Richard son of Richard Haddok	3 June
Anne dau. of Lawrance Nabbe	
Alice dau. of Henry Allens	
Susan dau. of Thomas Nabb	
Richard son of Nathan Nuttall	10 ,,
Alice dau. of John Whitehead	17 ,,
Anne dau. of John Howorth	
Ellin dau. of John Bury	
Mary dau. of Robert Scofeild	
Jane dau. of Oliuer Nabbe	1 July
Isaake son of Peter Holt of Bridge	18 ,,
Edmund son of Thomas Pilkinton	22 ,,
Sarah dau. of Edmund Pilkinton	
Elizabeth dau. of Robert Smeythurst	
Alice dau. of Thomas Warbuton	
Robert son of Robert Kay	5 August
Elizab dau. of James Holt	
John son of Richard Wild of Heape	12 ,,
John son of Thomas Wood	
William son of James Kay of Bury	19 ,,
Edward son of Richard Heald of Holc.	26 ,,
William son of William Lowe	9 September
John son of John Holt	
John son of John Bradshaw	
Alice dau. of James Gee	
Margret dau. of Oliuer Lomax	16 ,,
John son of James Atkinson	
Giles son of Thomas Rothwell	

Anne dau. of Richard Bentily		September
John son of Mathew Booth	19	,,
Alice dau. of Thomas Eckersall	30	,,
Thomas son of Tho. Livesay fil. petri.*		
Peter son of William Rothwell Curat	10	October
John son of Robert Sheaphard	14	,,
James son of Joseph Leach		
Richard son of Robert Hamar	21	,,
Edmund son of John Holt		
John son of James Whitaker		
George son of George Howorth		
b Anne dau. of Anne Ingam		
Richard son of Rodger Booth	28	,,
Alice dau. of Thomas Lomax		
Richard son of Robert Hitchenson	4	November
Thomas son of Thomas Nuttall		
Margret dau. of Henry Booth	11	,,
Jane dau. of Richard Hitchinson	18	,,
Mary dau. of Richard Fletcher		
Anne dau. of Edward Leach	25	,,
James son of John Smeythurst		
Fo. 103 Franches son of William Warberton	2	December
Thomas son of Charles Romsbotham		
Mary dau. of Samuell Shaw		
Bithiah dau. of Robert Dunster	9	,,
John son of John Kay		
Katharin dau. of John Buckly	16	,,
John son of John Greenhalgh		
Peter son of James Heaton	23	,,
Margaret dau. of John Crompton	30	,,
Mary dau. of Thomas Asmall & Mary Booth		
Thomas son of Thomas Holt	6	January
Katharin dau. of Thomas Melladew	10	,,
Mary dau. of James Stocke	13	,,
Anne dau. of Thomas Halliwell		
Mary dau. of John Aspinall		
Richard son of Richard Vnsworth		
Henry son of Henry Banister		
Henry son of Henry Holt	27	,,
Robert son of Edmund Howorth		
Henry son of Henry Pilkinton		
John son of John Marcroft	3	February
Peter son of Peter Holt	10	,,
Alice dau. of John Shippobotham		
William son of Mr. William Bamford	17	,,
Richard son of Thomas Liuesay		
Robert son of George Holt		
Elizab dau. of James Jenkinson		

* Apparently in later writing.

CHRISTENINGS.

James son of Thomas Kay	24 February
George son of Thomas Whitehead	3 March
Richard son of Thomas Kay	
Franches son of Edmund Holt	
James son of James Hardman	
John son of George Barnes	
Robert son of John Isherwood	
Mary dau. of James Isherwood	
Ellin dau. of Thomas Greenhalgh	10 ,,
Lawrance dau. of Lawrance Fletcher	17 ,,
Grace dau. of James Jenkinson	
Ellin dau. of John Hamar	

William Rothwell, Curat

1639.

John son of Richard Kay of Widdall	31 March
James son of James Kay of Gindles	
Thomas son of Thomas Howorth	7 Aprill
James son of Edward Kay	
Elizab dau. of Richard Grime	
James son of James Stocke	
Thomas son of Edmund Holt	
Alice dau. of Edward Hind	
James son of Margret Nabbe	
Alice dau. of Robert Greenhalgh de Barwick	14 ,,
William son of Richard Pilkinton	
Margret and Jane gemelli Richard Howorth of Ashworth	
Mary dau. of Robert Holt of Ashworth	
Jane dau. of Richard Kenian of Ashworth	21 ,,
Ellin dau. of John Holt of Holcom	
Anne dau. of Thomas Medowcroft	23 ,,
Deborah dau. of Zachary Kempe	25 ,,
George son of Ellis Howorth of Facid	5 May
Anne dau. of Edmund Haslom	
George son of John Ranson	19 ,,
William son of Peter Seddon of Holc.	
Dorathy dau. of Raphe Fish of Etonf.	23 ,,
James son of James Ashworth	
Alice dau. of Richard Romsbotha de Romsb.	13 June
Martin son of Martin Kay de littl: wood	16 ,,
Gideon son of Gideon Coupe of Holc.	
Samuell son of Richard Smeythurst de broody oke	19 ,,
Elizabeth dau. of Charles Holt	4 August
Elizabeth dau. of William Kay	
Mary dau. of Abraham Kay	
Mary dau. of Henry Hardman	

John son of James Tailor	11 August
Edmund son of Thomas Blakeley	
Richard son of Richard Lomax	
John son of Ellis Kay	18 ,,
Ellin dau. of John Yate	
Jane dau. of James Leach	21 ,,
Alice dau. of Thomas Ashley	25 ,,
Anne dau. of John Barlow	
Henry son of William Holt	1 September
George son of George Eckersley	8 ,,
Edmund son of Rodger Rigby	
Thomas son of Thomas Johnson	
Thomas son of Thomas Fletcher	9 ,,
Peter son of Peter Lomax	22 ,,
Jane dau of Francis Whittaker	29 ,,
Jane dau. of Edward Milnes	
Thomas son of James Gabbot	6 October
Edmund son of Edward Breerly	
Annice dau. of John Holes	
Alice dau. of Robert Scofeild	
Jane dau. of Edward Rausthorne	13 ,,
Anne dau. of William Greenhalgh	
Robert son of Robert Kay	
Henry son of Rodger Grime	27 ,,
James son of Robert Liuesay	
James son of Thomas Warberton	3 Nouember
Alice dau. of William Hitchenson	10 ,,
Mary dau. of Franches Booth	
Henry son of Henry Lort	17 ,,
Elizabeth dau. of James Brooke	
Richard son of John Brooke de Bury*	1 December
Richard son of Richard Taylor	8 ,,
Robert son of Ellis Leach	
Mary dau. of Thomas Wood	
Alice dau. of Bartholemew Stones de Bridge	
Jonathan son of Peter Holt	22 ,,
Sarah dau. of James Greenhalgh	
Richard son of John Kay	25 ,,
John son of Henry Bridge	27 ,,
Richard son of Thomas Nabbe	5 January
Elizab dau. of Peter Heald	
Mary dau. of Raph Seddon	
Elizab dau. of John Howorth	
Jane dau. of James Whitaker	14 ,,
Ellin dau. of Rodger Taylor	
James son of John Openshaw	15 ,,
Richard son of Hugh Greenhalgh	19 ,,
Samuel son of Richard Howorth	

* " De Bury " added in a later hand.

1639-1640   CHRISTENINGS.   263

James son of John Kay	26 January
Margret dau. of Hamlet Lowe	
Susan dau. of Edward Holt	
Richard son of Mathew Sutley	3 February
105 Mary dau. of John Hill	16 ,,
Elizabeth dau. of John Rausthorne	
Edmund son of Edmund Booth	19 ,,
Edmund son of Richard Battersby	23 ,,
John son of George Haughton	
John son of Thomas Shippobotham	
Dorathy dau. of Mr. James Ashton of Chadderton	
Richard son of Richard Rausthorne	8 March
Mary dau. of Thomas Lort	
Mary dau. of Robert Diggle	
Richard son of James Rothwell	15 ,,
William son of John Kay	
Edmund son of Edmund Holt	
Mary dau. of Robert Warberton	
Dorathy dau. of Gilbert Ogden	
Ellin dau. of Richard Booth of Booth	22 ,,
Dinah dau. of James Holt	

William Rothwell, Curat

1640.

Elizabeth dau. of Thomas Heald	29 March
Richard son of John Ormorod	
Alice and Ann gemelli Rodulphi Bridge	3 April
John son of Thomas Wood	5 ,,
Thomas son of Edmund Greenhalgh	
James son of Richard Fenton	
William son of George Lomax	
Dorathy dau. of Mathew Booth	
Dorathy dau. of John Warberton	7 ,,
Robert son of Robert Hamar	
Thomas son of Thomas Eckersall	12 ,,
John son of Robert Key	
Dorathy dau. of Thomas Key	
Thomas son of Thomas Whitehead	19 ,,
James son of Samuell Sayle	
Alice dau. of Edward Ogden	
Elizabeth dau. of Jeffry Brooke, Bury*	
Jane dau. of William Kay	
Nicholas son of Nicholas Rausthorne	
Ellin dau. of Hugh Bradshaw	
Susan dau. of James Ashton	
Susan dau. of John Penley	3 May
Susan dau. of Jarvice Greenhalgh	

* "Bury" in later handwriting."

BURY PARISH REGISTERS. 1640

James son of Edward Leach	May
Alice dau. of Robert Smeythurst	
Mary dau. of Robert Liuesay	
Elizabeth dau. of Thomas Mather	
Mary and Anne twins of Richard Aspinall	17 ,,
John son of Edward Hopkinson	
Raphe son of Thomas Aspinall	
John son of John Tabernacle	31 ,,
James son of Richard Rausthorne	
Thomas son of Edward Read	4 June
Richard son of James Jackson	7 ,,
Robert son of Robert Marcroft	
Alice dau. of John Hardus	
James son of Richard Ouerall	14 ,,
Henry son of Henry Nuttall	
Mary and Anne twins of Richard Jones	
Richard son of Andrew Read	

Fo. 106
John son of Thomas Greenhalgh	21 July
Susan dau. of Robert Duckworth	
Jane dau. of William Bamford gentl	
Alice dau. of Richard Haddoke	2 August
Lawrance son of John Fletcher	
James son of Martin Hopwood	
Thomas son of Thomas Warberton	9 ,,
Rodger son of Richard Isherwood	
Alice dau. of Richard Bury	
James son of Robert Sheaphard	
Margret dau. of Andrew Knowles	12 ,,
Elizabeth dau. of Mr. Hardye	13 ,,
Anne dau. of Edward Barlow	17 ,,
Anne dau. of Rodger Kay	
John son of Edward Barlow	30 ,,
Mary and Alice twins of James Whittaker	
Mary dau. of William Diggle	
Susan dau. of Thomas Kay	17 September
Anne dau. of Thomas Lomax	20 ,,
Judith dau. of Richard Bridge	
Alice dau. of John Buckly	
John son of James Howorth	
James son of James Fletcher	27 ,,
Richard son of John Booth	
Jeferie son of Jeferie Lomax	5 October
Dorathie dau. of Ric. Barlow	
Margarett dau. of Peter Smith	
Thomas son of Laurence Fletcher	
Isabell dau. of James Anderton	
Jefferie son of Oliuer Lomax	16 ,,
Thomas son of Robert Farros	
John son of John Lomax	

	John son of William Taylor	October
	Richard son of Richard Kay	
	Ann dau. of John Romsbothō	25 ,,
	Mary dau. of James Buckley	12 November
	Elizaƀ dau. of Abrahā Leach	
	Edmund son of John Shippobothā	
	Alice dau. of John Barlow	
	. . . .* Edmund Lort	
	Martha dau. of John Howorth	20 ,,
	John son of Raphe Whittaker	13 December
	Alice dau. of Richard Kay	
	Arthur son of James Crompton	22 ,,
	Thomas son of Francis Nuttall	
	James son of Richard Wild	1 January
	Mary dau. of Thomas Eccles	3 ,,
	Thomas son of Thomas Pilkinton	16 ,,
	James son of John Smeythurst	
	Alice dau. of James Gee of Bury	
	Anne dau. of Peter Hunter	
	Elizabeth dau. of Richard Fletcher	
107	Anne dau. of John Hopkinson	19 ,,
	Anne dau. of Will Rawstorne	24 ,,
	Susan dau. of John Ryley	
	Raphe son of John Stot	
	Margret dau. of Thomas Howorth	31 ,,
	John son of George Hunt	
	Ellin dau. of Thomas Hitchinson	
	Alis dau. of John Brooke, Bury †	7 February
	Mary dau. of George Liuesay	
	Thomas son of John Holt	
	Mary dau. of William Bury	14 ,,
	Judith dau. of Richard Hitchenson	
	Anne dau. of Arthur Smeythurst	
	James son of John Greenhalgh	
	James son of James Howorth	17 ,,
	Richard son of Richard Kenian	21 ,,
	George son of John Whitehead	
	James son of Rodger Booth	
	Jennet dau. of Richard Wigan	
	Rodger son of George Howorth	
	Mary dau. of Mr. Holt de Hollingreave	3 March
	John son of Robert Read	
	Faith dau. of Robert Dunster	7 ,,
	Lawrance son of Rodger Greenhalgh	
	Dorathy dau. of John Hunt	
	Mary dau. of James Adkinson	14 ,,
	Alice dau. of Francis Booth	17 ,,

* No christian name.
† "Bury" in later hand.

Mary dau. of Michael Howorth... ... ... March
Mary dau. of Edward Newport... ... ... 21 ,,
Anne dau. of Robert Holt ... ...
    William Rothwell, Curat

1641.

Thomas son of Thomas Shippobothā ... ... 4 April
Randoll son of Thomas Ashley ... ...
John son of John Cowpe ... ...
Mary dau. of James Gabbet ... ...
Mary dau. of James Jenkinson ... ...
Isabell dau. of John Kirkman ... ... 7 ,,
Anne dau. of Robert Kay ... ... 11 ,,
Richard son of James Turner... ... ... 14 ,,
Elizabeth dau. of Raphe Bridge ... ... 15 ,,
John son of James Wilson ... ...
Richard son of Thomas Kay ... ... 25 ,,
Oliuer son of John Ormorod ... ...
Marie dau. of Richard Lomax ... ... 2 Maij
Marie dau. of Francis Barlow ... ...
John son of James Gest ... ...
Ellin and William twinns of William Rothwell
 Curat ... ... 20 ,,
Roberte son of Gilbert Houlden ... ... 21 ,,
Marie dau. of Thomas Bidd ... ...
b Richard son of Richard Heaton and Elizabeth
 Hardmann ... ...
Robet & John twinns of Willim Barlow, Red. 3 June
Ann dau. of Thomas Woods ... ...
Thomas son of Thomas Walten ... ... 22 ,,
Ann dau. of Thomas Smethurst ... ...
Sara dau. of Francis Stott ... ... 23 ,,
Debera dau. of Richard Vnsworth of Eltō ... 27 ,,
Susan dau. of Thomas Nuttall of Tott. ... ...
Alis dau. of Ellis Fletcher de Holcome ...
Marie dau. of Willim Lowe de Hol. ... ... 1 Julij
Richard son of Raphe Howorth, Eltō ... ... 8 ,,
Tho. son of John Woods de Holcome ... ...
Fo. 108 John son of Thomas Booth ... ... 19 ,,
John son of Thomas Howorth ... ... 29 ,,
Mary dau. of Robert Kay ... ...
Alice dau. of Edward Rausthorne, Esqr ... ... 1 August
Mary dau. of Thomas Browne ... ... 5 ,,
Dorathy dau. of James Isherwood ... ... 8 ,,
John son of Thomas Tilsley of Ratcliffe ... ... 12 ,,
b Ellin dau. of John Whiticor and Dority Grenne
 of Bury ... ... 9 September
Samuell son of Mr. William Bamford ... ... 23 ,,

Susann dau. of Samuel Makonn	26	September
Ann dau. of Arthur Kay of Womersly*	30	,,
Alice dau. of Richard Jones	7	October
James son of Georg. Hoult of Tott.	10	,,
Catterin dau. of Georg. Clough		
Elizabeth dau. of Laurence Jackesonn		
Anne dau. of Raphe Seddon de heape	20	,,
Mary dau. of Tho. Flecher	4	November
Mary dau. of Ric. Smethurst		
John son of John Barlowe	7	,,
John son of Peter Hoult de holc.		
Margaret dau. of Edw. Rothwell		
James son of James Whiticor...		
John son of John Hoult de Holc.		
Debbera dau. of Henry Bridge...	17	,,
Thomas son of Edward Ogden, Bury		
b John son of John Brooke of Holc.		
Anne dau. of Tho. Medowcroft of Huntley	28	,,
Anne dau. of Thomas Holt	2	December
Robert son of Tho. Livesay	eodem	
Elizabeth dau. of Richard Booth	5	,,
Susan dau. of James Dison		
Mary dau. of Mr. William Ingham	16	,,
Susan dau. of John Openshaw		
Jane dau. of John Aspinwall		
Henry son of Henry Hardman	20	,,
Elizabeth dau. of Robert Greenhalgh	24	,,
Mary dau. of Robert Diggle		
Mary dau. of Peter Heald	2	Janū
Elizabeth dau. of Tho. Aspinwall		
Joseph son of William Booth	6	,,
Anne dau. of John Isherwood...		
b John son of John Lees and Jane Rothwell		
John son of . . .		
b Richard son of Rich. Low and Añ Hamer	13	,,
Mary dau. of John Barlow	eodem	
James son of John Smethurst	20	,,
Mary dau. of Tho. Whitehead of feilds	23	,,
Joseph son of James Livesay		
John son of Laurence Fletcher, Redivalls	24	,,
John son of William Kitchen	30	,,
109 Elizabeth dau. of Giles Vnsworth, Redivalls	6	February
John son of George Bradley of Cookhey	10	,,
James son of James Stocke	13	,,
Elizabeth dau. of Francis Macon of Heywood	10	March
Anne dau. of Edward Read		
Roger son of John Booth...		
Richard son of Charles Nuttall of Holcome		

* In left hand margin " Mr. Alte came."

James son of Richard Mather of Answorth ...	20 March
Isabell dau. of Raph Nuttall	
Elizabeth dau. of Thomas Holt of Walmsly ...	
Richard son of Richard Lomas of Bury hamell	23 ,,

1642.

Laurenc. son of Laurenc. Teallior of Bertle ...	27 March
Robert son of Henry Booth of Bury	
Anne dau. of Nathan Nuttall of Bury	7 Aprill
Anne dau. of John Rostron de Shutlewort ...	9 ,,
Martha dau. of William Grennoe de Bury ...	eodem
b Thomas son of John Ramsbothom	14 ,,
James son of John Kay de Reddivells	17 ,,
Robert and Issabell twines of Thomas Kay de Wallmersly	23 ,,
Robert son of Robert Whiticor de Eltō	24 ,,
Margret dau. of Thomas Howorth de Wallmersley	1 Maij
Bartholomew son of Bartholomew Stones ...	8 ,,
William son of William Hoult de Holcom ...	
James son of Frances Dozen de Walmersley ...	15 ,,
John son of Ellis Lomax de Eltō	
John son of John Gellder de Eltō	
James son of Richard Hardman de Reddivells	18 ,,
Ellin dau. of Thomas Woods	22 ,,
Ellizabeth dau. of John Marcroft*	
Robert son of Hugh Bartles of Eltō	5 June
Katherin dau. of Gillian Coupes de Holcome	6 ,,
Alice dau. of Thomas Warbortō	9 ,,
Sara dau. of Thomas Nabbs, Holc.	
Ellin dau. of Richard Aspinall	
Thomas son of James Hardman	
b John son of John Bikonsonn	
Lawrence son of John Fletcher de Bury ...	12 ,,
Tho. son of Thomas Hoult de Midletō pish...	19 ,,
John son of William Hoult de Holcome... ...	
Ric. son of Richard Lomax junior	26 ,,
Peter son of Peter Smith, Bury	
William son of Ric. Loe de Holcō	
Edward son of Andrew Knowles	29 ,,
Mary dau. of Laurence Babbs	10 Julij
Sarah dau. of Peter Lomax	
Jane dau. of Josephe Liuesy, Bury	14 ,,
Lawrence son of John Flecher	
Fo. 110 John son of Josephe Hargreavs	17 ,,
b Mary dau. of Elizabeth Kay	
John son of John Romsbothō, Holcō	24 ,,
Mary dau. of Ric. Lomax, Bury	31 ,,

* John Marcroft " in much later hand.

1642 CHRISTENINGS. 269

John son of John Aspinall	Julij
Alic. dau. of Tho. Haworth	7 August
John son of John Tabernacke	
Margret dau. of Ellis Lommax	
Mary dau. of William Booth	11 ,,
Ann dau. of Tho. Flecher	
Bernard son of John Ransome	18 ,,
Roger son of John Booth	
Alexander son of Robert Schofeeld, Bam.	21 ,,
Jane dau. of John Grennoe	24 ,,
Elizabeth dau. of Georg. Howorth	
Dorothy dau. of Robert Kay	
Ann dau. of Jeffery Brooke de Bury* ...	
Alice dau. of Robert Whiticor, Holcōe	4 September
Peter son of George Holt, Tott.	
Thomas son of Thomas Jacksonn	11 ,,
John son of Edward Reads	15 ,,
Mary dau. of Raphe Digle	21 ,,
Raphe son of Tho. Aspinall	
Alice dau. of Robert Tunge, Midletō p	25 ,,
Mary dau. of Richeard Kennion, Midletō	2 October
Ellinnor dau. of Thomas Blacklow	
James son of Josephe Leache	9 ,,
James son of Thomas Kay de Elton ...	15 ,,
Lauwrence son of James Lomax	19 ,,
Ellin dau. of Laurence Horrak	eodem
Catherin dau. of Mr. Laurenc̃ Rostrō ...	23 ,,
Jane dau. of Jo Grennoe, Midletō	
Gilbert son of Ric. Hadocke, Bury	30 ,,
Robert son of William Huchinsō, Tott :	3 November
Mary dau. of Robert Huchinsō, Bury ...	
Alis dau. of Thomas Flecher	6 ,,
Margret dau. of James Jackesō de Houghe	
Lawrence son of James Lomax, Walmersly	13 ,,
Ellin dau. of James Howorth, Bury	17 ,,
John son of Raphe Howorth, Eltō ...	20 ,,
Peter son of Tho. Lomax, Eltō	
Henry son of Henry Hoult, Walmer : ...	
John son of James Howorth, Walmer : ...	
Edward son of Robert Hamer, Tott. ...	24 ,,
James son of Edmund Hoult	4 December
Edmund son of Edmund Slake, Tott.	
Robert son of Robert Kay, Holcōe	
Alice dau. of Ric. Robbinsonn	19 ,,
Dorathy dau. of Edmund Mills of Bury... ...	22 ,,
111 James son of James Gis de Bury	26 ,,
George son of Tho. Warberton de Tot.... ...	1 January
Richeard son of William Horrax de Houlcō ...	3 ,,

* " De Bury " in later hand.

Alice dau. of John Wood de Holcō	15 January
Alice* dau. of Robert Dunster, Tottin.	
James son of Esaia Digle	
Elizabeth dau. of Tho. Whithead senior	
Elizabeth dau. of Jossua Teallior, Heawood	22 ,,
John son of Ellis Leach de Shutleworth	
Elizabeth dau. of Tho. Wood de red lees	25 ,,
Ellin dau. of Henry Allens, Bury	29 ,,
Elizabeth dau. of Abram Wood, Bury	
Richard son of Thomas Loort, Heawood	2 February
James son of Michaell Howorth, Ashworth	5 ,,
Charles son of Charles Nuttall, Holcome	
Easter dau. of James Hilton de Heiye	12 ,,
Elizabeth dau. of John Howorth	
Alice dau. of James Hoult, Tottingetō	15 ,,
Mary dau. of Laurence Flecher de Redd.	19 ,,
John son of John Anderton, Wallm.	
John son of Richard Fentō, Redd.	
Thomas son of Thomas Milladeu	
Mary dau. of Ric. Rostronn, Holcō	23 ,,
Ann dau. of John Bridd, Ashworth	
Richard son of Thomas Aspinall, Bury	26 ,,
Alice dau. of Henry Bury, Tottin.	5 Martij
John son of Abram Leach, Bury	
Dionis son of Ric. Howorth de Chesem	
Roger son of George Eckersly de Bury	9 ,,
Mary dau. of John Yate	12 ,,
Dorithy dau. of John Nuttall, Affside	19 ,,
Easter dau. of Robert Heald de Bury	
Mary dau. of Robert Barlow	23 ,,
b Sara dau. of Roger Kay	eodem

1643.

Elizabeth dau. of Nicholas Rostrō	26 March
John son of Ric. Romsbothom	
John son of Francis Huchinson	
Henry son of Tho. Brige	9 Aprill
Alice dau. of John Lomax	
Anthony son of Tho. Booth	
Elizabeth dau. of John Buckly	
John son of John Brooke de Bury †	16 ,,
Elizabeth dau. of John Kay	
Tho. son of William Teallior	19 ,,
Fo. 112 Elizabeth dau. of Rich. Brige, Tott.	27 ,,
Ann dau. of Robert Liuesay, Midltō	30 ,,
Margret dau. of William Kay	

* " Elizabeth " crossed out and " Alice " written over it.
† " De Bury " in later hand.

1643 CHRISTENINGS.

John son of Robert Eansworth, Midltō		Aprill
b Jane dau. of Ellin Hasleom		
Robert son of Robert Sheppeard	4	Maij
John son of Henry Booth de Bury	5	,,
Elizabeth dau. of John Heaton of Prestwich	7	,,
Mary dau. of James Hoult		
b Elizabeth dau. of Isaac Ranson & Ellen Overall		
Edward son of John Hamer of Bentileigh	11	,,
James son of James Leach of Bury	14	,,
John son of Robt Ainsworth of Middleton	18	,,
John son of George Bradly of Cockhey		
Mary dau. of Ellis Eccles	1	June
Ellen dau. of Thomas Fletcher seni⁹	4	,,
Robert son of William Kay		
Raph son of Raph Seddon of Heap.	8	,,
Richard son of Thomas Wood of Bury		
Jane dau. of Thomas Nuttall of Bury	11	,,
Jane dau. of Richard Vnsworth of Elton	18	,,
Martha dau. of John Barlow		
Margrett dau. of William Warberton		
Anne dau. of Edward Leach of Elton		
Thomas son of Richard Booth of Booth	22	,,
Susan dau. of George Walles of Rachdall	25	,,
Mary dau. of Thomas Hoult		
John son of William Hoult of Holcom̃		
Richard son of Rich. Bannister of Bury	29	,,
Roger son of John Taylor of Bury		
Sara dau. of John Buckley of Tottingtō	6	July
Edward son of John Whitehead of Bury		
Mary dau. of Josua Shaw of Heap		
John son of Ellis Grime, Scout	9	,,
Anne dau. of Henry Hardman of Heywood	15	,,
Richard son of Henry Nuttall of Holcome	26	,,
Thomas son of Thomas Kay of Shuttleworth	30	,,
Mary dau. of John Lort of Walmersley	6	August
Dorothy dau. of Henry Holt of Hollingreave	10	,,
Thomas son of Tho. Greenhalgh of Heape		
John son of John Duerden of Moreside	13	,,
Margrett dau. of Edward Hopkinson, Holcom̃	16	,,
Margrett dau. of Thomas Whitehead of Ratcliffe	20	,,
Elizabeth dau. of Francis Greenhalgh of Bury		
Thomas son of Richard Fletcher		
Anne* dau. of Richard Wild of Heap		
John son of John Clegge †	27	,,
113 Elizabeth dau. of John Ormroyd of Walm⁹ss	3	September
James son of James Jenkinson of Moorside		
Dorothy dau. of Tho. Mather of Walmersly		

* "Mary" crossed out and "Anne" written above.
† "John Clegge" in another handwriting.

Abraham son of Edward Barlow of Bury ...		September
Robert son of James Schofeild of Moreyate ...	7	,,
Robert son of Robt Marcroft	18	,,
Thomas son of Lawrence Turner of Birch hey		
Alice dau. of Francis Nuttall of Walmersly ...		
Henry son of Henry Booth	1	Octob
Richard son of William Smith		
Mary dau. of John Taylor of Bury	18	,,
Anne dau. of George Hull of Bury		
Charles son of James Gorton of Holcome ...	5	Novem
Anne dau. of Francis Whitaker		
Mary dau. of Rich. Booth of Holcom ...		
Anne dau. of Henry Taylor of Walmᵉsly ...	19	,,
John son of John Bently		
Mary dau. of James Milns		
Richard son of William Thornly	23	,,
Margrett dau. of James Chadwicke	27	,,
James son of John Rosthorn of Bury ham. ...	3	December
Elizabeth dau. of James Walworke		
b Peter son of Edmund Lort & An Crossly ...		
Anne dau. of Tho. Hoult of Heap		
Peter son of John Marcroft	10	,,
Margrett dau. of Thomas Jones	17	,,
Margrett dau. of Rolt Kay of Moreside	21	,,
Esther dau. of Rich. Lomax of Moreside ...		
Lydia dau. of John Hoult of Holcom ...		
Abraham son of Rich. Isherwood	31	,,
Dorothy dau. of James Greenhalgh		
Jane dau. of Robt Livesay, Midleton		
Alice dau. of John Wood of Bury		
Mathew son of Adam Jackson		
Thomas son of John Hind of Cock hey ...		
Grace dau. of Jeffray Taylor	3	Janū
b Ellen dau. of Dorothy Greenhalgh		
James son of Rich. Hoult	7	,,
Henry son of Thomas Jackson		
Anne dau. of Tho. Ashworth of Etenfeild ...	11	,,
Roger son of Roger Grime	15	,,
Robert son of Tho. Warberton of Holcom ...	18	,,
b Mary dau. of James Allens and Katherin Walker	28	,,
John son of John Howorth of Elton		
Mary dau. of Richard Wigan		
Hamlatt son of William Low of Holcom ...	31	,,
Fo. 114 Ellen dau. of John Hill of Tottington	4	Febr.
Mary dau. of James Mather of Ratcliffe		
Richard son of Thomas Livesay	8	,,
Henry son of George Livesay		
John son of John Medowcroft	11	,,
John son of Thomas Medowcroft		

CHRISTENINGS.

Francis son of John Ainsworth	Febr.
James son of John Kay of Burroughs	
James son of James Howorth of Midleton	
Robert son of Thomas Livesay of Birkhill	18 ,,
Martha dau. of Emor Ainsworth	25 ,,
Elizabeth dau. of John Bridge, Holcom̄	
Andrew son of Andrew Knowles, Holcome	
Elizabeth dau. of Robt Holt, Middleton	3 March
John son of John Lomax of Bury Bridge	7 ,,
Ellen dau. of Peter Heald	10 ,,
Mary dau. of Henry Jackson	
Henry son of Francis Nuttall	
Joseph son of Robt Marcroft	
Margrett dau. of Tho. Warburton of Holcom̄	14 ,,
Susan dau. of Raph Scoles of Middleton	
Elizabeth dau. of Edward Pilkington	17 ,,
Isabell dau. of Jo: Isherwood	
Abraham son of Samuell Nuttall, Holcom̄	24 ,,

1644.

Elizabeth dau. of Edmund Barlow of Tott.	31 March
Jane dau. of John Pate of Bury	
Ellen dau. of Richard Makon of Heywood	7 Aprill
Ellen dau. of Rich. Hutchinson of Bamford	11 ,,
Margrett and Anne twins of George Howorth of Walm's̄ly	
William son of Richard Nabbe of Holcome	
Mary dau. of Richard Lowe of Holcome	21 ,,
James son of Tho. Pilkington of Holcome	28 ,,
Richard son of Thomas Walker of Bury	
Mary dau. of Jerimy Barlow of Holcom̄	
John son of Thomas Fletcher of Black brook Bridg	2 May
John son of Raph Smithurst of Ratcliffe	5 ,,
Thomas son of William Greenalgh of Bury	
Richard son of Robert Duckworth of Heape	12 ,,
Anne dau. of John Greenalgh of Tottington	
Judeth dau. of John Birom, Mooersd	22 ,,
Abigall son of Michaell Bently de Haslcome heigh	
John son of Thomas Whithead de feelds	10 June
John son of Richard Batersbie	
Dorothie dau. of John Sheepobothum	
Elen dau. of Thomas Smethurst	
Elizabeth dau. of Thomas Holt of Walmersley	16 ,,
Añe dau. of Lawrance Flecher	23 ,,
Susan dau. of James Duckworth of Holcō	
Elias son of Thomas Ekorsall of Bury	30 ,,

Thomas son of John Kay of Readiuales		June
John son of Henerie Lort of Bury Lane		
Elizabeth dau. of Thomas Kitchin		
John son of Lawrance Jacksonne		7 Julij
Roger son of Thomas Greenehalgh		
James son of Thomas Sale		14 ,,
Alis dau. of George Cloogh		21 ,,
Richard son of Roger Hamer		
Deborah dau. of John Bury		
Edmund son of Edmund Haslam		
James son of James Stot of Heywood		28 ,,
John son of James Leach of Shuttleworth		
Alice dau. of Edward Holt of Elton		
Sara dau. of John Mather of Ainsworth		
Isabell dau. of Charles Nuttall of Holcom͂		4 August
Richard son of Roger Kay of Woofould		18 ,,
Elizabeth dau. of James Clarke of Birch hey		25 ,,
James son of Hugh Greenehalgh		1 September
Charles son of Charles Holt of Heape		8 ,,
Añe dau. of John Grenehalgh of Walshaw Lane		
Marie dau. of Raphe Crompton of Breighmist		15 ,,
Elizabeth dau. of Franches Doesun of Wallmersley		
Thomas son of Richard Rostrone of Totington		22 ,,
Robte son of Roger Taylor of Rughill Steele		
Roger son of John Coupe of Elton		24 ,,
Marie dau. of John Cockerill of Totington		
John son of Richard Barlow of Totington		
Edmund son of James Isherwood of Wallmer.		
John son of John Buckley of Bury		3 October
Marie dau. of James Rothwell of Houlcum		10 ,,
Elizabeth dau. of James Gee of Bury		
John son of Edmund Breareley of Eltō		13 ,,
Martha dau. of James Lech of Bury		
Fo. 116 John son of John Wood of Birch Hey		16 ,,
Thomas son of Ellize Flecher		
Margret dau. of Robte Whitticar		20 ,,
James son of Ric. Kay of Brid Hole		
Robte son of Robte Kay de Whittwall		27 ,,
b Elisse son of Margret Nabb		5 Nouember
James son of Josua Taylor of Heawood		7 ,,
Roger son of Edward Hamer of Buckden		10 ,,
Thomas son of Bartholemew Stones		14 ,,
Thomas son of John Ridings of Boultō pish		20 ,,
William son of Robte Kay of Cobbas		21 ,,
William son of Josua Hargreaves of Bury		24 ,,
Marie dau. of William Booth of Elton		
Alise dau. of Thomas Nabbe of Houlcom͂		1 December
Marie dau. of John Brooke of Bury		
Elizabeth dau. of John Jenkinsun		

CHRISTENINGS. 1644-1645

Margret dau. of Thomas Wood of Mill hous ..	5	December
Grace dau. of Franches Macon of Heawood ...	8	,,
Susan dau. of Edmund Slade		
Joseph and Marie twines of George Holt of Totington	12	,,
Roger son of Thomas Nuttall of Totington ...	15	,,
Sarah dau. of James Whiticar of Bury ...	22	,,
John son of Franches Huchinsun ...		
James son of James Liuesey		
Marie dau. of John Kay of Walmersley ...	29	,,
Alise dau. of John Shakeshaft		
John son of Jonathan Buterworth	9	January
Susan dau. of Richard Lomax of Bury	12	,,
John son of William Haslam		
Richard son of Edward Rothwall of Wamarsley*		
Elen dau. of Edward Roesun	19	,,
Thomas son of Joseph Leiusey	26	,,
Peeter son of Thomas Lomax	29	,,
Añe dau. of Thomas Smethurst	2	Februarie
b Elizabeth dau. of Katerin Bensū		
Marie dau. of Roger Kay	9	,,
Añe dau. of Raphe Brige	16	,,
Thomas son of Peeter Holt	2	March
Martha dau. of Robert Ridinges	6	,,
b Richard son of Elen Chowe	7	,,
Elizabeth dau. of John Warberton ...		
Thomas son of John Barlowe		
Alis dau. of William Bury of Woodrode ...		
Robert son of Thomas Liusey	16	,,
b Isabell dau. of Anne Lomax	17	,,
Marie dau. of John Buckley	23	,,
b James son of John Wood...		
Thomas son of Walter Wofenden ...		
Marie dau. of John Holt		

1645.

Marie dau. of Thomas Wood of Holcom	26	March
b Anne dau. of Grace Scoafeild	29	,,
Richard son of Henerie Kay of Hey Head	30	,,
Elizabeth dau. of John Smyth		
Marie dau. of Henerie Holt	3	Aprill
Marie dau. of John Romsbotom		
Elen dau. of Thomas Warberton	6	,,
Henery son of Thomas Lomax		
James son of Isaiah Diggle		
John son of John Hamer of Bentilee ...	13	,,
Margrett dau. of Richard Hadacke ...	16	,,

* Edward Rothwall, of Wamarsley. in later hand.

Marie dau. of John Lomax	17	Aprill
Thomas son of James Gabbit...		
John son of Lawrence Nab of Bury	19	,,
Elizabeth dau. of John Booth of Redivalls	24	,,
Jonathan son of James Nighell	27	,,
Samuell son of Samuell Shaw ...		
Jane dau. of Rich. Taylor ...	4	May
Elizabeth dau. of Robert Ainsworth of Cock Hey	15	,,
Mary dau. of Samuell Shaw of Bamford ...	18	,,
Thomas son of Richard Barlow posthumus	25	,,
Jane dau. of Peter Heald ...	1	Juñ
Fo. 118 Richard son of John Hardy	15	,,
Mary dau. of John Kay of Elton fold	22	,,
Anne dau. of John Greenalgh, Aphiside		
Rachell dau. of Tho. Brown, Holcome ...	29	,,
John son of Hugh Taylor of Bury ...		
Anne dau. of Andrew Lever of Washy Lane...		
Alice dau. of James Haworth, Gooseford		
James son of Robert Kay of Benteley	13	July
Elizabeth dau. of George Heaton of Fearngore		
John son of Raph Bridge of Tottingtō...	24	,,
Dorothy dau. of Tho. Jackson, Lemands hill...	27	,,
William son of William Grimeshaw		
Ellen dau. of James Brooke, Tottingtō ...		
John son of John Taylor of Bury	30	,,
Ellen dau. of William Thornley	3	August
Dorothy dau. of John Barlow of Heap		
Margret dau. of Tho. Livesay, Berkhill...		
Anne dau. of Raph Heaton of Vnsworth	10	,,
Margrett dau. of Josua Shaw of Bury		
Alice dau. of John Bird of Ashworth	14	,,
Elizabeth dau. of Henry Bridge of Holcoñ ...	20	,,
James son of Mr. Scholefeild, minister of Heywood	24	,,
Dorothy dau. of Francis Nuttall	31	,,
James son of James Lomax		
b John son of Abraham Asmall and Mary Booth	4	September
Mary dau. of Robert Hamer, Tott. ...	19	,,
Mary dau. of James Howarth ...	21	,,
William son of Tho. Eccles		
James son of James Whitaker of Tott. ...	28	,,
Edward son of Edward Read ...	2	October
Thomas son of James Gee	5	,,
Isaac son of James Holt ...		
William son of John Byrom	9	,,
Alice dau. of Tho. Holt, Walmᵖsly		
Richard son of William Taylor	16	,,
Robert son of James Gorton	29	,,

1645   CHRISTENINGS.

Raph son of Henry Nuttall	October
John son of John Kay, Goosford	2 Novem̃
Richard son of James Barlow, Whittle ...	
Thomas son of Thomas Heald, Moreside	5 ,,
Dorathy dau. of James Holt of Low ...	16 ,,
Abraham son of Ratcliffe Wrigley	
James son of Francis Greenalgh of Bury...	23 ,,
Robert son of Richard Fletcher of Elton	
John son of James Howorth, Littlewood	30 ,,
Thomas son of Edmund Booth, Elton ...	
William son of James Key, Walmᵒsly ...	4 Decem̃
Anne dau. of Robt Ridings, Woodyate hill	
Alice dau. of John Ormerode	14 ,,
Alice dau. of Thomas Sale	
Susan dau. of Richard Lomax of Bury ...	
James son of Edward Rawstorn, Walmᵒsly	17 ,,
James son of James Ainsworth	18 ,,
Jerimy son of William Holt, Holcome ...	21 ,,
Susan dau. of John Low	
Alice dau. of Roger Pilkington	
Martha dau. of Mary Marcroft	
John son of Thomas Aspinwall	28 ,,
John son of Francis Booth, Tott.	
Mary dau. of Rich. Lomax of Bury hamell	
Thomas son of Thomas Warberton, Holc.	
Thomas son of Ellis Lomax, Tott.	11 January
Elizabeth dau. of Thomas Earnshaw	
Rachell dau. of Mr. Laurence Rawstorn	15 ,,
John son of Lawrence Turner, Birchhey ...	18 ,,
James son of William Smith, Holcome	
Katherin dau. of Tho. Warberton, Stubbins ...	22 ,,
Sara dau. of John Lomax, Castlehill	
Margrett dau. of Henry Allen	
Mary dau. of Raph Hurst	25 ,,
John son of John Shakeshaft...	5 Febr.
Elizabeth dau. of John Romsden	
Georg son of Geo. Street and Mary Allen ...	
Andrew son of Adam Lever	8 ,,
Sara dau. of John Cockrill	
John son of Rich. Vnsworth of Elton	12 ,,
Mary dau. of Peter Lomax, Washy Lane ...	
Alice dau. of Ric. Baxenden	
Dorothy dau. of Gideon Coupe	15 ,,
Edmund son of Thos. Nuttall of Moorside ...	
John son of James Walworke	
Ellen dau. of John Isherwood, Tottington ...	22 ,,
Alice dau. of John Nuttall, Tott.	
Dorothy dau. of George Hull, Bury	
Peter son of Peter Rothwell	

Mary dau. of John Howorth, Tott. ...	Febr.
George son of James Dison ...	
Margrett dau. of Ric. Wigan, Tott. ...	
Mary dau. of John Wood of Bury ...	1 March
Peter son of Jame Greenhalgh, Tot. ...	
Anne dau. of Robt Livesay, Pilsworth ...	
Jane dau. of Robt Chadwicke, Bury ...	
Alice dau. of John Bridge ...	15 ,,
Noah son of Nicholas Cudworth, minister of Holcom ...	22 ,,
Alice dau. of Tho. Whitihead sen. ...	
John son of James Hartley ...	
Charles son of Abraham Leach ...	
Richard son of James Jenkinson ...	

1646.

	Anne dau. of John Pate ...	29 March
b	Thomas son of Tho. Godard & Isabell Birom...	
	Anne dau. of Peter Brooke born 31st bapt.*...	5 April
	Anne dau. of Jeffry Tayler ...	9 ,,
	James son of James Chadwicke ...	12 ,,
	Daniell son of James Leach ...	
	Dorothy dau. of Lawrence Taylor ...	
	John son of James Fletcher, Bury ...	
	Sara dau. of Edward Hopkinson ...	19 ,,
	James son of Joh. Marcroft, Birkhill ...	26 ,,
	Mary dau. of James Kay of Gindles ...	
	Richard son of Tho. Medowcroft, Huntly ...	
	Henry son of Henry Jackson, Tott. ...	
	Thomas son of Raph Wood, Tott....	3 May
	Edward son of Emor Ainsworth ...	
	Alice dau. of James Greenhalgh, Deane banke	4 ,,
	Elizabeth dau. of Rich. Wood, Holcome ...	7 ,,
	Anne dau. of Peter Holt, Lomax ...	10 ,,
	Margrett dau. of James Kay, Gloributts...	14 ,,
	Thomas son of Rich. Aspinwall, Tot. ...	17 ,,
	Samuell son of Martin Kay, Littlewood ...	24 ,,
	Mary dau. of John Whitehead of Bury...	31 ,,
	Catherine dau. of Rich. Tootell of Cockhey ...	
	Elizabeth dau. of Tho. Booth of Lommas ...	7 June
	Esther dau. of Charles Nuttall...	
Fo. 121	John son of William Hutchinson, Tott. ...	28 ,,
	Anne dau. of Tho. Nuttall ...	
	James son of Rich. Pilkington, Tott. ...	2 July
	Thomas son of Tho. Eccles ...	5 ,,
	Raph son of Robt Livesay, Birkhill ...	19 ,,

* This entry in later hand.

CHRISTENINGS.

Anne dau. of Rich. Bury, Walm.	26 July
Mary dau. of Abraham Barlow of Ratcliffe	
James son of Edward Booth, Tott.	2 August
Dorothy dau. of John Hoyle, Tott.	9 ,,
Anne dau. of Francis Whitaker, Walm.	
Rebeccah dau. of Tho. Kay, Elton	26 ,,
Elizabeth dau. of Nathan Low	30 ,,
Elizabeth dau. of Francis Hutchinson	
Elizabeth dau. of Mathew Booth, Elton	5 September
Sara dau. of James Hilton, Elton	
George son of Geo. Bradshaw, Ainsworth	
Thomas son of Edmund Slade	
Edmund son of Edmund Lowe, Tott.	
Raph son of Raph Brooke, Tott.	
Mary dau. of Roger Taylor	10 ,,
Elizabeth dau. of William Heald of Bury	13 ,,
George son of Thomas Wood of Bury	17 ,,
Esay son of Esay Diggle of Heap	
Anne dau. of Richard Banister	20 ,,
George son of Jonas Wood	24 ,,
Jerimy son of Jerimy Ainsworth, Tott.	27 ,,
Ellen dau. of William Low, Tott.	
Elizabeth dau. of Andrew Knowles	
Alice dau. of William Haslom, Walm.	
John son of John Nuttall, Tott.	
Dorothy dau. of Rich. Isherwood of Bury	4 Octob̃
John son of James Greenhalgh, Elton	
John son of Rich. Duckworth, Birkhill	
Mary dau. of John Rawsthorn, Elton	11 ,,
James son of James Whiticar, Elton	15 ,,
Thomas son of William Greenalgh, Bury	18 ,,
Jane dau. of Roger Booth, Tenters	25 ,,
Susan dau. of John Taylor, Bury	
Josias son of Robt Kirkman, Ainsworth	
John son of John Buckley, Tott.	1 Novem̃
Henry son of Tho. Smethurst, Barnbrooke	
Anne dau. of Henry Rawsthorn, Etenfeild	5 ,,
Susan dau. of Tho. Walker, Bury	8 ,,
Thomas son of Robert Kay	15 ,,
Mary dau. of John Kay, Littlewood	22 ,,
Mary dau. of Rich. Kay, Littlewood	
George son of George Clough	
Margrett dau. of Peter Heald	
Anne dau. of John Fletcher, Bury	6 Decem̃
Henry son of James Howorth, Elton	
John son of John Kay of Elton	
Katherine dau. of Hugh Taylor	13 ,,
Richard and William gemini Tho. Kay, Bury hamell	17 ,,

b Mary dau. of Tho. Rawstorn and Ellen Smethurst   Decem̃
Richard son of Richard Barlow, Tott. ... ... 20 ,,
Priscilla dau. of William Earnshaw ... ...
Elizabeth dau. of John Yate ... ... 27 ,,
Mary dau. of John Collins ... ...
Anna dau. of George Brookes ... ... 7 January
Ellen dau. of Georg. Howorth, Drygap ... ...
Richard son of Rich. Tootell, Bury ... ... 10 ,,
Alice dau. of John Cockrill ... ...
Robert son of Robert Duckworth, Heap ... 17 ,,
Peter son of Edmund Haslom ... ...
Dorothy dau. of John Shippobothã ... ... 24 ,,
Dorothy dau. of Oliver Lomax, Heap ... ... 31 ,,
Anne dau. of Richard Simond, Elton ... ... 2 Febr.
Lawrence dau. of William Grimeshaw ... ... 11 ,,
Ellen dau. of John Medowcroft, Haslom Hey...
Peter son of John Warburton, Tott. ... ... 15 ,,
Alice dau. of Richard Dewrden ... ... 21 ,,
John son of Owen Lomax, Bury h. ... ...
Margrett dau. of John Greenhalgh, Tott. ...
John son of Edward Barlow, Tott. ... ...
Alice dau. of Robert Kay, Cobbas ... ... 28 ,,
Jane dau. of Barthol. Stones ... ...
Thomas son of John Buckley, Bury ... ...
Joseph son of Lawrence Jackson ... ... 4 Mar.
Elizabeth dau. of James Gorton ... ... 7 ,,
John and Alice gemini John Kay, Redivalls... 12 ,,
Anne dau. of Tho. Eckersall, Bury ... ... 14 ,,
Margrett dau. of Tho. Nabbe, Holcom̃ ... ...
Mary dau. of John Booth, Redivalls ... ...
Alice dau. of Rich. Kay, Gooseford... ... ...
Richard son of Ellis Fletcher, Birch hey ...
William son of Edward Leach ... ...
Mary dau. of John Greenhalgh, Cathole ...
James son of Adam Jackson, Tott. ... ...
Mary dau. of Robert Kay, Whitewall ... ... 21 ,,
Robert son of John Brooke, Bury ... ...

          William Alte, pastor
          Año aetatis suae 46.

[The greatest part of this leaf has been cut away, only about five inches at the top remaining. After it there are the longitudinal remains of two leaves, upon one of which is written lengthways "William Alte, pastor."]

BURIALS.

Burialles Ano. Dni.
1617.

Fo. 167	Robert Kay of Bury	26	March
	Ann dau. of Peter Both…		
	Robert Battersby of Bury	27	,,
	Elizabeth dau. of John Grenhalhe	30	,,
e	Thomas Kay of Elton	1	April
e	George son of Thomas Warberton	2	,,
x	James Battersby of Benteley Lum	3	,,
	An Infant of Richard Healdes	5	,,
Fo. 168	Alice dau. of Richard Parseuall …	7	,,
	Elizabeth widdow of Henry Dunster	8	,,
	An Infante of Edmond Holtes	12	,,
x	Jefferey Haslome of Bury	14	,,
	Añe dau. of Abrahā Hauworth	15	,,
	Margaret Cowper of Tottington	16	,,
	Giles Haslome of Eues in Tot.	17	,,
x	Bartin Kay of Walmersley & Reignold Hauworth of Bury…	18	,,
x	John Cowap of Ashenbothome	23	,,
	Richard Stringer a wanderer drowned…	23	,,
	Wiłłm Benson of Chorley	24	,,
	Ann wiffe of Alexander Naden of Bur.	31	,,
	Edmond Fenton of Bamforthe		
	Elizabethe Hauworthe of Bury	9	Maij
	Dorithy Haslome of Wal.	15	,,
	Elizabeth wiffe of Emer Ainseworth …	16	,,
	Ellis sone of James Fletcher		
	Alisse wiffe of Thomas Rosthorne of Bu:	17	,,
	Ann Hopwood of Bamforth	25	,,
	Alisse wiffe of Richard Leache	27	,,
	An Infante of Richard Fletchers	30	,,
	Mary dau. of Leonard Asworthe	4	Jvnij
	Ellyn Kay of Goseforde	10	,,
	Mary dau. of Edmond Kay of Sheephey	14	,,
	Ellyn Pilkingtone of Holcome	15	,,
	Ann Pilkington of Holcome	18	,,
	An Infante of James Crosleyes		
	Robert Liuesay drowned	20	,,
	Alice dau. of Samuell Sale	22	,,

	Katheryn wiffe of Geo: Battersby	23	Jvnij
	James son of John Brooke, Holcō...	2	Julij
	Humphrey Kay of Bury	5	,,
	Mary dau. of Jefferey Lomax of Heap	6	,,
	John Hauworth of Tot. ...	11	,,
	Mary Digles of Bircle	12	,,
	Isabell wiffe of Ralphe Baron of Eden	29	,,
	An Infante of Robert Andertons...	31	,,
	Elizabeth dau. of Francis Grenhalhe...	9	August
	Jane Janion of Cokhey ...	12	,,
	Elizabeth wiffe of John Hauworthe	15	,,
x	Arthur Kay of Walmersley	23	,,
	An Infante of Robert Hauworthes	26	,,
	Añ Birtwisle of Skoute...	3	Septr.
	Francis Hardman of Bury	4	,,
	Ralphe son of Willm Rushton	16	,,
	Ralphe son of Henry Mather	17	,,
Fo. 169	Mr. Francis Holt of Grislehurst ...	28	,,
	An Infante of Ralphe Shepardes	29	,,
	Mary dau. of Richard Shawe	1	Octobris
M c	Thomas Bridge of Holcome & Thomas Brooke of Toting:	17	,,
	Robert Holte of Bury Hamel	21	,,
	Elizabeth Rothwell of B.	22	,,
	An Infante of Ralphe Leaches	30	,,
	Isabell dau. of Ellis Haslome	1	Nouembr
	James son of Richard Grenhalhe of Tot.	2	,,
	John son of John Wrigley of Heywode	11	,,
	James son of Willm Hauworth	18	,,
	Judethe Heywood of Brandlesam...	22	,,
pd x	Ellyn vid: Johanis Shephen de Bury ...	6	Decebr
	Robert son of Thomas Lomax of Croitsh ...	7	,,
	Lawrence Shaw of Brandl. ...	9	,,
	An Infante of John Wardeles		
	Lawrence Nabb of Bury	12	,,
pd x	Ellyn vidua Radulphi Brooke de Bury	16	,,
	Jony Sharpos of Affesyde		
	Robert Sedon of Bury ...	17	,,
	Ann Grenhalh of Fearnes		
	Henry Couper of Tottington	18	,,
	Richard Hey Collier of Bury	19	,,
	Ellyn wiffe of John Fletcher	22	,,
e	Isabell wiffe of John Hardman of Heywood...	23	,,
	Jony wiffe of James Hunte of Hol:		
	Jane wiffe of John Ashworthe	24	,,
	Anthony son of William Whitaker	26	,,
	Thomas Hauworth of Bury ...	27	,,
	Elizabethe wiffe of Thomas Key ...		
	Elizabeth widow of Tho: Kay of Birdh:	28	,,

x e	Isabell vidua of Ric. Holte of Hey:		Decebr
	Jane Smitherste of Bury	4	Janvarij
	Ann dau. of Owen Bury	6	,,
	Alisse dau. of Richard Whitheade	7	,,
	An infante of Elis Fletcheres of Birchey	8	,,
	Alisse w: of William Kay of Bury	12	,,
	Alisse w: of Richard Ramsbothom of Bu:...	14	,,
	Katheryn w: of John Powell	16	,,
	Robert Lomas of Bury	19	,,
	Edmond Pilkington of Totingtō	20	,,
	An Infante of Tho. Heywardes	23	,,
	An Infante of Thomas Kayes	25	,,
	John Bate of Bury	26	,,
	William Hamer of Bury		
	Margeret wiffe of Thomas Kay	27	,,
	Alisse vidua of Edmond Haslome	28	,,
	William son of Oliuer Nab	31	,,
x	Alisse vidua Wiłłmi Both of Tot.	vltimo	Febr.
	Christopher Both of Holcome	5	,,
	John son of Robert Hauworthe	6	,,
	Ellyn wiffe of John Horredge	7	,,
	John son of Richard Dukworthe	7	,,
x	Richard Rothwell of Bury	12	,,
	Ellis B. son of Ellis Farneworth		
e	Richard son of John Medicrofte	13	,,
	Gennet wiffe of Thomas Holte of Hag	15	,,
	Thomas son of Tho. Nuttall of Hol:	16	,,
	Richard Shippobotham of Hol:	18	,,
e	Ann dau. of Henry Hardman	20	,,
	Cicely Battersbue of Hol:	22	,,
	Katherin dau. of John Both of Hol:		
	Anthony Nabes of Bury	24	,,
	*b*Charles son of Charles Butterworth & Alisse Holt	25	,,
x e	Richard Smitherst of Brokshawe	27	,,
	Samuell son of James Skolefeild	26	,,
	Jane w: of Richard Holte of Fol	1	[March]
	Thomas son of John Grenhalh	3	,,
	Henry son of Thomas Nuttall		
	Jane vidua Williā Brooke of Hol:	4	,,
	Richard Bothe of Walmᵖs.	5	,,
	Richard son of Milles Holme of Walm̃	8	,,
	Richard son of John Heywod of Birkle	10	,,
	Francis son of Ric. Wood of Elton	14	,,
	Martyn Nuttall of Bury	17	,,
	An Infante of Mr. Dugdales		
	Margery w: of John Whithead of B.	18	,,
	Margeret w: of John Whitley	19	,,
	Thomas Key of Benteliye	24	,,
	Mary dau. of Richard Both of Wal.		

1618.

	John Leache of Walmer.	26	March
x	Tho: Kaye of Elton	29	,,
x	Richard Hauworthe of Bamfor:	31	,,
	Richard Holte of Holcome	1	April
e	Roger son of Roger Bothe of Rediu:	6	,,
	Elizabeth dau. of Richard Anderton		
	William Ogden	7	,,
x	Wiĥm Yate of Bury ham.	8	,,
	Thomas Grenhalghe	11	,,
	Ann Heywod dau. of Robert Heywode	14	,,
	Alisse wiffe of Robert Elton	15	,,
	Alisse dau. of John Bothe	16	,,
x	Margaret widowe of Robt Heald of Bury	17	,,
	Alisse dau. of John Wigon	22	,,
x	Robert Barlow of Bury	26	,,
	Susan dau. of John Kay of Bury	27	,,
	John Ainesworth of Toting:	30	,,
	Elizabeth Ankell of Walkf:		
	Elly dau. of Wiĥm Yate	2	Maij
	Thurstan son of Wiĥm Rausthorne	5	,,
	Genet Entwisle of Holcome		
Fo. 171	Henry Hauworthe of Edenfelde	12	,,
	Henry Broke of Tot.	14	,,
	Ellinar dau. of John Allen		
	Elizabeth Fletcher of Redi:	17	,,
	Ralphe sonne of Robt Crompton of Bury	18	,,
	Alisse dau. of Edmod Heliwell of Bury	22	,,
x	Thomas Grenhalghe of Heape	24	,,
	John son of John Holte de foulcoats	29	,,
	Alexander son of Tho. Heywood of Bu:	30	,,
	Elizabeth vidua of Edmond Kirshawe	4	Junij
	Jane dau. of Humphrey Kay of Bury		
	Alisse wiffe of Richard Wood of Hol:	6	,,
	Alisse wiffe of Ralphe Bukley of Foulcoats...	7	,,
	Margeret Allenes of Bury	11	,,
	Isabell wiffe of John Brearley of Heywood	14	,,
	Martha wiffe of Wm Romsbothom of Hol:	15	,,
	Richard son of James Grenhalghe	20	,,
b	John son of Richard Holte of Hauk....		
	Ellyn dau. of Francis Pilkington	22	,,
	Alisse dau. of Edmond Sedon of Heap	26	,,
	Mary dau. of John Hynde	27	,,
	An Infante of Peter Lomases	3	Jvlij
	An Infante of Peter Romsbothomes	10	,,
	John Baron of Walmᵖsley	11	,,
	Ann wiffe of Oliuer Chadweeke	12	,,
	Elizabeth dau. of John Hunte	14	,,

1618 BURIALS.

	George Nuttall of Nutall Lane	19 Jvlij
	Robert Holte of Birchhey	25 ,,
o	Elizabeth Kay of Holcome	26 ,,
	Isabell dau. of George Emerson	28 ,,
o	Richard Grehalh of Bur:	1 Aug.
	Ric. son of William Hargreues	
x	John Holte of Foultes	7 ,,
	Elizabeth Brokshaw of Holcom̃	10 ,,
o	Thomas Grenhalghe of Bu:	12 ,,
	Florence vid: Raignold Kay	15 ,,
	Thomas Kay of Shephey	21 ,,
	Alisse vidua Johannis Grenhalh	23 ,,
	An Infant of John Wodes of Birch	
	George son of George Battersby	22 ,,
	Alisse Rausthorne of Bury	25 ,,
	Thomas Bukley of Toting.	26 ,,
e	Thomas Battersby of Totting.	27 ,,
	John Whithead of Tot.	
	John son of John Jenkinsone	
	Alisse vidua Petrj Grenhalge	28 ,,
e	Diana w: of Richard Bridge, Leniet*...	3 Sep
	Alisse w: of Roger Nuttall of Totting	4 ,,
	Elizabeth w: of Richard Hey of B.	
	An Infante of Robt Hauworthes	
	Emyn w: of Francis Woolsnehã	5 ,,
	Elizabeth w: of Thomas Nuttall of Tot.	8 ,,
	Jennet w: of Thomas Bukley	12 ,,
x	Richard Wood of Tottingtõ	13 ,,
x	Ric. Welche of Tottington	
	William Hauworthe of Bur.	17 ,,
e	Katheryn v. Thomas Battersby of Tot.	19 ,,
e	Alisse dau. of Ric. Bridge	
	William Bukley of Tottingtõ	
	John Brearley of Heywood	23 ,,
	John son of Willm Rausthorne	25 ,,
x	Sara w: of Thomas Vnsworth & Katheryn w: of Abrahã Haworth of Tot.	29 ,,
	James Steele of Bury	6 October
	Alise dau. of George Emerson	12 ,,
	Alisse w: of Richard Beeman	14 ,,
	Mathew Both of Redi.	15 ,,
	Katherin w: of James Fogge	
	Thomas Smitherst of Brokshaw	22 ,,
	Jane wiffe of Robert Bothe	23 ,,
	Mary w: of John Roydes of Holcom̃	
	John Bothe of Holcome	24 ,,
	Lawrence Haslome of Walm̃	25 ,,

* Lieutenant, see March 23, 1620.

G

		Robert son of James Fogge		October
	b	Alisse dau. of George Romsbothome	26	,,
		An Infante of Rich. Grenhalghes		
		John Hauworth of Greenhill...	3	Novēb
x		James Hunt of Totting:	4	,,
		James Kay of Bawden	6	,,
		Thomas Vnsworthe of Burs	7	,,
	e	Ric. son of Richard Healde of Red.	9	,,
		Ann dau. of James Kay of Boden		
		An Infante of Gilbert Lawes	15	,,
		An Infante of James Crosleyes		
x		Alisse widow of George Holt of Tot.	20	,,
		Ellyn dau. of Ralphe Nuttall	23	,,
		John Brearley of Heywood	28	,,
		Constance Tayler of Walm⁹se	vltimo Novēbr.
	e	Ann vxor John Fletcher	7	December
	e	Wiłłm Rausthorne of Somerset	8	,,
		Margeret w: of Thomas Weston of Bury ...	12	,,
		Mary w: of Richard Grenhalh of Tot. ...	13	,,
		An Infant of Tho. Bothes of Holc.	20	,,
		Dorithy wiffe of Tho. Bury	21	,,
		Thomas Nuttall of Tottingtō		
		Jennet wiffe of Rich: Heald	25	,,
		Mary wiffe of Richard Heald	28	,,
		Isabell Nuttall of Tot.	2	Jany.
		Jane widow of John Taylor of Wal.	7	,,
		Agnes widow of Ellis Kay of Elton	8	,,
		An Infante of Michaell Wolsenas		
Fo. 173		Elizabeth dau. of Robert Hauworthe	12	,,
x e		Ellyn widow of Andrew Shepde	17	,,
x		Gabriell Wolsenham of Haslome Hey ...	19	,,
	o	Elizabeth w: of Thomas Grenhalh	22	,,
	e	Marg⁹t wiffe of Edmond Fenton	25	,,
	o	Katheryn w: of Abraham Kay	31	,,
		An Infant of Abraham Cowapes...	2	Febē
		Isabell w: of Anthony Nab of B.	5	,,
	e	John son of Edmond Fentones		
		John Wormold of Totting:	10	,,
	e	James Kay of Walms:	13	,,
		Elizabeth Rothwell of Rowley		
x e		John Nab of Holcome	22	,,
x e		John Shipobothome of Heape		
		Elizabeth dau. of Abrahā Holte		
	e	Elizabeth dau. of Richard Steele		
		Elizabeth w: of Oliuer Riley	4	March
		Ellyn dau. of John Wrigley		
		Elizabeth dau. of Edmond Parseuall		
—		John Grenhalghe of Tot:	10	,,
		Ann dau. of Thomas Turner		

An Infante of Robert Shepardes	11	March
Thomas son of John Harper	13	,,
Margeret w: of John Hardman	15	,,
Joseph son of Abrahā Cowap	16	,,
o Susan dau. of Roger Smitherst	18	,,
John son of Richard Kay		
Elizabeth wiffe of Richard Grenhalh	19	,,
Francis son of Thomas Hamar		
Katherin w: of Abraham Holte	21	,,
Katheryn dau. of Wiłłm Ramsbothom	23	,,
Edmond Hardman of Rediualls	24	,,
Elizaƀ dau. of John Harper	25	,,

Hu: Watmoughe
George Nuttall
Richard Rosthorne
Robert Shepert
Edmund Ashworth
Richard Houlden
Peter Lomas

1619.

— John Nuttall of Edenfeilde	31	March
Edward Holte of Birkle		
o Margeret wiffe of Richard Bridge	3	April
Mary dau. of James Brearley	2	,,
Elizabeth vid: Johaanis Hynd of Elton	5	,,
Thomas son of Thomas Bothe	7	,,
Elizabeth vid: of Richard Smitherste	13	,,
Jane widow of George Nuttall of Hol:	19	,,
John Vnsworth of Holcome	22	,,
Mary w: of John Hoyle of Crowelū (sic)	32	,,
Jane dau. of John Kay of Walmᵖsley		
Jony Macon of Ainseworth	30	,,
Alisse w: of Robert Cropp of Bamforth	3	Maij
e Ann dau. of James Barlow of Heap		
e Alisse dau. of John Bridge	6	,,
Jane dau. of Thomas Nuttall		
John son of Jeremy Ainseworthe	11	,,
Lawrence Hey of Edenfeilde	14	,,
John son of Roƀt Nab of Bur:	26	,,
Roger son of Richard Heald	28	,,
Alisse Lomax of Totington	13	Junij
e Ric. son of Richard Nuttall of Tot.	25	,,
Alisse dau. of Thomas Heywood of Bur:	27	,,
e Edward Romsbothome of Tot.	29	,,
Thomas Skolfeild of Elton	2	Jvlij
An Infant of Thomas Rushtons	3	,,

	Dorithy dau. of Richard Garstange	4 Jvlij
	Alisse w: of Edmond Grenhalhe	6 ,,
	Elizabeth dau. of Ellis Haslome	
	John son of John Brooke of Tot.	10 ,,
	Margeret Welche of Bury	13 ,,
	Hughe Holte of Ashworth	21 ,,
	Ellizibeth dau. of John Bothe	
	Elizabeth Tayler of Holcome	27 ,,
x e	James Grenhalhe of Chamb⁹s	21 August
	Elizabeth Grundy of Bury	22 ,,
	Elizabeth Holte of Ashworthe	2 Sepᵉ
	An Infante of John Heatones	7 ,,
	Margaret wiffe of John Wrigley	8 ,,
	Elizabeth Tayler of Walme⁹s.	12 ,,
	Alsse wiffe of James Bukley of Tot.	17 ,,
	Elizabeth dau. of Peter Lomax	20 ,,
	Alisse wiffe of Mathew Woode	28 ,,
	Ann dau. of James Grenhalghe of Bury ...	29 ,,
	Robert son of James Kays	6 Octobr
	Thurston son of John Rausthorne	12 ,,
M x	William Vnseworth of Holcome	14 ,,
	Jane Kay of Heyheade	
	Ann Warberton	16 ,,
Fo. 175 o	Elizabeth Hamer of Cheshā	18 ,,
	Margrey w: of William Sharoke	23 ,,
	Roger Nab of Birkle	26 ,,
o	James Grime of Edenfeild	30 ,,
	An Infante of James Crosleyes	6 Noveb
	An Infante of Robert Hauworthes	7 ,,
	Lawrence Battersby of Bury	12 ,,
	James son of Ric. Grime of Shutl.	17 ,,
	Sara dau. of James Fenton of Heywod ...	21 ,,
	An Infante of Thomas Tenants of Bentlye ...	26 ,,
	Isabell Lomax of Goseforde	1 December
	Elisabeth wiffe of John Kay	7 ,,
b	Edmond son of Edmond Law Jvn.	8 ,,
	Elizabeth w: of Robert Hauworth	13 ,,
	Jane w: of Thomas Rausthorne	15 ,,
	Ellyn w: of Ellis Mather	21 ,,
	Añ dau. of Willm Hauworthe	22 ,,
x	Richard Blakley of Bury	26 ,,
	Roger son of Thomas Fletcher & Alisse wiffe of John Pendlebury of Hol.	27 ,,
	Roger son of Thomas Cokshute	28 ,,
o	Isabell wiffe of Edward Hauworth of Edēf.	29 ,,
x e	Alisse Tayler vid: of Bury & John son of Thomas Haywood	30 ,,
	Edmond son of Abrahā Lort	4 Janv.
	John son of John Smithe of Holcome ...	6 ,,

	Alice w: of John Broghton of Hol:	10	Janv.
o	Isabell w: of Lawrence Nab of Bur:	12	,,
	James Birche of Bury		
o	A child of Mr. Heywoodes of Heyw:	16	,,
	A child of Rich: Romsbothomes of Bury	21	,,
	A child of Stephne Sagares		
	Margrey w: of Peter Romsbothom of Hol....	24	,,
e	Edward Rothwell of Walm⁹s.		
	Ric. son of Wiłłm Hauworth of Wal.	28	,,
x	Ric. Smitherst of Whā	1	February
	Jane dau. of Ellis Leach	2	,,
o	Margeret w: of James Nuttall		
	Dority dau. of John Wrigley		
	John son of John Wrigley of Heywood...	4	,,
	vzor James Bradley of Midleton	6	,,
x	vzor Roger Fildes of Bury	7	,,
	A child of John Grenhalhes of B. h. and John son of John Bothe of Bur:	9	,,
	A child of Samuell Nuttall of . .	15	,,
	Jennet wiffe of Francis Pilkington	16	,,
x	Ann vzor Thome Holte de Broke	21	,,
x	Josephe Nab of Walm⁹sly	26	,,
	Elizabethe fil: of John Heald		
176	Robert Ouldhā of Brandlesā	28	,,
	Ann dau. of Francis Warb⁹ton of Elt:	5	March
	Margeret dau. of Richard Dauēport	6	,,
	Margeret dau. of Francis Warbertō	7	,,
x	Thomas Warberton of Tott:	8	,,
	A child of Rich: Fletcheres	11	,,
	The wid: of Thurstan Broke of Tot.	12	,,
	Ric. son of Wiłłm Both of Tot.	13	,,
x e	Ric. Bridge Leiuetenante of Tot.	23	,,
e	vidua Jacobj Barlow of Croichlaw		

1620.

e	An Infant of Ric. Rothwelles of Hol:	27	March
	vxor Ric. Grime of Bury		
e	Alisse vzor John Heliwell of Bury	5	April
	A child of Richard Sedons of Bury	9	,,
	Elizaƀ dau. of Ralphe Kay of Walm⁹sley	13	,,
	A child of Wiłłm Leaches of Bamforth	28	,,
	Oliur Wigan of Tott.	26	,,
x	Ellen widow of Ric. Kay of Walmesley	27	,,
	Elizabeth vx: Rogʳ Sedon of Holc.	29	,,
	Jane vxor Roƀt Birde of Midleton	30	,,
x	Wiłłm Bury of Tottington	5	Maij
	Richard Heliwell of Totting:		
e	Letice vidua Gulielmi Bury de Tot.	9	,,

	Richard Nuttall of Crow lome	10	Maij
o	Margaret Ingham of Tottington		
	Thomas Kay of Walmesley & Margaret w: of Thomas Bothe of Tot.	12	,,
	Robt son of John Grenhalghe of Brand.	16	,,
	Mary dau. of James Rothwell of Bury	18	,,
	Richard son of John Barlow of Totting.		
	A child of John Wigons of Tot.	19	,,
	Mary dau. of Henry Dunster		
x e	Thomas Hamer of Walsawl	23	,,
	A child of Ric. Hameres of Bu:	27	,,
—	Margeret vidua Ric. Birch of Whitle	29	,,
— e	Francis Walworke of Bu:	30	,,
	Lawrence son of John Brogton of Tot:		
	Ric. Thornley of Midleton pishe	2	Jvnij
	Alisse v. John Grenhalh de Brandlesā	4	,,
	Thomas son of Ric. Battersby	10	,,
	Abrahā Fletcher of Birch hey		
	A child of Tho: Wodes of Tot.	17	,,
—	John Smithe of Elton	20	,,
	A child of Richard Grimes	21	,,
	Richard Sedon of Bury	22	,,
—	Andrew Holt of Holcome	23	,,
	John son of John Horrege	30	,,
	Alexander Maden of B.	3	July
Fo.177	Ric. son of Charles Nuttall of Hol.	9	,,
	Alisse w: of Thomas Heald of Bury	14	,,
	James Hardman of Heape	22	,,
	Eme the wiffe of Roger Kay	23	,,
	Elizabeth wiffe of Adam Rigby	27	,,
	Thomas Blakley of Bury	1	Aug.
	Robt son of Robert Kay of Benteley	13	,,
x	Christopher Nuttall of Tottington	14	,,
	Ann Brurcliffe of Bury	16	,,
x	Adam Rigbye of Bury	20	,,
x	John Lomax of Walshaw Lane	27	,,
e	A child of John Warbertons	28	,,
x	Katheryn wiffe of Robt Kay de Mosse	3	Sept
	John son of Edmond Law of Hol.	8	,,
	Willm Hilton of Brodoke	11	,,
	Willm son of Josua Ored	21	,,
	Margeret Estwood of Bury	5	Octobr
x	Thomas Hauworthe of Holehowse	9	,,
	A child of Edmond Heliwelles		
	A child of John Hiltons of Heape	27	,,
	Elyn wife of Oliuer Chadweeke	2	November
	Margeret Nuttall of Totington	3	,,
	John Barlow of Tot.	13	,,
	vzor Edmund Leach of Whā		

BURIALS.

	Wiłłm Leache of Bamford	16	November
	John son of George Holme	22	,,
	Alisse dau. of John Vnseworth	27	,,
	A child of Samuell Nuttales of Holcōe	29	,,
	Alisse wiffe of Edmond Ramsbothom of Tot.	1	Decebr
	Grace dau. of Thomas Kay de Wham	4	,,
	Elizab dau. of Robt Sharp de Hol:	6	,,
	Ric. son of Edmond Leache de Wal:		
x	Francis Warberton de Hethy hill	11	,,
	Jony wiffe of Wiłłm Benson de Bury	13	,,
	Robt Nab de Bury	14	,,
	A child of Daniell Stones of Bu:	15	,,
	A child of Wiłłm Bensons	17	,,
	Alisse dau. of Abrahā Rothwell of Hol.	23	,,
	Ester wiffe of Ralphe Leach of Tot:	27	,,
x	Henry Asmall de Skowte	30	,,
	A child of Robert Butterworthes		
	Thomas Wood of Tottingtō	5	Jañ
	Richard son of John Rothwell of Hol.	6	,,
	James son of Edward Symon	18	,,
	John son of Edward Lomax of Heywode	22	,,
	Jane w: of Arthur Holte of Bu:	23	,,
	Ann dau. of John Smith of Hol:	24	,,
	vxor Edward Lomax de Hey.	26	,,
178	Alisse dau. of Roger Hamer de Bukden	30	,,
	James Pacoke of Bury Hamell	1	Febr.
	Richard son of Thomas Liuesey	2	,,
	Margeret v. Thome Kay de Mosse	3	,,
	Richard son of James Leache of Walmᵍs.	11	,,
	Wiłłm son of Richard Duckworth		
	A childe of John Whitheades of Hasl.		
e	John Holte of Bury	12	,,
	Margeret wiffe of James Ridinges		
x	Francis Nuttall of Edenfelde	17	,,
	Margeret dau. of James Kay of Boden	19	,,
	James son of James Scolfeld of Eden.	21	,,
	Katheryn dau. of Thomas Pacoke of Holcome	27	,,
	Ellyn dau. of Robert Farneworth of Birch		
	Ann w: of Thomas Tennante of Walmᵍs.	1	March
	John son of Ric. Romsbothom of Bury	5	,,
	Ann dau. of John Brooke of Hol.	6	,,
	A child of Wiłłm Stotes of Heywood	8	,,
	Henry son of John Wrigley of Hey.	10	,,
	Lawrence Hey of Edenfeld		
	Margery w: of Adam Wolfenden	11	,,
	A child of Ricᵍ Buries of Woodrod	12	,,
	Richard Hauworth de Bury	17	,,
	Judeth w: of Ralph Baily of Whitle	19	,,
	Wiłłm son of Oliver Grime of Skoute	22	,,

1621.

	Ellen Vnseworth of Bury	2	April
	A child of Richard Shawes of Bamf.	3	,,
	Henry son of Roger Sedon of Hol.	8	,,
	Ellyn dau. of Ralphe Bayly of Whitle...	9	,,
	Ellyn dau. of Henry Bury of Tot.	15	,,
	Edward Kay of Bury		
	Willm son of Will Bancroft of Walm̃	18	,,
	Jony w: of Willm Rausthorn of Cokey	26	,,
	Elizabeth dau. of Edward Hynd	29	,,
	Edmond son of Richard Finche	1	Maij
	Ester wiffe of Henry Fildes of Bury	4	,,
	Ann dau. of Francis Grenhalh of Bury		
e	Isabell wiffe of Edmond Both de Redivales...	5	,,
	Alisse dau. of Thomas Hauworth de Tot.	10	,,
	Jane dau. of Roger Sedon of Hol.	17	,,
	Ann dau. of John Hardman	18	,,
	Ann Holte of Bury	19	,,
	Jane dau. of James Kay of Hartlee	20	,,
b	Edmond son of James Hauworth & Ann Beusweeke	21	,,
	John son of Henry Mather of Bur:	23	,,
	Ann w: of John Hardman of Heyw:	1	Jvnij
	Ellyn dau. of Rogr Kay of Elton	7	,,
o	Thomas Weston of Bury	9	,,
	A child of Samuell Nuttales of Hol:	16	,,
Fo. 179	Elizabeth dau. of John Barlow of Tot.	22	,,
x e	Thomas Rothwell of Walmesley	23	,,
	Mathew son of Charles Brooke	28	,,
	A child of Edmond Holtes	29	,,
	A child of Leonard Ashworthe	30	,,
	James son of John Rothwell of Hol:	1	Jvlij
x	Jony vxo: James Peacoke of Bury	3	,,
	Thurstan son of Willm Brooke	6	,,
	The wiffe of Abraham Lorte	8	,,
—	Margery vid: of Pel Boulton of Birtle...	9	,,
— e	Ann vid: Richard Heliwell of Elton	10	,,
o e	Thomas fil: Thomas Heliwell of Redi.	12	,,
	Jane dau. of John Crompton	20	,,
x	Thomas Healde of Bury	23	,,
	A child of Gilbard Halseyardes	28	,,
	James Ridinges of Bury	2	August
	Katheryn Hauworth of Heywood	6	,,
	Willm Heywood of Birkle	9	,,
	Edmond son of John Grenhalhe	11	,,
	James son of Richard Healde	19	,,
	Mary dau. of Abrahã Stringer	21	,,
	Elizabeth dau. of Jefferey Tayler of Edẽf.	24	,,
	Ellyn dau. of Francis Hauworth	25	,,

	John son of Thomas Waulker		August
b	Susan dau. of John Grenhalgh & . . Hunt	27	,,
b	A Bastard of Adam Holts & Ann Bate	28	,,
	Edward son of James Skolefeld of Tot:		
	Ann w: of George Haughe of Bury	29	,,
	James son of Richard Sydall of Bury	3	Sep.
	Prisilla Wilson of Elton	4	,,
	Susan dau. of Anthony Bothe	7	,,
	Mary dau. of Robert Heywood of Hey.		
o *b*	Jennet dau. of Edmond Fenton & Margeret Bate	9	,,
	Alisse dau. of Willm Bothe	19	,,
	Dorithy dau. of Thomas Buckley of Tot.	20	,,
	John son of Peter Totell of Bury	22	,,
	Leonard Asheworthe of Bury	27	,,
	A childe of Emer Ainseworthes		
	Ellyn dau. of Tho. Fletcher of Red:	29	,,
	Mary dau. of Willm Grenhalghe of Tot.	30	,,
	Elizabeth dau. of Ellize Haslome	5	Octob
	Alisse w: of Richard Heywood of Bur.	9	,,
	Richard son of John Warberton	12	,,
o	Ann wiffe of Thomas Hauworthe	14	,,
	Mary dau. of James Hardman	15	,,
b	Dority dau. of Abraham Tayler of Ratchd.	18	,,
	Lawrence Elton of Shutle:	20	,,
	Ralfe son of Henry Nuttall of Tot.	21	,,
	Thomas Finche of Walmesley	23	,,
180	Charles Nuttall of Holcome	10	November
	Ric: Wood of Tottington		
e	James Birche of Heape	13	,,
	A child of James Crosleyes of Hey.	14	,,
	Elizabeth w: of Robt Hauworth of Bamf.	16	,,
x	Oliuer Nabes of Walme⁹sley	28	,,
	Mary dau. of Richard Wigan		
	Thomas son of James Peacoke	4	Decebe
	Francis son of Franc: Pendlebury	20	,,
x	Thomas Whiteade of Bury	22	,,
	Richard Greenhalhe of Toting.	27	,,
	Richard Kay of Rediualles	29	,,
	A child of Edmond Bothes		
b	James son of Edmund Holte of Heap	6	Jañ
	A child of Robert Ashworthe of Midle.		
	John son of John Stot of Heywood	8	,,
o	Jane dau. of Alexand^r Naden	10	,,
	Elizabeth widow of Adam Tayler of Heywood	14	,,
	Richard Battersby of Bury		
	Jane vx: Edmond Ashworth of Heywood	18	,,
	Alisse widow of Willm Skolefeld of Hey.	19	,,
	Roger Bothe of Rediualles	21	,,

	James Totell of Bury	23	Jañ
	John Fenton of Bamford	24	,,
	Elizaƀ wiffe of Richard Nuttall		
o	James son of John Fletcher of Bu:	2	Feƀ
	Mary vz: John Stotte of Heywood	4	,,
	Elizabeth Romsebothom of Holc.	9	,,
	A child of James Cooperes of Bu:	10	,,
x	Thomas Bridge of Holcome	11	,,
x	Peter Shipobotham of Holcome	14	,,
	Willm son of Edward Hamer	17	,,
b	A child of Roƀt Wilsones & Jennet Hauworthes of Bury	19	,,
	Ann vz: of Miles Kay of Litlewood	24	,,
	Joan vz: of Thom: Wolsenhā of Has: ...	27	,,
	A childe of Ralphe Shepardes	6	Martij
	A child of George Bradshawes of Tot. ...	11	,,
	Jane w: of James Kay of Hartlee	16	,,

1622.

	Jennet w: of Ralfe Dewrden	25	Martij
	A child of Robert Andertons	27	,,
	A child of Richard Wigons	28	,,
	John Wigon of Tott.	29	,,
—	Williā Brooke of Holcome		
	Isabell dau. of George Hauworthe...	16	Apr
	A child of James Hauworthe		
—	Oliuer Chadweeke	19	,,
	A child of Roƀt Bothes of Wal:	23	,,
—	Ralphe Bridge of Holcome	26	,,
Fo. 181 —	Richard Rothwell of Holcome	1	Maij
—	Jane v. Richard Rothwell of Hol.	5	,,
	Elizabeth Butterworthe of Bury	17	,,
	Alisse Battersby of Holcome		
	Alisse Bukley of Bury	19	,,
	Isabell Bukley of Holcome		
—	John Roodes of Holcome	30	,,
o	Richard Bothe of Elton...	15	Jvnij
	Alisse dau. of John Holte	21	,,
e	Margret w: of Peter Liuesey of Mid:... ...	24	,,
	Alisse w: of Ralph Shephard	27	,,
	Richard Holte of Bury	1	Julij
	Ann dau. of Zachary Bridge	6	,,
	John son of Oliuer Grime of Skoute ...	15	,,
	Susan w: of Richard Dukworth of Bur: ...	17	,,
	Mary dau. of James Wrigley of Heywood ...		
	A child of Henry Bridges	19	,,
	Elizaƀ w: of Thomas Fletchᵽ of Red. ...		
o	Jane Smithe of Elton	28	,,

1622 BURIALS.

	Richard son of Richard Both of Hol:	1	Aug.
x	John Wood of the edge in Tott:	5	,,
	Katheryn Bats of Bury		
	Peter son of Peter Cloughe...	6	,,
o	Richard Grime of Bury hamel	8	,,
o	Thomas son of Robert Nab	9	,,
—	Samuell Kay of Elton	19	,,
	Ellis Fletcher of Hethy hill	29	,,
	Elizabeth dau. of John Turner	2	Sep
—	James Cooper of Bury	7	,,
o	Isabell Milles of Elton	11	,,
	Edmond son of Mathew Jakson	12	,,
	Ellyn v: of Francis Wardley of Pᵖstwch	15	,,
o	Thomas Grenhalghe of Birchehey	17	,,
	Jane dau. of Robert Crosley of Heywood	21	,,
o	Isabell Holte of Heape...	22	,,
	Margeret dau. of James Asmall	23	,,
	James Fletcher of Elton	24	,,
	Ann v. Symeon Lamb of Bury	29	,,
	Elizabeth v: Thurstan Fildes of Heap	4	Octobr
o	Roger son of Roger Fletcher of Elton	6	,,
	Thomas son of Roger Both of Bury		
	Lydia vx William Bury...	10	,,
x	James Barlow of Bury, Butcher	12	,,
	William Holte of Grislchurste	17	,,
	Ann vx. Thomas Fletcher	21	,,
	Edm̃d Shornley*		
Fo. 182	Elizabeth dau. of Peter Tayler	30	,,
	Ann vz. George Warberton	31	,,
e	Katheryn vx: of Thomas Holte	3	Noveb
	Thomas son of John Grenhalhe of Tot.	10	,,
	John Nab of Tottington	12	,,
	Ann vx: of Roger Fletcher of Eltō	19	,,
	Samuell son of John Hynde	23	,,
	Elizabeth dau. of Richard Heald		
e	Grace vx: Francis Barlow de Bury	28	,,
	Mary dau. of Henry Nuttall of Tot.		
	Ann vx: John Grene of Edenfelde	29	,,
	Ann dau. of Richard Heliwell of Bury	2	Deceb
	Thomas son of Williā Dikonson of Midl.	5	,,
e	Annes Haughe of Totington	13	,,
	Margeret Nuttall of Bury	16	,,
	Peter Walshawe's child...		
o e	Priscilla Nuttall of Bury	24	,,
o	A child of Ellis Haslome		
x	George Hauworthe of Skoute	26	,,
o	Elizabethe v: of Thomas Allens	29	,,
	Katheryn v: of Edmond Law of Hol:	30	,,

* Written below in later hand.

o	Emmyn v: of James Greenhahe of Tot.	3	Janv
o	Ann v: of Richard Barlowe		
	Grace w: of Thomas Nuttall of Aedenf.	4	,,
	A child of Richard Booth & Wormold	5	,,
o	Katheryn wiffe of Richard Kay of Wydell	7	,,
	Thomas Gartside of Edenfeilde	8	,,
o	Alisse v: Henry Cloughe of Ratchdale	10	,,
o	The Dikar of Holcome		
—	William Potto of Bury	11	,,
o	Ellyn Smithersthe of Brodoke		
o	Jane dau. of Roger Fletcher of Elton	14	,,
o	John Wigon v: of Tottington	16	,,
o	A sonne of the said John Wigan		
e	Alise w: of Ralphe Nuttall of Tot.	20	,,
	Ann w: of John Holte of Bury	22	,,
e	Ann w: of John Lomax of Tott.		
	William son of John Medocrofte of Bamf.	29	,,
	Margeret dau. of Richard Rausthorne	30	,,
o	William Kay of Bury	3	February
e	Margeret v: Richard Kay of Walmer:	8	,,
	Richard son of William Shipubothom		
o	James son of Robert Bothe of Bury	10	,,
Fo. 183	Elizabeth v: of John Smithe of Elton	17	,,
	Ann dau. of James Kay of Holcome	20	,,
	James Holte of Grislehurste Esquier		
o	Mary dau. of Robert Hauworthe	26	,,
o	Thomas Bridge of Walmersley	27	,,
—	Richard Leache of Shutleworthe	3	March
	George son of Richard Holt of Holc̄		
—	Robert Hauworthe of Bury hamē		
	A child of Mr. Greenhalghes	5	,,
	Richard Holt of Bury		
o	Jane dau. of Agnes Tayler of Hol:	6	,,
due	Grace dau. of Thomas Durden	8	,,
	James son of James Peacoke	13	,,
	Elizabeth dau. of Willm Hauworth of Tot.	15	,,
due	James son of Willm Horroks of Tot:	16	,,

1623.

	Thomas son of Mathew Bury	25	March
—	John Asheworthe of Tottington at Mr. Rausthornes		
o	Jane dau. of Robert Nab	26	,,
o	Roger Nuttall of Tot.	27	,,
	Alisse dau. of James Lomax of Midle.	28	,,
	Ann dau. of Willm Hauworthe	29	,,
o	An old man of Akrington	30	,,
o	Jane w: of John Wigan	31	,,

	Ann Hamer of Walmersley	2	April
	Thomas son of Thomas Hopwood of Baf :...	6	,,
	James Hardman of Bury	7	,,
e	John Rausthorne of Lume	8	,,
	Henry Knowles of Midleton	11	,,
	Adam son of Adā Jackson of Radcl :	14	,,
o	Alise Kay of Holcome	23	,,
	Lawrence Hardman of Bridge	24	,,
	Ann v. of William Nuttall of Holcome ...		
o	Ann Battersby of Holcome		
	Susan dau. of John Kay	25	,,
	Mary dau. of John Croston of Elton	30	,,
	Ann vidua of Thomas Bridge of Hol :... ...		
	Arther Smitherst of Wham	3	Maij
o	Elizabeth dau. of Edmond Leache	4	,,
	Ann dau. of John Barlow of Tott :	11	,,
o	Elizabeth dau. of Robert Nab	12	,,
	John son of Jerimy Barlowe	18	,,
o	Margret wiffe of Thomas Hynd	16	,,
o	Jane wiffe of William Tayler	18	,,
	Oliuer son of Willm Hauworthe		
	Alisse wiffe of William Hauworth	20	,,
	A child of John Crompton		
184	Alisse dau. of Richard Battersby & Elizab Kay	22	,,
	Beniamin son of Zachary Bridge		
	Ellyn dau. of Richard Rausthorne ...		
e	John Romsbothom, Fitter	25	,,
	Roger son of Thomas Nuttall	31	,,
	Edward son of John Dikson	5	Jvnij
	Jane w: of James Whitworthe	8	,,
	Thomas Nuttall of Elton	12	,,
	Arther Kay of Walmersley	23	,,
	Ralphe Pilkington of Chaterton	24	,,
	Ann dau. of Rich: Holt of Hauk: & Isabell Horroks		
	Isabell dau. of John Both of Bury...	25	,,
	John son of Joseph Ored of Bury	5	Julij
	James Kay of Walmer :	18	,,
	Thomas son of Hugh Sedon	21	,,
	Ann Holte of Tottington	23	,,
	Ann w: of Thomas Turner		
e	Ann w: of Richard Kay of Walm :	25	,,
	Ann w: of Richard Sedon of Heap	26	,,
	Ellis Haslome of Walm :	27	,,
	Jony w: of Robert Shepard of Cheshā ...	28	,,
	Isabell dau. of Arther Partington	2	August
o	Ann w: of Willm Leache of Bamford ...	3	,,
o	Ellnor Kaij of Walmersley	4	,,

o	Michill Kaij of Walmersley	9	August
o	Ann dau. of Richard Allence of Burie	13	,,
	Roger Haughton of Burie hamell	18	,,
x	A child of Willm Rosthorne of Elton	19	,,
	Mr. Hugh Watmoughe parson of Burie	21	,,
o	Richard Siddall of Burie	28	,,
o	Ann w: of John Isherwood of Tott:		
o	Henrie Hoyle of Huthersfeld pish		
x	A child of Richard Lomax of Tott:	1	September
	A child of Andrewe Holden of Musburie	2	,,
x	Richard Rosthorne of Lome	4	,,
—	Letisse w: of Henrie Nuttall of Holcom		
—	Ann w: of James Barlowe Butcher of Burie	5	,,
o	Ann Hilton of Burihamell	6	,,
o	Elizabethe Bouthe of Holcome	7	,,
o	Mathewe Wood of Tottington	10	,,
o	John Aspinall of Burihamell		
x	Raphe Woolsencrofte of Elton	13	,,
Fo. 185 x	Elizabeth Hellywell of Burie	16	,,
	bRichard son of Gyles Rothwell of Wal:	17	,,
x	Elsabethe w: of Thomas Kaij of Wal:	18	,,
o	A child of Samuell Vnsworthe of Burie	18	,,
	bRichard son of Richard Wood of Elton	19	,,
o	Ellis son of John Tayler of Birchey*	25	,,
—	Jinnie w: of Samuell Kaij of Elton		
x	Doritie dau. of Roberte Nabbe of Buriha:		
x	A child of Thomas Heald of Burie		
x	Thomas son of Michill Kaij of Tottington		
x	Thomas Turnor of Birchey	28	,,
x	Ann w: of John Vnsworthe of Holcom		
x	Grace w: of Richard Rothwell of Holcom		
x	Ann dau. of Edmund Hardman of Redivalls	30	,,
x	A child of John Hill of Elton		
x	James Wood of Midlton	2	October
x	A child of Richard Tuttell of Elton	3	,,
x	Margerie Moumforte of Burie		
x	Ollyver Royley of Burie	6	,,
x	Katrine w: of Thomas Woolsenham of Eltom	11	,,
x	A child of Roberte Smethurste of Redivalls		
x	Richard Hamer of Burie	14	,,
x	Jane Gest of Burihamell		
x	A child of John Aspinall of Burihamell		
x	John Turnor of Birchey	16	,,
x	John Buckley of Holcome	18	,,
x	Marie dau. of Dauid Nadden of Burieha:	20	,,
x c	Annis w: of Roger Kaij of Walmersley	21	,,
x	Alice Fletcher of Burihamell		
—	bWilliam Duckworthe of Burihamell	24	,,

* There has been here an erasure of a line.

1623   BURIALS.

x		Margerie w: of Willm Dowson of Rediualls...		October
x		A child of Willm Bouthe of Burihamell		
x		A child of Richard Hamer of Burie	26	,,
x		A child of Alexander Nadden of Burihamell		
x		Margreate w: of Jeffrey Lomax of Heape	28	,,
x		Richard Wood of Eltonn		
		Henrie Mather of Buriehamell	2	Nouember
	c	Isabell w: of John Nabbe of Holcō		
		Margreate w: of Christopher Smethurste of Burie		
	o	George Boothe of Rediuall	5	,,
	o	Ellen Kaij of Burie		
x		Richard Heywood of Midltonn	7	,,
x		vx⁹ Richard Siddall of Burie...		
x		Ellen Lomax of Burihamell	11	,,
x		Willm Byrome of Hewoode		
x c		Doritie w: Thomas Grinhalghe of Heape	15	,,
x		Peter Heywood of Burie		
x		A child of George Emerson of Burie		
x		A child of Roger Fletcher of Burie		
186 x		Thomas Howorthe of Burie		
x		Ann w: of Thomas Smethurste of Heape...		
x		Barnabie Birche of Burie	16	,,
x		Elsabethe Houlte of Burihamell	17	,,
x		Zacarie son of Zacarie Bridge of Holcom		
x		A child of Thomas Kaij of Wham	18	,,
x		Roberte Kaij of Burie		
x		Lawrance Smethurste of Heape	19	,,
x		Margreate Pendleburie of Burie	20	,,
x		A child of Roberte Smethurste of Rediualls...		
x		A child of Francis Holeleyes of Holcom	21	,,
x		James Ecckersall of Burie		
x		Edward Partington of Walmersley...		
x		Ollyuer Chadwicke of Burihamell		
x		Elsabethe Diggle of Burie	22	,,
x c		Raphe Duckworth of this hamell	23	,,
x		A child of Ellen Lomax of Tott....	28	,,
	o	Roger Duckworthe of Birchey	29	,,
x		Edmund Turnor of Birchey...	30	,,
x o		A child of Edmund Turnor of Birchey		
x c		Ann w: of John Shawe of Burie	3	December
x		Bessey Fletcher of Burie		
x		on of the Howorthes of Bamford		
x		Marie w: of James Leache of Burie	5	,,
x		A childe of Edwarde Kaies of Wal.*		
x c		Margreate Mackon of Heape	6	,,
x		Margreate w: of John Kaij of Wal:	7	,,
x c		Susan dau. of James Barlowe of Burie	8	,,

              * A line erased here.

x	Edmund Pilkington of Chatterton	9	December
x	Henrie Gryme of Scoute		
o	The w: of John Lomaxe of Heape		
x	Alice w: of James Scofeilde of Tott:	10	,,
x	Roberte Turnor of Tottington	11	,,
x	A child of Katrin Marland of Tott.	12	,,
x	Ould Biggman of Bamforthe		
— x	Josephe Hagge of Ferngore		
x o	Peter Romsbothom of Holcom̃	13	,,
x o	A child of John Wormill of Tott.	17	,,
x o	Elsabethe w: of John Wormill of Tott.	19	,,
x	John Kaij of Walmersley		
x o	Daniell Allence of Burie ha:		
x	Roberte Grinhalghe of Tott:	20	,,
x o	Richard Kaij of Burie	22	,,
x	The w: of Francis Woode of Tott.		
x o	Jane Kaij of Burie	23	,,
x o	A child of Thomas Boothe of Elton		
x	A poore criple borne of a barowe*		
	Ric⁹ son of John Asheworthe of Rosendall		
Fo. 187 x o	Thomas Smithe of Elton	24	,,
x o	Edmund Grinhalghe of Burie		
x o	Isabell Kaij of Walmersley	25	,,
x o	Elsabethe w: of Thomas Bridge of Holcom̃	26	,,
x o	A child of Henrie Nuttall of Tott.		
x o	Ellen w: of Edmund Lomax of Birchey		
x o	Ann w: of John Howorthe of Wal.	27	,,
x o	A child of John Wormill of Tott.		
x o	A child of Henrie Pilkington of Tott.	30	,,
x o	Abraham son of John Fletcher of Burie	1	Januarij
— x c	John Fletcher of Rediualls	2	,,
x c	Thomas Fletcher of Rediuals	5	,,
x	Raphe Aspinall of this hamell		
o	Ann w: of Edward Burton of this ha:	6	,,
o	A child of Edward Burton of this ha:		
o	A child of John Barlowe of Tott.	7	,,
o	Richard Nuttall of Tottington		
o	William Benson of Burie	10	,,
	Lenche of Rosendall		
o	Ann Kaij of Burih:	12	,,
o	Thomas Bridge of Tott.	15	,,
o	Michill Sall of Burie		
o	Marie w: of Thomas Lomax of Tott.	17	,,
o	Margreate Fletcher of Rediualls		
o	A pore child of Bamford	18	,,
o	A child of Richard Allence of Burie	20	,,
o	A child of John Aspinall of Burie		
x	Doritie w: of Mathewe Nuttall of Burie	21	,,

* This entry has been crossed through with a pen.

o	The w: of John Berie of Hewood	24	Januarij
x	Alice w: of James Lomax of Walmersley	26	,,
o	A child of Thomas Heald of Berie	27	,,
o	A child of Michill Saile of Rediuals		
o	A poor child died in Tottington	29	,,
o	The w: of Thomas Smythe of Elton		
o	Elsabethe Redgate of Burie...		
x	Henry Cuncliffe of Rediuals...	31	,,
o	A child of Edmund Leache of Wal:		
o	Thomas Bouthe of Tottington	3	Februarij
o	A child of Roger Nuttall of Tott.		
o	A child of Margerie Barlowes of Holcō		
o	Richard Kaij of Walmersley	6	,,
o	Jane Bouthe of Burihamell		
x	A child of Ellis Howorthe of Etenfeilde	10	,,
o	A child of Michill Kaij of Walmersley		
o	A child of John Taylor of Wal.	11	,,
o	The w: of Richard Barlowe of Holcom	12	,,
o	A child of Lawrance Taylor of Burie		
x	Elsabethe dau. of Mathewe Bouthe of Rediualls	13	,,
188 o	John son of John Hutton of Holcom	14	,,
	John son of Richard Rothewell of Holcom..	16	,,
	Marie dau. of Thomas Smythe of Eltonn		
	Isabell w: of George Houlte of Tottington...		
	Jane Boothe of Burie	18	,,
	John son of Lenard Asheworthe, Burihamell		
	A child of Michell Woolsenham of Elton	19	,,
	The w: of Gyles Rothewell of Wal.	20	,,
	The w: of Roberte Benson of Burie		
	Richard son of Richard Nuttall of Tottington	23	,,
	Ellen w: of John Iserwoode of Tottington...	28	,,
	Ann Hutton of Tottington	29	,,
	Genet w: of James Lomax of Wal.		
	Elsabeth dau. of Richard Rawsthorne of Tott.	1	Marche
	Francis son of Lawrance Cockrell of Tott....		
	Susan dau. of Arthure Kaij of Walmersley...	2	,,
c	Thomas Hellywell of Rediualls	3	,,
	A child of Johns of George of Rosendall	4	,,
	A child of Thomas Wood of Tott.	5	,,
	A child of Thomas Broucke of Tott.	6	,,
	Thomas Boothe of Tottington	7	,,
	Ellen w: of Richard Barlowe of Holcō	8	,,
	Alice w. of Samuell Sale of Buriha:	10	,,
	Alice dau. of Raphe Houlte of Ainsworthe...	11	,,
	Thomas son of Henrie Boardman of Burie...	12	,,
c	Margerie Turnor of Burie Hamell	13	,,
	George Durden of Etenfeild	14	,,
	Roberte Seddon of Burihamell	16	,,

H

Ann Scoles of Walmersley		Marche
Jane dau. of Willm Nabbe of Midletonn	18	,,
Ellen Greene of Holcoм̃	19	,,
Richard Parsiuall of Elton	22	,,
c A child of Lawrance Taylor of Burie		
Elsabeth w: of Thomas Hellywell of Rediuals		

1624.

A child of Elis Leache of Wal.	26	March
Genet w: of James Fogge of Elton		
A child of Richard Rawsthorne of Tott.	1	Aprill
Katrine dau. of Josephe Nabbe of Walmersley	3	,,
Henrie son of Henry Boothe of Etenfeild		
Richard son of Richard Overall of Burie	6	,,
c Thomas Whitheade of Burie	8	,,
Margreate w: of Lawrance Hardman of Litle bridge	11	,,
Alice w: of Ellis Lomax of Elton		
Ann dau. of James Howorthe of Wal.		
Alice dau. of Learnard Asheworthe of Burie	13	,,
A child of Richard Rothwells of Holcome	15	,,
Richard Broucke of Burie	16	,,
Thomas son of Thomas Kaie of Elton		
Fo. 189 Elsabethe Lomax of Tottington	19	,,
Roberte Smethurste of Rediuals	20	,,
c Emer Ainsworthe of Tottington	25	,,
Ann w: of Raphe Bridge of Holcome	27	,,
Charles Nuttall of Holcome	2	May
George son of the said Charles		
c Richard Grinhalghe of Tott.	3	,,
Jeremy Hynd of Tottington	6	,,
Ann w: of Francis Grinhalghe of Burie	8	,,
A child of Roberte Magnalls of Tott.		
Margreate w: of Francis Nabbe of Burie	10	,,
Ellis Lomax of Tottington	13	,,
Genet w: of James Rosthorne of Heape	14	,,
Josephe son of Zackerie Bridge of Holcome	15	,,
John Rothwell of Holcome	17	,,
Marie w: of Richard Bouthe of Holcō		
Roger Kaij of Burie	27	,,
Ann Woolsenham of Tottingtonn		
Jane dau. of Lawrance Smethurste of Heape	29	,,
c James Rothwell of Holcome	31	,,
Francis Taylor of Walmersley	1	Juñ
Elsabethe w: of Edward Nuttall of Etenfeild	2	,,
The w: of John Bouthe of Tottington	5	,,
c John Heatonn of Rediualls	7	,,
Alice dau. of Henrie Burie of Tott.	10	,,

1624 BURIALS.

Genet daughter of James Leache of Tott.	11	Juñ
Peter Rydinges of Heywood	13	,,
Margreate w: of John Smythe of Burieh:		
vx⁹ Owen Lomax of Burie hamell	17	,,
A childe of John Smethurste of Rediuals	26	,,
Alice dau. of Ollyuer Gryme of Scoute	27	,,
Richarde Fletcher of Eltonn	2	Julij
A child of Leonard Asheworthe of Burieh:		
A child of James Wilson of Holcom		
George Bromeley of Burie	6	,,
Richard Bouthe of Burie		
Alice w: of Henrie Gryme of Scoute		
A child wch died at Heywood	14	,,
A child of Edmund Grinhalghe of Burie	19	,,
A child of Willm Allence of Musburie	24	,,
Willm Bamford of Bamford	26	,,
Elsabethe Marcrofte of Burie		
cha Elsabethe w: of Thomas Whithead of Burie	27	,,
George Hamer of Banck laine	29	,,
Katrin Whithead of Burie	30	,,
A child of John Barlowe of Tott.	2	August
Grace Longworthe of Burie		
190 Elsabethe w: Roberte Marcrofte of Midlton	29	,,
c Michill Bentley of Elton	1	September
A child of William Hoult of Holcome	2	,,
Thomas son of Roberte Scofeild of Bamford	13	,,
Margreate w: of Roberte Brearlie of Heywood	18	,,
The wife of Thomas Greenall	21	,,
John Barlowe of Tottington	24	,,
A child of George Houlte of Tott.	2	October
Mathewe Wood of Walmershley	7	,,
John son of John Bouthe of Tottingtō	8	,,
William Whorockes of Midleton	17	,,
James Fletcher of Burihamell	19	,,
A child of Thomas Wilkingsonn of Wal.		
Ann w: of Ellis Haslome of Wal.	24	,,
A child of Leonarde Asheworthe of Burih:	25	,,
Ann w: of Roberte Howorthe of Sutleworth	29	,,
Ann w: of Thomas Hamer of Banclaine	6	Nouember
Margreate Hurle of Holcome	12	,,
Jony w: of Robert Dunster of Baleholte	21	,,
Roberte Kitchine of Tottington		
Ann dau. of Abell Tumlinson of Prestwiche	29	,,
Jane dau. of Thomas Andertonn of Walmersley	3	December
John son of Arthure Kaij of Walmersley	8	,,
A child of Arthure Partington of Walmersley	15	,,
Elizabethe dau. of Thomas Bouthe of Burie		
Roberte Howorthe of Bamford	23	,,
Elizabethe dau. of Symond Barlowe of Tott.		

Margreate Smethurste of Tottington	25	December
A child of Richard Nuttall of Tottington	27	,,
Elizabethe Wood of Tottington	31	,,
c Katrin w: of Thomas Nuttall of Tott.	2	Januarij
Sara w: of James Crosley of Heywood	11	,,
James Bate of Burie	15	,,
A child of Thomas Wilkingson of Wal.	16	,,
A child of Edmund Duckworthe of Burieha:		
The w: of Francis Walworthe of Burihamell	25	,,
A child of Francis Wood of Burihamell	26	,,
A child of Willm Stotte of Heywood	29	,,
c Joab son of Willm Rathborne of Tott.	30	,,
Ellen w: of John Rothewell of Holcome	2	Februarij
James Filden of Ratcliffe	9	,,
A child of Gilbert Lowe of Burihamell	15	,,
Isabell dau. of Willm Howorthe of Drigape	17	,,
Isabell dau. of James Kaie of Hartlie...		
Marie dau. of Roger Greenoucke of Burie...	20	,,
A child of Richard Woolsenham of Elton		
Fardinando Wild of this hamell	21	,,
Doritie Grinhalghe of Tottington...	1	Marche
A child of Abraham Collenge of Boulton	3	,,
Jane w: of Raphe Houlte of Burie	8	,,
A child of John Fletcher of Burihamell	11	,,
Fo. 191 Lamberte Shawe of Elton	13	,,
Ann w: of Francis Grinhalghe of Burie		
Marie dau. of Edward Rothwell of Elton	16	,,
Alice Rothewell of Burie		
Anne Hartley of Holcome		
Tho. son of Edward Rothewell of Elton	17	,,
c Francis Medowcrofte of Buriha:...		
Edward Rosthorne of Elton...	22	,,

1625.

Ann w: of James Houlte of Burihamell	29	Marche
Isabell w: of Edwar dAllence of Elton	1	Aprill
A child of Francis Medowcrofte of Burie	5	,,
c Genet w: of John Kaie of Walmersley		
A child of John Kaie of Walmersley		
A child of Richard Rothwell of Holcome	17	,,
A child of Andrewe Sale of Holcome...	21	,,
c Henrie Knowles of the pishe of Boulton		
A child of James Openshawe of Burie...		
John son of Richard Heye of Burie	28	,,
c Elsabethe w: of Ellis Rothewell of Burie	4	Maij
A child of Roger Wood, Tottington		
John Taylor of Walmersley...	12	,,
Bartyne Kaie of Walmersley		

1625   BURIALS.

John son of Richard Kaie of Widell	18	Maij
Raphe Marcrofte of Rachdall pishe	21	,,
Alice w: of Roberte Whiticar of Walmersley	24	,,
John son of James Howorthe of Walmersley	28	,,
Susan dau. of John Howorthe of Burie ...	3	Juñ
A child of Josephe Lyvsey of Burie	5	,,
Ann wiffe of Josephe Lyvsey of Burie... ...	9	,,
A child of James Kershawe of Burihamell...	15	,,
John Hynde of Tottington	18	,,
Elsabethe Nabbe of Birkle	1	Julij
Susan Elom of Bamford	3	,,
A child of Roberte Duckworthe of Buriha :	5	,,
A child of Willm Aspinall of Scoute	10	,
c A child of John Brigde of Holcome	13	,,
John Nuttall of Etenfeild	17	,,
Margreate w: of Richard Wood of Birklee ..	26	,,
A child of John Houlte of Holcome		
Ann Wilsonn of Holcome	8	August
A child of Thomas Fletcher of Rediuals ...	11	,,
Zacherie & Elsabethe children of Zackerie Bridge of Holcoñ	13	,,
Margreate dau. of Henrie Dunster of Blackhoulte	20	,,
Alice w: of Richard Houlte of Burie	21	,,
Thomas Woolfenden of Bamforde	26	,,
Marie w: of Arthure Scofeild of Bamford ...		
Alice w: of Christopher Nuttall of Holcome	27	,,
A child of John Hopkinson of Holcome ...	10	September
John son of Thomas Hamon of Litlewood...	27	,,
Elsabethe Howorthe of Etenfeild	28	,,
Ellen w: of Thomas Cockshutte of Burie ...	30	,,
Susan dau. of Abraham Nabbe of Wal: ...	7	October
Grace dau. of Roberte Howorthe of Bamford		
Fo. 192 Elizabethe Vnsworthe of Rediuals	16	,,
A child of Jeremy Hynd of Tottington ...	19	,,
The w: of Roberte Farworthe of Tottington	23	,,
Ellnor dau. of Christopher Bouthe of Rediuals	24	,,
A child of John Smythes of Holcome		
A child of James Giliam of Manchester ...	27	,,
Susan dau. of Roberte Magnall of Tott. ...	8	Nouember
c Edward Rothewell of Holcome	9	,,
Ann & Ellen daus. of Richard Smethurst of Brodoke	14	,,
Roger Scofeild of Etenfeild	16	,,
Henry Fyldes of Burihamell	17	,,
Peter son of Edmund Smethurste of Buriha :		
A child of John Bate of Burie	20	,,
The w: of Roberte Hiltonn of this hamell...	2	December
Jane w: of Roger Smethurste of Burie ...	6	,,

Ann dau. of James Kaie of Gosforthe	20	December
James Barone of Elton	21	,,
Richard Rothwell of Eues	6	January
Ann w: of James Croper of Bamford	7	,,
Abraham Rothwell of Eues		
Elsabethe dau. of Hugh Sedon of Burie	10	,,
Thomas Cromptonn of Buriham:	21	,,
John Sheaphard of Chesham		
A child of James Deanes of Wigan	24	,,
Genet w: of John Hardman of Buriha:	28	,,
A child of Edward Hamer of Bentilee Junor	29	.,
Thomas Wood of Holcome	30	,,
Elsabethe w: of Roberte Smethurste of Rediuals	31	,,
Ann dau. of Thomas Nuttall of Tottington...	3	February
Alice dau. of William Houlte of Holcome		
Grace Pasmond of Burie Hamell	7	,,
James Nabbe of Walmersley	12	,,
Ellen w: of Roberte Crompton of Burie	15	,,
Alice w: of John Taylor of Burihamell	17	,,
Thomas Grinhalghe of Chamber	24	,,
Henrie son of Thomas Rothwell of Tott.		
A poore child found dead on Burie more	26	,,
Henry Wood of Tottington	2	Marche
A child of Edmund Pilkington of Etenfeild...		
Francis Grinhalghe of Burie	7	,,
A poore child wch was found aboute Nuttall	11	,,
Roberte son of James Leache of Suttlewō	14	,,
Margreate Ratcliffe of Gosforthe		
Edmund Bouthe of Rediualls	22	,,
Roger Fletcher of Elton		
Fo. 193 Alice dau. of Edmund Pilkington, Chatterton	20	,,

1626.

A child of Roberte Howorthe of Drigape	30	Marche
Jane w: of Thomas Wofenden of Bamford...	31	,,
John Greane of Etenfeild	10	Aprill
Richard Grinhalghe of Burie	11	,,
A child of Richard Heward of Chatterton	12	,,
A child of Lawrance Taylor of Burie	14	,,
Doritie w: of Richard Howorthe of Holcome	16	,,
Alice w: of Peter Lomax of Tottington	17	,,
Alice w: of John Houlte of Heape	18	,,
James Barlowe of Burie	19	,,
Ann w: of Raphe Lyvsey of Heape	1	May
A child of Thomas Pilkington of Elton	4	,,
A child of George Battersbie of Wal.	6	,,
A child of John Crompton of Holcome	19	,,

1626 BURIALS.

	A child of Omphrey Barlowe of Burie...	21	May
	A child of James Wilsonn of Holcome	24	,,
	A child of John Ainsworthe of Buriha:	29	,,
	A child of Thomas Risheton of Buriha:		
c	Jeffray Greave of Suttleworthe	2	Juñ
	A child of Peter Tuttell of Burie...	8	,,
	A child of James Houlte of Burᵍha:...	11	,,
	Anis Nabbe of Walmersley ...	14	,,
	A child of Peter Toottell of Burie	17	,,
	John Bouthe of this Hamell	23	,,
	Elsabethe Houlte of this Hamell	24	,,
	Arthure Kaie of Houghe	28	,,
	A child of Edmund Bouthe of Rediuals	30	,,
	A child of Mathewe Woolsenham of Elton...	2	Julij
	Lawrance Stancfeild of Heape	7	,,
	Richard Grinhalghe of Tottington	8	,,
	A child of Edward Helliwell of Berie ...		
	A child of Richard Barlowe of Elton ...	24	,,
	A child of Andrewe Sale of Tottingtō ...		
	A child of Arthure Parkkington of Wal.	26	,,
	Thomas Hynd of Tottington	28	,,
	Richard Cropper of Bamford	30	,,
	William Wood of Tottington	7	Auguste
	Edmund Bouthe of Burie	13	,,
	William Fletcher of Walmersley ...	19	,,
	A child of Richard Rothwell of Holcom̄		
	A child of Richard Nuttall of Holcom̄	30	,,
	A child of Gilbert Lowe of this ham:	4	September
	Ann w: of Richard Parsivall of Elton...	7	,,
	Ann Smethurste of Lomas	19	,,
	Richard Kaie of Gosforthe ...	26	,,
chanc	Ellen w: of Peter Tutell of Burie	29	,,
	A child of Abraham Parsivall of Elton	6	October
	Elsabethe w: of James Grinhalghe of Burie		
	A child of Raphe Vnsworthe of this hamel...	10	,,
	Roberte Grinhalghe of Burie		
	A child of Elis Howorth of Etenfeild...	16	,,
	A child of Roberte Houlte of Bamford		
Fo. 194	A child of Richard Houlte of Holcome	26	,,
	A chid of Roger Fletcher of Burie	3	November
c	A child of Ric. Rothwell of Holcom̄	3	,,
	A child of John Broucke of Holcom̄	4	,,
b	A child of Edmund Leache of Burie	6	,,
	A child of Willm Sotte of Heywood	11	,,
	A child of Thurstan of Rosthorne of Elton...	16	,,
	Katrin dau. of Lawance Lort of this hamell	24	,,
	Roberte Duckworthe of Heape	4	December
	A child of Thomas Smethurste of Lomas		
	A child of James Kaie of Gosforthe	10	,,

A child of James Grinhalghe of Burie ...	11	December
Ann w: of Edward Hamer of Bentilee	12	,,
b A child of Lawrance Fletcher of Wal. ...		
c The w: of George Crostonn of Eltonn	16	,,
Joan Blacklowe of this hamell	18	,,
Martha & Mary daus. of John Walworke of Buriha:	21	,,
c A child of Thomas Nabbe of Holcome	26	,,
Edward Hamer of Burie hamell	28	,,
John son of Richard Whithead of Burie	4	Januarij
Ann w: of James Kaie of Burie	9	,,
James Fentonn of Bamford	7	February
Elsathe Seddon* of Burihamell	7	,,
A child found dead aboute the Bentilee	8	,,
chan Katrin dau. of Mr. Francis Houlte of Gristlhurste	12	,,
Margreate w: of Richard Rosthorne of Tottington	18	,,
Frauncis Grinhalghe of Burie	23	,,
c Dobora w: of Thomas Warbarton of Elton	1	Marche
A child of Abraham Strenger of Burie	3	,,
Joany Asheton of Tottington	5	,,
Peter son of Tharstan Rawsthorne of Elton	6	,,
A child of Richard Nuttall of Holcome	8	,,

1627.

Alice w: of Richard Barlowe of Elton	29	Marche
Abraham Stringer of Burie	3	Aprill
Susan w: of James Kaie of Burie	15	,,
A child of Thomas Houlte of Etenfeild	17	,,
A child of Thomas Fletcher of Burie	21	,,
Thomas Medowcrofte of Eltonn	22	,,
A child of George Howorthe of Burie	25	,,
John Bouthe of Walmersley	29	,,
James Dowsonne of Walmersley	12	Maij
Elizabethe Houlte of Lomax	16	,,
c Elizabethe w: of Edmund Pilkington of Holcome	18	,,
Elizabethe Broucke of Holcome	19	,,
c Judithe w: of John Warbarton of Holcome	21	,,
Fo. 195 A child of John Howorthe of Burie		
A child of John Howorthe of Burie	25	,,
A child of James Howorthe of Bamford	28	,,
c Alice w: of Raphe Pilkington of Chatterton	2	June
c Francis Barlowe of Burie	9	,,
A child of James Scofeild of Etenfeild	11	,,
chan Ann w: of Philip Martindale of Burie	16	,,

* "Seddon" written after "Buckley" crossed through.

A child of Thomas Fletcher of Redivals	19	June
Henrie Crosley of Midleton parishe ...	22	,,
Richard Whitehead of Burie	26	,,
c George Warbarton of Holcome	2	Julij
A child of Edmund Howorthe of Grinhill ...	3	,,
A child of John Warbarton of Holcome ...	7	,,
Cristopher Fletcher of Eltonn	15	,,
A child of John Lomax of Eltonn	16	,,
capell Thomas Houlte of Elton, gentleman	26	,,
chanc A child of Mr. John Grinhalghe of Brandlsome	28	,,
A child of Richar: Nuttall of Holcome ...		
Elizabethe *(sic)* of Thomas Garside of Etenfeild	31	,,
The wiffe of Edward Hamer of Burihamell ...	13	Auguste
A child of James Barlowes of Heape	15	,,
A child of John Lomax of Elton	22	,,
John son of James Lomax of Boulton parishe	1	September
Arthure son of Thomas Heward of Burie ..	10	,,
Elizabethe Howorthe of Burie Hamell ...	14	,,
A child of William Whiticar of Tottington...	29	,,
Thomas Hardman of Redivals	4	October
A child of Richard Nuttall of Tottington...	10	,,
A child of Peter Sythe of Burihamell	18	,,
A child of Thomas Mather of Wal:	29	,,
James Smetherste of Burihamell	1	November
A child of John Hamer of Burihamell ...	8	,,
A child of John Isherwood of Tottington ...	17	,,
Margreate w: of Richard Johoans of Heape	21	,,
A child of Charles Houlte of Tottington ...	24	,,
Alice w: of John Barlowe of Heape	26	,,
James Howorth of Midlton	3	Dēmber
chances Ann w: of Edmund Scofeild of Care ...	5	,,
A child of John Barker of Holcome	6	,,
Ollyver Rawsthorne of Eltonn	7	,,
A child of John Ainsworthe of Burihamell...	15	,,
A child of Alice Hoult & Edward Barlow, Burie		
A child of Marie Howorthe & Tho: Wood of Burie	17	,,
A child of Roberte Whiticar of Wal.	24	,,
Jane Suell of Eltonn	26	,,
A child of Edward Hamer of Burihamell ...	2	Januarij
Margreate w: of Thomas Milner of Etenfeild	6	,,
Thomas Houlte of Heywood	11	,,
Thomas Bridge of Holcome...	16	,,
The w: of Thomas Fyldes of Burihamell ...	17	,,
Margreate w: of Thomas Nabbe of Walmersley	25	,,
Frauncis Cowpe of Ollerbothom	29	,,
vx^p William Vnsworthe of Holcome	30	,,
Fo. 196 A child of William Lomax of Birchey ..	2	Februarij

c	Susan w: of William Holme of Heywood ...	5	Februarij
	Marie dau. of Emer Ainsworthe of Holcom	16	,,
c	The w: of Roberte Kaie of Sheephey ...	19	,,
	A child of Edward Hamer of Burihamell ...	24	,,
	A child of Richard Taylor of Burihamell ...	6	Marche
chap:	Edmund Houlte of Buriham:	10	,,
	A child of John Butterfeild of Boulton ...	11	,,
	Joan w: of Richard Duckworthe of Burihamell	12	,,
	A child of James Warbarton of Holcome ...	13	,,
	A child of Elsabethe Howorthe of Etenfeild	15	,,
	A child of James Warbarton of Holcome ...	17	,,
	A child of John Shawe of Burie	23	,,
	Richard Nuttall of Lumcare		
	The w: of James Grinhalghe of Burie ...	24	,,

1628.

	A child of John Kaie of Walmersley	29	Marche
	James Barlowe of Heape	31	,,
	Marie w: of James Greafe of Heywood ...		
	A child of Richard Duckworthe of Hamell...	5	Aprill
	A child of John Fletcher of Burie...	6	,,
	Doritie w: of Peter Heward of Burie	10	,,
	A child of Peter Heward of Burie		
	A child of Peter Lomax of Tottingtonn ...	18	,,
	A child of Richard Romsbothom of Holcome	26	,,
	Samuel Wood of the parishe of Midlton ...	27	,,
	A child of James Hardman of Burihamell ...	3	Maij
	A child of William Nabbe of Midlton	12	,,
	Ellis Scofeild of Etenfeild	13	,,
	Grace Huite of Burie	21	,,
	A child of Richard Bouthe of Tottington ...	22	,,
	A child of Henry Burie of Tottington		
	A child of John Fletcher of Burihamell ...	4	June
	A child of John Broucke of Haughshaw layne	16	,,
	A child of Zacarie Bridge of Houlcome ...	28	,,
	Mylles Kaie of Burihamell	1	July
	Ellen w: of John Nuttall of Etenfeild... ...	17	,,
chancell	Theophilus Houlte of Brandlesom, gent ...	23	,,
	Richard Fayrebancke of Burie	31	,,
	Edmund Kaie of Burie...	8	August
cha:	The w: of Mr. John Greenhalghe of Brandlesome	11	,,
	Mathewe Nuttall of Burie	13	,,
	Margerie Waddingtonn of Burie	21	,,
	A child of Roger Smethurste of Burie		
	Elizabethe Isherwood of Tottington	26	,,
Fo. 197	Isabell w: of John Kaie of Woodroad... ...	7	September
	Roberte Leache of Midleton parishe	9	,,

1628-1629 BURIALS. 311

A child of Samuell Mackon of Heywood	25	September
A child of Josephe Lyvsey of Midletonn	27	,,
Raphe Blacklowe of Burie	30	,,
The w: of Edmund Slade of Tottington	5	October
The w: of Raphe Nuttall of Holcome	12	,,
A child of John Broughton of Burie	25	,,
Katrin w: of John Romsbothom of Holcome	3	November
The w: of John Kaie of Widell	14	,,
A child of Alice Grinhalghe of Burie	17	,,
A child of John Longworthe of Burie	28	,,
James Cropper of Bamford	1	December
vx: Edmund Asheworthe of Heywood	8	,,
vx: Mathewe Berry of Tottington	17	,,
vx: Ollyver Seddon of Burihamell	23	,,
Tho. Heward of Burie	28	,,
Silvestris Wolfenden of Haslom Hey	5	January
Alice dau. of Richard Barlow of Bury		
Mary Hardman of Chesham	6	,,
Jone Partington of Walmersley	7	,,
Edmund Battersby of Bury	10	,,
Ratcliffe w: of Richard Romsbothom of Holcome	12	,,
Richard Barlow of Holcome	23	,,
The wife of Adam Warberton of Holcome	26	,,
Arthur Leach of Bamford	28	,,
Two Infants of Richard Battersby and Ellen Medowcroft of Bury	29	,,
The wife of Thomas Rothwell of Holcome	3	February
An Infant of John Warbertons of Holcome	code	
Bridgett ye w: of Francis Nuttall of Etenfeild	15	,,
A child of John Hunte of Tottington	20	,,
A child of John Greenhalgh of Tottington	21	,,
Jane Ratcliffe of Bury	24	,,
Jone Stones of Middleton	26	,,
Margrett Wilson of Holcome	27	,,
A child of John Mullenax of Tottington	2	March
A child of Peeter Lomas of Washy lane	4	,,
Richard Nuttall of Holcome	7	,,
Martha Wrigley of Haslom hey		
A child of Arthur Kay of Walmersley		
Mary dau. of Richard Lomax of Bury	9	,,
Richard Holt of Middleton	14	,,
The wife of Peter Horwich of Birch hey	16	,,

by mee Will Alte, Curat

1629.

o. 198	Mary Jackson of Bury	30	March
	Robert Ducksbury of Bury	2	April

	Thomas Greenleafe of Bury	5 April
	A child of Olliver Lomax of Walmersley ...	
	The wife of James Scofeild of Etenfeilde ...	8 ,,
	A child of John Wrigleys of Heywood... ...	10 ,,
	A child of William Overalls of Bury	12 ,,
	Edmund Holt of Heywood	13 ,,
	Thomas Buckley of Bury	
c	Ellen Nuttall of Holcome	15 ,,
chancell	The wife of John Greenhalgh of Bury... ...	18 ,,
	A child of John Broughtons of Bury	22 ,,
	Anne wife of James Heald of Bury hamell...	23 ,,
	A child of Henry Nuttalls of Birch hey ...	25 ,,
	A child of William Heald of Bury hamell ...	26 ,,
	John Fletcher of Redivalls	6 May
	The wife of Roger Hallywell of Redivalls ...	9 ,,

[On the margin is written what seems to be " Remember."]

An child of Edmund Holt of Tottington ...	
A child of Tho. Rawsthorn of Holcome ...	11 ,,
The wife of John Romsbothom of Walmersly	12 ,,
The wife of Tho. Wood of Tottington... ...	13 ,,
A child of Richard Fentons of Heape... ...	20 ,,
A child of Tho. Stott of Heywood	21 ,,
A child of Henry Nuttall of Birch hey ...	22 ,,
The wife of Mathew Bury of Tottington ...	3 June
A child of Roger Seddon of Bury	
Two children of Thomas Buckleys of Tottington	
The wife of Edmund Seddon of Bury hamell	4 ,,
The wife of Richard Medowcroft of Haslom hay	5 ,,
Samuell Bamford of Bamford	10 ,,
A child of George Vnsworth of Bury	12 ,,
A child of Mathew Nuttall & Anne Smethurst	13 ,,
Richard Holt of Bury a very godly man ...	18 ,,
Anne dau. of John Whithead of Bury hamell	19 ,,
A child of Thomas Stott of Heywood... ...	
Jonathan Machan of Heywood	3 July
A child of Edmund Holt of Bury hamell ...	
The wife of Thomas Haymer of Cheshā ...	4 ,,
A child of Edward Ashton of Midleton ...	
A child of John Kay of Walmersley	5 ,,
Catherine dau. of John Medowcroft of Haslom hey	9 ,,
The wife of John Howorth of Hornecliffe ...	
A child of Gideon Coupe of Holcome* ...	13 ,,
A child of Simon Barlowe of Holcome ...	16 ,,
A child of John Medowcroft of Haslom hey	18 ,,

* This was crossed out, and then written on the line below.

1629 BURIALS.

A child of Peter Clough of Bury … … …		July
A child of Thomas Nuttall of Bury hamell …	19	,,
A child of Richard Romsbothom of Walmersley	26	,,
Richard Holt of Middleton … … … …	29	,,
A child of John Fletcher of Bury hamell …		
The wife of Francis Medowcrofte of Bury …	6	August
A child of George Holt of Tottington … …		
John Fletcher of Bury hamell … … …	7	,,
A child of Abraham Nabbe of Walmelsrey …	8	,,
A child of Richard Nuttall of Holcome …	9	,,
The wife of William Byram of Heywood …	11	,,
The wife of Peter Heyld of Elton … … …	16	,,
Thomas Wood of Tottington … … …	19	,,
A child of James Byrom of Heywood… …		
A child of Francis Pens of Middleton… …	23	,,
A child of James Eckersall of Bury … …	26	,,
A child of Christopher Smethurst of Redivalls	27	,,
James Schofeild of Holcome … … …	28	,,
A child of John Brooke of Tottington …	1	September
A child of Edward Pilkington of Walmersley	2	,,
A child of Thomas Wood of Tottington …		
A child of George Haworth of Bury … …	7	,,
John Booth of Bury … … … … …	8	,,
The wife of Arthur Ashworth of Tottington…	14	,,
A child of George Livesay of Middleton		
A child of Thomas Bury of Tottington	15	,,
A child of James Liuesay of Heape …	27	,,
A child of James Greenhalgh of Elton		
Robte Booth of Bury … … … …		
Arthur Holt of Elton … … … …	30	,,
Sarah Fildes of Heape … … … …	4	October
Ellis Mather of Walmersly … … …	6	,,
A child of Richard Whitehead of Bury		
The wife of Mr. Holt of ye Hollin greave	28	,,
Ellen Medowcroft of Bamford … …	29	,,
A child of Richard Prescotts of Bury …	8	November
Elizabeth Scofeild of Etenfeild … …		
Anne Greenleafe of Bury … … … …	11	,,
Anne Vnsworth* of Bury hamell… … …		
The wife of Richard Greenhalgh of Bury	20	,,
The wife of William Romsbothom of Holcome	26	,,
Thomas Haworth of Walmersly … …	7	December
A child of John Barlowe of Bury… … …	12	,,
John Cunliffe of Bury hamell … … …	13	,,
Andrew Knowles of Shuttleworth… …	25	,,
The wife of Thomas Fildes of Bury … …		
Esther Nuttall of Nuttall … … …	5	January
Margrett Holt of Bury … … … …	7	,,

* "Unsworth" written over "Seddon" crossed out.

Richard Wolsenham of Haslom hey		January
Anne Rosthorne of Middleton	10	,,
A child of John Howorth of Bury	12	,,
A child of John Greenhalgh of Tottington	20	,,
A child of Robt Kay of Sheephey	22	,,
The wife of Robt Whitaker of Walmersley	24	,,
The wife of Richard Nuttall of Holcome		
Anne Howarth of Holcome	25	,,
A child of Robt Duckworth of Middleton	28	,,
The wife of Robt Battersby of Walmersly	5	February
A child of Mathew Bury of Holcome	10	,,
Laurence Rawsthorne of Elton	21	,,
Robt Leach of Shuttleworth	24	,,
Alice Wood of Bury	28	,,
A child of . . .* of Bamford	6	March
A child of Richard Kay Junio⁹ of Widell	7	,,
A child of Richard Worseley of Midletō	8	,,
John Aspinall of Midleton	13	,,
The wife of Laurance Lort of Bury hamell	15	,,
The wife of Martin Kay of Bury hamell	16	,,

1630.

Fo. 200 John Wilde of Heape	26	March
James Hardman of Rediualls	1	April
Jame Grinough of Elttonn	6	,,
A chillde of George Haworth of Eltton		
James Byrom of Heawood	15	,,
A chillde of John Buttrworth of Houlkom	16	,,
Sarah Houltt of Bury Hamell	22	,,
Kathern Reyds of Bury Hamell		
The wiffe of Zacheriah Bridge of Houlkom	23	,,
The wiffe of Thomas Buckley of Houlkom		
The wiffe of William Bridg of Houlkom	30	,,
Elizebeth Brooke of Houlkom		
A chillde of James Foggs of Bury	2	May
The wiff of James Fentton of Heawood	5	,,
Thomas Kay of Eltton		
Elizbeth Rothwell of Houlkom	16	,,
A childe of Charlls Vnsworths of Holkom	17	,,
A chillde of William Bury of Tottington	18	,,
Richard Witthead of Bury	1	June
A chillde of Thomas Nabs of Tottington	2	,,
Ellen Houltt of Heape	6	,,
The wiffe of Roger Grinaughe of Bury	7	,,
Thomas Witthead of Bury hamell	8	,,
A childe of James Shuttllworth of Houlkom		
A childe of Richard Hasselam of Rediualls	16	,,

* No name.

1630 BURIALS.

Jane Kay of Bury Hamell	20 June
A childe of Richard Boothe of Boothe	21 ,,
John Kay of Bury Hamell	24 ,,
The wiffe of Raphe Blakelowe of Bury hamell	25 ,,
The wiffe of Robertt Barllowe of Eltton	1 July
A chillde of John Kayes of Bury hamell	6 ,,
The wiffe of Franches Taylio[9] of Wallmerslay	11 ,,
Alice Nuttall of Holcome	22 August
Jennet Rothwell of Holcome	30 ,,
William Kay of Titchrode	eodem
Ellen Scolefeild of Holcome	2 September
A child of Richard Isherwood of Bury	4 October
Anne Holt of Middleton pish	25 ,,
The wife of Thomas Aspinall of Middleton	30 ,,
A child of John Heape of Redivalls	31 ,,
The wife of Christopher Nuttall	1 November
The wife of Thomas Greenhalgh of Bury	2 ,,
A child of Abraham Macon of Tottington	
A child of Richard Crosse of Bury	7 ,,
Mary Marcroft of Bury lane	8 ,,
The wife of Lambert Fletcher of Birch hey	9 ,,
Richard Shippobotha of Holcome	11 ,,
The wife of Raph Booth of Blakeholt	16 ,,
The wife of Christopher Cunliffe of Bury hamell	17 ,,
Anne Scofeild of Bury hamell	18 ,,
James Romsbotha of Holcome	30 ,,
Three children of George Nuttall of Golinrode	14 December
The wife of John Ishmalitt of Heape	
Oliver Lomax of Glorybutts	15 ,,
A child of James Fletcher of Elton	27 ,,
Ellen Kay of Bury	
John Peacocke of Holcome	28 ,,
A child of James Kay of Bury	
The wife of James Romsbotha of Holcome	2 January
A child of Thomas Smethurst of Bury	6 ,,
Robert Howorth of Shuttleworth	10 ,,
The wife of Emor Ainsworth of Holcome	29 ,,
A child of Gideon Coupe of Holcome	31 ,,
A child of Robert Duckworth of Woodgate hill	3 February
The wife of Thomas Whitehead of Tottington	6 ,,
The wife of George Shippobotha of Shuttleworth	11 ,,
Richard Nuttall of Holcome	14 ,,
Steven Sagar of Redivalls	18 ,,
A child of James Fletchers of Elton	21 ,,
A child of Arthure Furnace of Bury	23 ,,
Raph Livesay of Heape	7 March
William Duckworth of Woodgate hill	

o. 201

Giles Rothwell of Walmersley ...	17	March
Thomas Barlow of Holcome ...		
Mary Allens of Elton	23	,,

1631.

A child of Mathew* Bury of Tottington* ...	1	Aprill
The wife of Laurence Rausthorne of Elton...	2	,,
Katherine Wood of Tottington	4	,,
Elizabeth Booth of Bury	5	,,
A child of John Yates of Bury hamell		
A child of Robert Duckworth of Heape ...	7	,,
A child of Andrew Knowles of Drygap... ...	10	,,
Jane Shawe of Bamford...	17	,,
A child of James Holt of Birchen Bowre ...	20	,,
The wife of Richard Horabin of Tottington...	25	,,
Margrett Lort of Bury hamell	26	,,
Anthony Booth of Shuttleworth	29	,,
James Fenton of Bamford	4	May
The wife of Richard Nuttall of Holcome ...	5	,,
The wife of John Kay of Littlewood	6	,,
A child of David Naden of this hamell ...		
A child of James Scofeild of Etenfeild ...	10	,,
A child of Jerimy Barlow of Holcome ...	26	,,
John Knowles of Bury	9	June
The wife of Richard Greenhalgh of Tottington	10	,,
Robert Kay of Heape	13	,,
Edmund Booth of Redivalls...	17	,,
A child of Richard Howorth of Tottington ...		
Margrett Kay of Bury	20	,,
The wife of Robert Ridings of Heape	23	,,
A child of George Heaton of Heape	27	,,
William Wardleworth of Bamford	2	July
A child of Richard Howorth of Tottington...	3	,,
Fo. 202 A child of Thomas Smethurst of Bury	21	,,
A child of William Kay of Cobbas	22	,,
A child of William Hoult of Hollingreaue ...	3	August
The wife of Richard Barlow of Elton		
Raphe Leach of Wamersley	6	,,
The wife of Christopher Flecther of Elton ...	14	,,
The wife of Charls Ramsbothom of Houlcom	7	September
A childe of Richard Pecocks of Houlcome...		
Charls Nuttall of Houlcome	24	,,
A child of William Buys of Elton...	3	October
The wife of Richard Wood of Ernswoorrth ...	6	,,
Thomas Key of Houlcome	9	,,
John Lomaxe of Houlcome	10	,,

* "Mathew" over "William" crossed through and "Tottington" over "Woodrode."

A childe of Oumephrys Barlow of Bury ...	13	October
Raphe Buckley of Houlcome	20	,,
Catherine Grime of Shuttelworthe	26	,,
A child of Raphe Buckleys of Houlcome ...		
A childe of John Fentons of Bury	16	Nouember
Henery Bury of Tottington	20	,,
The wife D. Shaw of Bamford	26	,,
The son of George Batterseby	8	December
Añe Rombsebothom of Houlkom̃	16	,,
The wife of Richard Worsley of Haslom Hey	23	,,
The wife of John Hynde, Washe lane	27	,,
A childe of Peter Lomaxe of Washe lane ...	2	January
Robert Kay of Walmersley	14	,,
A childe of John Reys [? Keys] of Rediuolls	15	,,
Mr. Edmunde Hoult of Gristlhurst	25	,,
A childe of Richard Cuttlers of Tottington...	30	,,
A childe of John Barlows of Middelton ...	4	February
The wiffe of John Battersby of Shuttelworth	6	,,
A child of John Barlow of Middletō	14	,,
A child of Henry Nuttall of Birch hey ...	20	,,
The wife of Richard Greenhalgh of Birchhey	24	,,
The wife of Richard Battersby of Bury ...	26	,,
Mary Wild of Howlcom̃	28	,,
Mary Smethurst of Heape	4	March
A child of Oliver Nabb of Wamersley ...	5	,,
Williā Bridge of Howlcom̃	11	,,
The wife of Edmund Kershawe of this Hamel	15	,,
Edward Rostrō of ye Lume	16	,,
Richard Duckworth of Ruggilstile	19	,,
The wife of Roger Sedden of Heap		
A child of Rich. Barlow of Eltō	21	,,
A child of Geo. Haworth of Bury		

1632.

203	Valentine Haugh of Bury	2	April
	A child of Peter Heald of Bury		
	A child of Zacharie Bridg of Howlcō	11	,,
	Thomas Nuttall of Redivales	12	,,
	A child of James Lumas of Wamersley ...	14	,,
	The wife of Lawrence Key of Wamersley ...	16	,,
	Richard Symonds of Eltō	22	,,
	Alice Bowltō of this Hamell	3	May
	A child of Jephray Brookes of Bury	8	,,
	Anne Greenhalgh of this Hamel	13	,,
	Henry Nuttall of Crow lum̃	16	,,
	A child of Jeremy Answorth of Holcō ...	18	,,
	A ch: of Thomas Gauthroppe of Bury ...	22	,,

Añ Hardy, Holcom̃	27	May
A ch: of John Tayler, Tottentō	30	,,
Peter Walworke of this Hamel	13	June
Christopȟ Hopkinsonne of Holcome	20	,,
Thomas Whithead of Bury	18	July
Humphrey Barlowe of Bury	25	,,
A chil of Mathew Bury of Woodrood	29	,,
A child of Roƃt Ducworth, Heape	2	August
Elizaƃ Wood of Tottenton	12	,,
Edmond Hawworth of Shutelworth	17	,,
The wife of Richard Smethurst of this towne	18	,,
A child of John Stote of Haywood	20	,,
Raphe Booth of Blaucholte	5	September
A childe of Roberte Sheperde* of Chesom	6	,,
A childe of Robeart Sheperd of Chesem	9	,,
A childe of Peter Holte of Bridg hall	,,	,,
Marie Smethurst of Bruckeshe	14	,,
The wife of Henery Bordman of this towne...	18	,,
A child of John Booth of this towne	24	,,
The wife of James Kay of White Car	30	,,
A child of Richard Worsles of Elton	7	October
A childe of Roberte Dunster of this towne	12	,,
Añe a child of James Lech of this hamell		
A child of Rapth Nuttall of Tottington...	15	,,
Henery Wood of Tottingeton	20	,,
The wife of Barten Kay of Wamersle	29	,,
The wife of Oliuer Nabbe of Wamersle	1	November
A child of Roger Grime of Holcome	2	,,
Will Rostronme of Ensworth	5	,,
A childe of John Kay of Wamersle	11	,,
A childe of Edmond Kay of Bourh	12	,,
A childe of Richard Wigin of Tottington	14	,,
Marie Smith of this hamell	18	,,
A childe of John Barlowe of Tottingeton	19	,,
,The wife of Richard Smethurst of Brodocke	24	,,
Fo. 204 The wife of Richard Lomax of this towne	3	December
The wife of Mathew Jackson of Tottingeton	8	,,
Roberte Hawworth of Ashworth	10	,,
A child of John Fentons of Burie...	20	,,
A child of Roberte Hoppwood of Berkle		
A ch: of Rogr Sedens of Bury	23	,,
ch: of Edmund Law of Holcom̃	31	,,
The wyff of Thomas Fletcher of Holcom̃	6	January
George Harp of Aynsworth	12	,,
The wyff of Willm Haworth of Driegapp	18	,,
The wyff of Edmund Benson of Bury...		
Richard Tayler of Walmᵖsley	2	,,
A ch: of Richard Prescott of Bury	22	,,

* "Duckworth of Heape" crossed out and "Sheperde" written over it.

BURIALS.

The wyff of Arthur Holte of Lomax	26	January
A childe of Richard Holte of Bury		
Ralph Nuttall of Holcom̃	4	February
A ch: of Richard Romsbothome of Romsbothõ	8	,,
The wyffe of Thomas Woode of Holcome	14	,,
Peeter Bury of Heywood	18	,,
Elizebeth Rawsehorne of Som⁹sett	20	,,
George Fogg of Bury	24	,,
The wyffe of Thomas Woode of Birch hey	1	March
Margerett Blaklow of Bury	4	,,
Richard Rawscorne of Holcom̃	8	,,
Mr. Murrey Parson of Bury	12	,,
A ch: of Edmund Horoks	14	,,
John Halewell of Rediuals	19	,,
The wyff of Robert Leach of Bamford	21	,,
The wyff of Thomas Wood of Holcom̃	23	,,
Elizabeth Wadington of this towne	24	,,

1633.

Abram Buckle of this hamell	29	March
A child of Abram Bridge of Holcome		
Edmond Hallywell of this towne	6	April
A child of Edmond Mils of this hamell		
Abram Macon of Hollcome	11	,,
Edmond Duckworth of this hamell	13	,,
A chid of Thomas Barlow of Benle	14	,,
The wife of James Tayler of Hepe	18	,,
The wife of Abram Flecher of Berch hey	20	,,
A child of Robert Digle of Benle	26	,,
A child of Ather Furniss of this towne	29	,,
Debera Lifsi of this towne	4	May
John Limor of Holcome	6	,,
John Nabbe of Wamersle	9	,,
Thomas Holt of Wamersle	18	,,
The wife of William Burie of Totting.		
A child of George Haworth		
A child of Geferie Brookes of this towne	20	,,
Richard Greenalghe of this towne	31	,,
A child of Martins Kay	6	June
Jane Brooke of Wamerslee	16	,,
Ann Rothwell of Hollcome	30	,,
The wife of Richard Wood of Holcome	2	July
A chid of John Hawworth of Burie	16	,,
A chid of Charles Brooke	23	,,
The wife of Thomas Booth of Holcome	29	,,
Elen Tayler of Holcome	2	August
The wife of Roberte Fletcher of Rediualls	8	,,
A ch: of Thomas Wood	16	,,

A ch: of Richard Kay of Widill	20	August
A ch: of Richard Smethurst of Brodoke ...	24	,,
The wife of Josua Holt of this towne	26	,,
Richard Kay of Sheepe hey...	1	September
The wife of John Kay of Wamersle	6	,,
A child of Lawrence Flecher	12	,,
Elizabeth Holylee of Berchey	16	,,
Marey Brooke of Wamerslee	22	,,
Bartholemew Smethurst	6	February
The wife of Richard Burie of Hea :	3	March
A childe of Richard Nuttall of Hole.	17	,,
The wife of John Withingtō of this tow. ...	11	,,
Elizabeth Greenhalgh of Walm̄	12	,,
The wife of Mr. Richard Greenha :		
A child of Robte Kaie of Walm̄	18	,,
Elizabeth Rothell of Holcome	19	,,
The wife of Richard Birch of Whitt.	21	,,
A childe of Roger Booth of Rediuals		
A child of Robte Smethurst of Hagge ...	24	,,

[1634.]

	A child of Peter Fletcher of Elton	26	March
	A child of John Bridg of Holecom̄	29	,,
	Dorithie Blaklowe of Bamford	30	,,
	A child of Francis Greenhalgh	3	Aprill
	Ric. Lomax and John Greenhalgh	5	,,
	vxᵒ Francis Burie of Heawood	7	,,
	John Gryme of Scout	12	,,
	Ric. Gryme of Shuttleworth	15	,,
	A child of Oliver Gryme	16	,,
	Wife of Ric. Leach of Walm̄	18	,,
	Child of Ric. Kaie of Walm̄...	19	,,
Fo. 206	A childe of John Greenhalgh	20	,,
	A child of John Kaie of W :	21	,,
	A child of Robt Howorth of Bamford... ...		
	A child of Jeffraie Brooke	20	,,
	The wife of Thomas Hinde	22	,,
	Ric. Holt of Haslam hey	26	,,
	Peter Greenhalgh of Burie	3	May
	John Gorrell of Bamford	8	,,
	Mary Scofeld of Bamf :	12	,,
	Arthur Scofelde of Bamfo :...	19	,,
	Barbarie Crompton of Burie	22	,,
	Marie Furnas of Burie	27	,,
	A child of Jeffrey Brooke of Burie	3	June
	A child of John Longworth of Burie	9	,,
	Thomas Warberton of Stubbins	15	,,
	Dorithie Shawe of Bamford	24	,,

1634 BURIALS.

A child of Georg Wood of Burie	30	June
Tho. Barlowe of He :	4	July
Tho. Holt de Burie	10	,,
Marie Gorrell of Bamford	21	,,
The wife of Jeremie Barlowe	28	,,
Ellis Leach of Walmersley	9	August
The wife of Mr. Bamford	15	,,
Wiłłm Holt de Holcom	29	,,
A child of Wiłłm Holt de Holcom	2	September
The wife of Robt Butterworth	12	,,
George Howorth of Facide	16	,,
Ann Scofeld of Ainsworth	24	,,
Roger of Holcom		
The wife of Thomas Howorth of Wał	28	,,
James Warberton	7	October
The wife of Francis Greenhalgh	10	,,
Tho : Aspinwall of Ainsworth	18	,,
A child of Adam Scoles of Ains :	25	,,
John Scofeld of Bamford	28	,,
Georg Howorth of Shephey	30	,,
Ann Scofeild of Bamf:	31	,,
Marie Howorth of Shuttle :		
Wife of Ric. Gr [?]	3	November
Richard Kaie of Sheep hey	9	,,
Elizabeth Scofeld	20	,,
? Sara Hickopp	22	,,
The wife of Jeffrey Brooke	26	,,
John Benson of Burie	29	,,
James Failsworth of Holcom	4	December
The wife of Rich : Sturdicar	12	,,
Ester Butterworth of Bamfo :	16	,,
Robte Knowes de Holcom	19	,,
A childe of Ric. Roske of Holc.	21	,,
Robte Howorth of Bamford	24	,,
John Fenton of Bamford	26	,,
A child of Robte Fenton	19	,,
Marie Howorth of Bamford		
The wife of Robte Howorth of Bam	31	,,
Kathrin Barlow		
The wife of Robte Dunstier		
Edw : Rostron	4	January
A child of Robt Shepard		
John Stott	14	,,
Thurstan Rostron	16	,,
Daughter of Josua Holt	18	,,
A child of James Jackson		
Edward Pilkington	25	,,
Georg Emerson	29	,,
A child of Robte Heald	30	,,

A child of John Royley	4	February
Ann Kaie	7	,,
Peter Fenton	17	,,
A child of Richard Bannest	19	,,
Ann Rydings	21	,,
A child of John Barlow	22	,,
A child of John Fenton	23	,,
The wife of James Hardman	28	,,
The wife of Edm̄ Seddon *(sic)*	30	,,
A child of Edm̄ Hellywell		
The wife of James Shepard	2	March
A child of Ellis Kaie	7	,,
A child of Robte Leach	10	,,
James Heald	12	,,
Henerie Pilkingtō of Tott.	13	,,
Dorithie Blacklow	15	,,
A child of Peter Fletcher	16	,,

1635.

Fo. 208 Rodger Vnsworth the son of Raphe de Bury	31	March
Anne the dau. of Adam Scoles de Ainsworth		
Mary the dau. of Richard Vnsworth of Casle	1	April
James the son of Richard Haddok de Bury	6	,,
Jane the dau. of Mathew Bury de Elton	9	,,
Richard the son of Richard Haddok de Bury	12	,,
James Sheaphard de Chesam	13	,,
Anne the dau. of John Howorth de Horncliffe	15	,,
Richard Prescot de Bury	16	,,
Mary the dau. of John Whitehead de Bury		
Richard Maiorcroft de Bury	18	,,
Dorathy the dau. of James Lomax	19	,,
Richard the son of Henry Cuncliffe de Bury	21	,,
James Kay de Whitekar	25	,,
Elizabeth the wife of James Jackson de Bury	27	,,
John the son of James Greenhalgh de Tottington	30	,,
John the son of Thomas Stot de Heape	3	May
The wife of William Hey de Bury	11	,,
Isabel the wife of Edward Partington, Walm̄		
Thomas Hamar of Chesam	17	,,
A child of Richard Booth of Bury	20	,,
Annice the dau: of Richard Pilkinton of Tottington	21	,,
Edmund the son of Elis Howorth of Shuttleworth	22	,,
Thomas Nuttall of Edenfeild	24	,,
Anne Heaton of Heywood		
John Wood of Holcom̄	25	,,

Jane the wife of James Dawson	26	May
Anne dau. of Jeffrey Taylor of Holcom̃	26	,,
Mathew the son of Richard Wigan	31	,,
Mrs. Anne the w: of Samuell Bamford gentł		
John the son of Richard Wigan	2	June
Alice the dau. of John Hamar of Holcom̃	7	,,
John Fletcher the son of James de Bury	8	,,
Henry son of John Rigley	10	,,
Anne the dau. of John Hopkinson of Holcom̃	20	,,
Margaret the w: of John Barlow of Bury		
James Dawson of Walmsley	2	July
John Kay of Shuttleworth	4	,,
A daughter of Mr. Littleworth of Holcom̃	6	,,
A child of Gilbert Loe	10	,,
Jane the dau. of John Bolton	14	,,
The wife of Mathew Nuttall		
The wife of Thomas Allen	26	,,
A child of Richard Booth of Holcom̃	3	August
Susan the dau. of Tho. Allen	11	,,
A child of Richard Overall		
A child of Williã Lomax of Birchey		
Williã Bridge of Holcom̃		
A child of Williã Lomax	12	,,
The wife of Robert Whittaker of Holcom̃	14	,,
The wife of Thomas Fletcher of Bury		
A daughter of John Medowcroft of Bamford	19	,,
The wife of Robert Hopwood of Birtle	21	,,
William the son of William Overall of Bury	24	,,
Elizabeth Tayler of Holcom̃	26	,,
A child of Thomas Booth of Bury	2	September
A child of Thomas Fletcher of Bury	4	,,
A child of Richard Nuttall of Elton	5	,,
A child of Richard Ashworth of Baliden	7	,,
A child of James Kay de Walmesly	11	,,
A daughter of Williã Howorth of Facid		
A child of James Jenkinson of Bury	14	,,
Rodger Seddon of Bury	25	,,
John Barlow of Bury	1	October
Margret Hopwood	2	,,
A child of John Booth		
A bastard of Tho. Whitehead's wife	3	,,
A child of Oliver Nabbe of Walm̃	5	,,
A child of Tho. Nuttall of Etonfeild	7	,,
A child of Tho. Wood of Bury	8	,,
The wife of John Kay of Bury	10	,,
209 John Vnsworth of Redivals	21	,,
The wife of Richard Hoileley	22	,,
Margret Bridge of Holcom̃	26	,,
A child of Robert Taylor	28	,,

Thomas the son of John Hobkinson	2	November
A bastard of Tho. Rothwell & Izabell Nabbe		
The wife of William Hargraues of Bury ...	3	,,
A child of Martin Kay	4	,,
A child of George Howorth of Bury	5	,,
James Leach of Shuttleworth	7	,,
A child of George Howorth...	12	,,
A child of Robert Reade	13	,,
A child of Richard Duckworth's wife... ...	15	,,
A daughter* of Mr. Holt of the Bridge ...	17	,,
Arthur Whitaker	20	,,
A child of Georg Oldhā		
A child of Richard Prescot	21	,,
Jeremy Howorth of Holehouse	24	,,
A child of John Booth of Bury	25	,,
John Holt of Bamford	26	,,
The wife of Thomas Halliwell of Bury ...	27	,,
A daughter of James Warberton	29	,,
Richard Steele of Bury	3	December
The wife of William Holt of Holcom		
Jonas Howorth of Holehouse	7	,,
2 children of John Rauson	8	,,
A child of William Milnes		
The wife of James Kay of Walm...	11	,,
A child of Robert Maiorcroft	13	,,
The wife of Francis Emerson	18	,,
A child of Margret Bromeley...	28	,,
Edmund Lomax of Birch hey	1	January
A child of Francis Nuttall	3	,,
John Hind the son of John Hind		
Robert Leach of Sheep-hey	8	,,
A child of Tho: Booth of Bury	13	,,
A child of John Mullinex	16	,,
Mr. Richard Greenhalgh of Brandleshā ...	19	,,
Peter Heward of Bury	23	,,
A child of Edward Hind of Bury...	24	,,
A child of John Hardus		
Anne the wife of Abrahā Bridge of Holc. ...	25	,,
A child of Henry Lort	27	,,
A child of Robert Read	31	,,
Mr. Henry Bury of Bury qui dedid Scholae Buriensi 300 li et libros 666 pochiae ...	2	February
Elizabeth Haslom	3	,,
Jane the dau. of Mr. Bamford	5	,,
Ellin the dau. of Thomas Nuttall...	7	,,
The wife of Thomas Smethurst of Bury ...	11	,,
James son of Abel Tomlinson	17	,,
A child of Thomas Blakeley	19	,,

* "Katherine" in margin.

1635-1636. BURIALS.

James Greenhalgh of Tottington...	21 February
Anne Rausthorne of Lume ...	24 ,,
A child of Nathan Nuttall of Bury	26 ,,
The wife of Robert Cropper of Bamford	27 ,,
A child of Rich: Bury of Heywood	
The wife of Thomas Wood of Holcom̃	28 ,,
George Haulgh of Bury	29 ,,
A child of Francis Em̃erson of Tot.	
Mrs. Holt of Grizzlehurst	1 March
A child of George Howorth of Sum̃erset	2 ,,
Edward the son of Thomas Hind	10 ,,
The wife of John Warberton of Holcom̃	12 ,,
A child of James Kay of Gindles	18 ,,
Richard Booth of Smithy Yate	23 ,,
John Bridge of Holcom̃	
A child of Robert Duckworth	
The wife of Richard Worsley	24 ,,

(O.210 appears beside "The wife of John Warberton...")

William Rothwell, Curat

1636.

A child of Mr. Heywood of Heywood...	26 March
A child of Martin Kay ...	
William Overall of Bury	29 ,,
The wife of George Howorth	
A child of Richard Battersby of Bury...	1 April
A child of Robert Healds of Bury	
A child of Richard Wood of Elton	12 ,,
A child of Richard Wood of Holcom̃	
A child of Jonas Howorth	17 ,,
A child of John Holt	27 ,,
The wife of Zachary Bridge	29 ,,
A child of Robert Knowles	30 ,,
Richard Wood of Elton	2 May
A child of Abraham Nabb	5 ,,
A child of James Lomax	6 ,,
William Hargreaus of Bury ...	7 ,,
A child of William Hopwood	13 ,,
A child of Mr. Bamford of Bamf:	15 ,,
A child of Thomas Fletcher	17 ,,
A child of Peter Seddon of Holcom̃	
A child of Peter Smith of Bury	
A child of Robert Booth of Bury ...	
Mr. Richard Holt of Grizzlehurst...	5 June
The wife of Thomas Pilkinton of Elton	6 ,,
The wife of James Hunt of Holcom̃	14 ,,
Richard Gorton of Holehouse	20 ,,
A child of Reuben Howorth	21 ,,
The wife of Richard Holt of Haukshaw	5 July

John the son of John Nabbe of Walmͫ...	7	July
A child of Raphe Vnsworth of Bury	31	,,
Francis Warberton of Holc. ...	4	August
Lawrance Kay of Walmesley	1	,,
A child of James Openshaw ...	7	,,
The wife of Abraham Nabbe	8	,,
A child of James Openshaw...	11	,,
Richard Stones	19	,,
A child of Thomas Jackson of Tot.	28	,,
A child of Francis Warberton	10	September
The child* of William Bury of Woodrode ...		
The wife of Francis Warberton	16	,,
Adam Scofeild	19	,,
George Croston of Elton	26	,,
The wife of William Makon of Heywood	8	October
A child of Miles Holme		
Anne Bewsicke of Brookshaw	12	,,
A child of George Hull ...	15	,,
The wife of Giles Haslom	19	,,
A child of Richard Lomax of Gooseford	21	,,
A child of Samuell Nuttall of Holcomͫ...	22	,,
John Holt of Mooreyate	11	November
Edmund † Pilkinton of Holcomͫ	13	,,
James Kay of Bury	16	,,
The wife of James Fletcher of Totting.	27	,,
The wife of Robert Scofeild of Bamford	1	December
A child of John Coupe...	4	,,
Arthur Taylor of Walmͫ ...	8	,,
The wife of Peter Romsbothā	12	,,
Ellis Fletcher of Walmͫ ...	13	,,
Edmund Modes of Bircle	14	,,
Thomas Bridge of Holcomͫ		
A child of Richard Haddok of Bury	21	,,
The wife of Richard Birch of Whittle...	29	,,
The wife of Thomas Kay of Elton		
A child of James Kay of Gooseforth ...	30	,,
The wife of James Wood of Bircle	2	January
A child of Edmund Pilkinton	11	,,
The wife of Christopher Greason	15	,,
A child of Robert Sheaphard	17	,,
The wife of John Booth of Bury ...	20	,,
A child of James Howorth		
John son of Lawrance Lort of Bury	22	,,
The wife of John Lame of Bury ...	27	,,
The wife of Charles Holt of Holc.	28	,,
Robert Rockley	1	February
Jeremy Scofeild	3	,,

Fo. 211 (at Ellis Fletcher of Walmͫ)

* " Wife " crossed through and " child " written above.
† " Edmund " written over " Adam " crossed out.

BURIALS.

A child of Martin Kay		February
The son of William Romsbotham	13	,,
A child of Thomas Wharnby of Rediu : ...	16	,,
Arthur Smethurst of Chesam...	18	,,
Thomas Wood of Birch-hey	20	,,
A child of John Battersby of Shuttl.		
John Horwich of Standleyrake	22	,,
A child of Edward Leach	25	,,
The wife of Raphe Nuttall of Tott.	3	March
A child of Mary Greenhalgh of Bury	4	,,
A child of John Kay of Baudinstone		
George Nuttall of Gollinrode jugvlatus*	4	
Tho. Rothwel	5	,,
John son of Richard Heald of Bury	9	,,
James son of James Howorth of Shuttl : ...	10	,,
Abraham Wood of Holcom̃	11	,,
Anne Bate of Bury	19	,,
The wife of Mathew Bently	20	,,

William Rothwell, Curat

1637.

Mary the daughter of Thomas Heward of Bury	26	March
A child of Lawrance Bury	28	,,
A child of Charles Romsbotham	30	,,
The daughter of Rodger Holt	31	,,
A child of Edward Caly	1	Aprill
A child of Edmund Rothwell	3	,,
The wife of Rodger Breerly	4	,,
Margery Fenton	7	,,
Alexander son of Mr. Bamford	8	,,
Thomas Simond	9	,,
John Hunt	10	,,
A child of Thomas Bury	11	,,
A child of Thomas Whittle		
A child of Nathan Nuttalls	13	,,
George son of Thomas Nuttall of Bury ...	21	,,
Simon Lomax of Croichley	1	May
Robert Fletcher of Rediv :	6	,,
Ellis Leach	8	,,
The wife of Thomas Booth of Bury	9	,,
A child of Edward Halliwell	13	,,
The daughter of Robert Howorth	15	,,
The wife of Arthur Whitaker	16	,,
George Peacoke of Holcom̃		
A child of Robert Fenton		
A child of Thomas Warberton	17	,,
The son of Edmund Barlow	18	,,

* *i.e.* murdered.

John Lomax of Holcom̃	30	May
Richard Booth of Holcom̃	2	June
The wife of Richard Holt	3	,,
The wife of John Brooke	6	,,
A child of James Gee		
A child of William Howorth of Drygap	8	,,
William Nabb of Bircle	9	,,
The wife of John Hitchenson of Tott.	10	,,
A child of Robert Radcliffe	13	,,
The daughter of Edmund Duckworth	14	,,
Richard Holt of Haukshaw	21	,,
Richard Kay of Elton	22	,,
A child of John Fenton of Bury	1	July
Aemar Ainsworth of Holcom̃	2	,,
A child of John Battersby of Sheep hey	4	,,
Richard son of Raphe Leach	5	,,
Alice wife of Henry Mather		
A child of Richard Siddall	16	,,
Margret Nuttall	22	,,
The wife of John Howorth	24	,,
The daughter of John Lomax of Birch-hey	2	August
A seruant woman of Mr. Standly	6	,,
The wife of Rodger Nabbe	11	,,
A child of Raphe Leach	13	,,
James Fenton	20	,,
Richard Crosston	30	,,
Raphe Bridge		
The wife of William Pendlebury		
John Wardle	31	,,
John Brooke		
A child of Jeffry Lomax	5	September
A child of Robert Coptill	12	,,
A child of Henry Allens	13	,,
The wife of Robert Heald	28	,,
Elizabeth Medowcroft	1	October
The wife of Thomas Warberton	2	,,
A child of William Fish	2	,,
Rodger Kay of Widdall	6	,,
A child of Samuell Makon	18	,,
Francis Nuttall	24	,,
Andrew Sayle	26	,,
Edmund Parsivall	8	November
A child of Hugh Bradshaw	9	,,
Thomas Barlow	17	,,
Elizabeth dau. of George Croston	19	,,
Mrs. Rausthorne of Lume	20	,,
The wife of Henry Coupe of Owll		
A child of John Booth	22	,,
William Nabbe	3	December

1637 BURIALS.

A child of Henry Lort	4	December
The wife of Richard Lowe	6	,,
The wife of Robert Heald		
Arthur Holt	8	,,
The wife of James Kay	10	,,
The wife of Peter Shippobothā	11	,,
Robert Lomax	12	,,
William Howorth	13	,,
The wife of Bartholomew Smeythurst	14	,,
Isabell wife of George Croston	16	,,
A child of James Kay	17	,,
13 The son of James Holt	18	,,
The wife of John Booth	20	,,
Mary Smeythurst	22	,,
Hugh Seddon		
James Rushton	26	,,
A child of John Bury		
The wife of Edmund Greenhalgh	27	,,
A child of William Hopwood	1	January
Richard Jones		
The wife of . . .		
The wife of Robert Greenhalgh	2	,,
The wife of John Romsbothā	4	,,
The wife of Peter Smith	8	,,
A child of James Ashworth		
The wife of Robert Bridge	12	,,
Peter Cowpe	17	,,
b A child of . . .		
The son of John Romsbothom	21	,,
The wife of Henry Nuttall	25	,,
A child of William Rothwell minister	26	,,
A child of Edward Rausthorne	29	,,
A child of Henry Greaues	6	February
Robert Kay of Sheepe-hey	7	,,
Lawrance Haslom*	10	,,
The wife of Christopher Booth	9	,,
The son of William Romsbotham	17	,,
The wife of Richard Romsbothā of Holcoṁ	18	,,
The daughter of John Hind	12	,,
A child of Thomas Wharneby		
The wife of Henry Nuttall	22	,,
The wife of James Read	20	,,
James Kay of Hart-lee	26	,,
The wife of William Rothwell als Redgate	27	,,
The wife of James Ashworth		
A child of Adā Liuesay		
Thomas Booth	3	March
The wife of Raphe Nuttall	4	,,

* " A child of " crossed out.

The wife of Rodger Seddon...	8	March
The wife of John Scofeild of Etonꝭ:		
A daughter of William Rushton ...	9	,,
Rodger Vnsworth of Elton ...	10	,,
George Howorth of Lee ...		
Ellen Horrobin ...		
William Orrell of Holcom̃ ...	17	,,
A child of Robert Heald ...		
b A child of Anne Booth ...		
Abraham Nabbe ...	19	,,
Margret Taylor ...	22	,,

William Rothwell, Curaꝉ

1638.

Thomas Hamer of Bentiley ...	26	March
Jane Wild ...	29	,,
A child of Hamlet Lowe of Walm̃ ...	1	April
Thomas Smeythurst of Tacklee ...		
The wife of Robert Butterworth of Bamfꭍ:...	7	,,
A child of Richard Rausthorne of Etonꭍ:...	9	,,
A child of Richard Medowcroft ...	12	,,
Richard Walworke ...	14	,,
Edward Barlow ...	22	,,
A child of Arthur Holt ...		
Fo. 214 The wife of Lawrance Lort ...	23	,,
Jeffry Nuttall ...		
Rodger Halliwell ...	24	,,
The wife of Raphe Vnsworth...	26	,,
Rodger Grime...	27	,,
A child of Tho. Pilkinton & John Rausthorne	30	,,
A child of Tho. Lomax ...	1	May
The wife of Henry Prescot ...		
William Kay of Foultꭍ...	2	,,
Mary Hardman ...	9	,,
A child of John Mullinex ...		
vx : Daniell Lort ...	13	,,
The daughꭉ of Martin Kay ...	16	,,
Rodger Greenhalgh ...	18	,,
John Clough ...	20	,,
A child of Lawrance Fletcher ...	23	,,
vx : Richard Holt of Birch-hey ...		
A child of Tho : Gawthrop ...	24	,,
Edmund Smeythurst ...	25	,,
Robert Holt of Lomax...	29	,,
Jane Fenton ...		
The wife of John Stot ...	9	June
A child of Rodger Vnsworth...	10	,,

* "Rodger Grime" crossed out.

A child of Peter Seddon	17	June
The wife of Jeffray Taylor	26	,,
A child of Edward Rausthorne	27	,,
Peter Seddon of Holcom̃	30	,,
The wife of William Kay of Touchrode	1	July
The wife of Andrew Holt		
A daughter of Tho: Wood		
vxor Aemar Ainsworth		
A child of Oliuer Brendwood	9	August
vxor of Thomas Holt de Walm̃	9	September
Anne daugh: of John Harpur	14	,,
Peter Ramsbothā	16	,,
A daughtͬ of Richard Medowcroft	17	,,
vxor Richard Booth	20	,,
The son of Edmund Lowe	23	,,
The wife of Richard Howorth	2	October
The wife of Richard Rausthorne	3	,,
The wife of Thomas Wood	18	,,
The wife of Robert Howorth	19	,,
Richard Low of Walm̃	20	,,
Robert Bradly		
Mathew Woosnam		
Jane Kay de New house		
Alexander Worsley	26	,,
The wife of Abrahā Crossly	27	,,
A child of John Hardus	29	,,
Mr. Rigby	3	November
A child of Dorothy Floud	5	,,
The wife of Raphe Leach	6	,,
Richard Nuttall	15	,,
Richard Raustorne	18	,,
James Holt		
The son of Raphe Baron	24	,,
The wife of Robert Kay	29	,,
Alice Romsbothā	3	December
Fo. 215 The wife of Oliuer Booth	10	,,
The wife of Henry Dunster		
The wife of Abraham Wood		
The wife of George Howorth	15	,,
The wife of James Greenhalgh	20	,,
The wife of William Stot	22	,,
Raphe Leach	5	January
A child of John Crompton	11	,,
William Redgate	12	,,
Richard Kay	15	,,
Richard Rothwell	25	,,
A child of Richard Holt	26	,,
A son of Richard Bury	27	,,
The wife of Robert Liuesay	28	,,

The wife of John* Ormorod	29	January
Joseph Nabbe of Bury	7	February
Richard Holt	20	,,
John Cunliffe		
A child of Tho: Hopwood		
vx⁹ Ellis Fletcher	21	,,
Caleb Butterworth	24	,,
A child of Raphe Howorth	2	March
The wife John Kay	3	,,
The wife of John Greenhalgh de fernes	11	,,
John Boulton		
A child of John Asmall		
Daniell Leach	12	,,
A child of Thomas Mather		
The wife of John Asmall		

William Rothwell, Curat

1639.

Robert Butterworth	1	Aprill
Anne dau. of Henry Holt of Holling...	5	,,
Dorathy Kay	6	,,
Anne vx⁹ William Booth	7	,,
A child of John Kay of Gowse-ford	12	,,
A child of Francis Hamar	13	,,
Edmund Lort	27	,,
John Shaw	8	May
Mary Isherwood		
vx⁹ Henry Pendlebury	13	,,
vx⁹ Richard Wiggan		
A child of Henry Holt	16	,,
Richard Nuttall	27	,,
Ellin Horrocks	30	,,
Richard Fenton	31	,,
James son of Richard Overall	1	June
Susan dau. of Francis Warberton	12	,,
Edward Lomax of Heywood	21	,,
Peter Rausthorne	23	,,
The wife of Joseph Nabbe	3	July
A child of Edward Leach		
A child of James Howorth	6	,,
The wife of James Leach	27	August
Elizabeth † daught of Nicholas Rausthorne...		
Margret Hopwood	4	September
A child of James Holt	8	,,
A child of Lawrance Fletcher	22	,,
vx: Francis Kay	27	,,

* "Robert" crossed out and "John" written over.
† "The wife" crossed through and "Elizabeth" written over.

1639 BURIALS.

Thomas Pilkinton of Elton	3	October
6 Mary Ainsworth	6	November
Mary Jackson	7	,,
Mary Hamar	9	,,
A child of George Hull		
vx: Arthur Howorth	11	,,
A child of James Leach	12	,,
A child of Edward Hunt		
Dority wife of John Hopwood	16	,,
Richard Romsbotham	20	,,
Peter son* of Mr. Peter Heywood	25	,,
Rodger Walker	26	,,
vx: Raphe Duckworth	29	,,
vx⁹ Thomas Hamar	30	,,
Rodger son of Rodger Hamar	20	December
vx: George Howorth	25	,,
Thomas son of Richard Barlow	30	,,
Grace ye wife of Peter Holt of Bridge	1	January
Richard son of Richard Taylor		
Mary wife of Thomas Leach	8	,,
Mary wife of Francis Makon	14	,,
Alice wife of Samuell Shaw	15	,,
Thomas Rothwell		
Joan wife of Richard Fletcher	20	,,
Mary dau. of Robert Smeythurst	25	,,
Robert Anderton	26	,,
James Openshaw	1	February
Jane Wood		
A child of Martin Kay	2	,,
A child of John Ainsworth	4	,,
James son of William Whittaker		
Bartholomew son of John Greenhalgh	5	,,
Elizab wife of Thomas Nuttall		
Dorathy Ainsworth	6	,,
Margret Jannion	13	,,
Anne Peacoke		
Alice Nuttall	21	,,
Ellin Nuttall	23	,,
A child of John Howorth	25	,,
Ellis Fletcher of Birch-hey		
Ellin dau. of Frances Booth	29	,,
Elizabeth wife of Richard Booth	1	March
Mary wife of Rodger Smeythurst	3	,,
Elizabeth wife of Raphe Smeythurst	4	,,
Frances son of James Jackson	5	,,
Sarah wife of Henry Ainsworth	7	,,
Richard Booth	8	,,

* "A child" crossed out and "Peter son" written over it.

Isabell wife of Thomas Kay	10 March
A child of Henry Bridge	
John Smith	11 ,,
Ellin wife of Edmund Slate	16 ,,
Mary a child of Arthur Kay	
Isabell wife of Jeffry Riley	17 ,,
Anne dau. of Edmund Holt	18 ,,
William Whittaker	21 ,,
A child of Henry Booth	22 ,,

William Rothwell, Curat

Thomas Barlow } Churchward.
Henry Hardman }

1640.

Fo. 217 The wife of Robert Sheaphard	26 March
The wife of John Howorth of Ashworth	
Henry Howorth	
A child of Gideon Coupe	27 ,,
A child of Thomas Greenhalgh	28 ,,
A child of John Riley	3 Aprill
Anne Shippobotham	4 ,,
A daughter of Thomas Rothwell	6 ,,
The wife of Adam Scoles	7 ,,
John Whitehead	8 ,,
The wife of Thomas Nuttall	
John Maudsley	15 ,,
2 children of John Bridge	16 ,,
The son of Richard Romsbotham	21 ,,
A child of George Hull	
A child of Nicholas Rausthorne	23 ,,
Ellin Romsbotham	24 ,,
A child of Robert Stanfeild	25 ,,
The wife of William Nabbe	27 ,,
A child of Samuell Shawe	30 ,,
A child of John Duerden	
Francis Barlow	8 May
Abraham Crossly	10 ,,
vx^o John Booth	
A child of Charles Romsbotham	
A child of Thomas Eckersall	11 ,,
A child of Thomas Shippobothā	14 ,,
A child of Peter Holt of Bridge	16 ,,
A child of John Booth	18 ,,
Thomas Kay	23 ,,
A child of Edmund Holt	24 ,,
A child of John Warberton	
Anne Taylor	30 ,,
A child of Katharin Kay	2 June

1640   BURIALS.

A child of Miles Holme	4	June
Robert Horrobin	8	,,
James Adkinson	11	,,
vx: Robert Diggle	12	,,
Samuell Holt	13	,,
A child of Edward Barlow	25	,,
A child of Robert Diggle		
Alice Holt	28	,,
A child of James Gest	29	,,
Henry Rothwell	4	July
Ellin Fogge	5	,,
Elizabeth Barlow	9	,,
Anne Aspinall	11	,,
vx^9 Henry Rausthorne	23	,,
John Buckley	24	,,
Richard son of Richard Fletcher	7	August
John Greenhalgh	10	,,
A child of Richard Kay		
Frances a child of Thomas Wood	25	,,
Raphe Whittaker	29	,,
Isabell wife of Bartholomew Smeythurst	3	September
John Howorth	8	,,
Elizabeth Washaw	17	,,
vx^9 Edmund Kay	20	,,
Susan child of Richard Jones	23	,,
Isabell the wife of Thomas Whithead	13	October
Thomas the son of Jo: Wolfenden		
Ann the wife of Robert Greenō	15	,,
Jane the w: of Ric. Lomax of Burie	14	,,
Elizabeth the child of Jo: Kaye	23	,,
Richard Romsbothom of Burie	24	,,
A child of Richard Burie	26	,,
Francis Bury	2	November
Jane Leach	4	,,
Jane vx: of James Liuesay	16	,,
Thomas Wood	20	,,
A child of Henry Lort	24	,,
Elizabeth Rushton	23	,,
A child of Andrew Leuer	29	,,
Elizaƀ dau. of James Whittaker	18	December
Anthony Sheaphard	29	,,
A child of Jeffry Lomax	30	,,
Thurstan Brooke	14	January
A child of John Shippobothā		
Christopher Smeythurst	19	,,
Arthur Smeythurst	20	,,
Madame Mary Ashton of Brandlesha	25	,,
A child of Mr. Rausthorne de New-hall		
A child of Henry Greaue of Bircle	27	,,

o. 218

Richard son of James Fletcher	4	February
A child of Thomas Blakelow	12	,,
Roger Booth of Whitewall	14	,,
A child of Ellis Lomax	17	,,
Elizabeth Bury	25	,,
Alis vx: Mathew Suttliffe	4	March
Anne vx: Michaell Sale		
Jane Holme	7	,,
John Heywood		
John Kay de Woodrode	9	,,
Dorithy Fenton		
Dorathy Kay		
John son of Mathew Booth	10	,,
Thomas Nuttall	17	,,
A child of James Atkinson	20	,,
Rodger Greenhalgh	21	,,
Edmund Holt	22	,,
John Horrox	23	,,
Robert Gawthrop	24	,,

William Rothwell, Curat

1641.

Fo. 219	Richard Booth de Bury	25	March
	Anne vx: Robert Whittaker		
	A child of John Smeythurst		
	Henry Nuttall of Bury	1	Aprill
	Jane dau. of Thomas Mather	8	,,
	Richard Rausthorne	10	,,
	Edmund Lowe		
	Elizabeth Whitehead vid:	14	,,
	Jane vx: Elize Holt		
	John a child of Raphe Seddon	21	,,
	Franchis Whittaker	6	May
	A child of Gilbert Holden	8	,,
	Raph Baron	18	,,
	Thomas son of Thomas Pilkinton	27	,,
	John son of Robert Marcroft		
	A child of*	31	,,
	Richard Allen	1	June
	Elizabeth Booth		
	Anne the wife of Thomas Holt	5	,,
	Alice Eckersall	9	,,
	Ellin the wife of Thomas Pilkinton	10	,,
	A child of Peter Smith	14	,,
	A child of Edward Ogden		
	vx: Peter Seddon	24	,,

* This entry is struck through. The name is illegible.

1641 BURIALS.

Alice Houghton	2 July
Thomas Booth	5 ,,
Robert Kay	10 ,,
Elizabeth Wardleworth	13 ,,
Dorathy dau: of Thomas Kay of Elton	18 ,,
Anne Smeythurst	29 ,,
Mary dau. of James Jenkinson	30 ,,
Anne Leach	1 August
Ellin Waddington	
A child of John Fletcher	
A child of Wiliam Horrocks	2 ,,
A child of James Gorton	3 ,,
The wife of Raphe Bridge	15 ,,
Thomas Pilkinton of Bury	16 ,,
A child of James Holt of Turton	
A child of Mr. William Rothwell	1 September
A child of Richard Lomax de Bury	2 ,,
A child of Richard Lomax, taylor	5 ,,
Richard son of Thomas Lomax	7 ,,
Elizabeth dau. of Abraham Kay	18 ,,
A child of Laurance Fletcher*	25 ,,
A child of Samuell Makon	1 October
Henry son of Robt Dunster	,, ,,
Anne ye wife of James Crompton	14 ,,
Rich a child of Raph Howorth	
Rich son of Tho. Buckley of Holcom	1 November
A child of Edmund Holt of Tottingtō	2 ,,
A child of Peter Seddon of Holcom	4 ,,
Henry Romsbotham of Bury	5 ,,
A child of George Holt of Tottingtō	17 ,,
Mary † daughter of Josua Holt	18 ,,
Raphe Bridge	20 ,,
Samuell Macon } both buried together Elizabeth his wife }	3 Dec.
A child of James Disons	9 ,,
Margrett Winkley of Bury hamel	16 ,,
Fo. 220 Immin Lomax of Holcome, aged 107 years	
Elizabeth ye daughter of Richard Rosthorn of Holcom	25 ,,
Henry son of Richard Booth of Holcom	11 January
John Shaw of Bury	12 ,,
Elizabeth wife of Rich Booth	
Thomas Haymer	14 ,,
Richard Macon	15 ,,
Elizabeth Howorth	
Margrett Medowcroft	21 ,,
Mary Chadwicke	28 ,,

* Written in the margin.
† "Ellen" crossed through.

Robert Kay	31	January
John son of Edmund Seddon	10	February
A child of Richard Hayward	eodem	
Jennet wife of Charles Romsbothā	13	,,
A child of an Irish traveller	16	,,
Sarah ye wife of James Stocke	20	,,
Elizabeth ye child of John Romsbothā	22	,,
Elizabeth Rothwell	28	,,
A child of Mary Marcroft		
Elizabeth a child of Richard Booth, Totting.	3	March
A child of Margrett Cowp	eodem	
Roger Holt of Tottington	5	,,
Mary a child of Richard Heyward	7	,,
Anne ye wife of John Buckley		
Elizabeth ye wife of James Walwork		
A child of Robert Naab's daughter	8	,,
Edmund ye son of Richard Heward		
Elizabeth ye child of Francis Kay	13	,,
Susan the child of Edward Beacom	14	,,
George ye son of Edmund Barlow	15	,,
A child of Henry Lort of Bury hamell		
Richard ye son of James Lomax of Bercle	16	,,
William Holt ye son of James Holt of Holcome	20	,,

Will Alte, minister

1642.

Robert Hutchinson of Bury hamell	25	March
Mary wife of Andrew Sale	28	,,
A daughter of Robert Marcroft	30	,,
Susan wife of Robert Fletcher	3	April
A child of Nathan Nuttall		
Susan dau. of John Walworke	9	,,
James Fletcher of Moorside	23	,,
Henry son of William Aspinwall	25	,,
A child of Martin Kay	27	,,
A child of Ratcliffe Rigby	30	,,
Fo. 221 The wife of William Whitaker	1	May
A child of John Holt	3	,,
A child of John Booth		
A daughter of Robt Livesay of Heape	4	,,
James Shippobotham of Gigge	10	,,
The wife of Robert Marcroft	11	,,
A child of Ecclestones		
The wife of Rich. Holt of Holcom̃	13	,,
John Greenhalgh de Fearns	18	,,
William son of Will Holt of Holcom̃	23	,,
The wife of Roger Booth of Tenters	26	,,
Mr. Hardier, Vicar of Deane	29	,,

1642 BURIALS.

A child of Mary Holt	4 June
Deborah dau. of John Medowcroft of Haslum hey	6 ,,
A child of Dorothy Greenhalgh	7 ,,
James a child of Rich Jackson	
Josias Booth	8 ,,
A child of Alice Estler [? Essher or Esther]...	
A child of Tho. Fletcher of Fishpool juñ	10 ,,
Thomas son of Rich. Rosthorn of Tottingtō...	12 ,,
Mary Rawsthorn his daughter	14 ,,
Roger son of John Booth of Redivalls	15 ,,
Lawrence Pickopp	17 ,,
Jane ye wife of William Booth of Bury	18 ,,
A child of Robert Read	20 ,,
Edmund Benson	25 ,,
A child of Humphrey Broome	
The wife of Edmund Bury	3 July
Richard Duckworth	5 ,,
Roger son of Richard Isherwood	10 ,,
Mary dau. of George Bradly	15 ,,
Jane ye wife of Richard Heild	29 ,,
The wife of Thomas Gawthrop	31 ,,
Jane ye daughter of Emor Emarson	2 August
A child of Mathew Sutcliffe	eodem
A child of Tho. Kay of Gooseford	7 ,,
A child of James Ashworth	15 ,,
Edward Hamer of Bentiley	18 ,,
A child of Rich. Key seni^9 of Widell	19 ,,
A child of James Rothwell	
A child of Rich. Smethurst of Brodoke	21 ,,
A child of Robert Duckworth	
Martin Hopwood	23 ,,
John Kay of Lees Leach	30 ,,
A child of Jane Rothwell	eodem
Mr. William Orrell	16 September
The wife of Thomas Hamond, a gracious woman*	21 ,,
Alice dau. of James Greenhalgh	25 ,,
Margrett Seddon	26 ,,
A child of Rich. Fletchers	29 ,,
Ellen Hutchinson	3 October
A child of Rich. Rawsthorn	5 ,,
Richard Shaw	6 ,,
A child of Rich. Wigan	
A child of Francis Whitaker	
Mr. Edward Holt of Gristlehirst	7 ,,
Anne dau. of Tho. Livesay	8 ,,
Arthur a child of George Holt	10 ,,

* "A gracious woman" written in another hand.

A son of William Scoles	13 October
James Buckly of Mooreside	14 ,,
Dorothy wife of Edmund Low	23 ,,
Alice wife of Tho. Kay of Elton	31 ,,
Margrett wife of John Rosthorn	
Thomas Hind juñ	13 November
John Rawsthorn	5 December
Anne Howorth	6 ,,
A child of Ellen Marcroft	8 ,,
A child of Tho. Eccleston	14 ,,
Theophilus Smethurst	16 ,,
Wife of Tho. Heward	eodem
A child of Emor Ainsworth	17 ,,
Isabell* ye wife of Robert Kay	26 ,,
A child of James Isherwood	27 ,,
The wife of Robert Reade	1 January
The wife of John Bate señ	2 ,,
A child of James Gorton	5 ,,
The wife of Edmund Lort	11 ,,
Elizabeth Rushton	
The wife of George Heaton	12 ,,
Mary Lort	14 ,,
The wife of Giles Rothwell	19 ,,
A child of John Yates	2 February
Roger Grime of ye Scout	8 ,,
A child of Tho. Booth of Shuttleworth	16 ,,
Mary Fildes of Bury	17 ,,
An infant of Joñ Buckleys of Bury	22 ,,
A child of John Nightgales of Holcoñ	23 ,,
Elizabeth dau. of Martin Hopwood	28 ,,
Robert Chadwicke of Holcoñ	
A child of Tho. Holt of Walmersly	eodem
A child of Tho. Mellidew	2 March
A child of Rich. Wigan	3 ,,
Wife of William Yates	4 ,,
Elizabeth dau. of Mr. Edward Rawsthorn juñ	6 ,,
Isabell † ye dau. of Barthol Smethurst	7 ,,
Alice Kay of Bury	9 ,,
Alice dau. of Rich. Booth	
The wife of Richard Simond of Elton	12 ,,
A child of Edmund Lowes	13 ,,
A child of Francis Hamer of Walm'sly	14 ,,

Will Alte, minister

* "Isabell" written over "Anne" crossed through.
† "Isabell" written over "Catherine."

1643.

No. 223	The wife of Edmund Holt of Haslom hey	31	March
	James Kay, Bevis	3	April
	The wife of James Holt	4	,,
	The wife of Edmund Parcivall	7	,,
	The wife of John Bury	8	,,
	The wife of John Booth		
	Roger Brearley of Heywood	9	,,
	Thomas Woolner	13	,,
c	Richard Smethurst of Brodoke	15	,,
	Thomas Smith Saxton		
	A child of Thomas Kay		
	The wife of Peter Taylor	16	,,
	Anne Bury		
	Margrett Howorth of Harden Clough	21	,,
	A child of Edmund Holts of Tottingtō	23	,,
	Jerimy Briggs of Mooreyate	24	,,
	The wife of Tho. Barlow of Bury lane	29	,,
	Edmund Dugdale of Holcome	1	May
	A child of James Howorth of Ashworth	4	,,
	A child of Oliver Nabbe	5	,,
	Susan Eckersall of Bury	6	,,
	The wife of Frauncis Booth of Bury	11	,,
	Peter Greenhalgh of Tottington	14	,,
	Charles Nuttall of Tottington	18	,,
	A child of John Booth of Bury	25	,,
	Henry Romsbothom of Lees Leach	31	,,
	Thomas son of Rich. Haslom of Redualls		
	Arthur Taylor of Whitewall	5	June
	A child of Charles Nuttall of Elton	8	,,
	James Walworke of Walmersly	10	,,
	Ellen ye widow of James Kay of Hawkshaw lane		
	Katherin dau. of Thomas Kay of Shuttleworth	13	,,
	A child of James Ashworth of Moorside	15	,,
	Abraham Wood of Bury lane	19	,,
	Raph Nuttall of Holcome	21	,,
	The wife of Roger Pilkington of Bury	25	,,
	A son of Rich. Romsbothā of Romsbothō	3	July
	Elizabeth dau. of John Kay of Lees	6	,,
	The wife of John Chadwicke of Birkhill	15	,,
	Roger Vnsworth of ye Moore Yate	16	,,
	James Chadwicke of Bury hamell	17	,,
	Mary Baraclough of Hallifax vicarage sojourning at Heywood	21	,,
	A child of Martin Kay	1	August
	Edmund Whitaker of Brodoke	4	,,
	A child of Alice Broome	5	,,

	A child of William Greenleafe of Bury	9 August
	A child of Rich. Kay of Bridhole	14 ,,
	Jane Blakely of More yate	13 ,,
	Mr. John Croston of Elton	16 ,,
Fo. 224	Rich. Baron of Walmersley	18 ,,
	A child of Isaac Rauson	21 ,,
	The wife of John Harpur	
	James Rothwell of Holcom	
	A child of John Deurden of Moreside	22 ,,
	The wife of Robt Macon of Heywood	26 ,,
	Phebe Clay of Halifax Vicarage sojourning at ye parsonage house	1 September
	The wife of Robt Kay of Shipobotha	
	The wife of Edmund Whitaker of Brodoke ...	4 ,,
	William Scoles of Bury hamel	8 ,,
	A child of Harry Booth of Bury	
	James Livesay of Gristlehurst moore yate ...	14 ,,
	The wife of Mr. William Rawstorn of Tottingtō	
	The wife of James Rothwell of ye Edge ...	16 ,,
	The wife of Francis Stott of Heywood ...	18 ,,
	A child of James Holt of Low	23 ,,
	Peter Lomax of Washy lane	24 ,,
	John Lomax of Gloributts	30 ,,
	Elizabeth daughter a child of Geffray Brookes	5 October
	A child of John Hardus of Bury	6 ,,
	Thomas Wilkinson of Walmersly	9 ,,
	A child of James Greenhalgh of Heape ...	12 ,,
	A child of James Kay of Gindles	14 ,,
	John Taylor of Heywood	17 ,,
	The wife of James Crompton of Heywood ...	21 ,,
	Elizabeth Shepheard dau. of Robt of Chesha	24 ,,
	Richard Heald the elder of Redivalls	27 ,,
	Mary Lombe of Bamford	eodem
	The wife of Roger Kay of Horncliffe	28 ,,
	A child of James Lomax of Birchey	2 November
	Robert Broadly a very godly man exiled from Halifax sojourning at Heywood	6 ,,
	Oliver Holden of Rainshore	8 ,,
	An infant of Anthony Booth of Shuttleworth	
	John Bridge of Holcome	11 ,,
	Robert Fenton of Tottington	14 ,,
	An infant of John Aspinwall of Padock Leach	
	Michaell Bowker of Dean Banke	17 ,,
	Peter Leach of Shuttleworth	19 ,,
	Margret Whitehead of Bury	
	The wife of James Kay of Goosford	22 ,,
	The wife of John Jenkinsō of Moreside ...	
	John Kay of Gloributts	27 ,,
	Elizabeth dau. of Jerimy Barlow of Holcome	28 ,,

BURIALS.

John Hind son of Thomas of Elton	11	December
The wife of John Whitehead of Bury	12	,,
The wife of John Kay of Gloributts	13	,,
Mr. Bamford of Bamford	16	,,
Raph Duckworth of Woodyate hill	17	,,
The wife of Richard Holt of Haslom hey	21	,,
The wife of John Warberton of Holcom͠ hey	25	,,
Geffray Brooke of Bury	26	,,
225 The wife of William Taylor of White wal	5	January
James son of William Low of Holcome hey	13	,,
The wife of John Booth of Woodyate hill	14	,,
John Brooke a soldier of Yorkshire	21	,,
The wife of Jerimy Croston of Walmersley	1	February
The wife of Richard Haslom of Redivalls	2	,,
Esther Smith of Walmersley		
John son of John Battersby of Shuttleworth	3	,,
A child of William Grimeshaw of Walmersley	4	,,
The wife of Henry Dumster of ye Ball holt	7	,,
The wife of Henry Booth of Holcome	8	,,
A child of Peter Leach of Rachdall	18	,,
The wife of Henry Howorth of Bury bridge	20	,,
Mr. Cecill Holt of Gristlehurst	22	,,
Katherine Smethurst of Butchy lane	24	,,
A child of Thomas Lort of Heywood		
A child of Thomas Asheton of Midleton	27	,,
The wife of William Smith of Holcome	29	,,
The wife of William Bury of Chamber	2	March
The wife of James Greenalgh of Heap	3	,,
A child of Richard Lomax of Goosford	4	,,
Rob͠t Whitaker of Bentileigh Lum		
Geffray Lomax of Heape, a very zealous professor	7	,,
John Howorth of Sillinhurst	8	,,
The wife of Tho. Scolefeild of Bury	11	,,
The wife of Thomas Heald of Bury lane		
The wife of George Haughton of Holcom͠	16	,,
The wife of Henry Hamond of Little wood	19	,,
The wife of Henry Cowpe of Booth		
Thomas Barlow of Redivalls	22	,,

Will Alte, minister

1644.

Edward Simonds of Elton	25	March
A child of Robert Rawsthorn of Holcom͠	4	April
Jane dau. of George Nuttall of Golinrode	8	,,
The wife of Richard Taylor of Bury lane	9	,,
Richard son of Rich. Taylor		
John Bentley of Haslom hey	17	,,

Mary Filding of Bamford		April
The wife of Edmund Holt of Heywood ...		
Mary dau. of George Wood of Bury	18	,,
Elizabeth dau. of William Kay of Tichrode		
Martin Kay	21	,,
Jane Lort of Heywood	22	,,
William Nuttall of Tottington	23	,,
The wife of Martin Hopwood		
The wife of William Scoles		
The wife of Richard Duckworth of Berkhill	3	May
The wife of Tho. Fletcher of Blakebrook Bridg	4	,,
Richard Heald ye yonger of Redivalls		
A child of Peter Heald of Bury lane	10	,,
A child of James Taylor of Birkhill		
Fo. 226 Adam Sutcliffe of Bury	13	,,
A child of John Bury of Tott.		
Richard Allen a stranger stabd	18	,,
Roger Howorth of Scout	21	,,
The wife of James Holt of Cleg...		
A childe of Mathew Sutcliffe de Bury	25	,,
The wife of James Ray de Gindles	29	,,
A child of John Lomax of Bury Brige ...	30	,,
7 strange souldiores weare Buried this weeke		
Richard Peacock sonne of Holcom̃	7	June
Richard Fletcher of Bury	9	,,
A strange souldior A cavallier	10	,,
A child of James Howorths of Ashworth ...		
Henery son of Henery Holt of Holingreaue	12	,,
Richard Romsbothom of Ramsbothom gent	13	,,
A strange souldier A cavallier	14	,,
The wife of Henery Hardman of Chesum ...	18	,,
The wife of Richard Prescod	19	,,
Peeter Cloogh of Bury	22	,,
A child of Edward Barlowe of Bury	28	,,
Peter Taylor of Totington	30	,,
The wife of Franches Greenehalgh of Lomax	3	July
A child of Robert Hameres of Totington ...		
The wife of John Lomax of Caslehill	4	,,
Richard Kay of Bury	5	,,
Henery Booth of Totington	6	,,
James Flecher of Elton	15	,,
A child of Isaigh Diggle	16	,,
Richard Medowcroft of Lomax	17	,,
Richard Buckley of Bury mooreside	21	,,
The wife of Mathew Booth of Elton		
Richard Orell of Wallmersley		
The wife of William Rawsthorn of Brown hill	26	,,
A child of Rich Romsbothom of Romsbotham		
Robert Holt of Bamford	27	,,

1644 BURIALS.

Mary dau. of Francis Wolfenden		July
A child of Joseph Taylor of Heywood	28	,,
The wife of Tho. Heyward, Bury ...	29	,,
A child of Rich. Wigan of Tottingtō ...	eodē	
Elize Kay of Elton	2	August
A child of Thomas Jachuns...	5	,,
Elizabeth Knowles of Wharnetan ...	8	,,
⁁o. 227 The wife of Peeter Leach	10	,,
The wife of Richard Holt of Bury		
Roƀte Greenehalgh of Totington	14	,,
Roƀte Duckworth of Heape	19	,,
Roƀte Nabb of Elton	20	,,
Roƀte Sagar of Houlcom̃		
Richard Holt of Bamford		
The wife of John Hunt of Walmersley ..	21	,,
Thomas Orpe of Leemonshill	27	,,
A childe of Richard Nabbs of Houlcom̃ ...		
Peeter Greenhough of Bury	29	,,
A childe of James Gortons of Holehouse ..	2	September
A childe of Raph Leach of Totington ...	4	,,
A childe of Thomas Holts of Elton		
The wiffe of Richard Kay of Bury lane	9	,,
A childe of John Bothes of Shutleworth ..	eodem die	
A childe of Andrew Leauers of Walshaw lane	12	,,
Petrus Holt in artibus Magister filius Petri Holt de Bridghall, juvenis optimae spei ..	17	,,
James Fletcher of Bury		
The wife of James Milles of Birckle		
A childe of Thomas Lieseyes of Birckle ...		
Robert Dunster of Balehoult	24	,,
The wife of Jeramie Barlowe of Houlcom̃ ...		
A child of Thomas Fletchers of Blackworth brig	28	,,
A child of Robert Dunsters of Elton	1	October
John Barlow of Heawood	2	,,
A child of Anne Lomax of Totington	4	,,
William Stot of Heywood	5	,,
Nicolas Rowstron of Houlcom̃	7	,,
Elise Fletcher of Bury	15	,,
A child of Alise Haworthes		
A child of Jeramie Barlow	22	,,
James Scofield		
Roƀte Rothwell	25	,,
The wife of Lawrance Bury		
Edmund Sedon ⎫ booth of Heape Simeon Lotton ⎭	27	
Thomas Holt of Bury	30	,,
⁁o. 228 The wife of Edmund Holt of Brookesmouth	2	November
Jane dau. of Thomas Wood of Bury	5	,,

Adam Rostron of Totington	7	November
The wife of John Kay of Littlewood		
Lawrance Kay de Cobbas	8	,,
A ch: of Edward Hamer of Buckden	9	,,
John Scofeild of Holcom̃	12	,,
A child of Richard Holt of Birchey	18	,,
The wife of Arthur Holt of Lomax	22	,,
The wife of Thomas Wilkinsun		
Katteren Walker		
Two twines of Edmund Boothes of Smythie yate	18	,,
A child of Raph Woodes of Brookehouse	25	,,
Daniell Stones of Bury	26	,,
Richard Holt of Haslam hey		
Alise dau. of John Brookes of Bury		
The wife of Caleb Butterworth	2	December
The wife of Lawrance Smethurst	3	,,
The wife of John Chadwicke	5	,,
A child of James Hartleyes		
A child of William Greenehalgh	9	,,
Edward Kealey of Bury		
Joan Tootell	13	,,
The wife of Rob̃te Knowles of Totington	17	,,
Peeter Tootell of Bury	18	,,
The wife of Rob̃te Hopwood of Birkle	21	,,
A childe of Edward Hameres of Buckden		
A childe of Thomas Warbertones	22	,,
Richard Barlowe of Mooreside	25	,,
Robert son of Thomas Liuesey of Birkle	27	,,
A childe of Edward Holtes of Walmersley	29	,,
The wife of Anthonie Walles	30	,,
The wife of Thomas Lomax	2	January
A childe of Samwell Nuttalls of Holcom̃		
The wife of George Vnsworth	16	,,
A childe of Richard Lomax of Bury	18	,,
Franches Greenehalgh of Lomax	21	,,
The wife of Elize Haworth of Chaterton hey	25	,,
The wife of James Hardman of Chesam	29	,,
Fo. 229 James son of Samwell Nuttall of Houlcom̃	30	,,
A child of James Gee of Bury		
Rachhell Morrey	1	February
A child of William Taylores	6	,,
Alice Greenchalgh of Walshaw lane	10	,,
Two twines of Roger Bothes of Tentores	11	,,
Edward Marlor of Holcom̃	14	,,
An Infant of Oliuer Lomax of Ensworth	15	,,
Alise dau. of Robert Flecher	18	,,
John Haworth of Burie	19	,,
An Infant of Richard Romsbothomes		

1644-1645 BURIALS.

The wife of James Eckersall of Burie ...	3	March
The wife of Edward Holt of Walmersley	4	,,
Jeramie Barlowe of Holcom	7	,,
A childe Marie Kershawes		
A childe of Anne Horrobinnes	10	,,
The wife of John Bridge of Houlcom ...	11	,,
John Migley of Houlcom	12	,,
An Infant of John Flecheres of Bury ...	13	,,
Isabell dau. of John Holt of Bury ...		
A childe of Richard Fentones	16	,,
Añe dau. of Guiles Rothwell	17	,,
Anne Leach	23	,,

William Alte, minister

1645.

A childe of Anne Lomaxes	25	March
A childe of John Woodes	27	,,
The wife of Martin Kay	29	,,
The wife of John Rostron	15	Aprill
John Wood of Totington	16	,,
Marie Nuttall of Golinrode		
The wife of Thomas Pott	18	,,
George Holt of Haslam hey	19	,,
Jane Bridge	20	,,
The wife of Tho. Simond of Elton Car ...	23	,,
A child of John Aspinwall of Paddockleach...	26	,,
A child of Rich. Battersby of Bury	28	,,
Arthur Whitaker of Woolfold	29	,,
John Romsbotham of Rowley	1	May
A child of William Haslom of Berkhill ...	3	,,
A child of James Haworth of Littlewood ...	8	,,
The wife of Henry Holt of Hollingreave ...	9	,,
A child of Tho. Fletcher of Bury*		
Susan dau. of Samuell Holt of Bury ...	11	,,
Thomas Nuttall of Banke lane	13	,,
Richard Seddon of Heape	30	,,
Robert Heald of Redivalls	4	June
The wife of Tho. Haworth of Greenhill ...	7	,,
The wife of Raph Vnsworth of Moorside ...	15	,,
A child of Raph Seddon of Heap	16	,,
A child of Raph Seddon of Heap	25	,,
A child of Richard Lowes of Holcom	26	,,
Michaell Bentley of Haslom hey	2	July
The wife of Henry Cunliffe	4	,,
Isabell dau. of Edmund Seddon of Heap	8	,,
Charles Leach of Goodin	20	,,
A child of Francis Booth of Bury ...	25	,,

o. 230

* "Roger" written at foot of page.

A son of George Haughton of Holcome ...	30	July
A son of John Kay of Banke lane	31	,,
Richard Fletcher of Holcome	7	August
Dorothy dau. of John Buckley, Holc. ...	24	,,
Arthur son of Rich Kay, Widell	25	,,
The w: of Michaell Bentley, Haslom hey ...	26	,,
A child of Robt Shepheard, Chesham... ...	29	,,
James Chadwicke of Hough...	2	September
James son of James Brooke, Tott.		
Alice Romsbotham, Woodyate hill	5	,,
A child of Tho. Kay	7	,,
Laurence Yate	9	,,
A child of Peter Heald	11	,,
James son of Roger Fletcher...	15	,,
The wife of Robert Hamer	28	,,
A child of Edmund Holt, Tott.		
Thomas Kay of Heyhead	9	October
A child of Edw. Barlow of Bury	16	,,
Robert Greenhalgh	30	,,
A child of James Gorton	31	,,
A child of Thomas Eccles	3	November
Daniell son of Gilbert Low	5	,,
John son of Robert Greenhalgh	27	,,
John Hind	10	December
Mary Pilkington	19	,,
The wife of John Stott	21	,,
A child of James Ainsworth	23	,,
Elizabeth Redman	26	,,
The wife of William Overall	29	,,
Fo. 231 A child of Thomas Aspinwall	1	January
Elizabeth dau. of Roger Seddon	3	,,
Anne dau. of William Aspinwall, Scout ...	6	,,
Richard Livesay of Marland	7	,,
A child of Laurence Yates		
A child of Edward Holt of Walm9sly		
Edward Ogden of Bury	12	,,
Lawrence Lort		
Anne Booth, Woodyate Hill...		
Mrs. Rigby	14	,,
The wife of Raph Seddon	15	,,
Anne Hoyles	18	,,
The wife of Nicholas Rawstorn	20	,,
A child of Rich. Fenton, Redivalls	23	,,
A child of William Smith of Holc.		
Abraham Kay of Bury	6	February
The wife of Francis Stott		
The wife of Edward Simond	9	,,
James Holt of Goosford	12	,,
William Barlow	15	,,

A child of Joh: Cockrills	22	February
James son of Abraham Kay of Bury	27	,,
The wife of Joh: Ainsworth...	7	March
Mary dau. of Richard Bury of Heywood ...	8	,,
A child of Joh: Shakeshaft	11	,,
Mr. William Rawstorn, wrong priest	16	,,
A child of Joh: Romsbothā, Rowley	21	,,

William Alte, miñ

1646.

Margrett dau. of William Aspinwall, Scout...	26	March
An infant of Edward Leach	31	,,
The wife of Thomas Jones	2	April
A child of John Woolfendens	3	,,
A child of Tho. Jones		
The wife of John Woolfenden	5	,,
Elizabeth Buckley	7	,,
A child of Jeffry Riley	12	,,
The wife of Raph Fitton	15	,,
John Pate	17	,,
The wife of Robt Nabbe of Bury hamell ...	28	,,
Elizabeth Hull	30	,,
Isaac son of Capt. Peter Holt, Bridghall ...	1	May
A child of Joh: Brooke of Holehouse		
An infant of William Rifi	5	,,
An infant of Peter Seddon	10	,,
An infant of John Crompton...	15	,,
A child of Tho. Allens & Añ Howorth... ...	16	,,
A child of Lawrance Turners	18	,,
A child of George Hull	25	,,
A child of John Nuttall	26	,,
The wife of Williā Holt of Ainsworth	27	,,
Anne dau. of Mathew Woolsenham		
o. 232 The wife of John Rosthorne	2	June
John Seddon of Holcome	3	,,
Thomas Nuttall of Bury	5	,,
The wife of William Heald of Tott:	6	,,
The wife of John Booth...	9	,,
A child of James Crompton	21	,,
A child of Henry Nuttall, Tott	22	,,
A child of Hugh Greenhalgh...	26	,,
An infant of Rich. Pilkingtons, Tott.	2	July
The wife of Peter Lomax, Tott.	4	,,
Mary dau. of Christoph. Cunliffe	16	,,
A child of Edward Hopkinson	17	,,
The wife of Edmund Hey	22	,,
Hugh Bordman of Tott.	28	,,
A child of Geo. Houghton		

L

John son of Henry Lort...	29	July
Roger son of Rich. Vnsworth, Elton	7	August
James Lomax of Castlehill, a very godly man	10	,,
A base child of Joh: Anderton	17	,,
A child of Robert Hamer	23	,,
The wife of Richard Lomax of Tott.	25	,,
A child of Richard Hutchinsons	7	September
Margrett dau. of Francis Barlow	15	,,
Henry Dunster of Baleholt	16	,,
Martha dau. of James Leach...	18	,,
The wife of Henry Dunster of Baleholt	19	,,
A child of Thomas Chadwicke	2	October
John Warburton of Holcom̃	17	,,
The wife of Richard Romsbothã, Tott.	19	,,
A child of Tho. Lomax, Tott.		
Thomas Holt, moreyate	26	,,
A child of Richard Vnsworth	31	,,
Robert Kay of Shippobothã	16	November
Kerstabell dau. of Roger Kay		
The wife of Mr. Peter Holt of Bridghall, an ancient professor vocata Elizabeth...	21	,,
The wife of Richard Thornley	4	December
Richard Kay of Tichroade		
The wife of Tho. Rawsthorn, Holc.	8	,,
A child of Robert Smethurst, Heywood	10	,,
A child of Raph Howorth		
Fo. 233 A child of Andrew Knowles, Holc.	1	January
A child of Robt Smethurst, Heywood	2	,,
An infant of Rich. Taylor, Heap	6	,,
Mr. Robt Heywood of Heywood	19	,,
William Overall, Blacksmith	25	,,
Henry West miles jugulatus	30	,,
The wife of Richard Simond junior	2	February
An infant of Mr. Latham, minister	4	,,
Susan dau. of Francis Macon, Heywood	7	,,
William son of Mr. Peter Holt, Bridghall	9	,,
John Marcroft of Birkhill	16	,,
A child of John Howorth, Tott.	17	,,
Jane dau. of John Marcroft, Birchill	24	,,
Thomas Booth, Scout	26	,,
The wife of Arthur Smethurst of Heape, a very pious woman	3	March
An infant of Jonathan Crosley	5	,,
Thomas Warburton, Elton	10	,,
The wife of Tho: Smethurst, Barnbrook	12	,,
The wife of James Gabbitt, Moreyate	15	,,
A child of Tho: Kayes, Buryham	18	,,
Richard Kay of Sheephey	19	,,
The wife of William Smith, Heywood	22	,,

William Alte, minister

WEDDINGS.

1617.

251	Thomas Kay of Elton & Alisse Symones	24	April
	James Milles of Heywood & Sara Kay	1	March
	Ralphe Jakson & Alse Rausthorne	1	Maij
	Edmond Sedon of Heape & Alisse Kay	12	,,
	Roger Sedon of Bury & Eliza: Lomax	14	,,
	Robert Mankinoles of Tot. & Eliz: Fletcher	20	,,
	James Kay of Tichrod & Eliza: Barlow	9	June
	George Mañe [?] of Clithero & Jane Pilling		
	Robert Sedon of Bury & Emery Kay	22	,,
	Thomas Both of Hol: & Dority Nuttall	24	,,
	Jefferey Feldinge of Grisl: & Mary Hopwood	28	,,
	Willm Dikonson & Mary Redman of Bamf:	6	July
	Richard Grenhalhe of Tot. & Mary Whithead	12	August
	William Haslome of Bothhaule & Alise Bothe	26	,,
	Elise Fletcher of Birch hey & Mary Lomas		
	Thomas Smithe & Katheryn Monkes	23	September
	Roger Kay of P^{9}stwich & Isabell Both	25	,,
	Henry Hauworth of Haslingden & Añe Hauworth		
	Henry Bothe of Holcome & Alise Romsboth$\tilde{\text{o}}$ maried I know not wheare		
	Thomas Cropper of Bamforth & Ann Hakinge	30	October
	Miles Holmes of Radclife & Jane Whitak^9	2	November
	Ruben Hauworthe of Tot. & Ellyn Hamer	5	,,
	Williã Whitaker of Walm^{9}sley maried by W$\tilde{\text{m}}$ Rausthorne		
	Robert Barlow of Pilkin: & Emen Hardmã	18	,,
	Robert Crompton of P^{9}stwithe & Ellyn Jakson	7	December
	John Wardle of Ratchd: & Ellyn Shawe	9	,,
	Ralphe Bridge of Hol: & Alise Tayler	19	,,
	Gilbert Law of Redi: & Susan Jenkinson	13	January
	Robert Kay of Walm̃ & Jane Hamer	20	,,
	Simon Barlow of Croytchlaw & Ellen Lomas	26	,,
	John Garsyd of Edenf: & Ann Romsbothome	29	,,
	John Kay of Walmesley & Isabell Goose	2	February
	Williã Cronkshaw of Musb. & Eliz. Brooke		
252	Thomas Rosthorne of Bu: & Jane Hunte		
	Alexander Elmer of Bol: & Mary Lamb	10	,,
	Abrahã Crosley of Heape & Margeret Holt	13	,,

1618.

Thomas Rothwell of Cowap & Margete Grime	6	April
Isake Royd of Cowap & Gennet Shutleworth ...	23	,,
Richard Banis of B : & Marg⁹et Harison ...	14	,,
James Greane of Ratch. & Mary Nuttall (sic)	31	,,
John Fletcher collier & Alisse Ratcliffe of Midl :	3	May
Richard Damforth of P⁹stwich & Margeret Medowcroft	5	,,
John Horege of Birch & Ann Forde		
James Barnes of Bolton & Ann Rothwell	6	,,
Francis Croithlawe of Bolton & Alisse Kay ...	12	,,
James Fogge of Elton & Katheryn Brook ...	21	June
Samuell Grene of Ratch : & Jane Hamer of Ches :	29	,,
George Boukar of Manchesf & Jane Holte of B :	4	August
James Hauworth of Bamf : & Ann Holte ...	12	,,
Edward Hamer of Walmsley & Lucy Kay ...	1	September
James Fenton of Bamf : & Ann Marcrofte ...	8	,,
Thomas Liuesay of Birkle & Elizabeth Lawe ...	15	,,
John Shaw of Bury & Elizabeth Smitherst ...	23	,,
Ralphe Rosthorne, Shutlew & Elizabeth Gryme	12	October
John Durden of Edēf : & Alisse Pillinge	3	November
Peter Cowap & Alisse Hauworthe	8	,,
Peter Baron of Edenfeld & Eliza : Gryme ...	30	,,
Richard Baron & Marg : Longworth of Stubis...	21	December
Martyn Kay of Bury & Isabell Digle	22	January
John Rosthorne of Edenf : & Allise Grene ...	26	,,
Stephen Sagar of Walm⁹sley & Mary Hauworth	2	February
Robert Elton of Edenfeld & Alisse Radcliffe ...		
Thomas Rushton of Eltō & Elizaƃ Heywood ...	9	,,
Thomas Gauthrop of Elton & Ann Entwisle ...		
Thomas Tennant of Walms : & Añ Feeldinge		
Samuell Nuttall of Holcom & Ellyn Opēshaw...		

              Hu : Watmoughe
  George Nuttall   Richard Rosthorne
  Robert Shepert   Richard Houlden
  Edmund Ashworth   Peter Lomax

1619.

Fo. 253 Richard Romsbothome of Bury & Alisse Lee ...	30	March
Richard Dukworth of Hasl : & Ann Holte ...		
Richard Grenhalhe of Bu : & Mary Haslome ...	31	,,
Adam Rothwell of Eccles & Katherin Hardmā	23	April
Alexander Bradshaw of Bolton & Aliss Houworth	3	May
Richard Heald & Alisse Lyon		
John Fletcher of Redi : & Alisse Pilkington ...	11	,,
Gilbert Dukworth & Margeret Barnes	18	,,
James Bukley of Totting : & Alis Ensco	30	,,

WEDDINGS.

1619-1620

Mathew Wood of Tot : & Alisse Bury	9 June
Arthur Vsherwood of Boltō & Abigail Holte	24 ,,
Abrahā Nab & Alisse Rausthorne	5 July
James Fletcher of Elton & Ann Both	15 ,,
James Fogge of Elton & Genet Fairecloughe	23 August
Henry Bordman & Jony Haslome	24 ,,
Robert Tayler of Musby & Marg⁹t Hauworth	
Edmond Law of Tot. & Katryn Romsbothom	26 ,,
Edward Tayler of Mus : & Alise Hauworthe	28 ,,
John Holden of Musb : & Grace Tailer	7 September
Joseph Holte & Alisse Hauworthe	12 October
Ric. Grenhalh of Totin : & Clemence Williāson	19 ,,
Ric. Bury of Heywood & Susan Holte	29 ,,
James Leache & Alice Hauworthe	2 November
Willm Bankrofte of Ouldhā & Ann Rothwell	28 ,,
Abrahā Stringer of Ratch : & Alsse Sidall	20 ,,
Richard Core of B : & Alise Wood	7 December
Lawrence Tattersall & Margeret Ormeroyd	14 ,,
James Wolsenham & Jennet Hartley	24 ,,
Edward Rausthorne & Alise Prescot	26 ,,
Thomas Wood & Sara Leach of Bāf :	20 January
James Rothwell & Alisse Holden at Haslende	
John Pikop & Sara Fento	
George Hauworth & Elizaƀ Rausthorne	
Thomas Wood of Hol : & Eliza : Grenhalh	26 February
Edmond Wrigley of Elton & Martha Wolsenā	
John Lomax of P⁹stwitch & Eliz : Brooke	29 ,,
Thomas Rausthorne of B : & Jennet Gortō	6 March

1620.

John Smitherst of P⁹stwitch & Mary Dawsō	17 April
Hu : Watmoughe	
Roƀt Brearley & Ann Vnseworthe	2 May
Thom Wilkinson of Walm & Jane Bury	7 ,,
Willm Aspinall of Walm & Ann Rawsthorne	9 ,,
Henry Pendleton & Elizabeth Kay	7 ,,
Ralphe Blakley of Prestwitch & Ann Kay	16 ,,
James Fletch⁹ of Bu : & Ann Lomax	22 ,,
Ralphe Nutall of Holcome & Eliz : Nuttall	30 ,,
Richard Dukworth of Bury & Susan Longworth	
John Lord of Clithero & Alisse Ashworth eius	1 June
John Cropper of Bamf : & Jane Lache	3 ,,
Arther Smitherst of Heap & Eliz : Smith⁹st	5 ,,
Edward Hind of Eltō & Eliz : Holte	8 ,,
Jervis Grenhalhe & Dority Kay of Elton	2 July
Lawrance Haslome of Wal : & Elizaƀ Bothe	6 ,,
George Hargreues of Clithero & Marg⁹t Hauworth	19 ,,
John Hauworth & Eliza : Hauworth	23 ,,

Charles Nuttall of Hol: & Elizaḃ Johnson	27	July
Roḃt Hauworth of Edē & Añ Hauworth	30	,,
John Ashworthe of Hasl: & Alise Cowap	27	August
George Holme of Rad: & Ann Bury	5	September
John Cowap & Margret Bridge	3	October
Tho: Heald of Bury & Margeret Overall	11	,,
Alexander Lamb of Bamf: & Judeth Leache	22	,,
John Harison of Boulton & Alise Bridge	22	,,
Francis Warbᵖton & Eliz: Blaklow	30	,,
John Kay of Elton & Jane Heald	12	December
Charles Lort & Elnor Pikop	21	,,
Roḃt Skolfeld & Alisse Blakley	26	,,
Roger Sedon of Heap & Elizaḃ Grenhalhe	18	January
Francis Grenhalh & Ann Batersby of Bu:	30	,,
George Vnseworth & Ellyn Radley	5	February
Thomas Durden of Bur: & Susan Hauworth	7	,,
James Cowp of Bury & Margaret Kay	12	,,
James Aspinall of Walm̃ & Jane Nab		
Roger Hamer of Bukden & Eliz: Rausthorne	15	,,

1621.

Richard Cowap of Eden: & Isabell Tayler	3	April
Andrew Sale of Bury & Mary Bukley	10	,,
Roger Kay of Grenmosse & Alise Grēhalghe		
Francis Pilkington of Edenf: & Ann Fittõ	12	,,
Thomas Bury & Susan Lomax	18	,,
Wiłłm Wardleworth & Ester Turner		
James Hauworth of Midł & Jane Prascot [?]	10	May
James Wrigley of Mancᵉ & Elizaḃ Croop	21	,,
James Holt of Midłe & Alsse Hauworth	24	,,
Rich: Nutall of Hol: & Katheryn Rawshtorn	3	June
James Pikop & Mary Bromhead		
Roger Bromeley & Ann Hynd	9	,,
Fo. 255 William Bury of Tot. & Lydia Nuttall	12	,,
James Kay of Goseford & Ann Kay	24	,,
James Skolefeld & Jane Hardman of Bury	22	July
Ralphe Leache & Elizaḃ Hynd	29	,,
Thomas Bothe of Tot: & Margeret Noris	5	August
Oliuer Garstange & Jane Kay	13	,,
John Marcrofte & Elizabeth Noble [? Nab]	3	September
Edward Ingham & Susan Hauworth	4	,,
Robert Dunster & Mary Gerret	22	,,
Symeon Lamb & Annett Rothwell of Bury	6	November
Roḃt Hauworth of Eden: & Eliz: Hamer	13	,,
Richard Heyward of Chattõ & Ann Pilking	15	,,
John Brooke of Haukshaw & Eliz Hauworth	11	,,
Mathew Both of Redi & Eliz. Vnseworth	21	,,
Nicolas Walkeden & Ann Smithe	27	,,

WEDDINGS

Edmond Holte of Clithero & Susan Mere	15 Jan
Adam Skolefeld of Edenf: & Margeret Cronkshaw	19 ,,
George Hauworth of Edenf: & Jennet Grime ...	24 ,,
James Bukley of Hol: & Alisse Vnseworth	2 February
Robt Hauworth of Bamf: & Mary Warbᵒton ...	10 ,,
John Barnes of Haslyndē & Eliz: Holt of Bu:	24 ,,
John Tayler of Walmes: & Ellyn Wood	26 ,,
Roger Kay of Elton & Ann Pilkington	5 March
Edmond Barlow of Croithlaw & Dority Bukley	6 ,,
Thomas Smitherst of Bury & Eliz: Holte ...	

[1622.]

John Skolefeld of Edenf: & Elizaƀ Piccop	3 Junij
Arther Partington & Jennet Setle	4 ,,
James Dawson of Edenf: & Ann Michell	13 ,,
John Both ye son of Anthony at Edenfelde	28 ,,
William Kay of Tichrod & Jane Kay ...	3 September
James Holte of Bury & Eliz. Kay	1 October
Robert Hopwood & Priscilla Taylor ...	8 ,,
James Jackson of Bury & Alise Grenhalhe ...	29 ,,
Thomas Kay of Walmers: & Eliz: Skolefeld...	5 November
Michaell Bentley & Alisse Allenes of Midl	11 ,,
Ellis Hauworth of Walm & Martha Wilde ...	12 ,,
Roger Vnseworth of Wal: & Jony Smitherste...	20 ,,
Zachary Collinge of Midleton & Ann Crompto	10 December
John Stotte of Heywood & Judith Lamb ...	20 ,,
George Wharledale & Jane Pleasington ...	26 ,,
John Crompton of Bolton & Ann Holte	4 Feb
John Chadwicke of Bamf: & Elizaƀ Tayler ...	
Ralfe Fildes of Bury & Ann Knowles	17 ,,
Arther Smitherste & Jane Whitheade ...	18 ,,
John Pilinge of Lenches & Alles Ormeroid	24 ,,
John Battersby of Hasl: & Margeret Greine ...	
Richard Wood of Elton & Mary Haslome ..	25 ,,

1623.

Williā Bury & Ann Holte at Cokey...	25 March
Henry Hauworth of Ratch: & Jane Hardman...	3 May
Richard Hopwood of Midleton & Alise Kay ...	29 ,,
Francis Bridge & Isabell Howorthe of Musburie	9 October
John Kaie and Jenent Fenton of this p	2 February
George Houlte & Margreate Symond of this pisn	3 ,,
Ellis Haslome of ye pishe of Boulton & Alice Nabbe of pish	9
Richard Asheton and Jane Orell of Turtō	18

1624.

Olliver Nabbe of this parishe and Jane Scoles of the parishe of Prestwiche	26 March
Edward Lomax & Doritie Brearley both of this pishe	
Richard Hadocke & Ann Blacklowe both of pish	9 June
Roger Hamer and Alice Bridge both of this pish	15 ,,
John Broughton & Marie Chadwicke of Berie...	1 July
Richard Kaie & Doritie Kaie bothe of this parish	12 ,,
John Howorthe of this pishe & Susan Knote of the parishe of Midlton	24 ,,
James Taylor & Margreat Waterhouse of this pishe	29 ,,
Thomas Smythe of ye parishe of Manchester and Elizabethe of this parishe	14 September
Richard Mather of Walton pishe, Katrin Houlte of this parishe	29 ,,
Robert Taylor & Elsabethe Walker of Burie ...	5 October
Thomas Hoult & Katrin Roads of this pishe ...	19 ,,
James Lorte of Midlton pishe and Marie Berie of this pishe	19 November
George Haslome of the parishe of Ratcliffe and Margreate Winell of the parishe of Bolton	17 ,,
Henry Hargreaues & Elsabethe of this pishe ...	21 ,,
Roberte Fenton & Margreate Wood of this pishe	23 ,,
Thomas Boothe & Ellen Hewarde of this pishe	
John Hoyle of Clitherall pishe and Allice Gregorie of this pishe	28 ,,
Richard Chadwicke of Midleton pishe & Jane Howorth of this pishe...	30 ,,
Adam Rosthorne & Isabell Partington both of this parishe	30 January
Richard Bouthe and Elsabeth Broucke bothe of this parishe	15 February
John Bate & Elsabethe Houlte of this pishe ...	1 March

1625.

Richard Fisher of this parishe and Annis Durden of the parishe of Clitharall	26 May
Henry Rothwell & Annis Duckworthe of this pishe	
Richard Baron & Elsabethe Gryme both of pish	8 June
Thomas Wood and Katrin Hardie both of this pishe	15 ,,
Roger Taylor & Allen Stons of this pishe ...	17 ,,
Christopher Smethurste and Alice Kaie both of this parishe	2 July

WEDDINGS.

1625-1626

John Greaue and Elizabethe Burtwistle both of this parishe ...	5 July
Wittm Houlte and Ann Bridge bothe of this pishe ...	26 ,,
Roberte Sheaphard & Ann Houlte of this pishe	21 August
George Howorthe & Anis Howarthe of this pishe	18 September
Wittm Overall & Ellen Leyland of this pishe ...	20 ,,
John Longworthe & Marie Taylor of this pishe	27 ,,
Roberte Gregorie & Margreate Jacson of this pishe ...	18 October
John Broucke & Isabell of this pishe ...	8 December
James Turnor & Marie Croper of this pishe ...	12 ,,
Francis Mackon & Marie Wrigley of this pishe	20 ,,
Thomas Smethurste & Ann Adamson of this pishe ...	3 January
Edmund Houlte & Jane Howorthe of this pishe	16 ,,
Thomas Bate of Prestwiche & Annis Wilson of this pishe ...	31 ,,
Thomas Smithurste & Ellen Leache of this pishe	1 February
Thomas Fenton of ye pishe of Clitherall and Elizabethe Rosthorne of this parishe ...	7 ,,
Francis Grinall & Allice Haugh of this pishe ...	14 ,,
Roberte Grinall & Marie Harper of this pishe...	19 ,,
Wittm Dowson & Ann Nuttall of this pishe ...	21 ,,

1626.

Arthure Smethurste & Katrin Smithurste of this parishe ...	16 April
Wittm Durden of Rachdall & Ann Whithead of Burie ...	1 May
John Mulenex & Alice Bridge of this parishe ..	22 ,,
Thomas Millner & Margreate Greaue of this pishe ...	21 ,,
John Shawe & Jane Kaie of this parishe ...	22 ,,
James Walworke & Margreate Kaie of this pish	2 June
John Bouthe & Katrin Jacksonn of this parishe	2 July
Hugh Lomax of the parishe Rachdall and Isabell Rothwell of the parishe of Boulton ...	6 ,,
Richard Pilkington & Margerie Howorthe of this pishe ...	16 ,,
Mathewe Suttcliffe & Alice Howorthe of this pishe ...	
Josua Leache & Edithe Berie of this pishe ...	8 August
Jeffray Foster of the pishe of Leaygh and Elizabethe Nuttall of this pishe ...	15 ,,
Richard Duckworthe of this pishe and Ann Barlowe of the pishe of Ratcliffe ...	10 October
Gyles Vnsworthe of this pishe & Ann Harper of ye pishe of Midlton ...	1 November

John Johns of the parishe of Midltonn and Alice Kaie of this parishe ...	7 November
George Howorthe & Ann Longworthe of this pishe ...	21 ,,
John Kaie and Ann Kaie bothe this parishe ...	
James Buckley & Katrin Smethurste of this parishe ...	
Thomas Warbarton & Margreate Bridge of this pish ...	10 December
Richard Ashworthe & Ann Abat of this pishe...	24 ,,
Edward Ingham & Katrin Burie of this pishe...	7 January
James Grinhalghe & Margreate Bate of this pishe ...	
Richard Romsbothome & Elsabethe Lomax of this parishe ...	28 ,,
Thomas Wood and Ann Houlte of this parishe	2 February
Peter Heward and Doritie Grinhalghe of this parishe ...	5 ,,
Richard Crompton and Jane Boardman of Boulton pishe ...	6 ,,
James Chadwicke of Midltō & Ellen Lyon of this pishe ...	
John Isherwood and Martha Grinhalgh of this pishe ...	
Roberte Johnson of Prestwiche & Doritie Heward of this pishe...	
Thomas Leache and Susan Lambe of this pishe	

1627.

Fo. 258 John Wofenden of this pishe & Marie Rude of the pishe of Rachdall...	28 March
John Fletcher & Anne Harope of this parishe	25 April
George Howorthe & Ellen Greene of this parishe ...	24 May
John Blacklowe and Katrine Fletcher of this parishe ...	12 June
Thomas Nuttall and Margreate Rosthorne of this parishe ...	17 ,,
Thomas Kenion and Jane Duckworthe of Midltone	
Gyles Ored of ye Deane pishe & Alice Fletcher of this pishe ...	2 July
Peter Lomax of this parishe and Elisabeth Leache of Midlton pishe ...	6 August
Samuell Mackon of this pishe & Susan Heaton of Midlton pishe...	15 ,,
Richard Fletcher of Midlton pishe & Joan Mather of our pishe ...	19 ,,
James Crompton of our pishe & Alice Carter of Prestwiche ...	3 October

WEDDINGS.

Thomas Clifford and Elsabeth Grinhalghe of this pishe	12 October
Roberte Cropper and Ellen Thorneton of this pishe	13 ,,
Richard Barlowe & Isabell . . . of this pishe	4 November
Roger Kaie and Kerstabell Howorthe of this pishe	6 ,,
John Hill and Doritie Wood bothe of this parishe	24 ,,
John Hoult and Alice Ainsworthe bothe of this pishe	12 December
Thomas Durden of Rachdall pishe & Alice Whithead of this parishe	6 January
Edward Barlow and Francis Proctor of this parishe	
William Heald & Doritie Vnsworthe of this pishe	7 February
George Tumlinson and Alice Pilkington of this pishe	17 ,,
Edmund Rothwell and Isabell Lomax of this pishe	19 ,,
John Kaie of this pishe & Elnor Siddall of the pishe of Prestwiche	23 ,,
William Overall and Alice Smythe of this parishe	24 ,,
John Barlowe of Prestwiche & Ellen Grinhalghe of Bury pishe	26 ,,
Roger Wood of Boulton & Sara Bouthe of this parishe	

1628.

William Grinhalghe and Alice Fogge of this parishe	15 April
Richard Houlte & Margreate Grinhalghe of this pishe	17 ,,
Roberte Taylor & Letese Howorthe of this pishe	22 ,,
Richard Seddon & Margreate Howorthe of this pishe	May
Richard Sturdicar of Midelton pishe and Ellen Casson of this parishe	22 June
John Sickes of the parishe of Midelton and Margreate Bouthe of this parish	24 ,,
John Bouthe & Elizabeth Bouthe of this parishe	1 July
John Wrigley and Susan Hilton of Prestwiche pishe	25 August
John Warbarton & Elizabeth Kaie of this parishe	6 September
William Wilson & Jane Bridge of this parishe	9 ,,
Ellis Lomax and Margreate Medowcrofte of this pishe	14 ,,

Richard Barlowe and Elizabeth Horidge of this pishe	16	September
Roberte Whiticar and Ann Parsivall of this pishe	30	,,
Thomas Blacklowe and Ann Duckworthe of this p		
Barnard Townley of the parishe of Bromley and Margerie Bradshawe of the parishe of Boulton	19	November
Roberte Marcrofte of the parishe of Midleton and Ellen Houlte of this parishe	2	December
John Kaie and Ann Leache of this parishe ...	10	,,
James Hunte and Elsabeth Kaie of this parishe	23	,,
Robte Walworke & Elizabeth Kay of this pishe	24	,,
William Sharrocke of Manchester pish and Mary Haymer of this pish	30	,,
John Wardleworth of ye pish of Manchester and Mary Low of this pish	8	January
John Bury & Ellen Barlow both of this pish ...	3	February
Thomas Hoult & Margerett . . . both of this pish	16	,,
Fo. 259 Edward Slade of this parish & Ellen Haslom of ye pish of Middleton	17	,,

1629.

Robert Marcroft & Mary Holt both of this pish	19	April
James Wilson & Anne Vnsworth both of this pish	27	,,
Thomas Nabbe & Dorothy Kay both of this pish	5	May
John Whitley and Jane Brooke both of this pish	12	,,
Henry Booth of this pish & Jennett Longworth of Bolton	13	,,
Charles Ramsbothom & Margrett Horrockes both of this pish	14	,,
Thomas Rothwell & Isabell Wood both of this pish	29	June
John Greenhalgh & Anne Whitworth of this pish	15	July
Richard Yate of Blakeburne pish & Elizab Duckworth of this pish	10	August
Thomas Wood & Mary Peacocke both of this pish	28	,,
James Whittle of Ratcliffe pish & Esther Fogge of this pish...	1	September
John Barlow of Ratcliffe pish & Elizab Rothwell of Prestwich...		
John Heywood of Middleton pish & Ellen Liuesay of this pish	24	October
Edmund Seddon & Mary Baron both of this pish	4	November
Ashton Lever of Bolton pish & Eliz: Booth of this pish	12	,,
James Kay & Jane Holt both of this pish ...	27	December
William Berry & Anne Scofeild both of this pish	31	,,

WEDDINGS.

Robert Smethurst & Anne Haymer both of this ꝑish	5 January
William Johnson & Mary Diggle both of this pish	7 ,,
Adam Crompton of Bolton ꝑish & Elizabeth Holt of this parishe	2 February
Edmund Seddon & Elizabeth Crompton both of this ꝑish	
John Kay & Anne Hardman both of this parish	7 ,,
Thomas Jackson & Ellen Mather of this parish	8 ,,

1630.

John Marccroft of Boulton ꝑish & Añ Hinde of this parishe	30 March
Arthur Kay and Mary Kay both of this ꝑch ...	13 April
Thomas Smetherst and Ann Haslom both of this ꝑch	
Charles Vnsworth and Elizabeth Rothwell both of this ꝑish	19 ,,
Raphe Bucklay & Dorettey Lomax both of this ꝑish	20 ,,
Jame Jenkenson & Martha Taelio' both of this ꝑish	25 ,,
George Hulls of Prestwich ꝑish & Eliz: Pens of this ꝑish	2 May
Henry Henthorn of Rachdall ꝑish & Grace Maken of this ꝑish	4 ,,
Thomas Tong of Boulton psh & Alies Kay of this ꝑish	13 June
Robert Doason & Mary Hoult bothe of this ꝑish	6 July
John Walch of Rachdall pishe & Doretty Booth of this psh	8 ,,
Henry Prescott and Alice Grime both of this ꝑish	24 August
Richard Kenion and Anne Fogge both of this ꝑish	1 September
Henry Hill of Bolton ꝑish & Dorothey Brucke of this ꝑish	
Ellis Clegge and Margrett Hardmen both of Ratchdall ꝑish	10 October
James Scowles and Mary Taylor both of Prestwich ꝑish	23 ,,
James Marocke [?] of Prestwitch & Jane Duckworth of this ꝑish	20 November
James Taylor of Rachdall ꝑish and Mary Holt of this ꝑish	15 December
William Davis of Winwicke & Anne Barlow of this ꝑish	31 January
Thomas Warburton & Susan Heaton both of this ꝑish	2 February

Edmund Lort & Jane Rishton both of Middleton pish		February
Thomas Warburton & Alice Rothwell both of this pish	8	,,
Thomas Nuttall & Margrett Aspinall both of this pish	19	,,
George Howorth & . . . both of this pish . . . Rosthorne of this pish & Margrett Hoyle of Whaly	20	,,
Raph Seddon & Elizabeth Lomax both of this pish	21	,,
John Romsbothom & . . . Nuttall both of this pish	22	,,

1631.

Fo. 260 Samuell Wilde & Sara Hargreaves both of Rachdall pish	23	April
John Smith of this parish & Isabell Milnes of Rachdall	12	May
James Reade of Prestwich & Mary Booth of Bury	20	,,
Francis Kay and Alice Wood both of Bury pish	28	June
John Leigh of Whaley pish & Elizab Kay of Bury	5	July
William Makon of this pish & Susan Bury of Middleton	24	,,
John Holt and Mary Seddon both of this pish	26	,,
Richard Romsbothome & Alice Battersby both of this parish	3	October
James Fenton & Grace Howorth both of this parish	1	November
Richard Grenehalgh & Alice Roustornes of this parish	13	,,
John Berde of Midelton pish & Dorothy Battersby of this parish	24	January
John Wrigley of this parish ãd Mary Lees of Ouldham	31	,,

1632.

John Howldin of Ecles & Margret Nuttall of Bury	2	April
Francis Dawson & Ann Grenhawh of Bury p ...		
Roger Rogerson & Isabell Radelley of Manchester	11	,,
James Haworth, Bury & Caterine Grime, Midleſ	10	May
Rich. Both, Prestwich & Margret Hardman ...	3	July
Robt Hamer, Rochdale & Jane Holt, Bury ...	16	,,
Gyles Haslom, Grace Longworth, Bury	22	,,
Richard Cromptõ, Deane & Margret Holden ...	5	August
John Holt of Prestwich & Susan Stock, Bury...	14	,,
Samuel Heywood of Rachdall and Elen Taylor of this pish	5	September

John Warberton & Marie Pilkington booth of this pish	6 September
Robert Whitiker & Lettis Rothwell booth of this pish	11 ,,
Edmand Mills & Marie Kay booth of this pish	13 ,,
Richard Vnsworth and Martha Holt both of this pish	15 January
Frances Emerson and Jane Lifsi of Mdletō pish	
Frances Nutall of this pishe & Jane Wood of ye pish of Midleton	16 ,,
Edmond Holte and Alice Burie both of this pish	5 March
James Holt & Marie Jenkenson both of this pish	

1633.

261	Thomas Cluth and Susan Whithed both of this pish	24 April
	James Stott & Margret Scoufild both of this pish	2 May
	James Holt & Susan Pendleburie both of this pish	16 ,,
	Thomas Lort of Midleton pish & Susan Grime of this pish	6 June
	Thomas Nutall & Jane Greenalgh both of this pish	20 ,,
	Raph Smethurst of Rattlife & Ellen Crompton of this pish	5 July
	Roberte Moris and Elizabeth Holyley both of this pish	27 ,,
	Oliver Winterberow and Ann Orell both of Ratchdall pish	14 August
	Will Booker of Manchester and Caterin Simon of this pish	11 September
	Abraham Stot of Ratchdall pish and Susan Ashworth of this pish	15
	Edward Kayley and Alice Strenge both of this pish	
	Robert Benson and Ginnitt Tayler both of this pish	
	Edmand Bockome of Presswhich pishe and Margret Hull of this pish	
	John Kay and Mariy Digle both of this pish	
	Arthur Smethurst and Ann Smethurst both of this pish	
	John Wood and Mariy Booth both of this pish..	

1634.

Edmund Greenhalgh & Elizabeth Lort	8 April
Oliver Telior of this pish & Ann Holt of Rachdall	27 ,,
John Bellet of Blakeborne pish and Ellin Howorth	29 ,,

Arthur Smethurst & Ann Smethurst	3	June
John Milns of Rachdale & Ann Beasicke	3	July
John Greenhalgh & Añ Crosley	30	,,
Fo. 262 Roɓte Heald and Marie Fogg	14	August
Arthur Smethurst & Mary Nuttall	31	September
Richard Telior and Elizabeth Whitehead* ...	17	October
John Walworke* and Elizabeth Whitley	22	,,
Abraham Fildes and Marie Dunstier	20	November
John Haslam and Ellin Rothwell	27	,,
Roɓte Hichenson and Marie Hichenson Istius...	15	December
Samuell Holt & Susan Duerden	7	January †
Roger Kilshaw and Ann Lakershey	13	February

1635.

Fo. 263 Richard Grime & Anne Grime both of this parish	29	March
Thomas Jones & Anne Walworke	30	,,
Thomas Greenhalgh & Jane Taylor	6	April
Robert Smethurst & Katherin Bridge		
Jeffry Brooke & Alice Batersby both of this parish	14	,,
Francis Booth & Martha Bewsicke	26	,,
Mr. Richard Holt & Ms. Jane Greenhalgh both of this parish	1	May
James Dunster & Susan Fitton both of this parish	19	,,
Richard Haslam of Ratcliffe pish & Margret Duckworth of this pish		
Nathan Nuttall & Mary Booth both of this pish	20	,,
Mr. Edward Rosthorne & Ms. Mary Greenhalgh both of this pish	25	,,
Rodger Chadwicke of Rachdale pish & Alice Holt of this pish	28	,,
Arthur Howorth & Ellin Fletcher both of this parish		
Raphe Smethurst of Ratcliffe & Elizaɓ Wood of Middleton pish	16	June
Oliver Houlden & Issabell Bealie both of this parish	23	,,
John Coupe of this parish & Ratcliffe Frischo of Ratcliffe pish	2	July
William Heape of Rachdale pish & Susan Hanson of this pish	14	,,
William Wilson of Bolton pish & Alice Rosthorne of this pish	25	,,

* "Elizabeth Whitehead" and "Walworke" in Mr. William Rothwell's handwriting.
† From here to August, 1641, the entries are in Mr. Rothwell's beautiful handwriting.

WEDDINGS.

Lawrance Nab & Elizaḃ Smith both of this pish	4 August
Thomas Jackson of Ratcliffe pish & Anne Pilkinton of this pish	9 ,,
Richard Lomax & Katherin Coupe both of this pish	11 ,,
Adam Rosthorne & Ellin Rosthorne both of this pish	3 September
Edmund Holt & Margret Johnson both of this pish	8 ,,
John Bolton of this pish & Jane Parkin of Cawthorne pish	10 ,,
Thomas Nuttall & Jane Rushton both of this pish	5 October
Thomas Pilkinton & Ellin Symond both of this pish	
Robert Booth of this pish & Ellin Wood of Bolton pish	10 November
John Kay & Elizaḃ Lomax both of this pish ...	8 December
Thomas Lord & Elizabeth Coupe both of this pish	15 ,,
James Isherwood & Jane Smith both of this pish	1 January
Edward Lomax of Bolton pish & Joan Vnsworth of this pish	13 ,,
William Kay & Margret Barlow both of this parish	26 ,,
John Hoyle & Anne Bird both of this pish ...	28 ,,
John Howorth & Elizabeth Romsbotha both of this pish	31 ,,
Henry Smith & Elizabeth Seddon both of this pish	2 February
Rodger Grime & Dorathy Hunt both of this pish	16 ,,
Richard Croston & Ellenor Kay both of this pish	25 ,,
Edward Rausthorne & Anne Haddok both of this pish	29 ,,

William Rothwell, Curat

1636.

William Manne of Whaley pish, Alice Hargreaus of this pish	18 April
Henry Coupe & Rebecca Johnson both of this pish	26 ,,
Thomas Eckersall & Elizabeth Beamond both of this pish	27 ,,
Richard Howorth of Middl pish & Mary Bowers of this pish	5 May
Edward Rausthorne & Mary Scofeild both of this pish	15 ,,

M

Richard Rothwell & Katherin Foster both of Bolton pish ...	19 May
John Hardy of Middleton pish & Mary Kay of this pish ...	23 ,,
John Gleaden of Ratchdall pish & Mary Rydings of this pish ...	24 ,,
James Fenton & Margret Coup both of this pish	26 ,,
Bartholemew Stones & Alice Smeythurst both of this pish ...	1 June
Peter Coupe of this pish & Ellin Gorton of Stopford pish ...	14 ,,
Richard Clegge of Ratchdale pish & Katharin Scofeild of this pish ...	
Samuell Hollas of Ratchdale pish & Alice Pens of this pish ...	
John Tattersall of Whaley pish & Agnes Ashworth of this pish ...	
Thomas Greenhalgh of Bolton pish & Ellin Holt of this p ...	24 ,,
George Croston & Isabell Whitehead both of this pish ...	6 July
Richard Rosthorne & Mary Kay both of this pish	17 ,,
George Eckerslay & Alis Overall both of this pish ...	19 ,,
Fo. 264 William Holt & Margret Nabbe both of this pish	1 August
George Allens of Radcliffe & Anne Barlow of this pish ...	4 ,,
James Gabbet & Susan Newton both of this pish	23 ,,
Robert Taylor & Margret Taylor both of this pish ...	25 September
Robert Dunstere & Alis Fletcher both of this pish ...	27 ,,
Richard Kay & Anne Robinson both of this pish	28 ,,
William Rothwell & Anne Tootell both of this pish ...	2 October
Robert Leach & Alice Booth both of this pish	10 ,,
Thomas Halliwell & Alice Greenhalgh both of this pish ...	26 ,,
John Cronkshaw of Haslingden & Margret Cronkshaw of this pish ...	1 November
Thomas Kay & Mary Smethurst both of this pish	6 ,,
Thomas Baxenden & Alice Leach both of this pish ...	8 ,,
Francis Saxon of Middleton pish & Isabell Holt of this pish ...	
Joseph Taylor of Rachdale pish & Jennet Whitaker ...	29 ,,
Richard Siddall & Alis Haughton both of this pish ...	6 December

WEDDINGS.

Richard Booth & Mary Holt both of this pish...	8 December
George Barnes & Elizabeth Balshaw both of this pish ...	10 ,,
Abell Tomlinson of pestwich & Jane Bordman of Bolton pish ...	29 ,,
John Rausthorne & Elizabeth Coupe both of this pish ...	5 February
Charles Milnes of Rachdale pish & Isabell Grimes of this pish ...	21 ,,
Robert Kay & Elizabeth Heaton both of this pish ...	24 ,,
James Stocke & Sarah Kay both of this pish...	

William Rothwell, Curat

1637.

Joseah Stot & Alice Smeythurst both of this pish	18 May
Oliuer Taylor & Elizabeth Wood both of this pish	29 ,,
Robert Skofeild & Winifrid Barlow ...	6 June
Edmund Pilling of Bury pish & Alice Hoile of Rachdale ...	12 ,,
Leonard Diggle & Katherin Dauson both of this pish ...	25 July
James Crompton & Anne Greenhalgh ...	1 August
William Low & Ellin Rosthorne ...	
Raphe Whittaker & Grace Taylor ...	6 September
Francis Pilkinton & Susan Taylor ...	12 ,,
James Kay & Jane Greenhalgh ...	10 October
Edward Mawde & Alice Jones ...	19 ,,
Mr. James Ashton & Mrs. Katharin Greenhalgh	
John Buckley & Anne Nuttall ...	28 ,,
John Kay & Margret Kay ...	
Richard Wild & Joan Rausthorne ...	1 November
Raphe Heaton & Anne Holt ...	
Samuell Shaw & Alice Booth ...	7 ,,
John Crompton & Mary Dawson ...	29 ,,
Esau Diggle & Mary Breerley ...	6 December
Andrew Know & Elizabeth Duckworth ...	20 ,,
Richard Nuttall & Margret Scoles ...	30 January

William Rothwell, Curat

1638.

Charles Lee & Alice Whittle ...	26 March
Edward Pilkinton & Britchet Booth	9 April
John Rausthorne & Anne Vnsworth...	
John Rausthorne & Alice Howorth ...	
John Isherwood & Martha Bentley ...	15 ,,
Richard Hargreaues & Sarah Bushell	

No. 265 John Howorth & Isabell Nabbe...   20 June
         Thomas Fletcher & Anne Thirnough   24 „
         Edward Greenhalgh & Elizaḅ Wood ...
         James Leach & Elizabeth Cockshet   30 „
         Franches Pilkinton & Mary Mather ...   17 July
         Edmund Haslome & Anne Leach   24 „
         Humfry Beamond & Mary Crossly   15 August
         James Ashworth & Anne Lockwood ...   21 „
         Richard Low & Alice Brooke ...   11 September
         John Tabernacle & Alice Howorth ...   25 „
         Raphe Seddon & Elizaḅ: Aspinall   30 „
         Arthur Kay & Jane Woosnam ...   9 October
         Robert Lang & Elizaḅ: Pilling
         Thomas Rothwell & Diana Higson ...   21 „
         Richard Lomax & Jane Clough   30 „
         Thomas Hasleden & Elizaḅ: Wood...   19 November
         Robert Ashworth & Elizabeth Armorod ...   28 „
         Nicholas Raustorne & Anne Smeythurst ...   4 December
         Thomas Wood & Anne Scofeild   2 January
                     William Rothwell, Curaṫ

1639.

         Raphe Leach & Ellin Holt   16 April
         James Fletcher & Mary Duerden   1 July
         Thomas Fletcher & Mary Booth   2 „
         Richard Barlow & Jane Worthington   25 „
         Franches Whittaker & Elizaḅ . . .
         James Rushton & Anne Coupe ...   14 August
         John Ainsworth & Jane Horrabin
         James Greenhalgh & Susan Bewsicke   22 September
         James Whittaker & Mary Greenhalgh   1 October
         John Lomax & Alice Nuttall   8 „
         John Booth & Grace Bolton   23 „
         Hugh Greenhalgh & Izabell Kay   12 November
         William Taylor & Mary Hamar...   19 „
         Thomas Aspinall & Grace Wood   February
                     William Rothwell, Curaṫ

1640.

         Francis Hitchenson & Margret Booth   6 April
         John Barlow & Alice Taylor   11 „
         John Anderton & Alice Rushton   15 „
         Abrahā Leach & Anne Shaw   21 „
         Richard Crouxhaw & Margret Hargreaus   26 „
         Oliuer Romsbothā & Grace Scofeild
         John Heaton & Elizabeth Frisco   1 May
         Edward Rothwell & Mary Whitehead   18 „

George Howorth & Katharin Breerly	6 June
John Riley & Joan Pilkinton	14 ,,
F 266 John Makon & Ellin Seddon	7 July
Aemar Ainsworth & Alice Cocker	16 ,,
Edward Hobkinson & Elizab Anderton	3 September
Raphe Vnsworth & Anne Hamar	4 November
Oliuer Seddon & Jane Howorth	10 ,,
Robert Fletcher & Susan Scofeild	1 December
Arthur Howorth & Katherin Kay	27 January
Oliuer Brendwood & Elnor Hardman	2 February
Mr. William Ingham & Mary Howorth	2 March
William Booth & Anne Kay	6 ,,
Henry Booth & Alice Rodes	
Richard Kay & Alice Greenhalgh	9 ,,
William Rothwell, Curat	

1641.

William Thornley & Ellin Sheaphard	26 April
Richard Howorth & Elizabeth Holt...	27 ,,
Robert Rydings & Jane Leigh	5 May
Thomas Jackson & Dorathy Ainsworth	9 ,,
John Wolfenden & Margret Worrall	20 ,,
Richard Lomax & Isabell Buersill ...	1 June
John Kay & Mary Kay	3 ,,
Robert Whittaker & Margret Lomax...	6 July
Robert Heald & Elizabeth Bridge	17 August
Richard Fitton & Mary Redffearne	5 October
Josua Hargreaues & Sibbill Tealior	12 ,,
James Howorth & Mary Nabbs	November
James Livesay & Hellen Smethurst	
Humphrey Saundiforth & Alice Greenhalgh	Decemb
Richard Fletcher & Mary Smith	
Alexander Chadwich & Anne Johnson ...	
Thomas Fletcher & Alice Greenhalgh ...	2 Febr.
Edmund Slate & Elizabeth Booth	22 ,,
John Heward of Rachdall & Anne Fildes...	

1642.

Abraham Mather of Midleton & Mary Lomax ...	11 April
John Ridings & Esther Kershaw of this pish ...	28 ,,
Henry Taylor & Lettice Duckworth...	10 May
John Taylor & Margrett Stot	1 June
Henry Allens & Katherine Sale	10 July
James Leach & Katherin Percivall	21 ,,
Richard Holt & Anne Pollard	28 August
o. 267 Richard Bury of this pish & Martha Greenhalgh of Prestwich	29 September

John Buckley & Elizaḃ Stith	17 November
James Greenhalgh & Elizaḃ Hind	24 ,,
James Walworth & Alice Rothwell	26 ,,
Richard Bannister & Anne Emarson ...	13 December
Francis Greenhalgh & Ellen Shaw	24 January
John Howorth & Alice Jenkinson	14 February

1643.

Josua Shaw & Margrett Holt	4 April
John Taylor & Alice Steele	24 ,,
Ellis Grime & Alice Howorth	4 June
Robert Shepheard & Anne Fletcher	12 ,,
Henry Taylor & Mary Whitaker	18 ,,
Raph Smethurst & Isabell Henly	25 ,,
George Heaton & Elizaḃ Walworke	30 July
John Bridge & Catherin Nuttall	2 October
John Lomax and Mary Vnsworth	14 ,,
John Birom & Katherine Seddon	7 November
Thomas Lomax & Elizabeth Pott	18 ,,
Roger Pilkington and	20 ,,
Robert Kay & Elizaḃ Low...	12 December
Edward Bamford of Bamford & Elizabeth Rausthorn	4 March

1644.

John Jenkinson & Ellen Haworth	1 August
Mathew Booth & Elen Sandes...	8 ,,
Richard Nabb & Marie Crompton	15 September
James Stott & Marie Kenion	21 ,,
Franches Booth & Elizabeth Heaward	3 October
Hughe Longworth of Blackroade & Sarah Leigh of Ouldham pish	7 November
Lawrance Taylor & Ane Rosthorne of Bury ...	19 ,,
Johāthan Butterworth of Bury & Kateren Grenehalgh of Midleton	25 ,,
William Smyth of Holcom & Sarah Mather of Ratlife	30 ,,
John Holt of Prestwich & Marie Haworth of Bury	3 December
Richard Holt & Marie Heyes of Bury	4 ,,
Henery Dunster & Joan Orpe	
Thomas Heald & Elizabeth Kay	26 ,,
Samwell Shawe & Alise Booth	4 January
Richard Kay & Añe Flecher	27 ,,
Franches Booth of this pish & Marie Smethurst of Prestwich	28 ,,

Fo. 268

James Fletcher of Prestwich & Alise Kay of this pish	11	Februarij
Roger Holt of Brigehall & Jane Grenehalgh of Chamber	21	,,

1645.

Thomas Hilton & Margret Hatton of Leigh	8	April
Joseph Tomlinson & Mary Tayler	26	May
Peter Rothwell & Mary Scholefeild	29	,,
Thomas Hutchinson & Sara Royd	23	June
Roger Coupe & Isabell Leach ...	24	,,
Jeffrey Riley & Elizabeth Kay	22	July
Ellis Vnsworth & Katherin Longworth	6	August
Richard Taylor & Katherin Holt ...	18	,,
Richard Rothwell & Anne Cronkshaw	25	,,
Anthony Walls & Añ Howorth	28	,,
John Bury & Margrett Fenton		
Jeremy Thornly & Elizab Higginson ...	2	September
Jeremy Ainsworth & Mary Pilling	8	,,
Robt Fog of Ratcliffe & Margrett Whitaker	13	,,
Charles Pilkington & Mary Holt	15	,,
John Couper & Alice Whitehead ...	16	,,
William Earnshaw & Anne Lomax ...	18	,,
269 John Nuttall & Gennet Holden	22	,,
John Pilling & Alice Ormeroyd	30	,,
James Ainsworth & Elizab Smith		
Jonas Wood & Mary Kay	3	October
John Rawstorne & Alice Holt	6	,,
Dionisse Rothwell & Mary Tong ...	7	,,
William Heald & Margrett Wilson ...	8	,,
Robert Deurden & Mary Overall ...		
John Crompton & Margrett Pilkington	15	,,
Thomas Kay & Margrett Booth ...	20	,,
James Greenalgh & Susan Cockstey ...	23	,,
Edward Booth & Alice Booth	30	,,
John Broome & Grace Booth	3	December
James Hardman & Susan Lomax	11	,,
Richard Tootell & Isabell* Nuttall	23	,,
Richard Duckworth & Alice Kay ...	1	January
Arthur Holt & Susan Howorth ...	5	,,
Owen Lomax & Alice Howorth	6	,,
John Booth & Alice Nabbe		
William Rife & Ellen Booth	20	,,
Thomas Seddon & Alice Foster...	9	February
John Kay & Judith Scolefeild	10	,,
John Clegge & Mary Fletcher		
Richard Simond & Margrett Eckersall	21	March

* " Isabell " written in another hand over " Elizabeth " crossed through.

1646.

John Greenhalgh & Margrett Fentō...	30 March
John Salle & Ellenor Carlile	1 April
Richard Kay & Alice Smith	21 ,,
Robert Bury & Christian Barlow	
John Broome & Alice Kay	1 May
John Aston [?] & Alice Neeld...	5 ,,
Nicholas Aspinwall & Anne Wood*	2 June
John Mawde & Isabell Holme	9 ,,
James Smethurst & Susan Lomax	30 ,,
William Gabbit & Kirstabell Holden	
James Holt & Elizaƀ Leach	5 July
Jonathan Wardle & Jane Burgesse	5 August
Rich. Clegge & Elizaƀ Ashworth	10 ,,
Thomas Jones & Alice Booth	13 ,,
Ellis Vnsworth & Elizaƀ Nuttall	25 ,,
John Clough & Margrett Ored...	7 September
John Lang & Alice Broome †	22 ,,
Fo. 270 Mr. Robert Bath, Vicar of Rachdall & Elizabeth Hely	15 October
Richard Clough & Elizaƀ Nabbe	3 November
Thomas Howorth & Dorothy Howorth	5 ,,
Joseph Street & Ellen Heald	10 ,,
Richard . . . & Anne Lomax	16 ,,
John Long & Alice Stanford	24 ,,
John Hopwood & Alice Stanford	2 February
Richard Booth & Sara Hardman	9 ,,
Robert Howorth & Alice Romsbothō	
Richard Heaton & Alice Burns	2 March
Thomas Brierly & Jane Chadwick	9 ,,

William Alte

* John Taylor and Mary Lomax crossed through.
† "Broome" written over "Booth" crossed through.

[*The first volume of the Register ends here.*]

Indexes.

I.
INDEX OF SURNAMES AND CHRISTIAN NAMES.

```
Vol. 1.—C.   .  pp.   1— 90 inclusive.   Vol. 2.—C.   .  pp. 205—280 inclusive.
       B. .    ,,   91—168        ,,           B. .    ,,  281—350        ,,
       W. .    ,,  169—204        ,,           W. .    ,,  351—372        ,,
```

N.B.—As many variants of the same Surname occur, that variant has been selected for the Head-name which most closely resembles the modern form. The names in brackets are the other variants found in the period 1590-1646. Christian names have been given in their modern form.

An asterisk against the page number denotes that the name occurs more than once in the particular page.

At the top of each page will be found indicated the pages of this work which deal with Christenings, Burials, and Weddings respectively.

N.X.N.=Christian name left blank in original.

Entries relating to illegitimate children are Indexed under Surnames of Mother and reputed Father.

A

ABAT, Ann, 358
Adamson, Ann, 357
Adkinson [see Atkinson]
Accroyd, Prudence, 198
Ainsworth [Ainesworth, Ainesworthe, Ainseworth, Ainseworthe, Ainsworthe, Ainworth, Answorth, Aynesworth, Aynesworthe, Aynsworth, Aynsworthe, Eansworth, Ensworth, Ensworthe],
,, Alice, 62, 205, 226, 359
,, Amor (Emor), 4, 8, 52, 59, 85, 132, 157, 159, 192, 210, 222, 251,* 256, 273, 278, 281, c. of 293, 302, 310, w. of 315, 328, w. of 331, c. of 340, 369
,, Ann, 222
,, Dorothy, 214, 333, 369
,, Edward, 278
,, Elizabeth, 210, 249, 276, 281
,, Ellen, 3, 8, 80, 196, 221, 256
,, Francis, 273
,, George, 41, 127
,, Gennit, 248
,, Henry, 215,* 221, 228, 245, 248, 251, 333

Ainsworth, Isabel, 147
,, James, 35, 43, 52, 61, 64,* 71, 74, 80, 105, 121, 128, 129, 159, 194, 202, 205, 212,* 226, 237, 238, 246,* 277,* c. of 348, 371
,, Jane, 148, 159,* 203, 207, 221
,, Jeremie, 53, 62, 80, 138, 188, 206, 214, 221,* 225, 228, 230, 237, 245, 248,* 249, 279,* 287, c. of 317, 371
,, John, 3, 10, 11, 20, 53, 74, 80, 140, 153,* 159,* 203, 207, 209, 218, 225, 238, 271,* 273, 284, 287, c. of 307, c. of 309, c. of 333, w. of 349, 368
,, Katherine, 10, 159
,, Margaret, 20
,, Martha, 4, 61, 202, 273
,, Mary, 35, 41, 43, 71, 85, 157, 190, 206, 209, 310, 333
,, Richard, 221
,, Robert, 271,* 276
,, Sarah, 218, 251, 333
,, Simon, 57
,, Thomas, 11, 57, 147, 169, 230
,, William, 117
Allen [Allanes, Allence, Allene, Allenes, Allens],
,, Alice, 26, 216, 259, 355

374   BURY PARISH REGISTERS.

Vol. 1.—C. . *pp. 1— 90 inclusive. Vol. 2.—C.* . *pp. 205—280 inclusive.*
  B. . ,, 91—168 ,,   B. . ,, 281—350 ,,
  W. . ,, 169—204 ,,   W. . ,, 351—372 ,,

Allen, Ann, 87, 89, 220, 298
 ,, Christopher, 153
 ,, Daniel, 87, 209, 218, 300
 ,, David, 1
 ,, Deborah, 212
 ,, Dorothy, 246
 ,, Edmund, 6
 ,, Edward, 39, 117, 142, 152, 195, 304
 ,, Elizabeth, 51, 166, 184, 252, 295
 ,, Ellen, 270
 ,, Ellinor, 207, 284
 ,, Ellis, 53
 ,, George, 277, 366
 ,, Henry, 28, 238, 246, 252, 259, 270, 277, c. of 328, 369
 ,, Isabel, 304
 ,, James, 177, 272
 ,, Jane, 59
 ,, John, 6, 46, 81, 202, 207, 211,* 218, 284
 ,, Lawrence, 131, 205, 212
 ,, Margaret, 277, 284
 ,, Mary, 74, 205, 209, 272, 277, 316
 ,, Ralph, 53
 ,, Richard, 1, 7, 20, 25,* 31, 66, 91, 166, 175, 213, 216, 220, 298, c. of 300, 336, 344
 ,, Robert, 138
 ,, Roger, 39
 ,, Susan, 212, 323
 ,, Thomas, 4,* 7, 28, 31, 46, 51, 59, 66, 74, 81, 89, 130, 136, 155, 169, 186, 201, 212, 213, 238, 295, w. of 323,* c. of 349
 ,, William, 303
Alte, Elizabeth, 242
 ,, Mr., 242
 ,, William, 236, 239, 242,* 280, 311, 338, 340, 343, 347, 349, 350, 372
Alton, Anne, 210
 ,, Jane, 216
 ,, John, 210, 216
Amffidsey, Jane, 1
 ,, William, 1
Amon, Catherine, 201
Andarton [see Anderton]
Anderson, Jennet, 195
 ,, Margaret, 203
Anderton [Andarton, Andertonu; Anndertonn],
 ,, Alice, 74
 ,, Ann, 8, 24, 203, 235
 ,, Edmund, 96, 138, 152, 171
 ,, Elizabeth, 157, 167, 208,* 284, 369

Anderton, Genet, 235
 ,, George, 213,* 220
 ,, Isabel, 180, 207, 264
 ,, James, 144, 157, 264
 ,, Jane, 82, 95, 303
 ,, John, 221, 270,* c. of 350, 368
 ,, Katherine, 142
 ,, Mary, 220
 ,, Richard, 16,* 24, 107, 142, 208, 284
 ,, Robert, 203, 208, 218,* 221, inf. of 282, c. of 294, 333
 ,, Thomas, 8, 74, 82, 109, 125, 190, 207, 215,* 303
Ankell, Elizabeth, 284
Armeroyd [see Ormerod]
Arneworth, Richard, 158, 214
 ,, William, 214
Armorod [see Ormerod]
Ash, Ann, 85
 ,, William, 85
Asheton [see Ashton]
Ashley [see Astley]
Ashton [Asheton, Aston],
 ,, Dorothy, 263
 ,, Edward, c. of 312
 ,, James, 263,* 367
 ,, Joany, 308
 ,, John, 255, 372 [?]
 ,, Mary, 335
 ,, Mr., 263, 367
 ,, Richard, 355
 ,, Susan, 263
 ,, Thomas, 255, c. of 343
Asley [see Astley]
Ashworth [Asheworth, Asheworthe, Ashworthe],
 ,, Abraham, 231
 ,, Agnes, 366
 ,, Alice, 34, 149, 258, 302, 353
 ,, Ann, 94, 187, 272
 ,, Arthur, 149, w. of 313
 ,, Dorothy, 157
 ,, Edmund, 210, 287, 293, w. of 311, 352
 ,, Elizabeth, 92, 221, 224, 372
 ,, George, 246
 ,, Gennet, 246
 ,, Imyn, 46
 ,, James, 50, 62, 73, 85, 258, 261,* c. of 329, w. of 329, c. of 339, c. of 341, 368
 ,, Jane, 27, 62, 185, 235, 282, 293
 ,, John, 41, 46, 77, 177, 249,* 282, 296, 300, 301, 354
 ,, Jonathan, 67
 ,, Leonard, 34, 41, 50, 65, 73, 82,

INDEX OF NAMES.

Vol. 1.—C. . pp. 1— 90 inclusive. Vol. 2.—C. . pp. 205—280 inclusive.
    B. . ,, 91—168 ,,   B. . ,, 281—350 ,,
    W. . ,, 169—204 ,,   W. . ,, 351—372 ,,

Ashworth, Leonard, *continued*—
    131, 141, 180, 212, 221, 281,
    c. of 292, 293, 301, 302, c. of
    303*
,, Margaret, 199
,, Mary, 82, 212, 227,* 249,* 281, 335
,, Richard, 40, 65, 85, 126, 184, 224, 300, c. of 323, 358
,, Robert, 27, 67, 193, 231, 235, c. of 293, 368
,, Susan, 363
,, Thomas, 77, 157, 272
,, William, 170
Asmall [Asmal, Asmale, Asmaull],
  [see also Aspinall],
,, Abraham, 55, 276
,, Alice, 107, 217
,, Ann, 113, 152
,, Elizabeth, 13, 45
,, Francis, 7, 13, 23,* 29, 41, 127
,, Henry, 256, 291
,, James, 295
,, John, 41, 65, 145, 152, 159, 167, 190, 195, 217, 276, c. of 332, w. of 332
,, Katherine, 105
,, Margaret, 159, 295
,, Mary, 260
,, Peter, 7
,, Rauffe (Ralph), 37, 45, 55, 103
,, Robert, 29
,, Roger, 65, 167
,, Thomas, 37, 123, 260
,, William, 15,* 256
Asmand, Elizabeth, 77
,, John, 77
Aspinall [Asnall, Aspinwall]
  [see also Asmall],
,, Alice, 229
,, Ann, 4, 69, 238, 264, 335, 348
,, Elizabeth, 267, 368
,, Ellen, 217, 229, 268
,, Francis, 4
,, Henry, 4, 338
,, James, 16, 354
,, Jane, 267
,, John, 7, 69, 183, 209, 229, 238, 260, 267, 269, 277, 298, c. of 298, c. of 300, 314, inf. of 342, c. of 347
,, Margaret, 25, 349, 362
,, Mary, 260, 264
,, Nicholas, 372
,, Rauffe (Ralph), 4, 7, 16, 25, 99, 264, 269, 300
,, Richard, 264, 268, 270, 278

Aspinall, Susan, 209
,, Thomas, 264, 267, 269, 270, 277, 278, w. of 315, 321, c. of 348, 368
,, William, 108, 217, 229, c. of 305, 338, 348, 349, 353
Astley [Ashley, Asley, Asselay],
,, Alice, 262
,, James, 240
,, Randle, 266
,, Robert, 224
,, Thomas, 262, 266
,, William, 202, 224, 240
Aston [see Ashton], John, 372
Atkinson [Adkinson], James, 259, 265, 335, c. of 336
,, John, 259
,, Mary, 265
Atton [see also Hatton],
,, Elizabeth, 222
,, John, 222, 234, 241*
,, Thomas, 234
Aynesworth [Aynsworth]
  [see Ainsworth]

B

Babbs, Laurence, 268
,, Mary, 268
Baguley [Bagley, Bageley],
,, John, 197, 216
,, Richard, 216
,, William, 202
Baily, Balie [see Bayley],
Balshaw, Elizabeth, 367
Bamford [Bamforde, Bamforth, Bamforthe, Bamforte],
,, Alexander, 254, 327
,, Ann, 247, 323
,, Edward, 370
,, Gennet, 167
,, Henry, 189
,, James, 13
,, Jane, 264, 324
,, John, 29
,, Margaret, 157
,, Mary, 242
,, Mr., 254, 260, 266, w. of 321, 324, c. of 325, 327, 343
,, Mrs., 323
,, Samuel, 266, 312, 323
,, Susan, 29
,, Thomas, 13
,, William, 156, 167, 242, 247, 260,* 264, 266, 303
Banaster [see Bannister]
Bancroft [Bancrofte, Bankrofte],

Vol. 1.—C. . pp. 1— 90 inclusive. Vol. 2.—C. . pp. 205—280 inclusive.
   B. . ,, 91—108 ,,   B. . ,, 281—350 ,,
   W. . ,, 109—204 ,,   W. . ,, 351—372 ,,

Bancroft, Ann, 213
   ,, William, 212,* 213, 292,* 353
Banks [Banckes], Alexander, 117
Bannister [Banaster, Banester,
   Banister, Banistr,
   Bannest, Bannester],
   ,, Ann, 279
   ,, Elizabeth, 234
   ,, Henry, 258, 260*
   ,, James, 195
   ,, Lawrence, 216
   ,, Mary, 222
   ,, Richard, 210,* 216, 222, 234,
       240, 248, 258, 271,* 279, c. of
       322, 352, 370
   ,, Roger, 248
   ,, William, 240
Baraclough, Mary, 341
Barker, John, 15, 88, c. of 309
   ,, Richard, 43, 79,* 88, 199
   ,, Thomas, 15, 43, 179
Barlow [Barllowe, Barlowe,
   Barlowes],
   ,, Abraham, 272, 279
   ,, Alice, 25, 49, 78, 155, 189, 227,
       232, 237, 239,* 241, 254, 265,
       308, 309, 311
   ,, Ambrose, 133, 165
   ,, Ann, 32, 35, 63, 67, 92, 121, 127,
       180, 230, 238, 243, 246, 254,
       262, 264, 287, 296, 297, 298,
       357, 361, 366
   ,, Bartholomew, 42
   ,, Charles, 144
   ,, Christian, 372
   ,, Dorothy, 9, 204, 222, 223, 225,
       226, 264, 276
   ,, Edmund, 1, 15, 41,* 86, 89, 106,
       202, 225, 233, 254, 258, 273,
       s. of 327, 338, 355
   ,, Edward, 41, 232, 264,* 272, 280,
       309, 330, c. of 335, c. of 344,
       c. of 348, 359
   ,, Elizabeth, 35, 45, 46, 178, 180,
       195, 217, 224, 233, 273, 292,
       303, 335, 342, 351
   ,, Ellen, 30, 32,* 240, 301, 360
   ,, Francis, 18, 22, 34,* 91, 92,* 103,
       105, 126, 181, 220, 232, 266,
       295, 308, 334, 350
   ,, George, 32, 54, 338
   ,, Grace, 295
   ,, Humphrey, 41, 227, 232, 238,
       c. of 307, c. of 317, 318
   ,, Isabel, 165
   ,, James, 6, 14, 15, 18,* 22, 26, 32,
       34, 37, 41, 45, 49, 56, 61, 67,

Barlow, James, continued—
       68, 73,* 78,* 103, 121, 127,
       130, 135, 141, 147, 155, 157,
       160, 195, 206, 207, 208, 214,
       222, 227, 232, 277, 287, wid. of
       289, 295, 298, 299, 306, 309,
       310
   ,, Jane, 243
   ,, Jerimy, 207, 214, 221, 223, 227,
       230, 241, 242, 273, 297, c. of
       316, w. of 321, 342, c. of 345,
       w. of 345, 347
   ,, Joan, 201
   ,, John, 21, 23, 26,* 27,* 32, 37,
       43,* 45, 54, 61, 63, 65, 67, 73,
       81, 89, 107, 114, 118, 119, 146,
       148, 174, 175, 178, 203, 210,
       217, 221, 222, 225,* 227, 230,
       231, 237, 242, 243, 246, 248,*
       254, 255,* 262, 264, 265, 266,
       267,* 271, 274, 275, 276, 280,
       290,* 292, 297,* c. of 300, c. of
       303, 303, 309, c. of 313, c. of
       317,* c. of 318, c. of 322, 323,*
       345, 359, 360, 368
   ,, Katherine, 21, 41, 179, 321
   ,, Margaret, 1, 68, 133, 180, 222,
       323, 350, 365
   ,, Margerie, 53, c. of 301
   ,, Martha, 271
   ,, Mary, 5, 86, 146, 214, 228, 266,
       267, 270, 273, 279
   ,, Ralph, 56, 210, 235
   ,, Richard, 5, 6, 26,* 30, 32, 34,
       41, 42, 53, 54, 67, 72,* 75,*
       81, 96, 101, 115, 119, 134, 141,
       147, 148, 179, 181, 182, 206,
       222, 228, 230, 232, 235, 243,
       246, 258, 264, 274, 276, 277,
       280,* 290, 296, w. of 301, 301,
       c. of 307, 308, 311,* w. of 316,
       c. of 317, 333, 346, 359, 360,
       368
   ,, Robert, 9, 18, 21, 25, 41, 42,*
       120, 133, 134, 206, 246, 266,
       270, 284, w. of 315, 351
   ,, Roger, 73, 78, 157
   ,, Sarah, 220
   ,, Simon, 208, 218, 224, 227, 240
       (Symond), 303, c. of 312, 351
   ,, Susan, 45, 78, 218, 299
   ,, Thomas, 14, 21, 23, 46, 54, 65,
       73,* 82, 206, 214, 222, 226,
       231, 275, 276, 316, c. of 319,
       321, 328, 333, 334, w. of 341,
       343
   ,, William, 82, 266, 348

INDEX OF NAMES. 377

Vol. 1.—C. . pp. 1— 90 inclusive. Vol. 2.—C. . pp. 205—280 inclusive.
      B. . ,, 91—168 ,,   B. . ,, 281—450 ,,
      W. . ,, 169—204 ,,   W. . ,, 451—572 ,,

Barlow, Winifred, 367
Barnes, Adam, 174
,, Ellen, 144
,, George, 261, 367
,, Henry, 141, 144
,, James, 352
,, John, 261, 355
,, Margaret, 352
Baron [Barren], Ann, 55, 69
,, Elizabeth, 7
,, Ellis, 7
,, Isabel, 282
,, James, 3, 11,* 22, 117, 119, 229, 306
,, John, 11, 284
,, Mary, 360
,, Peter, 3, 12, 119, 352
,, Ralph, 12, 21, 28,* 132, 136, 171, 191, 282, s. of 331, 336
,, Richard, 21, 55, 69, 229, 342, 352, 356
,, Thomas, 22
Barres, John, 182
Bartles, Hugh, 268
,, Robert, 268
Bate [Bates, Bats], Alice, 39, 55
,, Ann, 176, 217, c. of 293, 327
,, Elizabeth, 95
,, Ellen, 33, 152
,, Ellinor, 73
,, James, 304
,, Jennet, 214, 293
,, John, 14, 24,* 33, 39, 55, 73, 95, 103, 121, 133, 152, 245,* 283, c. of 305, w. of 340, 356
,, Katherine, 295
,, Margaret, 14, 214, 293, 358
,, Mary, 217
,, Thomas, 357
,, William, 177
Bath, Mr., 372
,, Robert, 372
Battersby [Batersbie, Batersby, Battersbie, Battersbue, Batterscby, Battursby],
,, Alice, 8, 9, 25, 49, 75, 154, 203, 221, 294, 297, 362, 364
,, Andrew, 136
,, Ann, 31, 37, 297, 354
,, Cicely, 283
,, Dorothy, 29, 53, 302
,, Edmund, 91,* 107, 171, 263, 311
,, Edward, 167
,, Elizabeth, 6, 36, 43, 144, 176, 228
,, Ellen, 65, 214
,, George, 25, 37, 53, 71,* 174, 213,

Battersby, George continued—
   228, 231, 245, 282, 285,* c. of 306, s. of 317
,, Isabel, 47, 189
,, James, 49, 100, 133, 134, 169, 176, 191, 255, 281
,, Jane, 151
,, John, 38, 151, 224,* 255, 273, w. of 317, c. of 327, c. of 328, 343,* 355
,, Katherine, 161, 282, 285
,, Lawrence, 154, 288
,, Margaret, 231
,, Margerie, 190
,, Mary, 19, 80, 195, 196
,, "One," 105
,, Ralph, 85,* 96, 214, 230*
,, Richard, 2,* 8, 23,* 31, 38, 43, 51, 61, 67, 75, 80, 107, 111, 123, 135, 143, 161, 176, 213, 221, 253, 256, 263, 273, 290, 293, 297, two infants of 311, w. of 317, c. of 325, c. of 347
,, Robert, 174, 281, w. of 314
,, Susan, 196
,, Thomas, 6, 9, 19, 29, 36, 47, 65, 67, 245, 255, 256, 285,* 290
,, William, 51, 61, 253
Baule, Jennet, 200
,, John, 162
,, Mary, 162
Baxenden, Alice, 277, 366
,, Richard, 277
,, Thomas, 366
Bayley [Baily, Balie, Bayle, Bayly],
,, Ellen, 292
,, Jeffery, 81
,, Jodrell, 7
,, Judith, 291
,, Ralph, 202, 291, 292
,, Roger, 81
,, Thomas, 7
Beacom [see Beckome]
Bealie, Isabel, 364
Beamond [Beaman, Beamman, Beeman, Bemon, Bemonde, Bymonde],
,, Alice, 33, 285
,, Ann, 111
,, Elizabeth, 365
,, Humphrey, 368
,, Jane, 29
,, Lawrence, 33
,, Richard, 147, 285
,, Susan, 29
Beasicke [see Beswicke]
Beckome [Beacome, Bockome],

Vol. 1.—C. . pp. 1— 90 inclusive. Vol. 2.—C. . pp. 205—280 inclusive
    B. . ,, 91—168 ,,   B. . ,, 281—350 ,,
    W. . ,, 169—204 ,,   W. . ,, 351—372 ,,

Beckome, Arthur, 252
  ,, Edmund, 252, 363
  ,, Edward, 338
  ,, Susan, 338
Becman [see Beamond]
Beirch [see Birch]
Belfelde, Dorothy, 188
Bellet, John, 363
Bemon [see Beamond]
Benson [Bensone, Bensonn, Bensun],
  ,, Caleb, 206
  ,, Edmund, 86,* 201, 210, w. of 318, 339
  ,, Elizabeth, 275
  ,, James, 210
  ,, Jane, 163
  ,, John, 71, 321
  ,, Jony, 201
  ,, Katherine, 275
  ,, Mary, 81
  ,, Robert, 71, 81, 150, 196, 206, w. of 301, 363
  ,, William, 92,* 135, 163, 169, 190, 281, 291,* 300
Bentley [Bentily, Bently],
  ,, Abigal, 273
  ,, Abraham, 206
  ,, Ann, 260
  ,, Edward, 248
  ,, Isabel, 255
  ,, Katherine, 250
  ,, Jane, 41
  ,, Jennet, 203
  ,, John, 29, 243, 255, 272,* 343
  ,, Martha, 64, 367
  ,, Matthew, w. of 327
  ,, Michael, 20,* 29, 41, 52, 64, 76, 173, 206, 243, 248, 250, 254, 273, 303, 347, w. of 348, 355
  ,, Richard, 76, 260
  ,, Sarah, 254
  ,, Thomas, 52
Berche [see Birch]
Berde [see Bird]
Berie, Berry, Berrye, [see Bury]
Beswicke [Beasicke, Beusweeke, Bewsicke, Bexwicke, Bexwike, Busicke],
  ,, Ann, 52, 210, 216, 231, 292, 326, 364
  ,, Edmund, 216, 292
  ,, Hugh, 29
  ,, Martha, 364
  ,, Mary, 231
  ,, Richard, 29
  ,, Robert, 52
  ,, Susan, 368

Beswicke, Thomas, 210
Bicrofte, Thomas, 141
Bidd [see Bird], Marie, 266
  ,, Thomas, 266
Biggman, Ould, 300
Bikonsonn, John, 268*
Birch [Beirch, Berche, Birche, Byrche],
  ,, Alice, 22
  ,, Ann, 38, 45, 223
  ,, Barnaby, 299
  ,, Elizabeth, 196
  ,, Francis, 38
  ,, Henry, 240
  ,, Isaak, 252
  ,, James, 22, 215, 289, 293
  ,, John, 205, 218
  ,, Katherine, 161, 218
  ,, Margaret, 290
  ,, Mary, 186, 245
  ,, Owen, 123
  ,, Ralph, 18*
  ,, Richard, 26, 45, 103, 114, 117, 140, 290, w. of 320, w. of 326
  ,, Sarah, 230
  ,, Susan, 26, 185
  ,, Thomas, 205, 215, 223, 230, 240, 245, 252
  ,, Ursula, 182
Bird [Berde, Bidd, Birde, Brid, Bridd, Bridde, Byrd],
  ,, Alice, 276
  ,, Ann, 79, 149, 270, 365
  ,, Jane, 253, 289
  ,, John, 149, 174, 246,* 253, 270, 276, 362
  ,, Mary, 266
  ,, Robert, 79, 113, 289
  ,, Thomas, 266
Birrie [see Bury]
Birom, Birome [see Byrome]
Birstall, Edward, 159
Birtwistle [Birtwisle, Burtwistle],
  ,, Ann, 282
  ,, Elizabeth, 357
Blakeley [Blacklawe, Blakelawe, Blakeleye, Blakely, Blakley],
  ,, Alice, 26, 354
  ,, Ann, 37
  ,, Dorothy, 52
  ,, Edmund, 262
  ,, Ellen, 154
  ,, James, 198
  ,, Jane, 44, 342
  ,, John, 99, 158, 172, 217
  ,, Katherine, 164
  ,, Margaret, 18

INDEX OF NAMES.

Vol. 1.—C. . pp. 1— 90 inclusive. Vol. 2.—C. . pp. 205—280 inclusive.
 B. . ,, 91—168 ,, B. . ,, 281—350 ,,
 W. . ,, 169—204 ,, W. . ,, 351—377 ,,

Blakeley, Ralph, 1, 18, 26, 37, 44, 52, 123, 217, 257, 353
,, Richard, 154, 288
,, Thomas, 1, 257, 262, 290, c. of 324, c. of 336
Blakey, Mary, 201
Blacklow [Blacklowe, Blakclow, Blakelowe, Blaklow, Blaklowe],
,, Ann, 356
,, Dorothy, 320, 322
,, Elizabeth, 354
,, Ellen, 246
,, Ellinor, 269
,, Joan, 308
,, John, 358
,, Margaret. 319
,, Ralph, 311, w. of 315
,, Thomas, 246, 269, 290, c. of 336, 360
Blomley [Blomeley, Blomeleye],
,, Ann, 146
,, John, 13
,, "One," 110
,, Samuel, 13
,, William, 107, 146, 169
Boardman [Bordman],
,, Elizabeth, 34
,, George, 34
,, Henry, 51,* 301, w. of 318, 353
,, Hugh, 349
,, Jane, 358, 367
,, Robert, 70
,, Thomas, 70, 301
Bockome [see Beckome]
Bolton [Boulton, Bowlton],
,, Adam, 180
,, Alice, 317
,, Ann, 70
,, Elizabeth, 123
,, Francis, 23
,, Grace, 368
,, Isabel, 49
,, Jane, 57, 323
,, John, 15, 23, 32, 42, 49, 57, 70, 81,* 174, 323, 332, 365
,, Margaret, 32
,, Margery, 292
,, Peter, 42, 121, 292
,, Richard, 15
,, Rosamund, 177
Booker [see Bowker]
Booth [Boothe, Both, Bothe, Bouth, Bouthe],
,, Alice, 9, 24, 38, 51, 65, 69, 72, 82, 149, 151, 156, 165, 197,* 206, 212, 224, 226, 229, 234,

Booth, Alice, continued—
265, 283, 284, 293, 340, 351, 366, 367, 370, 371, 372
,, Ann, 4, 23, 34, 52, 80, 83, 87, 93, 161, 162, 178, 181, 200, 206, 213, 220, 243,* 244, 281, c. of 330, 332, 348, 353
,, Annis, 23
,, Anthony, 15, 23, 33, 46, 63,* 64, 127, 143, 144, 193, 194, 270, 293, 316, inf. of 312, 355
,, Bridget, 75, 367
,, Charles, 75
,, Christopher, 7, 12, 17, 25, 29, 58, 84, 93, 100, 103, 112,* 114, 118, 135, 161, 163, 164, 283, 305, w. of 329
,, Dorothy, 5, 39, 41, 42, 155, 159, 235, 263, 361
,, Edmund, 9, 40, 46, 73,* 79, 82, 93,* 126, 154,* 184, 197, 207, 225, 258, 263,* 277, 292, c. of 293, 306, c. of 307, 307, 316, two twines of 346
,, Edward, 218, 279, 371
,, Elizabeth, 6, 7, 17, 27, 29, 35, 43, 53, 58, 60, 61, 70, 72, 156, 178, 205, 207, 213, 218, 221, 224, 226, 239, 258, 267, 276, 278, 279, 288, 298, 301, 303, 316, 333, 336, 337, 338, 353, 359, 360, 369
,, Ellen, 27, 35, 63, 79,* 81, 157, 181, 201, 209, 212, 250, 263, 333, 371
,, Ellinor, 207 305
,, Elsabell, 222
,, Frances, 333
,, Francis, 6, 11,* 27, 33, 38, 48, 51,* 55, 58,* 61, 83, 101, 108, 145, 151, 162, 168, 179, 208, 223, 255 * 258, 262, 265, 277, w. of 341, c. of 347, 364, 370*
,, Geffraye, 130
,, George, 12, 228, 241, 299
,, Gervis, 106
,, Grace, 249. 371
,, Harry, c. of 342
,, Henry, 28, 72, 151, 156, 197, 233, 236, 243, 244, 254, 260, 268, 271, 272,* 302,* c. of 331, 337, w. of 343, 344, 351, 360, 369
,, Humphrey, 251
,, Isabel, 6, 27, 35, 56, 185, 292, 297, 354
,, James, 28, 38, 49, 265, 279, 296

Vol. 1.—C. . pp. 1— 90 inclusive. Vol. 2.—C. . pp. 205—280 inclusive.
B. . „ 91—168 „ B. . „ 281—350 „
W. . „ 169—204 „ W. . „ 351—372 „

Booth, Jane, 23, 26, 34, 48, 68, 152, 243,* 279, 285, 301,* 339
„ Jennet, 156
„ John, 15, 23,* 27, 32, 34, 35,* 42, 43, 44, 48, 52, 54, 57, 58,* 62, 63, 65, 67, 69,* 72, 75, 76,* 79,* 82, 83,* 86,* 87, 88,* 89, 119, 128,* 133, 136, 140, 145, 149, 150, 152,* 157, 159, 161, 162, 181, 192, 196, 205,* 211,* 212, 213, 218, 221, 223, 226, 227, 230, 232, 236,* 237, 242, 244, 250, 258, 260, 264, 266, 267, 269, 271, 276,* 277, 280, 283, 284, 285, 288, 289,* 297, w. of 302, 303,* 307, 308, 313, c. of 318, c. of 323, c. of 324, w. of 326, 328, w. of 329, w. of 334, c. of 334, 336, c. of 338, 339, w. of 341, c. of 341, w. of 343, c. of 345, w. of 349, 355, 357, 359, 368, 371
„ Jonie, 184
„ Joseph, 267
„ Josias, 238, 339
„ Katherine, 26, 28, 48, 76, 87, 115, 145, 155, 180, 196, 233, 249, 257, 283
„ Margaret, 6, 35, 38, 50, 67, 76, 79, 158, 186, 198, 230, 254, 260, 290, 359, 368, 371
„ Margerie, 150, 164
„ Mary, 26, 27, 46, 55, 67,* 151, 178, 185, 192, 206, 208, 211,* 225, 231, 237, 241,* 243, 244, 260,* 262, 269, 272, 274, 276, 280, 283, 302, 362, 363, 364, 368
„ Mathew, 6, 25, 51, 134, 162, 189, 206, 222, 241,* 260, 263, 279, 285, 301, 336, w. of 344, 354, 370
„ Maude, 149
„ Maudlen, 150
„ Oliver, 33, 41, 51, 61, 76, 80,* 123, 155, 181, 206, w. of 331
„ Peter, 53, 68, 13, 152, 165, 188, 281
„ Ralph, 34, 44, 47, 129, 132, 170, 186, 187, 234, w. of 315, 318
„ Ranulph, 62
„ Richard, 17, 47, 49, 50, 60, 65,* 67, 69,* 70, 71,* 72, 75, 79, 82,* 83, 87, 92, 97, 131, 145,* 151, 195, 196, 206,* 208, 209, 212, 213, 218, 220, 221, 224,

Booth, Richard, continued—
226,* 227, 229, 230,* 234, 235, 236, 238, 239,* 241,* 242, 244, 249, 251, 254, 257, 258, 260, 263, 264, 267, 271, 272, 283,* 289, 294, 295,* c. of 296, 302, 303, c. of 310, c. of 315, c. of 322, c. of 323, 325, 328, w. of 331, 333,* 336, 337,* 338, 340, 356, 362, 367, 372
„ Robert, 28, 38,* 39, 46, 51, 53, 57, 61, 65, 72, 76, 80, 82, 84,* 143, 158, 178, 197, 207, 230, 268, 284,* 285, c. of 294, 296, 313, c. 325, 365
„ Roger, 4, 9,* 16, 35, 48,* 50,* 55, 58, 60,* 63, 70,* 72, 82, 83,* 99, 106,* 127, 135, 138, 150, 155,* 179, 191, 198, 199, 206, 208, 213, 216,* 220, 228, 234, 243, 244, 260, 265, 267, 269, 279, 284,* 293, 295, c. of 320, 336, w. of 338, 339, two twines of 346
„ Sarah, 88, 359
„ Susan, 33, 230, 254, 293
„ Thomas, 5, 6,* 13, 23, 24, 26, 35,* 44, 47, 48, 51, 53, 54, 56, 58, 67,* 69,* 79,* 80, 82, 89,* 96, 97, 112, 122,* 131, 133, 135, 136,* 141, 150, 151, 152, 156, 158, 159, 164, 169,* 177, 186, 192, 199, 205, 213, 214, 219, 220, 221, 224, 226, 227,* 231, 232, 234, 236, 241, 243, 255, 266, 270, 271, 277, 278, inf. of 286, 287,* 290, 295, c. of 300, 301,* 303, w. of 319, c. of 323, c. of 324, w. of 327, 329, 337, c. of 340, 350, 351, 354, 356
„ William, 13, 16, 17, 58, 67, 72, 81, 89, 97,* 100, 122, 126, 143, 190, 198, 212,* 214, 219, 234, 249, 258, 267, 269, 274, 283, 289, 293, c. of 299, 332, 339, 369

Bordman [see Boardman]
Both, Bothe [see Booth]
Boukar, Bowkar [see Bowker]
Boulton [see Bolton]
Bouth, Bouthe [see Booth]
Bower, Mary, 365
„ Samuel, 190
Bowker [Booker, Bowker, Boukar, Bouker],
„ George, 352
„ Grace, 198

Vol. 1.—C. . *pp.* 1— 90 *inclusive*. *Vol. 2.—C.* . *pp.* 205—280 *inclusive.*
      B. . ,, 91—108 ,,   *B.* . ,, 281—350 ,,
      W. . ,, 109—204 ,,   *W.* . ,, 351—377 ,,

Bowker, John, 254
,, Michael, 342
,, William, 254, 363
Bradley [Bradleye, Bradly],
,, Ann, 217
,, Daniel, 28
,, George, 267, 271, 339
,, James, 26, 178, w. of 289
,, John, 4, 107, 267, 271
,, Katherine, 26
,, Margaret, 199
,, Mary, 339
,, Nathaniel. 28
,, Robert, 217, 331
,, Roger, 4
Bradshaw [Bradshawe],
,, Alexander, 252, 352
,, Ann, 88, 257
,, Elizabeth, 218
,, Ellen, 263
,, Ellis, 180
,, George, 88, 211, 218, 222, 279,*
     c. of 294
,, Hugh, 252, 263, c. of 328
,, Jane, 181
,, John, 135, 189, 191, 211, 259*
,, Lawrence, 257
,, Margerie, 360
,, Mary, 222
Brady, Esther, 200
Brearley [Brealey, Breareley, Brearlie,
     Breerlaye, Breerley, Breerly,
     Brerley, Brerleye, Brerly,
     Brierly],
,, Dorothy, 18, 356
,, Edmund, 257. 262, 274
,, Edward, 262
,, Henry, 257
,, Isabel, 284
,, James, 58, 65,* 85, 165, 205,
     217, 226, 233, 251, 287
,, John, 7, 274, 284, 285, 286
,, Jonathan, 226
,, Katherine, 369
,, Margaret, 6, 303
,, Margarie, 202
,, Martha, 233
,, Mary, 85, 165, 205, 217, 219,
     287, 367
,, Richard, 219
,, Robert, 168, 303, 353
,, Roger, 7, 18, 202, w. of 327, 341
,, Samuel, 153
,, Sarah, 58
,, Thomas, 251, 372
Brendwood, Elizabeth, 256
,, Oliver, 256, c. of 331, 369

Brid, Bridd, Bridde [see Bird]
Bridge [Bridg, Bridge, Brige]
     [see also Briggs],
,, Abraham, 128, 206, 319, 324
,, Alice, 29, 56, 160, 182. 188, 189,
     219, 224, 263, 278, 285, 287,
     354, 356, 357
,, Ann, 36, 57, 179, 193, 207, 258,
     263, 275, 294, 297, 302, 324,
     357
,, Annis, 26
,, Bartholomew, 13, 110, 172
,, Benjamin, 221, 297
,, Christopher, 119
,, Deborah, 267
,, Diana, 223, 285
,, Edmund, 13, 31, 118, 153, 155,
     180, 219,* 223, 230, 237
,, Elizabeth. 7, 35, 39, 154, 155,
     183, 190, 204, 206, 209, 215,
     230, 237, 247, 266, 270, 273,
     278, 300, 305, 369
,, Ellen, 177, 217
,, Francis, 73, 84, 152, 355
,, Geffray, 127
,, Henry, 39, 99, 223, 231, 239,
     252,* 262, 267, 270, 276, c. of
     294, c. of 334
,, James, 84, 99
,, Jane, 7, 19, 194, 347, 359
,, John, 5, 7, 11, 19, 25, 36, 69, 72,
     79, 80, 122,* 126, 130, 149,
     150, 169, 170, 182, 196, 207,*
     210, 213, 217, 219, 225, 240,
     254, 262, 273, 276, 278, 287,
     c. of 305, c. of 320, 325, two
     c. of 334, 342, w. of 347,
     370
,, Joseph, 221, 302
,, Joshua, 229
,, Judith, 11, 264
,, Katherine, 12, 63, 230, 364
,, Lawrence, 102
,, Margaret, 3, 118, 179, 180, 202,
     237, 256, 287, 323, 354, 358
,, Mary, 5, 56, 68, 202, 238, 241,
     249, 252, 257
,, Ottiwell, 183
,, Ralph, 11,* 17,* 19, 25, 28, 29,
     36, 39, 47, 55, 57, 69, 72, 79,
     95, 111, 114, 118, 125, 128,
     138, 140, 162, 171, 174,*
     191, 209, 210, 224, 230,* 238,
     248,* 250, 256, 257, 263, 266,
     275, 276, 294, 302, 328, w. of
     337, 357, 351
,, Ranulph, 63

O

Vol. 1.—C. . pp. 1— 90 inclusive. Vol. 2.—C. . pp. 205—280 inclusive.
  B. . ,, 91—168 ,,   B. . ,, 281—350 ,,
  W. . ,, 169—204 ,,   W. . ,, 351—372 ,,

Bridge, Richard, 12, 17, 26, 39, 47, 165, 171, 210, 231, 237, 241, 247, 248, 252, 254, 258, 264, 270, 285,* 287, 289
  ,, Robert, 73, 152, 202, w. of 329
  ,, Sarah, 223
  ,, Susan, 162
  ,, Thomas, 6, 19, 24,* 28, 31, 32, 35, 80, 92, 114, 121, 123, 136, 142, 142, 159, 164, 176, 234, 238, 239, 240, 249, 270, 282, 294, 296, 297, 300,* 309, 326
  ,, William, 32, 68, 186, 193, 225, 230, 238, 248, 250, w. of 314, 317, 323
  ,, Zachary, 207, 213, 215, 219,* 221, 224,* 229, 234, 294, 297, 299,* 302, 305,* c. of 310, w. of 314, c. of 317, w. of 325
Bridgman, Thomas, 337*
Briercliffe [Bruerchff, Bruercliffe, Bruerclyffe, Brurcliffe],
  ,, Ann, 290
  ,, James, 145, 180
  ,, Katherine, 197
Brierley [see Brearley]
Briggs [Brige, Brigge, Bridges], [see also Bridge],
  ,, Ann, 64, 231, 275
  ,, Elizabeth, 53, 270
  ,, Henry, 270
  ,, James, 64
  ,, Jerimy, 341
  ,, Judith, 38, 53, 193
  ,, Laurence, 38
  ,, Martin, 159
  ,, Ralph, 275
  ,, Richard, 270
  ,, Thomas, 231, 270
Brindle, Alice, 116
  ,, Elizabeth, 156
  ,, Ellen, 176, 213
  ,, John, 213
  ,, Richard, 156, 270
Broadly, Robert, 342
Broghton [see Broughton]
Broke [see Brook]
Brokshaw, Elizabeth, 285
Bromley [Bromelie, Bromeley, Bromeleye, Bromely, Bromileye, Bromileye, Bromilee, Bromille, Bromlee, Broomle],
  ,, Adam, 121
  ,, Ann, 198, 242
  ,, Dorothy, 246
  ,, Elizabeth, 15

Bromley, Ellen, 45
  ,, George, 8, 15, 26,* 35, 45, 55, 144, 151, 155, 170, 225, 303
  ,, Humphrey, 225
  ,, Jane, 144
  ,, John, 225, 234
  ,, Katherine, 55, 155
  ,, Margaret, 226, 253, c. of 324
  ,, Margerie, 55, 238, 246
  ,, Robert, 82*
  ,, Roger, 8, 219,* 226, 234, 242, 253, 354
  ,, Sarah (Zara), 225
  ,, Thomas, 35, 151, 238
Bromhead, Henry, 71*, 197
  ,, Mary, 354
Broomle [see Bromley]
Brook [Broke, Brooke, Brookes, Broncke, Brucke],
  ,, Abraham, 35, 125
  ,, Adam, 57
  ,, Alice, 12, 75, 151, 179, 180, 243, 265, 346, 368
  ,, Ambrose, 19, 22, 37, 116, 123, 175
  ,, Ann, 24, 115, 215, 269, 278, 280, 291
  ,, Charles, 223, 292, w. of 319
  ,, Dorothy, 41, 361
  ,, Edward, 208
  ,, Elizabeth, 3, 89, 130, 151, 162, 223, 262, 263, 308, 314, 342, 351, 353, 356
  ,, Ellen, 158, 193, 276, 282
  ,, Geffray, 44, 238, 244, 250, 253, 259, 263, 269, c. of 317, c. of 319, c. of 320,* w. of 321, 342, 343, 364
  ,, George, 211, 280
  ,, Giles, 150*
  ,, Henry, 104, 162, 174, 202, 259, 284
  ,, Isabel, 19
  ,, James, 37, 38, 87, 167, 205, 254,* 262, 276, 282, 348*
  ,, Jane, 41, 61, 73, 131, 248, 283, 319, 360
  ,, John, 22, 25, 33, 41, 50,* 60, 61, 73, 74, 88, 90, 104, 105, 108, 110, 112, 115, 120, 126, 131, 144, 148, 151,* 166, 178, 205, 211,* 215, 243, 262, 265, 267,* 270,* 274, 280, 282, 288,* 291, c. of 307, c. of 310, c. of 313, w. of 328, 328, 343, 346, c. of 349, 354, 357
  ,, Katherine, 18, 352

INDEX OF NAMES.

Vol. 1.—C. . pp. 1—90 inclusive. Vol. 1.—C. . pp. 205—280 inclusive.
     B. . ,, 91—168 ,,   B. . ,, 281—350 ,,
     W. . ,, 169—204 ,,   W. . ,, 351—372 ,,

Brook, Laurence, 90
 ,, Margaret, 66, 148
 ,, Mary, 33, 41, 57, 152, 166, 221, 274, 320
 ,, Matthew, 292
 ,, Peter, 206, 278
 ,, Ralph, 3, 12, 13, 25, 27, 38, 100, 108, 111, 136,* 156, 158,* 164, 279,* 282
 ,. Richard, 18, 24, 34,* 44, 56, 60, 66, 74, 75, 87, 89, 91, 120, 135, 152, 167, 174, 206, 238, 244, 250, 262, 302
 ,, Robert, 280
 ,, Roger, 56
 ,, Thomas, 198, 208, 211, 253, 282, 301
 ,, Thurstan, 27, 137, 217, wid. of 289, 292, 294, 335
 ,, William, 13, 35, 88, 130, 143, 170, 217, 221, 248, 283, 292, 294
Broome [Broume], Alice, c. of 341, 372
 ,, Grace, 257
 ,, Humphrey, 220, 238, 257, c. of 339
 ,, John, 371, 372
 ,, Margaret, 220
 ,, Mary, 238
Broucke [see Brook]
Broughton [Broghton, Broughtonn],
 ,, Alice, 180, 289
 ,, Elizabeth, 221
 ,, John, 213, 221, 231, 289, 290, c. of 311, c. of 312, 356
 ,, Lawrence, 213, 290
 ,, Sarah, 231
Brown [Browne], Anthony, 10
 ,, Edmund, 230
 ,, Humphrey, 230
 ,, Jony, 180
 ,, Mary, 266
 ,, Rachell, 276
 ,, Thomas, 266, 276
 ,, William, 10
Brownlow [Brownlowe, Brownelowe],
 ,, Dorothy, 180
 ,, Katherine, 189
Brucke [see Brook]
Bruercliffe [see ante Briercliffe]
Bruntliffe, James, 28*
Brurcliffe [see Briercliffe]
Brusame, William, 103
Buckley [Bucklay, Bucklaye, Buckle, Buckleye, Buckly, Buckley, Bukley],
 ,, Abraham, 319

Buckley, Alice, 190, 212, 264, 284, 288, 294
 ,, Allen, 7, 16, 40, 45, 52, 60, 118, 126, 136, 155
 ,, Ann, 7, 66, 180, 195, 226, 338
 ,, Dorothy, 13, 16, 176, 212, 293, 348, 355
 ,, Elizabeth, 40, 49, 60, 62, 78, 193, 201, 270, 349
 ,, George, 246
 ,, Isabel, 294
 ,, James, 7, 42, 125, 230,* 238, 246, 255, 265, 288, 340, 352, 355, 358
 ., Jennet, 285
 ,, Joan, 202
 ,, John, 2, 13, 73, 99, 208, 213, 226, 237, 243, 248, 255, 260, 264, 270, 271, 274,* 275, 279,* 280, 298, 335, 338, inf. of 340, 348, 367, 370
 ,, Katherine, 36, 260
 ,, Laurence, 213
 ,, Mary, 73, 217, 265, 275, 354
 ,, Michael, 248
 ,, Owen, 2
 ,, Ralph, 7, 45, 243, 284, 317, c. of 317, 361
 ,, Richard, 35, 42, 49, 123, 137, 181, 220, 238, 337, 344
 ., Sarah, 237, 271
 .. Thomas, 52, 62, 66, 68,* 72,* 73,* 78, 148,* 154,* 194, 268, 212, 217, 220, 227,* 280, 285,* 293, 312, c. of 312, w. of 314, 337
 ,, William, 285
Buersill, Isabel, 369
Bukley [see Buckley]
Burgesse, Jane, 372
Burns [Burnes], Alice, 372
 ., Margaret, 106
Burton, Ann, 45, 300
 ,, Edmund, 66
 ,, Edward, 45, 83, 300, c. of 300
 ,, Margaret, 66
 ,, N.N.N., 83, 211
 ,, Wife of 211
Burtsall, Edward, 183
Burtwistle [see Birtwistle]
Bury [Berie, Berry, Berrye, Birrie, Burie],
 ,, Alice, 31, 223,* 230, 264, 270, 275, 302, 353, 363
 ,, Andrew, 180, 223, 232,* 252
 ,, Ann, 3, 139, 185, 189, 205, 216, 279, 283, 341, 354

Vol. 1.—C. . pp. 1— 90 inclusive. Vol. 2.—C. . pp. 205—280 inclusive.
   B. . ,, 91—168 ,,   B. . ,, 281—350 ,,
   W. . ,, 169—204 ,,   W. . ,, 351—372 ,,

Bury, Bestian, 23
,, Deborah, 29, 204, 274
,, Dorothy, 286
,, Edith, 357
,, Edmund, 16, 28, 117, 224, w. of 339
,, Elizabeth, 201, 243, 248, 258, 336
,, Ellen, 16, 259, 292
,, Francis, 15, 29, 53, 67, 78, 102, 146, 147, 172, 177, 235, 249, 255, w. of 320, 335
,, Grace, 58, 196
,, Henry, 7, 44, 82, 202, 213, 223, 226,* 233, 238, 252, 270, 292, 302, c. of 310, 317, 324
,, Isabel, 177, 224
,, James, 36, 235, 238, 244, 252
,, Jane, 23, 73, 252, 322, 353
,, John, 6,* 7, 11, 12, 16, 22, 29, 36, 44, 51, 53, 58, 84, 92, 167, 224, 226, 227, 232, 233, 240, 246, 249, 251, 252, 254,* 259, 274, w. of 301, c. of 329, w. of 341, c. of 344, 360, 371
,, Katherine, 29,* 196, 358
,, Laurence, 165, 205, 212,* 218, 222, 224, 230, 234, c. of 327, w. of 345
,, Lettice, 289
,, Lydia, 295
,, Margaret, 67, 99, 147
,, Martha, 28, 238
,, Mary, 6, 22, 23, 78, 210, 265, 349, 356
,, Mathew, 7, 16, 23, 31, 40,* 50, 51, 63, 134, 136, 157, 169, 189, 216, 222, 226, 230, 252, 254, 296, w. of 311, w. of 312, c. of 314, c. of 316, c. of 318, 322
,, Owen, 82, 210, 283
,, Peter, 4, 6, 11, 15, 22, 28, 99, 101, 115, 116, 136, 214, 319
,, Ralph, 50, 107, 126
,, Richard, 3, 4, 12, 62, 73, 84, 112, 165, 213, 214, 216, 218, 223,* 227, 234, 238, 244, 249, 251, 252, 253, 255, 264, 279, c. of 291, w. of 320, c. of 325, s. of 331, c. of 335, 349, 353, 369
,, Robert, 51, 372
,, Roger, 230
,, Sarah, 249, 253
,, Susan, 22, 232, 362
,, Thomas, 7, 62, 73,* 159, 216, 224, 230, 240, 246, 248, 256,* 286, 296, c. of 313, c. of 327, 354

Bury, William, 28, 63, 67, 142, 146, 224, 230, 236,* 243,* 246, 251,* 252, 254, 258, 265, 275, 289,* 295, c. of 314, c. of 316, w. of 319, c. of 326, w. of 343, 354, 355, 360
Bushell, Isabel, 27
,, John, 27
,, Roger, 116
,, Sarah, 367
Buterworth [see Butterworth]
Butler, Bartholomew, 254
,, Thomas, 254
Butson, Edmund, 47
,, Priscilla, 47
Butterfield, John, 234,* c. of 310
Butterworth [Buterworth, Buterworthe, Butterworthe, Buttrworth],
,, Ann, 206
,, Caleb, 193, 332, w. of 346
,, Charles, 207,* 283*
,, Edmund, 156
,, Elizabeth, 294
,, Esther, 321
,, Grace, 185
,, John, 70, 153, 239, 253, 275, c. of 314
,, Jonathan, 75, 275, 370
,, Joseph, 156
,, Mary, 57
,, Robert, 51, 57, 70, 75, 120, 129, 134, 189, 206, 253, c. of 291, w. of 321, w. of 330, 332
,, Ruth, 239
,, Thomas, 153, 155, 197
Bymonde [see Beamond]
Byrche [see Birch]
Byrd [see Bird]
Byrom [Birom, Birome, Byram, Byrome, Byron],
,, Agnes, 146
,, Ann, 228
,, Christopher, 11, 160
,, Elizabeth, 87, 165, 179, 237
,, Henry, 230
,, Isabel, 214, 245, 278
,, James, 195, 233, c. of 313, 314
,, Jane, 233
,, John, 4, 85, 87, 165, 206,* 214, 228, 230, 237, 273, 276, 370
,, Judith, 273
,, Mr., 230, 245
,, Nicholas, 93
,, Richard, 85
,, Thomas, 278
,, William, 4, 11, 276, 299, w. of 313

INDEX OF NAMES. 385

Vol. 1.—C. . pp. 1— 90 inclusive. Vol. 2.—C. . pp. 205—280 inclusive.
B.   .   ,, 91—168   ,,   B.   .   ,, 281—350   ,,
W. .   ,, 169—204   ,,   W. .   ., 351—372   ,,

C

Caly [see Kealey]
Carlile, Eleanor, 372
Carter, Alice, 358
,, Ann, 256
,, Lawrence, 256
Cartwright, Dorothy, 195
Casson, Ellen, 359
,, Mary, 40
,, Samuel, 40
,, Susan, 187
Cawdell [see Cowdrell]
Cawdowe, John, 119
Cawoppe [see Cowpe]
Chadwick [Chadwicke, Chadweeke, Chadweeke],
,, Alexander, 369
,, Alice, 22, 88, 183
,, Ann, 16, 284
,, Deborah, 243
,, Dorothy, 253
,, Elizabeth, 10, 14, 221, 222, 229, 240
,, Ellen, 157, 207, 290
,, Grace, 259
,, James, 1, 10, 16, 22, 30, 37,* 44, 50, 78, 88, 129, 130, 157, 193, 222, 231, 236,* 243, 253, 259, 272, 278,* 341, 348, 358
,, Jane, 278, 372
,, John, 1, 227, 231, 240, 253, w. of 341, w. of 346, 355
,, Jonathan, 253
,, Lawrence, 227
,, Margaret, 30, 229, 272
,, Mary, 188, 192, 221, 337, 356
,, Oliver, 14, 68, 78, 103, 207, 284, 290, 294, 299
,, Richard, 44, 50, 356
,, Robert, 278, 340
,, Roger, 364
,, Thomas, c. of 350
Chalenger, Alice, 201
Cheesden, Edmund, 61*
Chew [Chowe], Ellen, 275
,, Richard, 275
Clarke, Anthony, 54, 138
,, Elizabeth, 274
,, Ellen, 54
,, James, 274
,, Richard, 12
,, Thomas, 12
Clarkson [Clarkesonne], Alice, 185
,, Ann, 222
,, John, 257
,, Raphe, 222, 257

Clarkson, Richard, 199
Clay, Phebe, 342
Clegg [Cledge, Clegge],
,, Alexander, 86, 209
,, Elizabeth, 209
,, Ellis, 361
,, Jane, 194
,, John, 95,* 271,* 371
,, Jonie, 92
,, Mary, 86
,, Richard, 366, 372
Clifford, Thomas, 359
Clough [Cloogh, Cloughe, Cluth],
,, Alice, 274, 296
,, George, 267, 274, 279*
,, Henry, 296
,, Jane, 368
,, John, 8, 19,* 31, 46, 207, 330, 372
,, Katherine, 267
,, Mary, 31
,, Peter, 204, 207, 216,* 222, 237, 295,* c. of 313, 314
,, Richard, 8, 222, 372
,, Robert, 46, 237
,, Thomas, 363
Cocke, Robert, 69*
Cocker, Alice, 369
Cockerill [Cockre.l, Cockrill, Cokerell],
,, Alice, 280
,, Francis, 87, 301
,, John, 274, 277, 280, c. of 349
,, Laurence (Lance), 87, 301
,, Mary, 274
,, Sarah, 277
Cockshead [see Cockshutt]
Cockshutt [Cockshead, Cockshet, Cockshutte, Cokshot, Cokschead, Cokshead, Cokshute],
,, Edward, 82, 166
,, Elizabeth, 72, 368
,, Ellen, 305
,, Roger, 205, 288
,, Susan, 215
,, Thomas, 72, 82, 166, 197, 205, 215, 288, 305
Cockstey, Susan, 371
Cokerell [see Cockerill]
Coleson, Ellen, 257
,, William, 257
Colleer, John
Collinge [Collenge, Collings],
,, Abraham, 82, c. of 304
,, James, 193
,, Jonas, 192

Vol. 1.—C. . pp. 1— 90 inclusive. Vol. 2.—C. . pp. 205—280 inclusive.
B. . „ 91—108 „ B. . „ 281—350 „
W. . „ 109—204 „ W. . „ 351—372 „

Collinge, Mary, 82
„ Zachary, 355
Collins [Collyns, Collens],
„ Ellen, 157
„ James, 157
„ John, 193, 280
„ Mary, 280
Conlife [see Cunliffe]
Cooke [Kooke], Elizabeth, 77
„ John, 77, 192
Cooper [see Cowper]
Coptill, Robert, c. of 328
Core, Richard, 353
Couper [see Cowper]
Cowap, Cowape [see Cowpe]
Cowburn [Cowborne, Cowburne],
„ Jane, 200
„ John, 43, 54, 128
„ Margery, 54, 191
„ Mary, 43
Cowdrell [Cawdell], Robert, 82, 161
Cowpe [Cawoppe, Coup, Coupe,
    Cowap, Cowape, Cowp],
„ Abraham, 200, 210, 286, 287
„ Alice, 113, 241, 354
„ Ann, 187, 243, 368
„ Dorothy, 277
„ Elizabeth, 197, 212, 254, 365, 366, 367
    Francis, 44, 47, 58,* 63, 64, 82, 129, 132, 143, 144, 163,* 186, 187, 193, 194, 309
„ Genet, 104
„ Gideon, 238, 241, 245, 251, 261,* 277, c. of 312, c. of 315, c. of 334
„ Gillian, 268
„ Henry, w. of 328, w. of 343, 365
„ Isabel, 11
„ John, 82, 105, 107, 183, 223,*238, 254, 266,* 274, 281, c. of 326, 354, 364
„ Joseph, 210, 287
„ Katherine, 32, 251, 268, 365
„ Lawrence (Laurence), 102
„ Margaret, 200, c. of 338, 366
„ Margery, 196
„ Peter, 24, 212, 223, 320, 352, 366
„ Richard, 354
„ Roger, 32, 274, 371
„ Susan, 246*
„ Thomas, 19,* 24, 104,* 108, 113, 115, 117, 118, 129, 169
Cowper [Cooper, Coopere, Couper],
„ Alice, 12, 88
„ Deborah, 38

Cowper, Elizabeth, 61, 212
„ Emarie, 7
„ Henry, 38, 61,* 282
„ Isabel, 190
„ James, c. of 294, 295, 354
„ Jane, 70
„ John, 164, 251, 371
„ Margaret, 61, 163, 177, 281
„ Mary, 12
„ Owen, 142
„ Richard, 7, 38,* 88, 163,* 164
„ Susan, 212, 251
„ Thomas, 70
Crampton [see Crompton]
Croft [Crofts], James, 165*
Croichlawe [Croithlawe, Croitshlawe],
„ Alice, 200
„ Ellis, 190
„ Francis, 352
Crompton [Crampton, Cromptonn],
„ Adam, 361
„ Alice, 40
„ Ann, 239, 337, 355
„ Arthur, 265
„ Barbarie, 320
„ Elizabeth, 228, 235, 361
„ Ellen, 306, 363
„ George, 189
„ Genet, 149
„ Isabel, 220
„ James, 200, 235, 239, 244, 265, 337, w. of 342, c. of 349, 358, 367
„ Jane, 292
„ John, 194, 217,* 220, 228, 260, 292, c. of 297, c. of 306, c. of 331, inf. of 349, 355, 367, 371
„ Margaret, 260
„ Mary, 200, 244, 274, 370
„ Ralph, 207, 274, 284
„ Richard, 358, 362
„ Robert, 207, 284, 306, 351
„ Roger, 179
„ Thomas, 149, 306
„ William, 31,* 40, 126, 178, 243*
Cronshaw [Cronikshaw, Cronkshaw, Cronkshawe, Cronnshaw, Cronshawe],
„ Alice, 198
„ Allen (f), 193
„ Ann, 187, 371
„ Christopher, 36, 122, 182
„ Elizabeth, 195
„ Ellen, 190
„ Grace, 180
„ John, 190, 366

INDEX OF NAMES. 387

Vol. 1.—C. . pp. 1— 90 inclusive. Vol. 2.—C. . pp. ???—289 inclusive.
B. . ,, 91—198 ,,   B. . ,, 287—450 ,,
W. . ,, 199—??? ,, W. . ,, 451—??? ,,

Cronshaw, Margaret, 355, 366
 ,, Richard, 55, 138
 ,, William, 351
Crooke, Grace, 184
 ,, James, 177
Cropper [Crooper, Croper],
 ,, Alice, 73, 287
 ,, Ann, 306
 ,, Elizabeth, 152, 354
 ,, James, 306, 311
 ,, Jane, 40, 193
 ,, John, 96, 220,* 353
 ,, Mary, 40, 357
 ,, Richard, 307
 ,, Robert, 73, 152, 287, w. of 325, 359
 ,, Thomas, 86,* 95, 351
Cross [Crosse], Edward, 240
 ,, Grace, 220
 ,, John, 225
 ,, Joshua, 240
 ,, Richard, 220, 225, 240, c. of 315
Crossley [Crosle, Crosley, Crosleye, Crossleye, Crosly, Crossly],
 ,, Abraham, w. of 331, 334, 351
 ,, Alice, 85
 ,, Ann, 199, 209, 212, 272, 364
 ,, Anonimus, 212
 ,, Dorothy, 252
 ,, Edward, 156
 ,, Elizabeth, 192, 205
 ,, Francis, 99, 129, 148, 157, 188
 ,, Henry, 212, 221, 225, 230, 309
 ,, Isabel, 156
 ,, James, 84, 200, 212, 230, 240, inf. of 281, inf. of 286, inf. of 288, c. of 293, 304
 ,, Jane, 217, 293
 ,, John, 247
 ,, Jonathan, 225, inf. of 350
 ,, Joshua, 221
 ,, Katherine, 148
 ,, Mary, 57, 84, 198, 368
 ,, Peter, 9, 13, 57, 224, 272
 ,, Richard, 205, 209, 214*
 ,, Robert, 13, 209, 217, 224, 233,* 240, 247, 252, 293
 ,, Sarah, 304
 ,, Susan, 9, 197, 209
 ,, Thomas, 85
Croston [Crosston, Crostonn, Crostonne],
 ,, Edward, 209
 ,, Elizabeth, 258, 328
 ,, Esther, 224
 ,, George, 61, 258, w. of 308, 326, 328, 329, 366

Croston, Henry, 75, 227
 ,, Isabel, 243, 329
 ,, Jeriiny, 216, w. of 343
 ,, John, 61, 68, 75, 90,* 154, 2 63, 209, 216, 221, 224, 227, 234, 238, 243, 247, 257, 297, 342
 ,, Jonas, 234
 ,, Mary, 154, 221, 287
 ,, Mr., 221, 227, 234, 342
 ,, Richard, 68, 257, 328, 365
 ,, Sarah, 238
 ,, Susan, 247
Croaxhaw, Richard, 368
Cudworth, Nicholas, 278
 ,, Noah, 278
Cunliffe [Conlife, Cundlife, Cunlef, Cunlieffe, Cunlife, Cunlifi],
 ,, Abraham, 90
 ,, Alice, 74
 ,, Christopher, 71, 80, 90, 213, 228, w. of 315, 349
 ,, Ellis, 2
 ,, Henry, 2, 62,* 71, 74, 83, 191, 301, 322, w. of 347
 ,, Kirstabell, 181
 ,, John, 83, 313, 332
 ,, Mary, 349
 ,, Nathan, 213
 ,, Richard, 322
 ,, Susan, 228
Cutlers [Cuttle], Richard, c. of 317

D

Dalamonce [Delamonce], Ann, 150
 ,, Robert, 150
Damforth [Damport, see Davenport]
Dancy, Anna, 90
 ,, Mr., 90
Darlinge, John, 58
 ,, Peregrine, 53
Darwyn, Anne, 51, 191
 ,, Katherine, 51
Davenport [Damforth, Damport, Damporte, Dauemport, Davenporte],
 ,, John, 4, 166
 ,, Margaret, 56, 213, 289
 ,, Richard, 4, 213, 216,* 289, 352
 ,, Thomas, 56
Davis [see also Devis], William, 361
Dawson [Dauson, Dawso, Dawsonn, Dawsonne, Doason, Doesun, Doson, Doueson, Dowson, Dowsonne, Dozen].
 ,, Ellinor, 33, 162
 ,, Elizabeth, 274

Vol. 1.—C. . pp. 1— 90 inclusive. Vol. 2.—C. . pp. 205—280 inclusive
B. . ,, 91—108 ,, B. . ,, 281—350 ,,
W. . ,, 109—204 ,, W. . ,, 351—372 ,,

Dawson, Francis, 60, 246, 249, 257, 268, 274, 362
,, Grace, 176
,, Henry, 242, 249*
,, James, 6, 15, 23,* 40, 50, 60, 149, 155, 242, 249, 268, 308, 323,* 355
,, Jane, 257, 323
,, John, 50, 155
,, Katherine, 367
,, Margaret, 81, 161
,, Margery, 299
,, Mary, 24, 40, 60, 246, 249, 353, 367
,, Richard, 6, 93, 149
,, Robert, 81, 161, 249, 361
,, Thomas, 15, 154, 242*
,, William, 24, 33, 60, 138, 143, 162, 189, 299, 357
Deane, James, c. of 306
Dearden [Derden, Deurden, Dewrden, Duerden, Durden],
,, Alice, 146, 280
,, Annis, 356
,, Elizabeth, 23, 184
,, Ellen, 195
,, Genet, 23, 190
,, George, 301
,, Grace, 296
,, Isabel, 189
,, James, 105
,, Jennet, 294
,, John, 197, 271,* c. of 334, c. of 342, 352
,, Mary, 368
,, Ralph, 294
,, Richard, 100, 172, 280
,, Robert, 32,* 118, 146, 177, 371
,, Susan, 364
,, Thomas, 26, 29, 32, 36, 40, 44, 47, 51, 55, 59, 114, 116, 119, 122, 126, 129, 132, 134, 138, 141, 178, 179, 181, 182, 184, 186, 187, 189, 191, 192, 296, 354, 359
,, William, 357
Delaware, Elizabeth, 30
,, William, 30
Derden [Deurden, see Dearden]
Devis [? Davis], Benjamin, 231
,, John, 231
Dewhurst [Dewherste], John, 15
,, Mary, 8
,, Richard, 8, 15
Dewrden [see Dearden]
Dickinson [Dickenson, Dickonson],
,, Mary, 216

Dickinson, Thomas, 208, 295
,, William, 208, 216, 295, 351
Dickson [Dicksonn, Dikson],
,, Edward, 60, 297
,, John, 48,* 149, 187, 297
,, Richard, 60, 71
,, Robert, 71, 202
Diggle [Digle, Digles],
,, Daniel, 49, 60, 183
,, Elizabeth, 299
,, Esau, 51, 279,* 367
,, George, 248
,, Hugh, 219
,, Isabel, 352
,, Isaiah, 270, 275, c. of 344
,, James, 257, 270, 275
,, Leonard, 367
,, Martha, 246
,, Mary, 51, 263, 264, 267, 269, 282, 361, 363
,, Peter, 248
,, Ralph, 238,* 269
,, Robert, 49, 239, 246, 263, 267, c. of 319, w. of 335, c. of 335
,, Thomas, 219
,, William, 60, 239, 257, 264
Dikson [see Dickson]
Dison [see Dyson]
Doason [see Dawson]
Dobson [Dobsonn], George, 184
Doesun [see Dawson]
Doson [see Dawson]
Douesun [see Dawson]
Doughty, Henry, 201
Dowson [see Dawson]
Dozen [see Dawson]
Draper, Johanna, 183
Drinkwater, Dorothy, 190
Ducksbury, Robert, 311
Duckworth [Ducworth, Duckworthe, Dukworth, Dukworthe],
,, Alice, 41, 152, 227, 233
,, Ann, 30, 31, 69, 193, 360
,, Annis, 356
,, Deborah, 235
,, Dorothy, 86
,, Edmund, 15, 39, 46, 69, 227, 235, c. of 304, 319, d. of 328
,, Elizabeth, 9, 149, 186, 227, 234, 360, 367
,, Ellen, 19, 23, 26, 183, 185
,, Emme, 88
,, Francis, 16, 86, 156
,, Gilbert, 352
,, James, 273
,, Jane, 40, 54, 200, 234, 239, 358, 361

INDEX OF NAMES.

Vol. 1.—C. . pp. 1— 90 inclusive. Vol. 2.—C. . pp. 205—280 inclusive.
B. . ,, 91—168 ,, B. . ,, 281—350 ,,
W. . ,, 169—204 ,, W. . ,, 351—372 ,,

Duckworth, Joan, 251, 310
,, John, 19, 60, 156, 194, 207, 211, 256, 279, 283
,, Lettice, 369
,, Margaret, 58, 62, 210, 364
,, Mary, 49, 222, 228
,, Ralph, 9, 16, 23, 31, 41, 46, 54, 62, 69,* 86, 108, 120, 130,* 141, 152, 183, 236, 209, w. of 333, 343
,, Richard, 26, 27, 30, 40, 49, 52, 58, 60, 69, 88, 153, 156, 180, 192, 202, 207, 208*, 210, 216, 222, 223, 227, 233, 239, 273, 279, 283, 291, 294, 310, c. of 310, 317, c. of 324, 339, w. of 344, 352, 353, 357, 371
,, Robert, 15, 18,* 27, 39, 52, 55, 69, 86, 124, 138, 160, 173, 191, 211, 220,* 223, 228, 229, 235, 236, 245, 251, 256, 264, 273, 280,* c. of 305, 307, c. of 314, c. of 315, c. of 316, c. of 318, c. of 325, c. of 339, 345
,, Roger, 145, 193, 299
,, Sarah, 153, 235, 245
,, Susan, 264, 273, 294
,, Thomas, 220
,, William, 127, 216, 229, 291, 298, 315
Dnerden [see Dearden]
Dugdale, Edmund, 341
,, Mr., inf. of 283
Dukworth [see Duckworth]
Dunsforth, Richard
Dunster [Dunsted, Dunstere, Dunstier, Dunsture],
,, Alice, 78, 195, 233, 270
,, Ann, 157
,, Bithiah, 260
,, Daniel, 27, 219, 226
,, Elizabeth, 19, 192, 211, 245, 281
,, Faith, 265
,, Henry, 2, 4,* 11,* 19, 27, 36, 37, 45, 49, 54, 62,* 70, 78, 90, 91, 94, 129, 147, 148, 202, 208, 211, 215,* 222, 226, 233, 238, 244, 245, 251,* 258, wid. of 281, 290, 305, w. of 331, 337, w. of 343, 350, w. of 350, 370
,, Isabel, 37, 148
,, James, 36, 107, 251, 364
,, John, 2, 49, 91, 222
,, Jonie (Jony), 192 303
,, Margaret, 54, 234, 305
,, Mary, 208, 238, 241, 290, 364

Dunster, Richard, 90
,, Robert, 11, 45, 113, 219, 234, 241, 244, 251, 258, 260, 265, 270, 303, c. of 318, w. of 321, 337, 345, c. of 345, 354, 366
,, Thomas, 70, 95
,, William, 11, 105, 124, 128, 157
Durden [see Dearden]
Dutton, Margaret, 236
,, William, 236
Dyson [Dison], George, 278
,, James, 267, 278, c. of 337
,, Susan, 267

E

Eansworth [see Ainsworth]
Earnshaw, Elizabeth, 277
,, Priscilla, 280
,, Thomas, 277
,, William, 280, 371
Eastwood [see Estwoode]
Eccarsall [Eccarsell, Eccersall, see Eckersall]
Eccles, Ellis, 271
,, Mary, 265, 271
,, Thomas, 265, 276, 278,* c. of 348
,, William, 276
Eccleston [Ecclesiones],
,, N.N.N., a child of 338
,, Thomas, c. of 340
Eckersall [Eccarsall, Eccarsell, Eccersall, Eckersall, Eckersley, Eckersly, Ekersall, Ekarsall, Ekorsall],
,, Alice, 86, 260, 336
,, Ann, 280
,, Elias, 273
,, Ellen, 207
,, Ellis, 111
,, George, 262,* 270
,, James, 72,* 79, 86, 96,* 164,* 207, 212, 218, 222,* 256, 299, c. of 313, w. of 347
,, Margaret, 96, 218, 371
,, Robert, 75
,, Roger, 270
,, Susan, 212, 341
,, Thomas, 79, 256, 260, 263,* 273, 280, c. of 334, 365
,, William, 75, 152*
Eckersley [Eckerslay, Eckersly],
,, Alice, 257
,, George, 257, 262, 270, 366
,, Roger, 270
Edge [Edgh], Alice, 23
,, Ann, 17

P

Vol. 1.—C. . pp. 1— 90 inclusive. Vol. 2.—C. . pp. 205—280 inclusive
B. . ,, 91—168 ,,   B. . ,, 281—350 ,,
W. . ,, 169—204 ,,   W. . ,, 351—372 ,,

Edge, Elizabeth, 30
,, Robert, 17, 111, 112
,, Thomas, 23, 30, 33, 118, 123, 125, 135
Ellcock [Elcoke], Elizabeth, 144
,, Henry, 155, 159, 170
,, Katherine, 159
Ellison, Grace, 183
Elmer, Alexander, 351
Elom, Susan, 305
Elton [Eltonn], Alice, 284
,, Lawrence, 293
,, Margaret, 186
,, Robert, 187, 284, 352
,, Thomas, 109
Emerson [Emarson, Emersome, Emmerson, Emorson],
,, Alice, 208, 285
,, Ann, 213, 215, 255, 370
,, Elizabeth, 85, 164, 245, 250
,, Emor, 339
,, Francis, 236, 240, 245, 250, 252, 255, w. of 324, c. of 325, 363
,, George, 85, 86,* 164, 208, 213, 215, 222,* 285,* c. of 299, 321
,, Isabel, 208, 285
,, Jane, 339
,, Peter, 252
,, Richard, 236
,, Thomas, 240
Emotson, George, 202
Emott, Edward, 78
,, Mary, 78
Ensco, Alice, 352
Ensworth [see Ainsworth]
Entwisle [Entwysle],
,, Alexander, 105, 182
,, Ann, 352
,, Ellen, 189
,, Genet, 284
,, Katherine, 202
,, Ralph, 132, 177
,, Richard, 182, 188
,, William, 170
Essher [? Esther, Estler],
,, Alice, c. of 339
Estwood [Estwoode], Jane, 135
,, Margaret, 230

F

FAILSWORTH, James, 321
Fairebancke [Fayrebancke],
,, Richard, 183, 310
Fairclonghe [Faireclenghe],
,, Elizabeth, 192
,, Genet, 353

Farer, Henry, 247
,, Michael, 247
Farnworth [Farneworth, Farworthe],
,, Ellen, 209, 291
,, Ellis, 283*
,, Robert, 209, 220,* 291, w. of 305
Farros, Robert, 264
,, Thomas, 264
Fayrebancke [see Fairebancke]
Feeldinge, Feildinge, Feldinge [see Fielden]
Fenton [Fentone, Fennton Fento, Fentonn, Fentton],
,, Alice, 227, 232
,, Anne, 257
,, Dorothy, 9, 218, 256, 336
,, Edmund, 73, 89, 124, 131, 209, 213, 214, 281, 286,* 293
,, Edward, 240
,, Francis, 240
,, George, 1, 256
,, Henry, 248
,, Isabel, 228
,, James, 4, 29, 68, 78,* 88, 116, 155, 156, 169, 179, 195, 198, 212, 218, 223, 240, 245, 248, 249, 256, 263, 288, 308, w. of 314, 316, 328, 352, 362, 366
,, Jane, 156, 330
,, Jeffery, 234
,, Jennet, 94, 214, 215, 293, 355
,, John, 4, 9, 14, 21, 34,* 111, 119, 209, 210*, 213, 215, 220, 223, 227, 230, 234, 238, 240, 243, 245, 256, 270, 286, 294, c. of 317, c. of 318, 321, c. of 322, c. of 328
,, Jonathan, 238
,, Katherine, 201
,, Margaret, 286, 371, 372
,, Margery, 327
,, Mary, 14
,, Peter, 1, 89, 101, 128, 220, 322
,, Richard, 46,* 73, 88, 115, 166, 187, 230, 252,* 257, 263, 270, c. of 312, 332, c. of 347, c. of 348
,, Robert, 162, 228, 232, c. of 321, c. of 327, 342, 356
,, Roger, 249
,, Sarah, 21, 212, 288, 353
,, Thomas, 68, 195, 243, 357
Fielden [Feeldinge, Feildinge, Feldinge, Filden, Filding],
,, Ann, 352
,, James, 304
,, Jane, 188

Vol. 1.—C. . pp. 1— 90 inclusive. Vol. 2.—C. . pp. 205—280 inclusive.
,,   B. . ,, 91—168   ,,   ,,   B. . ,, 281—350   ,,
,,   W. . ,, 169—204   ,,   ,,   W. . ,, 351—372   ,,

Fielden, Jeffery, 209, 351
 ,, Mary, 209, 344
 ,, Richard, 47
 ,, William, 47
Fildes [Fieldes, Fields, Filds, Fyldes, Fylds, Fyles, Fylles],
 ,, Abraham, 19, 25, 42, 54,* 81, 364
 ,, Alice, 81, 179, 233
 ,, Ann, 88, 369
 ,, Elizabeth, 295
 ,, Ellen, 52
 ,, Ester, 292
 ,, George, 37
 ,, Henry, 64, 78, 88, 101, 128, 145, 194, 212, 292, 305
 ,, James, 64
 ,, Jane, 129
 ,, Mary, 42, 78, 194, 240, 340
 ,, Ralph, 227,* 233, 240, 355
 ,, Richard, 82,* 163.* 199, 210
 ,, Roger, 25, 37, 52, 116, 131, 150, 159, w. of 289
 ,, Sarah, 19, 180, 210, 212, 313
 ,, Thomas, 115, 202, w. of 309, w. of 313
 ,, Thurstan, 295
Finch [Finche Fynche], Alice, 149
 ,, Ann, 75
 ,, Edmund, 217, 292
 ,, Elizabeth, 56
 ,, Richard, 46, 56, 75, 90, 149, 217, 292
 ,, Robert, 90
 ,, Thomas, 46, 293
Fish [Fishe, Fyshe], Alice, 186
 ,, Ann, 32
 ,, Dorothy, 261
 ,, Elizabeth, 177
 ,, Isabel, 168, 204
 ,, John, 200
 ,, Lawrence, 32, 119
 ,, Ralph, 261
 ,, Robert, 91, 168
 ,, Thomas, 103, 122, 157
 ,, William, c. of 328
Fisher, Richard, 356
Fitton [Fytton], Abraham, 25
 ,, Ann, 354
 ,, James, 25
 ,, Ralph, w. of 349
 ,, Richard, 369
 ,, Susan, 364
Fletcher [Flecher, Flechere, Flechor, Flecther, Fletchar, Fletchr, Fletchere],
 ,, Abraham, 9, 15, 22, 34, 68, 237, 290, 300, w. of 319

Fletcher, Alice, 84, 105, 266, 269, 298, 346, 358, 366
 ,, Ann, 17, 54, 67, 181, 191, 249, 269, 273, 279, 286, 295,* 370
 ,, Bartyn, 18, 98, 100, 118, 121, 174
 ,, Bessey, 293
 ,, Christopher, 309, w. of 316
 ,, Dorothy, 32, 188
 ,, Edmund, 241
 ,, Elizabeth, 17, 22, 58, 62, 79, 81, 144, 163, 185, 187, 188, 193, 206, 207, 226, 249, 256, 265, 284, 294, 351
 ,, Ellen, 15, 66, 84, 271, 282, 293, 364
 ,, Ellis, 6, 17, 29, 34, 65, 84, 93, 100, 124, 131, 209, 237, 241, 245, 247, 249, 253, 257, 266, 274, 280, 281, inf. of 283, 295, 326, w. of 332, 335, 345, 351
 ,, Francis, 245
 ,, George, 32*
 ,, Genet, 102, 154
 ,, Henry, 48
 ,, Isabel, 7, 76, 168
 ,, James, 9, 12, 29, 37, 46,* 50, 51, 57, 60, 67, 68, 79, 80, 81, 84, 87, 95, 115, 126, 151, 153, 163, 167, 172, 188, 191, 198, 199, 212, 213, 221,* 225, 226, 231, 233, 259, 264, 278, 281, 294, 295, 303, c. of 315,* 323, w. of 326, 336, 338, 344, 345, 348, 353,* 368, 371
 ,, Jane, 28, 56, 70, 74, 152, 182, 184, 186, 191, 267, 296
 ,, Joan, 333
 ,, John, 17, 29, 39, 41, 49, 51, 55, 59, 60, 68, 74, 83, 91,* 93,* 120, 134, 137, 141,* 142, 167, 187, 191, 192, 195, 207, 216, 226, 229,* 233,* 236,* 242,* 243, 247, 248, 253, 257, 259, 264, 267, 268,* 273, 278, 279, 282, 286, 294,* 300,* c. of 304, c. of 310,* 312, c. of 313, 313, 323, c. of 337, inf. of 347, 352,* 358
 ,, Katherine, 42, 156, 247, 248, 358
 ,, Lambert, 151, 152, w. of 315
 ,, Lawrence, 17, 27, 48, 50,* 122, 147, 229, 242, 247, 256, 261,* 264,* 267, 268,* 270, 273, c. of 308, c. of 320, c. of 330, c. of 332, c. of 337
 ,, Margaret, 11, 146, 180, 191, 229, 233, 242, 300

Vol. 1.—C. . pp. 1— 90 inclusive. *Vol. 2.—C.* . pp. 205—280 inclusive.
  B. . ,, 91—168 ,,   *B.* . ,, 281—350 ,,
  W. . ,, 169—204 ,,   *W.* . ,, 351—372 ,,

Fletcher, Margerie, 68, 148
,, Martyn, 67
,, Mary, 16, 83, 87, 151, 206, 226, 233, 235, 240, 250, 252, 260, 267, 270, 371
,, Nathaniel, 28
,, N.X.N., 249
,, Peter, 56, 66, 81, 106, 190, 207, c. of 320, c. of 322
,, Richard, 11, 16, 17, 20, 30,* 38,* 46, 55, 62, 68, 72, 77, 79,* 108, 110, 118, 122, 131, 136, 146, 148, 174, 181, 207, 209, 212, 213, 215, 216, 226, 233, 236, 245, 254,* 258,* 260, 265, 271, 277, 280, inf. of 281, c. of 289, 303, 333, 335,* 336, c. of 339, 344, 348, 358, 369
,, Robert, 40, 42, 61,* 72, 81, 126, 206, 214, 221, 245, 277, w. of 319, 327, 338, 346, 369
,, Roger, 12, 41, 48, 56, 68, 72, 80, 83, 107, 126, 145, 148, 151, 154, 176, 206,* 214, 219, 225, 231, 233, 236, 240, 247, 288, 295,* 296, c. of 299, 306, c. of 307, 348
,, Rosamund, 153
,, Susan, 253, 338
,, Thamer, 18, 167
,, Thomas, 6, 32, 34,* 39, 40, 46, 48, 49, 50, 54, 56, 58, 65, 72, 77, 78,* 83, 84, 98, 119, 130, 140, 142, 157,* 180, 186, 197, 206, 208,* 215, 226, 230,* 233, 235, 237, 243, 244,* 247, 249, 250, 252, 253, 258, 262,* 264, 267, 269,* 271,* 273, 274, 288, 293, 294, 295, 300, c. of 305, c. of 308, c. of 309, w. of 318, w. of 323, c. of 323, c. of 325, c. of 339, w. of 344, c. of 345, c. of 347, 368,* 369
,, William, 7, 17, 27, 37, 70, 76, 84, 122, 152, 168, 195, 237, 307
Flether [? Fletcher], Jane, 153
,, John, 153
Floud, Dorothy, c. of 331
Fogg [Fog, Fogge, Foge],
,, Alice, 41, 190, 359
,, Ann, 234, 361
,, Elizabeth, 36, 39, 186
,, Ellen, 22, 335
,, Ellis, 31
,, Esther, 360
,, George, 22, 31, 36, 41, 79, 118, 123, 126, 176, 189, 319

Fogg, Gennet, 302
,, James, 209, 215, 227,* 234, 285, 286, 288, 302, c. of 314, 352, 353
,, John, 30
,, Katherine, 285
,, Mary, 79, 364
,, Richard, 136
,, Robert, 209, 215, 286, 371
Forde, Ann, 352
Foster, Alice, 371
,, Jeffray, 357
,, Jony, 199
,, Katherine, 366
Fourness [see Furness]
Fowler [Foullor], James, 83, 219
,, Mary, 83
,, Margaret, 219
Fox, Ann, 62
,, George, 62
France [Francs], Ann, 197
,, Thomas, 105
Frisco [Frischo], Elizabeth, 368
,, Ratcliffe 364
Furness [Fourness, Furnace, Furnas, Furnes, Furnis, Furniss],
,, Arthur, 224, 230, 236, 241,* 244, c. of 315, c. of 319
,, Edward, 236
,, Martha, 224
,, Mary (Maria), 224, 230, 320
,, Sarah, 244
Fyldes, Fylds, Fyles, Fylles [see Fildes]
Fynche [see Finch]
Fyshe [see Fish]
Fytton [see Fitton]

G

Gabbit [Gabbet, Gabbitt, Gabbot],
,, James, 56, 255,* 262, 266, 276, w of 350, 366
,, Jeremy, 182
,, Mary, 266
,, Thomas, 56, 161, 262, 276
,, William, 372
Gaudie, Alice, 181
Garshed [see Gartside]
Garstange, Dorothy, 288
,, Oliver, 354
,, Richard, 288
,, William, 114
Gartside [Garshed, Garside Garsyd, Gartesyde],
,, Elizabeth, 144, 309
,, Jane, 94

Vol. 1.—C. . pp. 1— 90 inclusive. Vol. 2.—C. . pp. 205—280 inclusive.
B. . „ 91—168 „ B. . „ 281—350 „
W. . „ 169—204 „ W. . „ 351—372 „

Gartside, John, 351
  „ Ralph, 159
  „ Robert, 40*
  „ Thomas. 144, 296, 309
Gawthropp [Gauthrop, Gauthroppe, Gawthrop, Gothcrope, Gothrope],
  „ Elizabeth, 236
  „ Robert, 231, 336
  „ Thomas, 231, 236, c. of 317, c. of 330, w. of 339, 352
  „ Susan, 231
Gee [Gie, Gis], Alice, 259, 265
  „ Ann, 255
  „ Elizabeth, 207,* 274
  „ Ellen, 138
  „ James, 246, 255, 259, 265, 269, 274, 276, c. of 328, c. of 346
  „ John, 246
  „ Thomas, 276
Gellder, John, 268*
George, of Johns, 301
Gerret, Mary, 354
Geste [Gest], James, 266, c. of 335
  „ Jane, 298
  „ John, 94, 266
Gibson, Jane, 167
  „ William, 167
Giliam, Alice, 227
  „ James, 227, c. of 305
Gillibrand [Gilibrande, Gilibrunde],
  „ Elizabeth, 138
  „ Grace, 186
Gis [see Gee]
Gleaden, John, 366
Glover, Elizabeth, 177
Goar, Mary,
Goddard [Godard], Thomas, 211*, 278*
Goiltey, John, 149
Goose, Isabell, 351
Gorrell [Goreld, Gorelde, Gorell],
  „ Ann, 73
  „ John, 33, 59, 73, 81, 92, 192, 320
  „ Lawrence, 33
  „ Mary (Marie), 81, 321
  „ Thomas, 107
Gorton, Charles, 272
  „ Elizabeth, 280
  „ Ellen, 366
  „ James, 257,* 272, 276, 280, c. of 337, c. of 340, c. of 345, c. of 348
  „ Jennet, 353
  „ Richard, 325
  „ Robert, 276
Gotherope, Gothrope [see Gawthropp]

Gr (?), Richard, w. of 321
Greame [see Grime]
Greason, Christopher, w. of 326
Greave [Greafe, Greaue],
  „ Geoffray, 170, 307
  „ Grace, 178
  „ Henry, 143,* c. of 329, c. of 335
  „ James, 310
  „ John, 112, 177, 357
  „ Margaret, 186, 357
  „ Mary, 310
  „ Richard, 133
  „ Thomas, 91
Green [Greane, Greene, Greine, Grene, Grenne],
  „ Alice, 352
  „ Ann, 295
  „ Dorothy, 266
  „ Ellin, 266, 302, 358
  „ James, 352
  „ John, 210, 295, 306
  „ Margaret, 355
  „ Samuel, 210, 352
Greenall [see Greenhalgh]
Greenhalgh [Greenahalgh, Greenalgh, Greenalghe, Greenall, Greenalgh, Greenealgh, Greenehalgh, Greenha', Greenhabe, Greenhalghe, Greenhalh, Greenhalhe, Greenhough, Greeno, Grehalh, Grenalgh, Grenall Grenealg, Grenealgh, Grenehalgh, Grenchalghe, Grenchall, Grenhal, Grenhalge, Grenhalgh, Grenhalghe, Grenhalh, Grenhalhe, Grenhall, Grenhallh, Grenhawh, Grennoe, Grinalghe, Grinall, Grinallgh, Grinaughe, Grinealghe, Grineall, Grinehalge, Grinehalgh, Grinehalghe, Grinehayhe, Grinhalgh, Grinhalghe, Grinhalh, Grinough],
  „ Alice, 1, 4, 15, 17, 25,* 26, 31, 33,* 35, 62, 86, 160, 188, 208, 213, 218, 221, 222, 232, 234, 261, 278, 285,* 288, 290, c. of 311, 339, 346, 354, 355, 366, 369*
  „ Ann, 16, 19, 30, 35, 44, 65, 66, 67, 77, 81, 82, 88, 90, 95, 145, 179, 204, 211, 217, 226, 250, 254, 262, 273, 274, 276, 282, 288, 292, 302, 304, 317, 335, 367

Vol. 1.—C. . pp. 1— 90 inclusive. Vol. 2.—C. . pp. 205—280 inclusive.
B. . ,, 91—168 ,, B. . ,, 281—350 ,,
W. . ,, 169—204 ,, W. . ,, 351—372 ,,

Greenhalgh, Arthur, 248
,, Bartholomew, 125, 333
,, Clemence, 230
,, Deborah, 256
,, Dorothy, 9, 10, 26, 35, 62, 74, 182, 198, 272,* 299, 304, c. of 339, 358
,, Edmund, 22,* 23, 26, 39,* 41, 49, 66, 93, 98, 99, 107, 108,* 112, 117, 119,* 125, 131, 175, 178, 212, 241, 247, 256,* 263, 288, 292, 300, c. of 303, w. of 329, 368
,, Edward, 368
,, Elizabeth, 10, 19, 23, 25, 41,* 54, 61, 65, 66, 82, 97, 140, 214, 222, 230, 237, 239, 240, 254, 267, 271, 281, 282, 286, 287, 307, 320, 353, 354, 359
,, Ellen, 45, 66, 196, 218, 261, 272, 359
,, Emmyn, 296
,, Francis, 16, 17, 82, 89, 106, 116, 140, 184, 199, 211,* 217, 222, 229, 271, 277, 282, 292, 302, 304, 306, 308, c. of 320, w. of 321, w. of 344, 346, 354, 357, 370
,, George, 245
,, Gennet, 167
,, Grace, 41, 224
,, Hugh, 54, 262, 274, c. of 349, 368
,, Isabel, 81, 146
,, Israel, 83, 162
,, James, 3, 5,* 10, 17, 23,* 25, 44, 54, 64,* 71,* 74, 78, 80, 82, 86, 89, 90, 109, 127, 130, 134, 157, 159, 162, 163,* 164, 167, 173, 198, 206,* 208, 211, 216, 218, 222, 226, 230,* 237, 244, 250, 251, 253, 262, 265, 272, 274, 277, 278,* 279, 282, 284, 288, 296, 307, c. of 308, w. of 310, c. of 313, 314, 322, 325, w. of 331, 339, c. of 342, w. of 343, 358, 368, 370, 371
,, Jane, 61, 68, 89, 109, 216, 227, 228, 233, 247, 269,* 363, 364, 367, 371
,, Jervis, 216, 221, 226, 232, 257,* 263, 353
,, John, 1, 4, 5,* 6, 9, 19, 26,* 30, 31,* 42, 44, 46, 49, 54, 62, 64, 70, 74,* 77, 80, 82,* 83, 89,* 90,* 97, 114, 115, 116, 123, 134, 137, 138, 139, 141,

Greenhalgh, John, continued—
145,* 146, 147, 151, 161, 167,* 194, 199, 205, 209, 212, 213, 216, 218, 220, 224, 228, 230, 233,* 234, 238, 241,* 245, 246, 247,* 248,* 249, 251,* 254,* 257,* 258, 260,* 264, 265, 269,* 273, 274, 276, 279, 280,* 281, 283, 285, 286, c. of 289, 290,* 292,* 293, 295, c. of 309, w. of 310, c. of 311, w. of 312, c. of 314, 320, c. of 320, 322, w. of 332, 333, 335, 338, 348, 360, 364, 372
,, Katherine, 1, 62, 93, 113, 198, 217, 218, 248, 367, 370
,, Laurence, 90, 167, 265
,, Margaret, 61, 280, 359
,, Margerie, 114
,, Martha, 63, 268, 358, 369
,, Mary, 17, 19, 25, 77, 205, 206, 214, 219, 221, 226, 228, 230, 233,* 250, 252,* 253, 280, 286, 293, c. of 327, 364
,, Mr., 224, 253, c. of 296, 309, 310, 320, 324
,, Mrs., 364, 367
,, Peter, 5, 49, 115, 128, 180, 219, 226, 227, 230, 278, 285, 320, 341, 345
,, Richard, 3, 11,* 14,* 15, 19,* 23, 26, 31, 38, 42, 45, 53, 54, 57, 64,* 68, 78, 79, 80,* 88, 99, 104,* 105, 106,* 108, 122, 157, 160, 167, 169,* 183, 186, 201, 206, 209, 214,* 216, 218,* 219,* 222, 230, 238, 247, 258, 262, 282, 284, 285, inf. of 285, 286, 287, 293, 302, 306, 307, w. of 313, w. of 316, w. of 317, c. of 319, w. of 320, 324, 351, 352, 353, 362
,, Robert, 6, 18,* 26, 35, 38, 46, 57, 66, 89, 146, 174, 206, 230,* 238,* 240, 244, 245, 249, 250, 252, 256, 261, 267, 290, 300, 307, w. of 329, 335, 345, 348,* 357
,, Roger, 1, 10, 16, 30,* 35, 44, 54, 57, 63, 66, 67, 77, 90, 101, 118, 178, 208,* 213, 217, 219, 221, 222, 226, 230, 233, 239, 248, 257, 265, 274, w. of 314, 330, 336
,, Sarah, 246, 262
,, Susan, 82, 167, 216, 263, 293
,, Thomas, 4,* 14, 16, 23, 26, 35,

INDEX OF NAMES.

Vol. 1.—C. . pp. 1— 90 inclusive. Vol. 2.—C. . pp. 205—280 inclusive.
B. . ,, 91—168 ,, B. . ,, 281—350 ,,
W. . ,, 169—204 ,, W. . ,, 351—372 ,,

Greenhalgh, Thomas, continued—
    44, 47, 49, 53, 56,* 57, 61, 64,
    70, 79, 90, 92, 93, 106, 112,
    115, 129, 132, 133, 137, 146,
    174, 186, 187, 206, 228, 247,
    251,*258,*261, 263, 264, 271,*
    273, 274, 279, 283, 284,* 285,
    286, 295,* 299, w. of 303, 306,
    w. of 315, c. of 334, 364, 366,
    368
,, Tomazin, 178
,, William, 90, 213, 214,* 220, 229,
    245, 250,* 252, 257, 258,* 262,
    268, 273, 279, 293, c. of 346,
    359
Greenhough [see Greenhalgh]
Greenleafe, Alice, 238
,, Ann, 313
,, Thomas 312
,, William, 238, c. of 342
Greeno [see Greenhalgh]
Greenoucke, Mary, 304
,, Roger, 304
Greenwood [Grenwood], Isabel, 85
,, Richard, 85
Gregory [Gregorie], Alice, 356
,, Robert, 357
Greine, Grene, Grenne [see Green]
Grennoe [see Greenhalgh]
Grey, Ann, 19
,, John, 19
Grime [Greame, Gryme],
,, Alice, 303,* 361
,, Ann, 105, 146, 154, 245, 250, 364
,, Edward, 5
,, Elizabeth, 14, 147, 195, 198, 261,
    352* 356
,, Ellis, 40, 47, 49, 74,* 154, 181,
    234, 271, 370
,, Grace, 47
,, Henry, 67, 70, 126, 171, 262, 300,
    303
,, Isabel, 27, 166, 367
,, James, 102, 120, 139, 153, 195,
    234, 288*
,, Jennet, 355
,, John, 220, 249, 271, 294, 320
,, Jone, 195
,, Katherine, 317, 362
,, Margaret, 5, 89, 352
,, Oliver, 108, 147, 220, 291, 294,
    303, c. of 320
,, Renald, 27, 163, 166
,, Renard, 100
,, Richard, 28,* 49, 61, 67, 70, 79(?),
    89, 122, 146, 167, 178, 192, 203,
    207,* 256, 261, 288, w. of 289,
    c. of 290, 295, 320, 364

Grime, Roger, 40, 61, 245, 249, 250,
    256, 262, 272,* c. of 318, 330,
    340, 365
,, Susan, 363
,, Thomas, 79(?), 111, 167
,, William, 14, 106, 118, 122, 291
Grimshaw [Grimeshaw].
,, Laurence, 280
,, William, 276,* 280, c. of 313
Grinalghe, Grinall, Grinaughe,
    Grinough [see Greenhalgh]
Grundy [Grundie], Elizabeth, 3, 33,
    177, 288
,, Ellen, 197
,, John, 3, 98
,, Margerie, 177
,, Thomas, 33, 132, 139, 181, 192
Gryme [see Grime]

H

HABERGAM [Habergame], Ann, 33
,, John, 124
,, Thomas, 33
Haddock [Hadach, Hadacke,
    Hadocke, Haddok,
    Haddoke],
,, Alice, 238, 264
,, Ann, 225, 365
,, Gilbert, 269
,, Hellen, 245
,, James, 251, 322
,, Jane, 231, 255
,, Margaret, 275
,, Richard, 225, 231, 238, 245, 251,*
    255, 263,* 264, 269, 275, 322,
    c. of 326, 356
,, Robert, 165
Hagge [Haghe], Alice, 25
,, George, 25
,, Joseph, 300
Hakinge, Ann, 351
Halgh [Halghe, Haugh, Haughe,
    Haulgh],
,, Alice, 21, 357
,, Ann, 293
,, Annis, 295
,, Elizabeth, 45, 89
,, George, 9, 16, 21, 32, 39, 45,
    111, 293, 325
,, John, 32
,, Mary, 16, 89
,, Peter, 39
,, Valentine, 9, 317
Halewell, Haliwell [see Helliwell]
Hall [Halle], Elizabeth, 26
,, George, 247
,, Jane, 30

Vol. 1.—C. . pp.   1— 90 inclusive. Vol. 2.—C. . pp. 205—280 inclusive.
         B. . ,, 91—168   ,,   B. . ,, 281—350 ,,
         W. . ,, 169—204   ,,   W. . ,, 351—37? ,,

Hall, Nicholas, 26, 30, 115, 119
  ,, Peter, 247
Halliley [see Holliley]
Halliwell [see Helliwell]
Hallowes, Isabel, 196
  ,, Sarah, 204
Halseyarde, Gilbert, 292
Halsom [see Haslam]
Halstead, Henry, 71, 78, 158, 160, 161, 201
Halton, Alice, 86
  ,, John, 86
Hallywell, Halywale [see Helliwell]
Hambage, Mr., 102
Hamer [Hamar, Hamere, Haymer],
  ,, Alice, 26, 224, 230, 245, 291, 323
  ,, Ann, 8, 18, 24, 38, 58, 88,* 166, 226, 228, 254, 267, 291, 297, 303, 308, 361, 369
  ,, Bartholomew, 243
  ,, Deborah, 48
  ,, Edmund, 45, 110
  ,, Edward, 3, 18, 25, 86, 103, 110, 142, 146, 177, 216, 221, 226, 257,* 269, 271, 274, 294, c. of 306, 308,* w. of 309, c. of 309, c. of 310, 339, c. of 346,* 352
  ,, Elizabeth, 35, 85, 217, 288, 354
  ,, Ellen, 18, 86, 153, 256, 261, 351
  ,, Francis, 11, 30, 146,* 193, 216, 230, 237, 244, 250, 251, 254, 287, c. of 332, c. of 340
  ,, George, 3, 11, 130, 143, 303
  ,, Henry, 11, 18, 25, 26, 35, 103, 146*
  ,, James, 22, 55, 146, 162, 217
  ,, Jane, 1, 11, 12, 146,* 213, 244, 250, 251, 351, 352
  ,, Jennet, 159
  ,, Jeremy, 69
  ,, John, 3, 38, 88,* 161, 200, 202, 213, 221,* 226, 232, 239,* 243, 245, 255, 257, 261, 271, 275,* c. of 309, 323
  ,, Katherine, 11, 75, 94, 187
  ,, Margaret, 25, 88, 143, 147, 176, 255
  ,, Mary, 19, 209, 226, 245, 276, 333, 360, 368
  ,, Ralph, 166
  ,, Richard, 3, 48, 147,* 217, 228, 260, 267, 274, c. of 290, 293, 298, c. of 299
  ,, Robert, 224, 231, 238, 245, 246, 257, 260, 263, 269, 274, 276, c. of 344, w. of 348, c. of 350, 362

Hamer, Roger, 25, 64, 96, 159, 221, 231, 256, 274,* 291, 333,* 354, 356
  ,, Thomas, 1,* 11, 12, 17,* 18, 19, 22, 26,* 30, 38, 48,* 58, 75, 85, 88,* 92, 94, 106, 114, 140, 162, 166,* 178, 190, 209, 217, 232, 237, 238, 246, 287, 290, 303, w. of 312, 322, 330, w. of 333, 337
  ,, Thurstan, 64
  ,, William, 8, 18, 24, 38, 45, 55, 69, 98, 100, 153, 173, 216, 283, 294
Hammond [Hamand, Hamon, Hamond],
  ,, Ellen, 242
  ,, Esther, 247
  ,, Henry, w. of 343
  ,, James, 236
  ,, John, 229, 305
  ,, Sarah, 254
  ,, Thomas, 229, 236, 242, 247, 254, 305, w. of 339
Haneworth, Alice, 87
  ,, Anne (Ann), 87
  ,, Edward, 87
  ,, Ellis, 87
Hanson, Susan, 364
Hardie [see Hardy]
Hardier, Mr., 338
Hardis [see Hardus]
Hardman [Hardmann, Hardmen],
  ,, Alice, 40, 77, 156, 192, 240
  ,, Ann, 20, 54, 68, 74, 156, 202, 217, 227, 271, 283, 292,* 298, 361
  ,, Edmund, 20, 30, 287, 298
  ,, Edward, 52, 187
  ,, Elizabeth, 32, 60, 63, 68, 155, 191, 200, 231,* 266
  ,, Ellen, 51, 178, 252
  ,, Ellinor, 369
  ,, Emen, 351
  ,, Francis, 140, 282
  ,, Gennet, 306
  ,, Henry, 11, 22, 83, 145, 183, 234, 261, 267,* 271, 283, 334, w. of 344
  ,, Isabel, 50, 60, 282
  ,, James, 17, 54, 60, 63, 68, 70, 77,* 78, 86, 133, 155, 156, 166, 173, 189, 191, 208, 209, 217, 222, 227, 234, 240, 246, 252, 261* 268,* 290, 293, 297, c. of 310, 314, w. of 322, w. of 346, 371

INDEX OF NAMES.

Vol. 1.—C. . pp. 1— 90 inclusive. Vol. 2.—C. . pp. 205—280 inclusive.
B. . ,, 91—168 ,, B. . ,, 281—450 ,,
W. . ,, 169—204 ,, W. . ,, 451—572 ,,

Hardman, Jane, 354, 355
,, Jeffry, 257*
,, John, 17, 36, 52, 74, 82,* 83, 86, 150, 165,* 194, 203, 206,* 208, 217, 222, 282, 287, 292,* 306
,, Jonie, 187
,, Katherine, 11, 181, 191, 352
,, Laurence, 17, 22, 36, 48, 68, 106, 297, 302
,, Mar: [f.], 246
,, Margaret, 42, 50, 60, 195, 287, 302, 361, 362
,, Mary, 17, 48, 86,* 217, 261, 293, 311, 330
,, Richard, 40, 78, 93, 126, 137, 138, 183, 266, 268
,, Robert, 206, 209, 212
,, Roger, 212
,, Sarah, 372
,, Thomas, 30, 32, 42, 51, 68, 70, 77, 156, 163, 179, 268, 309
,, Zachary, 176
Hardus [Hardis], Alice, 264
,, Elizabeth, 253
,, John, 253, 264, c. of 324, c. of 331, cf of 342
Hardy [Hardie, Hardye], Ann, 318
,, Elizabeth, 264
,, Gilbert, 71, 150, 196
,, Jane, 71
,, John, 276, 366
,, Katherine, 356
,, Mr., 264
,, Richard, 276
Hargreaves [Hargraues, Hargraves, Hargreaus, Hargreave, Hargreavs, Hargreue, Hargreues, Hargreves],
,, Alice, 177, 196, 365
,, George, 353
,, Henry, 356
,, John, 77, 199, 268
,, Joseph, 268
,, Joshua, 213, 274, 369
,, Margaret, 89, 167, 368
,, Richard, 194, 197, 208, 285, 367
,, Sarah, 66, 362
,, William, 66, 77, 89, 167, 194, 208, 213, 274, 285, w. of 324, 325
Harper [Harpur], Abigail, 58
,, Alice, 43, 59
,, Ann, 83, 331, 357
,, Elizabeth, 48, 287
,, George, 44, 58, 106, 318
,, James, 69

Harper, Jane, 44
,, John, 43, 59, 83, 287,* 331, w. of 342
,, Mary, 357
,, Peter, 69
,, Roger, 48, 175
,. Samuel, 59
,, Susan, 59
,, Thomas, 287
Harrison [Harison, Haryson],
,, John, 67, 84, 354
,. Katherine, 84, 196
,. Margaret, 352
,. "Ould," 106
,, Richard, 67
Harrope [Harope], Ann, 358
,, Edmund, 15
,, Ellen, 15
Hartington, Alice, 42
,, John, 42
Hartley [Hartleye, Hartly], Ann, 304
,, Gilian, 235
,, Henry, 241
,, James, 194, 229, 235, 241, 257, 278, c. of 346
,, Jennet, 353
,, John, 229, 278
,, Richard, 257
Haslam [Halsom, Haslame, Hasleom, Haslom, Haslome, Haslum, Hasselam],
,. Alice, 17, 36, 68,* 76, 79, 87, 102, 148, 154, 157, 197, 201, 224, 252, 279, 283
,, Ann, 34, 247, 261, 303, 361
,, Charles, 112
., Dorothy, 24, 198, 281
,, Edmund, 6, 10, 15, 18, 24, 30, 35, 42,* 43, 48, 52, 72, 79, 87, 90, 96, 99, 103, 128, 136, 152, 154, 158, 163, 170, 210, 227, 261, 274,* 280, 283, 368
,, Elizabeth, 35, 57, 154, 183, 184, 206, 211, 217, 226, 288, 293, 324
,, Ellen, 52, 158, 177, 219, 271, 360
,, Ellis, 4,* 10, 60, 68, 72, 78, 125, 139, 148, 152, 161, 166, 191, 211, 217, 224, 282, 288, 293, 295, 297, 303, 355
,. Emeric, 48
,, Geffray, 17, 34, 115, 154, 173, 180, 199, 281
., George, 353
,, Giles, 281, w. of 326, 362
,, Isabel, 43, 282

Q

Vol. 1.—C. . pp. 1— 90 inclusive. Vol. 2.—C. . pp. 205—280 inclusive.
  B. . ,, 91—168 ,,   B. . ,, 281—350 ,,
  W. . ,, 169—204 ,,   W. . ,, 351—372 ,,

Haslam, James, 36, 213
 ,, Jane, 30, 76, 188, 240, 242, 271
 ,, John, 62, 66,* 72, 79, 92, 145, 158,* 193, 214, 275, 364
 ,, Jony, 353
 ,, Katherine, 60, 235
 ,, Lawrence, 15, 62, 68, 72, 75,* 81, 90, 145, 191, 213, 214, 221, 226, 235, 285, 329, 353
 ,, Margaret, 202
 ,, Margerie, 96
 ,, Mary, 6, 81, 166, 233, 352, 355
 ,, "Oulde" 191
 ,, Peter, 280
 ,, Richard, 10,* 18, 81,* 155, 199, 203. 206, 210, 214,* 219, 223, 227, 233, 240, 242, 247, 252, 257, c. of 314, 341, w. of 343, 364
 ,, Thomas, 78, 109, 209, 221, 223, 257, 341
 ,, William, 4, 198, 209, 275, 279, c. of 347, 351
Hasleden, Thomas, 368
Haslom, Haslum, Hasselam [see Haslam]
Hatton [see also Atton], John, 227
 ,, Margaret, 371
 ,, Mary, 227
Haugh, Haughe [see Halgh]
Haughton [see Houghton]
Haulgh [see Halgh]
Haworth [Hauworth, Hauworthe, Hawarthe, Hawathe, Haweorth, Haworthe, Hawworth, Houworthe, Howarth, Howoorth, Howorth, Howorthe, Howworth],
 ,, Abraham, 79,* 162, 281, 285
 ,, Adam, 56, 105
 ,, Alexander, 106, 138, 230, 242
 ,, Alice, 28, 89, 115, 168, 190, 202,* 213, 228, 232, 239, 269, 276, 292, 297, c. of 345, 352,* 353,* 354, 357, 367, 368, 370, 371
 ,, Ann, 60, 82, 166, 182, 202, 210, 218, 242, 245, 256, 258, 259,* 273, 281, 288, 293, 296, 300, 302. 303, 314, 322, 340, 349, 351, 354, 371
 ,, Annis, 357
 ,, Arthur, 106, w. of 333, 364, 369
 ,, Charles, 29, 63
 ,, Diana, 36
 ,, Dionis, 270

Haworth, Dorothy, 26, 29, 85, 113, 219, 246, 253, 306, 372
 ,, Edmund, 3, 39, 89, 101, 109, 127, 166, 204, 216, 237, 238, 242, 247, 251, 253, 256, 260, 292, c. of 309, 318, 322
 ,, Edward, 83, 186, 288
 ,, Effan (f), 197
 ,, Elizabeth, 20, 27, 56, 57, 63, 78, 151, 194, 198, 199, 208,* 217, 223, 225,* 230, 236, 238, 262, 269, 270, 281, 282, 286, 288, 293, 296, 305, 309, c. of 310, 337, 353, 354
 ,, Ellen, 3, 4, 17, 51, 201, 202, 211, 226, 269, 280, 292, 363, 370
 ,, Ellis, 200, 208, 215, 222, 226,* 230, 231, 237, 243, 249,* 261, c. of 301, c. of 307, 322, w. of 346, 355
 ,, Francis, 8, 89, 195, 211, 219, 228, 292
 ,, Geffray, 180, 249
 ,, George, 5, 11, 13, 55, 73,* 138, 142,* 161, 173, 191, 197, 210, 217, 225,* 230, 232,* 234,* 239, 243, 245,* 247, 250, 253,* 254, 260,* 261, 265, 269, 273, 280, 294, 295, c. of 308, c. of 313, c. of 314, c. of 317, c. of 319, 321,* c. of 324,* c. of 325, w. of 325, 330, w. of 331, w. of 333, 353, 355, 357, 358,* 362, 369
 ,, Gilbert, 193
 ,, Grace, 23, 226, 229, 305, 362
 ,, Henry, 51, 63, 77,* 89, 121, 130, 133, 137, 142, 149, 156, 162, 163, 188, 193, 199, 212, 279, 284, 334, w. of 343, 351, 355
 ,, Imyn, 42
 ,, Isabel, 29, 138, 222, 288, 294, 304, 355
 ,, Jacob, 15
 ,, James, 1, 9,* 10,* 29, 53, 56,* 58, 70,* 74, 81, 83,* 124, 207,* 210, 211, 216, 223,* 252, 255,* 259, 264, 265,* 269,* 270, 273,* 276,* 277, 279, 282, 292, c. of 294, 302, 305, c. of 308, 309, c. of 326, 327,* c. of 332, c. of 341, c. of 344, c. of 347, 352, 354, 362, 369
 ,, Jane, 29, 38, 74, 226, 247, 261, 356, 357, 369
 ,, Jennet, 184, 239, 294
 ,, Jeremy, 232, 249, 324

ID## INDEX OF NAMES.

Vol. 1.—C. . pp. 1— 90 inclusive. Vol. 2.—C. . pp. 205—280 inclusive.
B. . ,, 91—168 ,, B. . ,, 281—350 ,,
W. . ,, 169—204 ,, W. . ,, 351—372 ,,

Haworth, John, 1, 5, 10,* 11, 12, 15, 16, 20,* 23, 31, 45, 48, 51, 53, 56, 66, 74, 78, 81, 83, 86,* 104,* 107,* 108,* 116, 120, 125,* 134, 136, 147, 148, 156, 162, 172, 181, 183, 186, 189,* 194, 207,* 211, 215, 225, 228, 231, 240, 241, 243, 246, 247, 249,* 252, 259, 262, 264, 265, 266, 269,* 270, 272,* 277, 278, 282,* 283, 286, 300, 305,* c. of 308,* w. of 312, c. of 314, c. of 319, 322, w. of 328, c. of 333, w. of 334, 335, 343, 346, c. of 350, 353, 356, 365, 368, 370
,, Jonas, 245, 324, c. of 325
,, Jone [Jonie], 48, 149, 164, 247
,, Katherine, 77, 150, 243, 254, 285, 292
,, Kerstabell, 359
,, Lawrence, 226
,, Letcse, 359
,, Margaret, 29, 51, 74, 78, 157, 183, 203, 261, 265, 268, 273, 341, 353,* 359
,, Margerie, 357
,, Martha, 265
,, Mary, 4, 50, 89, 159, 205, 221, 232, 234, 236, 255, 266, 276, 278, 296, c. of 309, 321,* 352, 369, 370
,, Michael, 196, 266, 270
,, Nathaniel, 211
,, Oliver, 91, 113, 117, 120, 154, 187, 213, 207
,, Otwell, 109
,, "One of the," 299
,, Ralph, 99, 124, 166, 266, 269, c. of 332, 337, c. of 350
,, Renard, 131
,, Renold, 168, 198, 226, 281
,, Reuben, 211, 218, 225, 235,* 253, c. of 325, 351
,, Richard, 3, 12, 23, 28, 36, 43,* 50, 60, 66, 76, 78,* 83, 99, 106, 127, 128, 150, 157,* 159, 178, 183, 192, 198, 208, 219, 228, 232, 239, 253, 261, 262, 266, 270, 284, 289, 291, 306, c. of 316,* w. of 331, 337, 365, 369
,, Robert, 2,* 4, 6,* 10, 16, 17, 21,* 23, 26, 27, 29, 31, 38, 42, 96, 101, 102, 103, 119, 120, 121, 128, 129,* 134, 157, 164, 171, 174, 194, 203, 207, 221,

Haworth, Robert, *continued*—
222,* 226, 229, 231, 235,* 249,* 250, 253, 254, 260, inf. of 282, 283, inf. of 285, 286, inf. of 288, 288, 293, 296,* 303,* 305, c. of 306, 315, 318, c. of 320, 321, w. of 321, d. of 327, w. of 331, 354,* 355, 372
,, Roger, 212, 265, 344
,, Samuel, 262
,, Susan, 56, 78, 149, 157, 239, 241, 249, 305, 354,* 371
,, Thomas, 3, 12, 15,* 25,* 28, 29, 39, 45, 51, 57, 63,* 74,* 85, 89, 99, 110, 114, 120, 122, 130, 135, 137, 143, 156, 176, 190, 204, 207, 210, 213,* 218, 219, 231, 234, 236,* 240, 242, 247, 250, 251, 259,* 261,* 265, 266, 268, 269, 273, 282, 290, 292, 293, 299, 313, w. of 321, w. of 347, 372
,, Widow, 147
,, William, 4, 8, 10, 20, 58, 71,* 76, 82, 83, 113, 120, 124, 125,* 157,* 199, 205, 213, 218, 253, 254, 282, 285, 288, 289, 296,* 297,* 304, w. of 318, d. of 323, c. of 328, 329
Haymer [see Hamer]
Hayward [see Heyward]
Haywood [see Heywood]
Heald [Healde, Heild, Heyld],
,, Alice, 220, 233, 253, 290
,, Ann, 42, 53,* 182, 213, 216, 232, 242, 312
,, Annis (Annes), 151
,, Edward, 259
,, Elizabeth, 31, 213,* 220, 239, 262, 263, 279, 289, 295
,, Ellen, 19, 42, 218, 273, 372
,, Esther, 270
,, Isabel, 216, 229, 242
,, James, 63, 135, 193, 216, 237, 292, 312, 322
,, Jane, 22, 276, 339, 354
,, Jennet, 286
,, John, 19, 85, 106, 221, 220, 289, 327
,, Katherine, 177, 215
,, Margaret, 279, 284
,, Mary, 223, 245, 267, 286
,, Peter, 39, 227,* 253, 259, 262, 267, 273, 276, 279, w. of 313, c. of 317, c. of 344, c. of 348
,, Richard, 13, 22, 28, 39, 53, 80*, 208, 213, 216,* 218, 220, 223,

Vol. 1.—C. . *pp. 1— 90 inclusive.* *Vol. 2.—C.* . *pp. 205—280 inclusive.*
    B. . ,, *91—168* ,,   *B.* . ,, *281—350* ,,
    W. . ,, *169—204* ,,   *W.* . ,, *351—372* ,,

Heald, Richard, *continued—*
 228,* 233, 239, 243, 258, 259,
 inf. of 281, 286,* 287, 292,
 295, 327, 339, 342, 344, 352
,, Robert, 28, 58, 125, 232, 239,
 245, 253, 258, 270, 284, c. of
 321, c. of 325, w. of 328, w. of
 329, c. of 330, 347, 364, 369
,, Roger, 208, 287
,, Thomas, 31, 53, 58, 70,* 85, 118,
 135, 189, 215, 220, 253, 263,
 277,* 290, 292, c. of 298, c. of
 298, c. of 301, w. of 343, 354,
 370
,, William, 13, 63, 121, 132, 216,
 221, 237, 242,* 243, 259, 279,
 c. of 312, w. of 349, 359, 371
Heap [Heape, Heavpp], George, 144
,, John, 44, 47, 59, 129, 132, 186,
 187, 227, c. of 315
,, Richard, 227
,, William, 59, 364
Heaton [Heatone, Heatonn],
,, Alice, 217
,, Ann, 10, 82, 276, 322
,, Elizabeth, 87, 271, 276, 367
,, George, 82, 200, 207, 217, 231,
 243, 276, c. of 316, w. of 340,
 370
,, Grace, 207
,, Isabel, 202
,, James, 37, 43, 67. 179, 260
,, John, 43, 174, 215, 271, inf. of
 288, 302, 368
,, Katherine, 188
,, Margaret, 231
,, N.N.N., 243
,, Peter, 260
,, Ralph, 37, 276, 367
,, Richard, 10, 67, 87, 100,* 266,*
 372
,, Sarah, 215
,, Susan, 358, 361
Heavpp [see Heape]
Heaward [see Heyward]
Heild [see Heald]
Heleye [Hely], Elizabeth, 184, 372
Helliwell [Halewell, Haliwell,
 Halliwell, Hallywell,
 Halywall, Heliwell,
 Heliwelle, Hellywell],
,, Alexander, 108, 151, 154
,, Alice, 39, 84, 284, 289
,, Ann, 18, 28, 39, 192, 260, 292,
 295
,, Edmund, 75,* 84, 193, 253, 284,
 c. of 290, 319, c. of 322

Helliwell, Edward, 68, 90, 211, 218,
 c. of 307, c. of 327
,, Elizabeth, 33, 44, 48,* 164,*
 253, 257, 298, 302
,, Ellen, 10, 45, 203
,, Hamer (Emor), 92
,, James, 218
,, Jane, 122
,, John, 10, 90, 201, 289, 319
,, Joshua, 71
,, Margery, 154
,, Ralph, 10
,, Richard, 18,* 28, 37, 44, 111,
 125, 157, 289, 292, 295
,, Robert, 37, 71
,, Roger, 45, 136, 211, w. of 312
 330
,, Thomas, 10, 19,* 33, 68, 95, 108,
 118, 137, 257, 260, 292,* 301,
 302, w. of 324, 366
Henly, Isabel, 370
Henthorne, Henry, 361
Heward, Hewarde, Hewward [see
 Heyward]
Hewood, Hewoode, Hewwood [see
 Heywood]
Hey [Heye, Heyes],
,, Abraham, 57, 58, 153,* 156, 191
,, Alice, 27, 65, 76, 114, 183, 202
,, Ann, 149
,, Dorothy, 9, 85
,, Edmund, w. of 349
,, Edward, 27, 155, 196
,, Elizabeth, 193, 195, 285
,, Ellen, 58, 153, 195
,, John, 20, 65,* 157, 208, 304
,, Lawrence, 55, 287, 291
,, Margaret, 55, 163
,, Mary, 149, 370
,, Ralph, 129
,, Richard, 57, 65, 76, 85, 149, 156,
 157, 163, 198, 208, 282, 285,
 304
,, Thomas, 17
,, William, 9, 13,* 17, 20, 100, 102,
 105, 115, 160, w. of 322
Heyld [see Heald]
Heyward [Hayward, Heaward,
 Heward, Hewarde,
 Hewward, Heywarde],
,, Alexander, 96, 102, 169, 207
,, Alice, 30
,, Ann, 27, 76, 212
,, Arthur, 309
,, Dorothy, 310, 358
,, Edmund, 338
,, Elizabeth, 370

INDEX OF NAMES.

Vol. 1.—C. . pp. 1— 90 inclusive. *Vol. 2.—C.* . pp. 205 – 280 inclusive.
    B. . ,, 91—168 ,,   B. . ,, 281—350 ,,
    W. . ,, 169—204 ,,   W. . ,, 351—372 ,,

Heyward, Ellen, 46, 356
  ,, Ellinor, 218
  ,, Humphrey, 96
  ,, Jane, 27, 30
  ,, Jeffery, 76
  ,, John, 76, 212, 369
  ,, Margaret, 120
  ,, Mary, 212, 327, 338
  ,, Peter, 55, 258,* c. of 310, 324, 358
  ,, Richard, 211, 218, c. of 306, c. of 338, 338,* 354
  ,, Thomas, 46, 55, 76, 186, 207, 212, inf. of 283, 309, 311, 327, w. of 340, w. of 345
  ,, William, 211
Heywood [Haywood, Hewood, Hewoode, Hewwood, Heywod, Heywode, Heywoode],
  ,, Alexander, 284
  ,, Alice, 57, 62, 67, 122, 152, 212, 287, 293
  ,, Ann, 217, 253, d. of 284
  ,, Caleb, 147
  ,, Dorothy, 52, 116
  ,, Edmund, 4, 11, 19, 62, 245
  ,, Elizabeth, 18, 56, 210, 352
  ,, Ellen, 18, 202, 212, 229
  ,, Em [sic], 85
  ,, Henry, 57, 158
  ,, Isabel, 162
  ,, James, 74, 116, 155
  ,, Jane, 71
  ,, John, 4, 18, 70, 85, 87, 110, 154, 174, 203, 207, 210, 217, 223,* 229, 237, 245, 283, 288, 336, 360
  ,, Judith, 282
  ,, Mary, 80, 124, 293
  ,, Mr., 253, c. of 289, c. of 325, 333, 350
  ,, Peter, 19, 114, 120, 299, 333*
  ,, Richard, 11, 71, 207, 237, 283, 293, 299
  ,, Robert, 48, 52, 56, 61,* 70, 74, 80, 87, 154, 155, 284, 293, 350
  ,, Samuel, 362
  ,, Susan, 48
  ,, Thomas, 67, 144,* 152, 284, 287, 288
  ,, William, 19, 136, 162, 292
Hichenson [see Hutchinson]
Hickopp [?], Sarah, 321
Higgins [Higgyns], John, 95
Higginson, Elizabeth, 371

Higson, Diana, 368
  ,, John, 151
Hilelee [see Holliley]
Hill, Alice, 25, 157
  ,, Ann, 2, 91
  ,, Bridget, 2, 93
  ,, Dorothy, 237
  ,, Edmund, 193
  ,, Ellen, 272
  ,, Henry, 361
  ,, John, 222,* 237, 256, 263, 272, c. of 298, 359
  ,, Mary, 25, 293
  ,, Sarah, 256
  ,, Thomas, 2
  ,, William, 25, 91, 93
Hilton [Hiltonn], Alice, 157
  ,, Ann, 298
  ,, Elizabeth, 188
  ,, Esther, 270
  ,, James, 84, 270, 279
  ,, John, 206,* 214, c. of 290
  ,, Joshua, 84
  ,, Mary, 214
  ,, Robert, w. of 345
  ,, Sarah, 279
  ,, Susan, 359
  ,, Thomas, 157, 371
  ,, William, 270
Hind [Hinde, Hynd, Hynde, Hyne],
  ,, Alice, 45, 84, 261
  ,, Ann, 21, 55, 217, 219, 227, 254, 361
  ,, Edward, 209, 215, 219, 224, 230, 237, 243,* 255,* 261, 292, c. of 324, 325, 353
  ,, Elizabeth, 13, 88, 180, 209, 211, 215, 224, 287, 292, 354, 370
  ,, Ellen, 16, 20, 51
  ,, Jane, 154
  ,, Jeremy, 51, 84, 136, 181, 200, 215, 302, c. of 305
  ,, John, 11, 13, 20, 31,* 45, 55, 63, 70,* 75, 84, 102,* 114, 138, 141, 174, 159, 172, 208, 211, 219,* 227, 236, 237, 272, 284, 287, 295, 305, w. of 317, 324,* c. of 329, 343, 348
  ,, Katherine, 201
  ,, Margaret, 207
  ,, Mary, 208, 236, 284
  ,, Richard, 11, 66, 106, 224
  ,, Robert, 66
  ,, Samuel, 84, 295
  ,, Thomas, 16, 21, 63, 74, 80, 88, 110, 159, 177, 194, 209, 215, 217, 224, 230, 272, 297, 307, w. of 320, 325, 340, 343

Vol. 1.—C. . *pp. 1— 90 inclusive.* *Vol. 2.—C.* . *pp. 205—280 inclusive.*
B. . ,, *91—108* ,, *B.* . ,, *281—350* ,,
W. . ,, *169—204* ,, *W.* . ,, *351—372* ,,

Hiptrotte, Isabel, 96
,, Peter, 96
Hitchenson, Hitchinson, [see Hutchinson]
Hobken, John, 42
,, Margaret, 42
Hobkinson [see Hopkinson]
Hodgekinson [Hodgekinsonn],
,, Jane, 194
,, Otiwell, 197
,, Roger, 190
Hoile [see Hoyle]
Holcome, Alice, 228
,, John, 228
Holcroft [Holcrofte], Ann, 8
,, John, 8
,, Mr., 107
Holden [Houlden, Houldenn, Howldin],
,, Alice, 188, 353
,, Andrew, 31, 38, 47, 54, 65, 149, 179, c. of 298
,, Ann, 31
,, Christopher, 160, 161
,, Dorothy, 65, 149
,, Elizabeth, 203
,, Genet, 177, 371
,, Gilbert, 266, c. of 336
,, John, 54, 353
,, Katherine, 38
,, Kirstabell, 372
,, Margaret, 362
,, Mary, 81
,, Oliver, 342, 364
,, Peter, 66
,, Ralph, 81
,, Richard, 210, 287, 352
,, Robert, 66, 194, 266
Hoileley, Holeleye, Holelie [see Holliley]
Holes, Annice, 262
,, John, 262
Hollilie [see Holliley]
Holland [Hollande, Hollon],
,, Edmund, 198
,, Ellen, 192
,, Francis, 299
,, John, 71
,, Mary, 33
,, Peter, 10
,, Richard, 33, 71
,, William, 10
Hollas, Samuel, 366
Holliley [Halliley, Hlilalee, Hoileley, Holeleye, Holelie, Holilee, Holilie, Holylee, Holyley],
,, Alice, 5

Holliley, Elizabeth, 16, 320, 363
,, Ellen, 89
,, Francis, 299
,, George, 1,* 5, 9, 16, 67, 201
,, Jane, 9
,, Jonas, 253
,, "One," 98
,, Richard, w. of 323
,, Robert, 89
,, Thomas, 67, 195, 253
Hollon [see Holland]
Holme [Holmes, Houlme], Ann, 220
,, Francis, 40
,, George, 215,* 291, 354
,, Isabel, 372
,, James, 241
,, Jane, 336
,, John, 207, 212, 291
,, Michael, 254
,, Miles, 207, 212, 220, 232, 241, 283, c. of 326, c. of 335, 351
,, Rauffe, 40
,, Richard, 232, 283
,, Susan, 310
,, William, 254, 310
Holt [Haulte, Hollt, Holte, Holtes, Houllt, Hoult, Houlte, Houltt, Howlt],
,, Abigail, 246, 353
,, Abraham, 21, 57, 71,* 79, 99, 140, 153, 166, 216, 237, 286, 287
,, Adam, 47, 217, 293
,, Alexander, 92
,, Alice, 12, 13, 22, 29,* 32,* 41, 46, 73, 76, 78, 81, 86, 96, 120, 121, 156, 157, 162, 179, 186, 188, 193, 195, 199, 205, 206, 207, 208, 211, 212, 215, 220, 225, 226, 227, 229, 232, 239, 243, 245, 252, 256, 270, 274, 276, 283, 286, 294, 301, 305, 306,* c. of 309, 335, 354, 364, 371
,, Andrew, 12, 15, 22, 27, 55, 67, 78, 83, 111, 122,* 123, 157, 172, 186, 212, 290, w. of 331
,, Ann, 1,* 2, 3, 16, 17, 20, 23, 30, 34, 37, 40, 42, 49, 52, 57, 62, 72,* 81, 85, 125, 154, 201, 202, 205, 208, 215, 216, 235,* 236, 237, 240, 243, 257, 266, 267, 272, 278, 289, 292, 296, 297,* 304, 312, 315, 332, 334, 336, 352,* 355,* 357, 358, 363, 367
,, Arthur, 2, 12,* 22, 30,* 39, 58, 60, 72, 85, 92, 101, 124,* 133,

INDEX OF NAMES.

Vol. 1.—C. . pp. 1— 90 inclusive. Vol. 2.—C. . pp. 305—380 inclusive.
B. . ,, 91—168 ,, B. . ,, 281—350 ,,
W. . ,, 169—204 ,, W. . ,, 351—372 ,,

Holt, Arthur, *continued*—
    136, 181, 242,* 243, 244, 247, 291, 313, w. of 319, 329, c. of 330, 339, w. of 346, 371
,, Benjamin, 41
,, Charles, 3, 45, 93, 207, 235, 241, 261, 274,* 283, c. of 309, w. of 326
,, Christopher, 83, 101
,, Cicell (Cecill), 77, 343
,, Deborah, 3
,, Dinah, 263
,, Dorothy, 2, 7, 26, 27, 32, 36, 40, 49, 52, 53, 58, 188, 198,* 199,* 231,* 245, 271, 277
,, Edmund, 7, 12, 13, 16, 19, 21,* 30, 31,* 36, 40, 85, 89, 105, 133, 164, 167, 172, 201, 204, 205, 211, 212, 220, 227, 231, 237,* 239,* 240, 246, 250, 252, 256, 257, 260, 261,* 263,* 269, inf. of 281, 292, 293, 310, 312,* c. of 312, 317, 334, c. of 334, 336, c. of 337, w. of 341, c. of 341, w. of 344, w. of 345, c. of 348, 355, 357, 363, 365
,, Edward, 14, 29, 38,* 49, 59, 64, 67, 89, 132, 141, 172, 175, 192, 201, 212, 229,* 253, 263, 274, 287, 339, c. of 346, w. of 347, c. of 348
,, Elizabeth, 3, 8, 17, 22, 27, 29, 36, 40, 43, 46, 53, 54, 56, 62, 79, 81, 83, 100, 122, 151, 153, 183, 185, 196, 201,* 208, 220, 236, 259, 261, 268, 273,* 286, 288, 299, 307, 308, 350, 353, 355,* 356, 361, 369
,, Ellen, 13, 18, 29, 41, 46, 67, 71, 73, 75, 144, 159, 160, 177, 200, 213, 246, 261, 314, 360, 366, 368
,, Ellinor, 94
,, Ellis, 12,* 20, 25, 27, 36, 44, 55, 68, 106, 149, 151, 153, 173, 257, 336
,, Francis, 10, 14, 15, 27, 38, 41, 59, 64, 66, 69, 77, 82, 88, 92, 93, 127, 136, 147, 232, 261, 282, 308
,, George, 16, 22, 29, 33, 38, 39, 47, 51, 52, 57, 61, 67, 76, 83, 86, 117, 120, 130, 147,* 152, 159, 173, 185, 189, 205, 213, 221, 225, 229, 235,* 240, 244, 248, 249, 250,* 251, 256,* 260, 267, 269, 275, 286, 296, 301,

Holt, George, *continued*—
    c. of 303, c. of 313, c. of 337, 339, 347, 355
,, Gennet, 283
,, Grace, 202, 220, 244, 333
,, Henry, 2, 8, 17, 30, 43, 45, 47, 73, 159, 216, 243, 251, 255, 256, 258, 260,* 262, 269,* 271, 275, 332,* 344,* w. of 347
,, Hugh, 288
,, Humphrey, 48, 95, 122, 131, 143
,, Inya, 46
,, Isaac, 37, 47, 66, 81, 124, 147, 259, 276, 349
,, Isabel, 33, 194, 222, 229, 283, 295, 301, 347, 366
,, James, 3, 15, 16, 23,* 26,* 30, 33, 36, 38,* 40, 44, 46,* 51, 54, 56, 60, 66, 73, 77, 81, 92, 93, 123, 131, 137, 144, 156,* 161, 165, 173, 176, 190, 205, 208, 215, 216, 220, 222,* 228,* 231, 234,* 242,* 245, 253, 254, 255, 258, 259, 263, 267, 269, 270, 271, 272, 276, 277, 293, 296, 304, c. of 307, c. of 316, s. of 329, 331, c. of 332, c. of 337, 338, w. of 341, c. of 342, w. of 344, 348, 355, 363,* 372
,, Jane, 15, 16, 44,* 46, 54, 187, 222, 229, 249, 251, 253, 283, 291, 304, 336, 352, 360, 362
,, Jeremy, 277
,, John, 1, 2, 3, 10, 17, 22,* 24, 29, 33,* 35, 37, 40, 41, 42,* 43,* 49,* 51, 52,* 53, 57, 58, 63, 66, 74,* 75, 77,* 88,* 89, 92, 98, 100, 124,* 126, 127, 130, 135, 136, 137, 148, 150, 162,* 167,* 174, 180, 182, 185, 187, 193, 207, 212, 225,* 228, 229, 231, 235, 239, 242, 243, 245, 248, 250,* 251, 253, 254, 255, 259, 260, 261, 265, 267, 268, 271, 275, 276, 281,* 285, 291, 294, 296, c. of 305, 306, 324, c. of 325, 326, c. of 338, 347, 354, 362,* 370
,, Johnie (Joan), 249
,, Jonathan, 82, 262
,, Joseph, 28,* 49, 71, 82, 121, 135, 216, 275, 353
,, Joshua, 54, 188, 207, 216, w. of 320, d. of 321, 337
,, Katherine, 5, 13, 39, 54, 69, 147, 163, 177, 178, 179, 188, 198, 240, 287, 295, 308, 356, 371

Vol. 1.—C. . pp. 1— 90 inclusive. Vol. 2.—C. . pp. 205—280 inclusive.
B. . „ 91—168 „ B. . „ 281—350 „
W. . „ 169—204 „ W. . „ 351—372 „

Holt, Lucie, 57
„ Lydia, 272
„ Margaret, 12, 16, 31, 36, 39, 46, 61, 92, 95, 110, 143, 158,* 165, 177, 205, 215, 227, 237, 240, 256, 313, 351, 370
„ Margerie, 52, 147, 194
„ Martha, 42, 253, 363
„ Mary, 8, 22, 27, 31, 36, 40, 41, 51,* 57, 68, 82, 86, 163, 190, 198, 205, 206, 212, 217, 225, 235, 239, 243,* 245, 249, 250, 253, 255, 261, 265, 271,* 275,* 337, c. 339, 360, 361,* 367, 371
„ Mr., 27, 265, 282, 308, w. of 313, 317, d. of 321, 325, 339, 343, 350,* 364
„ Mistress, 104, 325
.. Oliver, 41
„ "One," 110
„ Peter, 14, 44, 57,* 72, 93, 101, 129, 139, 218, 222,* 225, 228, 234, 239, 244, 247, 254, 255, 259, 260,* 262, 267, 269, 275, 278, c. of 318, 333, c. of 334, 345,* 349, 350*
„ Priscilla, 73
„ Ralph, 1, 10, 17, 19, 58, 72, 78, 115, 146, 157, 226, 232,* 238, 242, 246, 257, 301, 304
„ Richard, 2, 3, 5, 8, 10,* 12, 14, 15, 17,* 18, 25, 26, 32,* 34, 36,* 37,* 40, 46,* 47, 48, 51, 53, 54, 55, 57, 61,* 68, 73, 76, 81, 85, 88, 89,* 91, 95, 98,* 101,* 112, 113, 119, 121, 123, 126, 133, 136, 137,* 142,* 143, 144,* 147, 154, 157, 158,* 159, 160, 162,* 163,* 164, 170, 174, 181, 184, 198, 200, 201, 202, 207, 221,* 222, 229, 232,* 233, 235,* 236, 237, 239, 240,* 241, 242, 245,* 248, 249, 250, 252, 256,* 257, 272, 283,* 284,* 294, 296,* 297, 305, c. of 307, 311, 312, 313, c. of 319, 320, 325, w. of 325, w. of 328, 328, w. of 330, c. of 331, 332, w. of 338, w. of 343, w. of 345, 345, c. of 346, 346, 359, 364, 369, 370
„ Robert, 21, 24, 36, 55, 70, 72, 77, 93, 96, 97, 131, 139, 151, 152, 201, 205, 231, 257,* 260, 261, 266, 273, 282, 285, c. of 307, 330, 344

Holt, Roger, 24, 31, 36, 42, 50,* 51, 57, 62, 95, 98, 127, 139, 145, 167, 207, 218, 220, 233, 236, d. of 327, 338, 371
„ Rosamund, 35
„ Samuel, 20, 42, 49, 253, 335, 347, 364
„ Sarah, 314
„ Susan, 15, 32, 39, 63, 157, 221, 222, 253, 263, 347, 353
„ Theophilus, 59, 235, 310
„ Thomas, 3, 8, 12, 13,* 20,* 21, 24, 29, 30, 32, 34, 37, 39, 40, 44, 48,* 49, 51, 57,* 66,* 70, 76, 86, 95, 96, 99, 100, 106, 109, 111, 119, 127, 130, 134, 143, 148, 150, 152, 170, 171, 184, 186, 201, 212,* 235, 238, 244, 248, 250, 252, 255, 260,* 261, 265, 267, 268,* 271, 272, 273, 275, 276, 283, 289, 295, c. of 308, 309,* c. of 319, 321, w. of 331, 336, c. of 340, 345, c. of 345, 350, 356, 360
„ William, 8, 17, 30, 33, 41, 48,* 51,* 62, 134, 159, 189, 227, 231, 234, 239, 242, 243, 245, 249, 254, 257, 262, 268,* 271, 277, 295, c. of 303, 306, c. of 316, 321, c. of 321, w. of 324, 338,* w. of 349, 350, 357, 366

Holylee, Holyley [see Holliley]
Hooke, John, 200
Hope, Alice, 189
„ Ann, 190
Hopewood [see Hopwood]
Hopkinson [Hobkinson, Hopkinsonne],
„ Ann, 265, 323
„ Christopher, 318
„ Edward, 264, 271, 278, c. of 349, 369
„ John, 264, 265, c. of 305, 323, 324
„ Margaret, 271
„ Sarah, 278
„ Thomas, 324
Hopwood [Hopewood, Hoppwood, Hopwoode],
„ Alice, 19, 88
„ Ann, 213, 281
„ Annis, 96
„ Dorothy, 333
.. Edmund, 223
„ Elizabeth, 177, 213, 225, 235, 340
„ Ellen, 9

INDEX OF NAMES. 405

Vol. 1.—C. , pp. 1— 90 inclusive. Vol. 2.—C. , pp. 205- 280 inclusive.
 B. , ,, 91 -168 ,, B. , ,, 281 -350 ,,
 W. , ,, 169—204 ,, W. , ,, 351—372 ,,

Hopwood, James, 34, 100, 264
 ,, Jane, 233, 237
 ,, John, 22, 213, 217, 221, 223, 231, 244, 250, 253, 257, 333, 372
 ,, Judith, 34, 225
 ,, Katherine, 199
 ,, Margaret, 167, 197, 256, 323, 332
 ,, Martin, 88, 203, 213, 221, 227, 235, 256, 264, 339, 340, w. of 344
 ,, Mary, 59, 217, 227, 233, 257, 351
 ,, Matthew, 196
 ,, Richard, 19, 202, 214,* 228, 244,* 250,* 253, 355
 ,, Robert, 11, 22, 59, 124,* 202, 225,* 231, 237, 258, c. of 318, w. of 323, w. of 346, 355
 ,, Susan, 258
 ,, Thomas, 9, 13,* 104, 297,* c. of 332
 ,, William, 11, 98, 105, 138, 167, 244, 250, c. of 325, c. of 329
Horobin [Horabin, Horabyn, Horrabin, Horrobin, Horrobinne],
 ,, Ann, 220, c. of 347
 ,, Ellen, 330
 ,, Jane, 368
 ,, John, 161
 ,, Richard, 220, 241, 252, w. of 316
 ,, Robert, 241, 252, 335
Horredge [Horege, Horidge, Horrege, Horwich],
 ,, Ann, 215
 ,, Elizabeth, 360
 ,, Ellen, 283
 ,, John, 215, 283, 290,* 327, 352
 ,, Peter, 201, w. of 311
Horrobin [see Horobin]
Horrocks [Horockes, Horoks, Horrak, Horrax, Horrockes, Horroks, Horrox, Whorockes, Whorrockes],
 ,, Ann, 231
 ,, Edmund, c. of 319
 ,, Elizabeth, 79
 ,, Ellen, 210, 269, 332
 ,, Isabel, 297
 ,, James, 228, 296
 ,, Jane, 50
 ,, John, 32, 94, 112, 214, 228, 336
 ,, Lawrence, 210, 231, 269
 ,, Margaret, 56, 360
 ,, Richard, 79, 214, 269
 ,, Roger, 51, 56, 134

Horrocks, Susan, 32
 ,, William, 50, 51, 185, 269, 296, 303, c. of 337
Houghe, Elizabeth, 185
 ,, John, 192
Houghton [Haughton, Houghtonn],
 ,, Alice, 337, 366
 ,, Ann, 9, 193
 ,, George, 263, w. of 343, s. of 348, c. of 349
 ,, John, 263
 ,, Roger, 9, 109, 126, 298
 ,, Richard, 113, 139
Houlden [see Holden]
Houlme [see Holme]
Hoult, Houlte, Hoaltt [see Holt]
Howarth, Howorth, Howworth [see Haworth]
Howldin [see Holden]
Howlt [see Holt]
Hoyle [Hoile], Alice, 367
 ,, Ann, 211, 348
 ,, Dorothy, 279
 ,, Henry, 298
 ,, John, 203, 211, 279, 287, 356, 365
 ,, Margaret, 179, 361
 , Mary, 287
Huchinson [see Hutchinson]
Huite, Grace, 310
Hull [Hulls], Ann, 272
 ,, Dorothy, 277
 ,, Elizabeth, 238, 349
 ,, George, 34, 236,* 242, 254, 258, 272, 277, c. of 326, c. of 333, c. of 334, c. of 349, 361
 ,, Margaret, 363
 ,, Mary, 254, 258
 ,, Ralph, 238
 ,, Susan, 242
 ,, Thomas, 34, 186
Hunt [Hunte], Alice, 3, 163, 256
 ,, Ann, 158
 ,, Dorothy, 39, 265, 365
 ,, Edmund, 91, 156, 235
 ,, Edward, 4, 17,* 90, 107, 235, 256, c. of 333
 ,, Elizabeth, 85, 208, 216, 235, 284
 ,, Ellen, 20
 ,, George, 265
 ,, Grace, 226
 ,, James, 3, 16, 23, 39, 121, 128, 156, 163, 206, 282, 286, w. of 325, 360
 ,, Jane, 4, 351
 ,, John, 10, 16, 18, 85, 100, 118, 158, 172, 201, 208, 220, 235,

R

Vol. 1.—C. . *pp. 1 - 90 inclusive.* *Vol. 2.—C.* . *pp. 205—280 inclusive.*
     B. . ,, *91—168* ,,   *B.* . ,, *281—350* ,,
     W. . ,, *169—204* ,,   *W.* . ,, *351—372* ,,

Hunt, John, *continued*—
    240, 253,* 265,* 284, c. of 311, 327, w. of 345
,, Jony, 282
,, Margaret, 145, 215, 220
,, Margerie, 164
,, Mary, 86, 208, 240
,, N.X.N., 203
,, Oliver, 235
,, Richard, 86, 90, 164, 215, 226, 235
,, Robert, 10, 18, 208
,, Samuel, 42*
,, Sarah, 206
,, Susan, 216
,, Thomas, 20, 23
Hunter, Ann, 265
,, Peter, 265
Hurle, Margaret, 303
Hurst [Hurste],
,, Alice, 149
,, Ann, 84
,, Edmund, 171
,, Jane, 68, 147
,, John, 56
,, Margaret, 52
,, Mary, 277
,, Ralph, 277
,, Thomas, 68, 84, 147
,, William, 52, 56, 135,* 149,* 188
Hurtleingtonn, Ann, 194
Hutchinson [Hichenson, Hitchenson, Hitchensonne, Hitchinson, Hitchinsonne, Huchinson, Huchinsun, Hutchenson],
,, Alice, 232, 262
,, Elizabeth, 279
,, Ellen, 265, 273, 339
,, Francis, 76, 270, 275, 279, 368
,, Jane, 249, 260
,, John, 34, 42, 51, 76, 163, 270, 275, 278, w. of 328
,, Judith, 265
,, Mary, 269, 364
,, Richard, 51, 260,* 265, 273, c. of 350
,, Robert, 42, 253,* 260, 269,* 338, 364
,, Thomas, 34, 254, 265, 371
,, William, 232, 239,* 249, 254, 262, 269, 278
Hutton, Ann, 301
,, John, 65,* 158, 301*
Hynd, Hynde [see Hind]
Hyndleye, Elizabeth, 29
,, John, 29
Hyne [see Hind]

I

Ince, Robert, 105
Ingham [Ingam, Ingamm, Inghame],
,, Ann, 260*
,, Edward, 354, 358
,, Henry, 58
,, John, 185
,, Margaret, 290
,, Margery, 58
,, Mary, 267
,, Mr., 267, 369
,, William, 267, 369
Ingles [Engles], Isabel, 148
,, John, 148, 197
Isherwood [Iserwoode, Isherworthe, Usherwood, Usherwoode, Ushwood, Vsherwood, Ysherwoode, Yssherwoode],
,, Abraham, 272
,, Alice, 68
,, Ann, 233, 267, 298
,, Arthur, 353
,, Dorothy, 266, 279
,, Edmund, 274
,, Elizabeth, 310
,, Ellen, 277, 301
,, Francis, 53
,, Isabel, 273
,, James, 255,* 261, 266, 274, c. of 340, 365
,, John, 53, 68, 80, 83,* 181, 208, 233, 261, 267, 273, 277, 298, 301, c. of 309, 358, 367
,, Mary, 261, 332
,, Oliver, 199
,, Ralph, 80
,, Richard, 240, 244, 257, 264, 272, 279, c. of 315, 339
,, Robert, 192, 261
,, Roger, 240, 244, 264, 339
,, William, 208, 257
Ishmalitt, John, w. of 315

J

Jachuns, Thomas, c. of 345
Jackson [Jackeson, Jackesonn, Jacksonn, Jacksonne, Jacson, Jakson],
,, Abraham, 252
,, Adam, 56,* 79, 272, 280, 297*
,, Dorothy, 276
,, Edmund, 217, 295
,, Elizabeth, 73, 267, 322
,, Ellen, 8, 351
,, Francis, 241, **333**

INDEX OF NAMES. 407

Vol. 1.—C. . pp. 1— 90 inclusive. Vol. 2.—C. . pp. 205—280 inclusive.
   B. . ,, 91—168   ,,   B. . ,, 281—350 ,,
   W. . ,, 169—204   ,,   W. . ,, 351—372 ,,

Jackson, Henry, 137, 205, 272, 273, 278*
,, Jacob, 246
,, James, 8, 19, 30,* 224,* 230, 235, 241, 246, 264, 269, 280, c. of 321, 322, 333, 339, 355
,, John, 274
,, Joseph, 280
,, Katherine, 19, 221, 357
,, Lawrence, 267, 274, 280
,, Margaret, 269, 357
,, Mary, 230, 273, 311, 333
,, Matthew, 55, 73, 79, 154. 190, 205, 217, 272, 295, w. of 318
,, Ralph, 351
,, Richard, 221, 264, 339
,, Thomas, 55, 154, 173, 192, 235, 252, 269,* 272, 276, c. of 326, 361, 365, 369
Janian [Janion, Jannion],
,, Ellen, 181
,, George, 112
,, Jane, 282
,, Margaret, 333
Jenkinson [Jenkenson, Jenkingson, Jenkinsone, Jenkinsun, Jenkynson, Jenkynsonn],
,, Alice, 255, 370
,, Elizabeth, 219, 260, 274
,, Grace, 261
,, James, 60, 241,* 255, 260, 261, 266, 271,* 278, c. of 323, 337, 361
,, John, 50,* 55, 60, 76, 134, 138, 188, 208,* 213,* 219, 274, 285* w. of 342, 370
,, Katherine, 55
,, Mary, 76, 266, 337, 363
,, Richard, 278
,, Susan, 351
Jobson [Jobsonn], Ann, 194
,, James, 203
Johnes, Johnns, Johoanes [see Jones]
Johns of George, c. of 301
Johnson [Johnsonn], Ann, 239, 369
,, Edward, 258
,, Elizabeth, 61, 354
,, Margaret, 365
,, Otwell, 61, 73*
,, Rebecca, 365
,, Richard, 255
,, Robert, 358
,, Susan, 258
,, Thomas, 255, 262*
,, William, 239, 361
Jollie, Ellis, 36
,, Margaret, 36

Jones [Johnes, Johnns, Johoanes, Johns],
,, Alice, 267, 367
,, Ann, 87, 220, 264
,, John, 250, 358
,, Katherine, 211
,, Margaret, 272, 309
,, Mary, 264
,, Richard, 67,* 77, 87, 192, 211, 220, 250, 258,* 264, 267, 309, 329, 335
,, Susan, 335
,, Thomas, 77, 106, 272, c. of 349, w. of 349, 364, 372

K

KARY, Katherine, 243
,, Robert, 243
Kay [Kaie, Kaij, Kaye, Keie, Key, Keye],
,, Abel, 213
,, Abraham, 34,* 38, 43, 46, 52, 56, 63, 64,* 76, 80, 84,* 89, 93, 117, 120, 126, 157, 180, 207,* 219, 226, 240, 261, 286, 337, 348, 349
,, Adam, 27, 93, 227
,, Agnes, 286
,, Alice, 3, 4, 5, 6, 27, 32, 39, 44, 50,* 57, 58, 65, 69, 71, 77, 139, 147, 156, 167, 180, 181, 185, 188, 196, 197, 198, 207, 220, 221, 224, 226,* 227, 237, 240, 265, 280,* 283, 297,* 340,* 351, 352, 355, 356, 358, 361, 371,* 372
,, Andrew, 93, 148
,, Ann, 4, 8,* 31, 35, 40, 46, 47, 63, 69, 73, 84, 87, 88, 94, 96, 123, 153,* 158, 160, 179, 187, 188, 191, 194, 196, 199, 200, 203, 209,* 211, 230, 238, 239, 241, 242, 243, 244, 251, 255, 264, 266, 267, 286, 294, 296, 297, 300, 306, 308, 322, 353, 354, 378,* 369
,, Annis, 298
,, Arthur, 14, 15, 24,* 29, 39, 45, 46, 54,* 57, 66, 71, 76, 84,* 85, 86, 99, 103, 116, 132, 171, 178, 179, 192, 209, 216, 220, 233, 235, 241, 242,* 248, 250,* 267, 282, 297, 301, 303, 307, c. of 311, 334, 348, 361, 368
,, Bartyn, 7, 11,* 19, 27, 32, 36, 50, 75, 104, 119, 123, 157, 172, 191, 214, 281, 304, w. of 318

408   BURY PARISH REGISTERS.

Vol. 1.—C. . pp.   1— 90 inclusive. Vol. 2.—C. . pp. 205—280 inclusive.
      B. . ,, 91—108 ,,   *B. . ,, 281—350 ,,*
      W. . ,, 109—204 ,,   *W. . ,, 351—372 ,,*

Kay, Charles, 29
,, Christopher, 46, 92,* 98, 122, 232
,, Constance, 87
,, Denis, 3, 7, 16, 251
,, Dionis, 98, 172, 173, 209
,, Dorothy, 13, 18, 22, 23, 30, 43, 46, 56, 179, 218,* 226, 229, 232, 234, 241, 244, 245, 249, 250,* 263, 269, 332, 336, 337, 353, 356, 360
,, Douse (f), 161
,, Edmund, 2, 22, 29, 44, 52, 53, 57, 66, 69, 71,* 77, 82, 83, 117, 120, 136,* 146, 163, 174, 190, 205, 206, 207, 209, 213, 220, 223, 243, 281, 310, c. of 318, w. of 335
,, Edward, 5, 6, 49, 54, 69, 108, 114, 115, 132, 144, 149, 151,* 261, 292, c. of 299
,, Elizabeth, 11, 20, 22, 33, 36, 42, 45, 47, 54, 66, 69, 71, 73, 76, 77, 79, 85, 86, 107, 121, 122, 149, 150,* 152, 155, 178, 179,* 181, 184, 189, 193, 197, 199, 200, 209, 211, 218, 219,* 224, 235, 236, 237, 239, 245, 247, 248, 250, 252, 255, 261, 268, 270, 282,* 285, 288, 289, 297, 298, 335, 337, 338, 341, 344, 353, 355, 359, 360,* 362, 370, 371
,, Ellen, 2, 21, 49, 53, 95, 209, 212, 217, 232, 233, 247, 251, 281, 289, 292, 299, 315, 341
,, Ellenor, 15, 61, 297, 365
,, Ellis, 30, 117, 127,* 251, 255, 262, 286, c. of 322, 345
,, Eme, 290
,, Emery [f.], 351
,, Florence, 285
,, Francis, 15, 29, 53, 227, 245, w. of 332, 362
,, George, 45, 228, 229
,, Gennet, 107, 194, 304
,, Grace, 158, 214, 291
,, Henry, 42, 71, 252,* 253, 275
,, Humphrey, 73, 79, 87, 196, 282, 284
,, Imyn, 187
,, Isabel, 12, 18, 19, 38, 54, 79, 93, 186, 189, 190, 191, 195, 202, 221, 224, 229, 241, 248, 268, 300, 304, 310, 334, 340, 368
,, James, 2,* 3,* 11, 14, 21,* 24,* 25, 28, 30,* 33,* 37, 39, 40,* 43,* 46, 47, 50, 52, 53,* 57,*

Kay, James, *continued*—
58,* 63, 64,* 65, 70, 71, 72, 76, 78, 80, 82, 86, 91, 107, 108, 113, 116, 117, 122, 126, 128, 130,* 134,* 145, 149, 150,* 151, 153, 156, 160, 161, 162, 165, 166, 170, 175, 182, 184, 192, 193, 201, 202, 206, 208, 209, 211,* 214, 215, 216, 219,* 220, 222, 223,* 224,* 227,* 230, 233,* 237, 240, 241, 244,* 245, 247,* 251,* 252,* 255, 256, 257, 258,* 259, 261,* 263, 268, 269, 273, 274, 276, 277, 278,* 286,* 288, 291, 292, 294, 296, 297, 304, 306, c. of 307, 308, c. of 315, w. of 318, 322, c. of 323, w. of 324, c. of 325, c. of 326, 326, w. of 329, c. of 329, 329, 341,* c. of 342, w. of 342, 349, 350, 351, 354, 360, 367
,, Jane, 14,* 19, 24, 31, 33, 34, 40, 52, 76, 77, 79, 83, 86, 150, 154, 160, 163, 181,* 190, 202, 216, 256, 263, 284, 287, 288, 292, 294, 300, 315, 331, 354, 355, 357
,, Jeremy, 74, 76, 85, 135, 187, 254
,, Jinnie, 298
,, John, 1,* 4,* 5, 10, 14,* 19, 25, 27,* 33,* 34, 37, 39, 47, 49, 52, 53,* 56, 61, 63,* 64, 65,* 66,* 73, 74,* 76, 83,* 84, 87, 88,* 91,* 96,* 97, 104, 109, 113, 122, 126,* 130,* 139, 143, 144, 148, 150, 151, 153, 155, 158,* 162, 167, 168, 171, 181, 186, 193, 194, 203, 205, 209, 210, 211, 213, 214,* 217, 218,* 219,* 220, 223,* 224, 226,* 227, 229, 232, 233, 235, 236, 237,* 238, 239, 241, 242, 243,* 244,* 245,* 246,* 248, 251, 252, 254, 255, 256,* 260,* 262,* 263,* 268, 270, 273, 274, 275, 276, 277,* 279,* 280,* 284, 287,* 288, 297, 299, 300, 303, 304, c. of 304, 305, 310, c. of 310, w. of 311, c. of 312, 313, c. of 315, w. of 316, c. of 317 [? Reys], c. of 318, w. of 320, c. of 320, 323, w. of 323, c. of 327, w. of 332, c. of 332, 335, 336, 339, 341, 342, w. of 343, w. of 346, s. of 348, 351, 354, 355, 358, 359, 360, 361, 363, 365, 367, 369, 371

INDEX OF NAMES.

Vol. 1.—C.   pp. 1— 90 inclusive.   Vol. 2.— C.   . pp. 205—280 inclusive.
B.   ,,   91—168   ,,   B.   . ,, 281—350   ,,
W.   ,, 169—204   ,,   W.   . ,, 351—372   ,,

Kay, Katherine, 138, 143. 150, 181, 183, 185, 187,* 224, 229, 233, 257, 286, 290, 296, c. of 334, 341, 369
,, Kerstabell, 350
,, Lawrence, 57, 137, 192, w. of 317, 326, 346
,, Lucy, 352
,, Lydia, 82
,, Margaret, 3,* 7, 12, 24, 33, 60, 63, 69, 72, 74, 81,* 93, 105, 107, 144, 149, 160, 161,* 166, 167, 197, 198, 204, 218, 219,* 225, 233, 270, 272, 278,* 283, 291,* 296, 299, 316, 354, 357, 367
,, Margerie, 137, 138
,, Martin, 91, 161, 169, 213, 218, 223, 228, 246, 252, 253, 256. 257, 259, 261,* 278, w. of 314, c. of 319, c. of 324, c. of 325, c. of 327, c. of 330, c. of 333, c. of 338, c. of 341, 344, w. of 347, 352
,, Mary, 9, 26, 47, 55, 60, 63, 64, 71, 74, 75,* 77, 85, 134, 144, 151, 197, 205, 206, 210, 222, 223,* 225, 231, 235, 239,* 243, 245,* 254, 255, 256, 258, 261, 266, 268, 273,* 276, 278, 279,* 280, 281, 334, 361, 363, 366,* 369, 371
,, Michael, 68, 76, 85, 194, 298,* 301
,, Miles, 14, 110, 141, 294, 310
,, Owen, 95
,, R., 12
,, Ralph, 12, 95, 127, 158, 160, 164, 171, 186, 259, 289
,, Rebeccah, 279
,, Renald, 122, 167, 285
,, Richard, 1, 3, 5, 12,* 16, 18, 21, 28, 33,* 37, 39, 43,* 45, 49, 50, 52, 53, 54, 55,* 62,* 64,* 65,* 66, 67, 68, 69,* 73,* 78, 79, 80,* 82, 86, 88, 89, 93,* 94, 96, 99,* 100, 107, 110, 116, 124, 131, 143,* 148,* 149, 150, 152, 153, 162, 164, 171, 188, 189, 193, 197, 209, 210,* 211, 212, 216, 217,* 218, 219,* 220, 223, 224, 225,* 229,* 233, 236,* 237, 239,* 242, 244, 245, 248, 250,* 251,* 253, 254,* 257,* 258, 261,* 262, 265,* 266, 274,* 275, 279,* 280, 287, 289, 293,

Kay, Richard, *continued* 296,* 297, 300, 301, 305, 307, c. of 314, c. of 320,* 320, 321, 328, 331, c. of 335, c. of 339, c. of 342, 344, w. of 345, 348, 350,* 356, 366, 369, 370, 372
,, Robert, 4,* 7, 8, 11, 14, 16, 23, 24, 27, 30, 31, 35, 36, 37, 40, 42, 45,* 46, 50,* 54, 57,* 60,* 63, 65,* 71, 74, 84, 88, 91, 94, 99, 101, 105, 122, 127, 130, 131, 140, 144, 145, 147, 149, 152, 156, 161, 162, 172, 177, 182, 188,* 189, 200,* 211, 213, 214,* 215, 218, 220, 222, 226, 228, 233,* 237, 239, 241,* 247, 248,* 259,* 262,* 263, 266,* 268, 269,* 271, 272, 274,* 276, 279, 280,* 281, 288, 290,* 299, w. of 310, c. of 314, 316, 317, c. of 320, 329. w. of 331, 337, 338, 340, w. of 342, 350, 351, 367, 370
,, Roger, 3,* 10, 14,* 20,* 24, 30, 38,* 45, 53, 54,* 55, 64, 67, 71, 82,* 88, 89, 99, 105, 116, 124,* 126, 144, 154, 155, 160, 162,* 174, 188, 199, 207,* 210,* 217, 221, 224,* 225,* 232, 233,* 235, 239, 242, 243, 245, 246, 249, 250, 253, 264, 270, 274, 275, 290, 292, 298, 302, 328, w. of 342, 350, 351, 354, 355, 359
,, Samuel, 20, 26, 29, 30, 31, 45, 53, 77, 85, 115, 116, 134, 179, 180, 206, 220, 278, 295, 298
,, Sarah, 45, 64, 145, 217, 228, 252, 255, 270, 351, 367
,, Susan, 32, 84, 181, 205, 209,* 247, 257, 264, 284,* 297, 301, 308
,, Thomas, 1, 3,* 4, 5, 7, 9, 13, 14, 16, 18, 25,* 26, 27,* 29, 30, 33,* 39, 42, 45, 50, 54, 56,* 57, 63, 71, 79, 84, 86, 89, 93, 94, 96, 105, 108, 110, 114,* 115, 117, 122, 123,* 126, 127, 130, 137, 139, 144, 150,* 156, 157, 160,* 162, 166, 169, 173, 177, 178, 181, 182, 187, 193, 198, 200, 208, 214, 218, 219,* 221, 222, 224,* 228, 229, 231, 232, 237, 240, 241, 245,* 254, 255,* 257,* 261,* 263, 264, 266, 268, 269, 271,* 274, 279,*

Vol. 1.—C. . pp. 1— 90 inclusive. Vol. 2.—C. . pp. 205—280 inclusive.
  B. . ,, 91—168 ,,   B. . ,, 281—350 ,,
  W. . ,, 169—204 ,,   W. . ,, 351—372 ,,

Kay, Thomas, continued—
    281, 282,* 283,* inf. of 283,
    284, 285, 290, 291,* 298,*
    c. of 299, 302,* 314, 316,
    w. of 326, 334,* 337,* c. of
    339, 340, c. of 341, 341, c. of
    348, 348, c. of 350, 351, 355,
    366, 371
,, Thurstan, 115
,, William, 4, 5, 7, 8, 11, 14,* 15,
    22, 28,* 35, 40, 47, 51, 56, 57,
    62, 66, 70, 71,* 75, 82,* 93,
    105, 112, 115, 116, 121, 125,
    131, 133, 134, 142, 143, 157,
    162,* 176, 189, 204, 213, 219,
    222,* 224, 228, 234, 235, 237,
    241, 244, 248, 250, 256, 257,*
    259, 261, 263,* 270, 271, 274,
    277, 279, 283, 296, 315, c. of
    316, 330, w. of 331, 344, 355,
    365
Kayley [Caly, Kealey],
,, Edward, c. of 327, 346, 363
Keie [see Kay]
Kelshawe, Grace, 163
Kempe, Deborah, 261
,, Zachary, 261
Kenyou [Kenian, Kenion, Kennion],
,, Ann, 107
,, Ellen, 237
,, Jane, 261
,, Mary, 37, 244, 269, 370
,, Richard, 23, 37, 244, 261, 265,*
    269, 361
,, Robert, 23, 209, 244
,, Thomas, 204, 234,* 237, 244,
    256,* 358
,, William, 78,* 209
Kerkman [see Kirkman]
Kershawe [Kirsha, Kirshaw,
    Kirshawe, Kirshughe,
    Kirsowe],
,, Abraham, 23,* 29, 176
,, Ann, 202, 242
,, Edmund, 29, 284, w. of 317
,, Elizabeth, 284
,, Ellen, 54*
,, Esther, 369
,, James, 206, 214, 225,* 228,*
    242, c. of 305
,, Mary, 206, c. of 347
,, Peter, 214
,, Sarah, 200
Kersleye, John, 185
Key, Keye [see Kay]
Kilshaw, Roger, 364
Kirkman [Kerkman, Kirkeman],
,, Abel, 20

Kirkman, Ann, 34
,, Edmund, 20
,, Elizabeth, 17, 52
,, Ellen, 181
,, George, 17, 34, 52
,, Isabel, 34, 266
,, Jane, 87
,, John, 45, 87, 208, 215,* 266
,, Josias, 279
,, Lambert, 72
,, Lamwell, 14, 34, 45, 52, 62
,, Margerie, 14
,, Richard, 72, 79, 208
,, Robert, 52, 279
,, Samuel, 79
,, Thomas, 62
Kirsha, Kirshaw, Kirshawe,
    Kirshughe, Kirsowe [see
    Kershawe]
Kitchen [Kitchin, Kitchine, Kitchyn],
,, Elizabeth, 274
,, John, 267
,, Robert, 89, 217, 303
,, Susan, 217
,, Thomas, 89, 274
,, William, 267
Knote, Susan, 356
Knowles [Know, Knowes], Alice, 199
,, Andrew, 224, 259, 264, 268,
    273,* 279, 313, c. of 316, c. of
    350, 367
,, Ann, 355
,, Edward, 268
,, Elizabeth, 11, 279, 345
,, Henry, 11, 93, 297, 304
,, John, 316
,, Margaret, 264
,, Robert, 224, 230,* 259, 321, c.
    of 325, w. of 346
,, Thomas, 226*
Kooke [see Cooke ante]

L

LACHE [see Leach]
Lackershey, Ann, 364
Lamb [Lame, Lombe], Alexander, 354
,, Ann, 295
,, John, w. of 326
,, Judith, 355
,, Mary, 342, 351
,, Simeon, 295, 354
,, Susan, 358
Lang, John, 372
,, Robert, 368
Langley [Langleye], Deodatus, 160
,, Robert, 243*

INDEX OF NAMES.

Vol. 1.—C. . pp. 1—90 inclusive. Vol. 2.—C. . pp. 205—280 inclusive.
 B. . ,, 91—108 ,,   B. . ,, 281—350 ,,
 W. . ,, 109—204 ,,   W. . ,, 351—372 ,,

Langworthe [see Longworth]
Latham, Mr., inf. of 350
Law [Lawe, Loe, Low, Lowe],
 ,, Abraham, 246
 ,, Alice, 192
 ,, Ann, 17, 29, 193
 ,, Daniel, 228, 241, 348
 ,, Dorothy, 340
 ,, Edmund, 24,* 42, 143, 144, 176, 193, 194, 215, 218, 223, 229, 237, 246, 279,* 288,* 290, 295, c. of 318, c. of 331, 336, 340, c. of 340, 353
 ,, Edward, 63, 64
 ,, Elizabeth, 222, 224, 279, 352, 370
 ,, Ellen, 279
 ,, Esther, 212
 ,, Gilbert, 212, 218, 222, 228, 235, 241, 245, 249, inf. of 285, c. of 304, c. of 307, c. of 323, 348, 351
 ,, Hamlet, 20, 109, 128, 211, 224, 232, 242, 258, 263, 272, c. of 330
 ,, Isaac, 246
 ,, James, 87, 245, 249, 343
 ,, Jarvice, 252
 ,, John, 68, 125, 215, 222, 223, 242, 277, 290
 ,, Katherine, 229, 295
 ,, Margaret, 263
 ,, Mary, 42, 59, 218, 252, 266, 273, 360
 ,, Nathan, 218, 279
 ,, Rebecca, 246
 ,, Richard, 13,* 17, 20, 29, 52, 102, 106, 117, 143, 232, 235, 237, 267,* 268, 273, w. of 329, 331, c. of 347, 368
 ,, Robert, 258
 ,, Susan, 143, 277
 ,, William, 29, 52, 59, 68, 80,* 87, 116, 132, 179, 211, 222, 259,* 266, 268, 272, 279, 343, 367
Laych, Layche [see Leach]
Laycocke, N.X.N., 212
 ,, Richard, 212
Lea [Lee, Lees, Lies], Alice, 1, 352
 ,, Charles, 367
 ,, Ellen, 7, 35
 ,, John, 1, 7, 267*
 ,, Mary, 362
 ,, William, 35
Leach [Lache, Laych, Layche, Leache, Lech],
 ,, Abraham, 79, 104, 213, 265, 270, 278, 368

Leach, Alice, 21, 44, 75, 205, 281, 366
 ,, Ann, 11, 15, 21, 40, 51, 88, 155, 197, 201, 209, 228, 260, 271, 297, 318, 337, 347, 360, 368
 ,, Arthur, 311
 ,, Charles, 15, 22, 32, 43, 54, 138, 140, 173, 202, 207, 213, 278, 347
 ,, Daniel, 34, 43, 55, 74, 166, 241, 278, 332
 ,, Daughter of 79
 ,, Edmund, 32, 66, 75, 81, 104, 206, w. of 290, 291, 297, c. of 301, c. of 307
 ,, Edward, 235,* 243, 255, 256, 260, 264, 271, 280, c. of 327, c. of 332, inf. of 349
 ,, Elizabeth, 34, 43, 154, 166, 192, 206, 243, 247, 265, 297, 358, 372
 ,, Ellen, 14, 32, 74, 77, 181, 357
 ,, Ellis, 11, 21, 25,* 31, 40,* 43, 44, 50, 60, 68, 81, 103, 106, 112, 115, 117, 121, 125,* 132, 137, 142, 176, 229, 238,* 247, 262, 270, 289, c. of 302, 321, 327
 ,, Emery, 206
 ,, Esther, 194, 291
 ,, Francis, 54
 ,, Genet, 53, 94, 303
 ,, Hamlet, 161
 ,, Isabel, 19, 158, 205, 371
 ,, James, 6,* 7,* 9, 16, 21, 24, 38, 42,* 53,* 68, 77, 88, 99, 109, 111, 13`, 148, 154, 155, 171, 207, 229,* 232, 239, 255, 260, 262, 264, 269, 271,* 274,* 278, 291, 299, 303, 306, 318, 324, w. of 332, c. of 333, 350, 353, 368, 369
 ,, Jane, 9, 21, 40, 43, 154, 187, 189, 211, 212, 262, 289, 335, 353
 ,, John, 66, 108, 211, 230, 243, 270,* 274, 284
 ,, Jonathan, 249
 ,, Joseph, 230, 249, 260, 269
 ,, Joshua, 43, 241, 357
 ,, Judith, 22, 354
 ,, Katherine, 239
 ,, Leonard, 232
 ,, Margaret, 103
 ,, Martha, 274, 350
 ,, Mary, 53, 54, 195, 229, 299, 333
 ,, Nicholas, 140
 ,, Peter, 24, 43, 51, 60, 134, 216, 342, c. of 343, w. of 345

Vol. 1.—C. . pp. 1— 90 inclusive. Vol. 2.—C. . pp. 205—280 inclusive.
B. . „ 91—168 „ B. . „ 281—350 „
W. . „ 169—204 „ W. . „ 351—372 „

Leach, Ralph, 14, 19, 43, 50, 54, 72, 88,*
    108, 163, 181, 200, inf. of 282,
    291, 316, 328, c. of 328, w. of
    331, 331, c. of 345, 354, 368
  „ Richard, 16, 31, 83, 84, 127, 205,
    209, 211, 216, 243, 281, 291,*
    296, w. of 320, 328
  „ Robert, 21, 38, 55, 68,* 72, 84,
    104, 128, 148, 154,* 158, 161,
    203, 205, 211, 228, 259, 262,
    306, 310, 314, w. of 319, c. of
    322, 324, 366
  „ Samuel, 45
  „ Sarah, 83, 163, 353
  „ Thomas, 256, 259, 333, 358
  „ William, 32, 45, 125, 131, 134,
    189, 212, 280, c. of 289, 291,
    297
Leaner [see Lever]
Lech [see Leach]
Leigh, Jane, 369
  „ John, 362
  „ Sarah, 370
Leiusey [see Livsey]
Lenche [?], N.X.N., 300
Lenisel, Deborah, 82
  „ Robert, 82
Lever [Leauer, Leuer],
  „ Adam, 277
  „ Andrew, 276, 277, c. of 335, c. of
    345
  „ Ann, 276
  „ Ashton, 360
Lewes, Alice, 187
Leyland, Ellen, 357
Lies [see Lea]
Lifsi, Lifsie [see Livsey]
Lightollers, James, 16
  „ William, 16
Limor, John, 319
Linney, Mary, 194
Lister [Lyster], James, 195
  „ Margaret, 178
  „ William, 114
Littleworth, Mr., d. of 323
Livsey [Leiusey, Lieuesley, Lifsi,
    Lifsie, Liuecey, Lieusaie,
    Lieusay, Liucsey, Liueseye,
    Liuesy, Liusey Livesay,
    Livesaye, Livesey, Lyffsaye,
    Lyfsaie, Lyfsay, Lyfsaye,
    Lyvesaie, Lyvesey, Lyvsey,
    Lyvseye],
  „ Adam, 43, 253, c. of 329
  „ Alice, 220*
  „ Ann, 16, 61, 74, 150, 155, 204,
    254, 270, 278, 305, 306, 339

Livsey, Deborah, 319
  „ Dorothy, 252
  „ Edmund, 12, 215
  „ Elizabeth, 50, 234, 259
  „ Ellen, 26, 190, 242, 360
  „ Esther, 236
  „ George, 18,* 26, 36, 50, 61, 74,
    150, 153, 212, 234, 259, 265,
    272, c. of 313
  „ Henry, 272
  „ James, 7, 20, 155, 207, 212, 220,
    227, 237, 243, 248, 262, 267,
    275,* c. of 313, 335, 342, 369
  „ Jane, 36, 50, 56, 212, 259, 268,
    272, 335, 363
  „ Jeremy, 34
  „ John, 1, 2, 7, 16, 22, 30, 34,*
    43, 56, 73, 242, 253
  „ Joseph, 10, 73, 215, 220, 267,
    268, 275, c. 305, 305, c. of 311
  „ Katherine, 178
  „ Margaret, 276, 294
  „ Mary, 248, 264, 265
  „ Peter, 18, 27, 39, 50, 125, 174,
    240, 241, 260, 294
  „ Ralph, 12, 21, 30, 31, 173, 278,
    306, 315
  „ Richard, 2, 10, 20, 21, 39, 216,
    220, 221, 226, 234,* 236, 241,
    242, 260, 272, 291, 348
  „ Robert, 1, 18, 20, 145, 149, 183,
    195, 207, 215,* 221, 227, 233,
    240, 242, 243, 252, 257, 259,
    262, 264, 267, 270, 272, 273,
    275, 278,* 281, w. of 331,
    d. of 338, 346
  „ Susan, 34, 207, 233, 257
  „ Thomas, 22, 27, 31, 41,* 207,
    212, 216, 220, 226, 237, 247,*
    254, 260,* 267, 272, 273, 275,*
    276, 291, 339, c. of 345, 346,
    352
Lockwood, Ann, 368
Loe [see Law]
Lomax [Lomas, Lomaxe, Lommax,
    Lumas, Lummas, Lummax],
  „ Abraham, 16, 256
  „ Alice, 3, 20, 27, 30, 41, 48, 50,
    90, 195, 197, 222, 223, 227,
    242, 257, 260, 270, 287, 296,
    301, 302, 306
  „ Ann, 3, 11, 28, 46, 51, 74, 81,
    83, 88, 163, 184, 195, 216,*
    231, 246, 249, 254, 255, 264,
    275, 296, c. of 345, c. of 347,
    353, 371, 372
  „ Arthur, 1

INDEX OF NAMES.

Vol. 1.—C. . pp. 1— 90 inclusive. Vol. 2.—C. . pp. 205—280 inclusive.
B. . ,, 91—168 ,, B. . ,, 281—350 ,,
W. . ,, 169—204 ,, W. . ,, 351—372 ,,

Lomax, Dorothy, 246, 248, 280, 322, 361
,, Edmund, 5, 7, 17, 40, 47,* 95, 126, 171, 184, 212, 226,* 249, 300, 324
,, Edward, 177, 199, 205, 224, 235, 256, 291, vxor of 291, 332, 356, 365
,, Elizabeth, 5, 13, 38, 43, 61, 66,* 83, 146, 152, 156, 164, 203,* 210, 215, 227, 228, 232, 233, 235, 239, 249, 254, 288, 302, 351, 358, 362, 365
,, Ellen, 54, 156, 183, 236, 240, 299, c. of 299, 300, 351
,, Ellinor, 96
,, Ellis, 7, 43, 83, 185, 227, 233, 241,* 247, 257, 268, 269, 277, 302,* c. of 336, 359
,, Em, 152
,, Esther, 272
,, Francis, 106
,, Geffray, 61, 63, 64, 71, 81, 86, 92, 94, 143, 144, 161, 165, 182, 193, 194, 205, 209, 214, 222, 236, 245, 256, 264,* 282, 299, c. of 328, c. of 335, 343
,, George, 234, 248, 263
,, Genet, 34, 301
,, Henry, 222, 275
,, Hugh, 357
,, Immin, 337
,, Isabel, 31, 187, 194, 222, 275, 288, 359
,, James, 3, 21,* 31,* 38, 41, 48, 50, 52, 54, 57, 61,* 63, 64, 66, 69,* 74, 79, 81, 83, 84, 85,* 92, 96, 127,* 135, 140, 142, 144, 146, 152,* 156,* 180, 187, 190, 192, 205, 208, 208, 211, 216,* 218, 224, 227, 228, 232, 234, 235, 240, 244, 246, 258,* 269,* 276,* 296, 301,* 309, c. of 317, 322, c. of 325, 338, c. of 342, 350
,, Jane, 244, 335
,, Jeremy, 256
,, John, 1, 3, 7, 9,* 17, 18, 27, 43, 46, 51, 56, 61, 63, 66,* 69,* 86,* 117, 131, 132, 133, 140, 157, 163, 164, 165, 167, 171, 185, 194, 204, 205, 207, 208, 214,* 216, 222,* 224, 226,* 231, 232, 235, 238, 246, 247, 248,* 257, 258, 264,* 268, 270, 273,* 276, 277, 280, 290, 291, 296, w. of 300, c. of 309, 309,

Lomax, John, *continued*—
316, 328, d. of 328, 342, w. of 344, c. of 344, 353, 368, 370
,, Joseph, 95
,, Joshua, 224
,, Katherine, 61, 215, 222, 253
,, Lawrence, 43, 57, 78, 232, 269*
,, Lettice, 156
,, Margaret, 75, 167, 178, 190, 207, 208, 222, 259,* 263, 299, 369
,, Margerie, 190, 251
,, Mary, 3, 55, 73, 76, 166, 195, 205, 208, 209, 211, 227, 235,* 266, 268, 276, 277, 282, 300, 311, 351, 369
,, N.X.N., 164
,, Oliver, 59, 69, 71, 76, 84,* 90, 93, 140, 141, 167,* 191, 192, 195, 210,* 216, 226,* 234, 235, 259, 264, 280, c. of 312, 315, inf. of 316
,, Owen, 3, 87, 91, 280, w. of 303, 371
,, Peter, 11, 67,* 72,* 88, 122, 128, 147,* 195, 210,* 211, 214, 215, 222, 223, 234,* 240, 247,* 249,* 255, 262,* 268, 269, 275, 277, inf. of 284, 287, 288, 306, c. of 310, c. of 311, c. of 317, 342, w. of 349, 352, 358
,, Priscilla, 205
,, Ralph, 64, 144
,, Renald, 101
,, Richard, 18, 30, 43,* 49,* 55, 60,* 63, 73, 79, 83,* 87, 88, 136,* 152, 166, 181, 183, 200, 202, 206, 208, 222, 235,* 240, 245, 249, 252, 253,* 258, 259, 262,* 266, 268,* 272, 275, 277,* c. of 298, 311, w. of 318, 320, c. of 326, 335, c. of 337,* 337, 338, c. of 343, c. of 346, w. of 350, 365, 368, 369
,, Robert, 88, 208,* 226, 232, 282, 283, 329
,, Roger, 11, 13, 78, 81, 86, 161, 199, 208, 215, 222, 227, 235, 242, 252
,, Samuel, 81
,, Sarah, 87, 218, 268, 277
,, Simon, 44, 47, 97, 129, 132, 148, 186, 187, 212, 327
,, Susan, 84, 216, 226, 236, 238, 275, 277, 354, 371, 372
,, Tamar, 157
,, Thomas, 11, 16, 20, 28, 41,* 52, 56, 64, 69, 75, 81, 92, 119,

s

Vol. 1.—C. . pp. 1— 90 inclusive. Vol. 2.—C. . pp. 205—280 inclusive.
 B. . ,, 91—168 ,, B. . ,, 281—350 ,,
 W. . ,, 169—204 ,, W. . ,, 351—372 ,,

Lomax, Thomas, continued—
    128, 144, 147, 148, 152, 156, 172, 179, 216, 232, 235,* 239, 260, 264, 269, 275,* 277, 282, 300, c. of 330, 337, w. of 346, c. of 350, 370
,, William, 7, 113, 116, 164, 226,* 236, 246, 251, 257, 263, c. of 309, c. of 323*
Lombe [see Lamb]
Lommax [see Lomax]
Long, John, 372
Longworth [Langworthe, Longworthe],
,, Abraham, 14, 22, 33, 38, 42, 108, 120, 124, 139, 173, 238
,, Alice, 29, 62
,, Ann, 41, 248, 250, 358
,, Elizabeth, 62
,, Ellen, 33, 185
,, Grace, 303, 362
,, Hugh, 370
,, James, 38, 187, 196
,, Jenet, 360
,, John, 25, 42, 230, 238, 248, 250, 254, c. of 311, c. of 320, 357
,, Katherine, 51, 371
,, Margaret, 199, 352
,, Mary, 230
,, Peter, 25, 29, 114
,, Roger, 25
,, Susan, 22, 254, 353
,, William, 14, 25, 32,* 41, 51, 108,* 152, 173, 176
Lord [Loort, Lorde, Lort, Lorte, Lortt],
,, Abraham, 71, 162,* 196, 225, 288, 292
,, Alice, 36
,, Anna, 71, 79, 84
,, Charles, 354
,, Daniel, 255,* w. of 330
,, Dorothy, 243
,, Edmund, 55, 208, 254, 265, 272, 288, 332, w. of 340, 362
,, Elizabeth, 14, 28, 36, 48, 72, 74, 95, 188, 247, 363
,, Ellen, 215
,, Henry, 6, 247, 253, 255, 262,* 274, c. of 324, c. of 329, c. of 335, c. of 338, 350
,, James, 50, 84, 200, 225, 230, 236,* 243, 356
,, Jane, 54, 121, 344
,, John, 88, 271, 274, 326, 350, 353
,, Joseph, 28
,, Josias, 253

Lord, Katherine, 21, 307
,, Lawrence, 6, 14, 21, 38,* 48, 50, 54, 55, 61, 72, 74, 79, 88, 91, 95, 111, 124, 126, 133, 134, 138, 187, 188, 207, 208, 215, 307, w. of 314, 326, w. of 330, 348
,, Margaret, 316
,, Mary, 207, 230, 263, 271, 340
,, Peter, 272
,, Ralph, 225
,, Richard, 225, 254, 270
,, Robert, 255
,, Thomas, 61, 263, 270, c. of 343, 363, 365
Lotton, Simeon, 345
Low, Lowe [see Law]
Loynes [see Lyon]
Lumas, Lummas, Lummax [see Lomax]
Lyffsaye, Lyfsaie, Lyfsay, Lyfsaye [see Livsey]
Lyon [Loynes], Alice, 8, 352
,, Ellen, 358
,, John, 8
Lyster [see Lister]
Lyvesaie, Lyvesey, Lyvsey [see Livsey]

M

Machan, Machon, Mackcon, Macken, Mackon, Macond, Maconde [see Makin],
Maden, Alexander, 290
,, Mary, 12
,, Robert, 12
Magnalles [Magnall, Magnals],
,, Ralph, 223
,, Robert, 223, 226, c. of 302, 305
,, Susan, 226, 305
,, William, 184
Maiorcroft [see Marcroft]
Makin [Machan, Machon, Mackcon, Macken, Mackon, Macon, Macond, Maconde, Maconn, Makand, Makande, Makelande, Maken, Makende, Makon, Makonn, Makyn],
,, Abraham, 225, 232, 239, c. of 315, 319
,, Alice, 248
,, Ann, 230, 248, 250
,, Daniel, 15
,, Dorothy, 232
,, Elizabeth, 267, 337

INDEX OF NAMES.

Vol. 1.—C. . pp. 1— 90 inclusive. Vol. 2.—C. . pp. 205—280 inclusive.
B. . ,, 91—168 ,,   B. . ,, 281—350 ,,
W. . ,, 169—204 ,, W. . ,, 351—372 ,,

Makin, Ellen, 46, 273
,, Ellis, 46, 131
,, Francis, 8, 24, 25, 118, 143, 229, 234, 239, 245, 258, 267, 275, 333, 350, 357
,, Grace, 15, 275, 361
,, Hannah, 239
,, James, 67, 152, 246, 252
,, John, 24, 49, 234, 369
,, Jony, 287
,, Jonathan, 214, 246, 312
,, Lambert, 5, 8, 16, 170
,, Lamwell, 117
,, Margaret, 225, 299
,, Mary, 152, 205, 229, 333
,, Randall, 16
,, Richard, 75, 243, 273, 337
,, Robert, 5, 41, 201, 246, 250, 251, w. of 342
,, Samuel, 25, 32,* 41, 49, 58, 67, 75, 151, 164, 179, 205, 214, 235,* 243, 245, 248, 250, 267, c. of 311, c. of 328, c. of 337, 337, 358
,, Sarah, 250
,, Susan, 251, 267, 350
,, William, 58, 246, 248, 252, 258, w. of 326, 362
Makinson [Makynson, Meakinsoun, Mekinson],
,, Elizabeth, 145
,, Roger, 23, 43,* 145
,, William, 23
Makonn, Makyn [see Makin]
Mallocke, Mary, 256
,, Thomas, 256
Manchester, James, 185
Mane [?], George, 351
Mankenols [Mankinoles],
,, Ann, 168
,, Robert, 168, 351
Manne, William, 365
Marche, John, 170
Marcroft [Maiorcroft, Marecroft, Marcrofte, Matorcroft, Mercroft, Mercrofte],
,, Alice, 154, 238
,, Ann, 22, 167, 223, 244, 352
,, Elizabeth, 8, 179, 183, 190, 203, 218, 228, 242, 268, 303*
,, Ellen, 25, 257, c. of 340
,, George, 8, 25, 36, 47, 61, 149, 152, 237, 251
,, Henry, 114
,, James, 278
,, Jane, 66, 149, 255, 350
,, Jeffery, 251

Marcroft, John, 22, 35, 44,* 54, 66, 89, 218, 223,* 228, 234,* 255, 260,* 268, 272, 278, 336, 350,* 354, 361
,, Joseph, 89, 273
,, Martha, 277
,, Mary, 11, 61, 87,* 167, 201, 277, 315, c. of 338
,, Peter, 272
,, Ralph, 305
,, Richard, 11, 54, 105, 154, 203, 322
,, Robert, 7, 35, 36, 237, 238, 242, 244, 257, 264,* 272,* 273, 303,* c. of 324, 336, d. of 338, w. of 338, 360*
,, Thomas, 223
,, William, 7, 47
Marland, Katherine, c. of 300
Marlor, Edward, 346
Marocke, James, 361
Martincroft, Mary, 255
,, Robert, 255
Martindale [Martindele, Martyndall],
,, Alice, 160, 200
,, Ann, 308
,, James, 14
,, Martha, 248
,, Mary, 14, 238
,, Matthew, 7
,, Mr., 7
,, Philip, 238, 248, 308
Mather, Abraham, 369
,, Alice, 37, 51, 56, 79, 328
,, Dorothy, 271
,, Elizabeth, 264
,, Ellen, 288, 361
,, Ellis, 29, 37, 123, 173, 288, 313
,, Henry, 27, 32, 39, 45, 51, 56, 65, 79, 111, 125, 135, 141, 147, 175, 282, 292, 299, 328
,, James, 268, 272
,, Jane, 336
,, Joan (Jonie), 39, 45, 358
,, John, 27, 259, 274, 292
,, Margerie, 5
,, Mary, 236, 272, 368
,, Peter, 29
,, Ralph, 32, 282
,, Richard, 268, 356
,, Sarah, 274, 370
,, Susan, 250
,, Thomas, 65, 104, 147, 236, 250, 259, 264, 271, c. of 309, c. of 332, 336
,, William, 5, 169, 204
Matorcroft [see Marcroft and Meadowcroft]

Maude [Maud, Maude, Maudes, Mavd, Mavdes, Mawde, Modes],
,, Alice, 33
,, Anthony, 139
,, Edmund, 33, 35, 49,* 155, 326
,, Edward, 367
,, Ellen, 155
,, John, 35, 372
Maudsley [Modesley, Modesleye],
,, Jane, 12
,, John, 12, 334
,, Symonde, 93
Mayer, Robert, 104
Meadowcroft [Meadowecrofte, Medcrofte, Medicroft, Medicrofte, Medocroft, Medocrofte, Medowcroft, Medowcrofte],
,, Alice, 152, 165, 210
,, Ann, 89, 201, 217, 230, 261, 267
,, Deborah, 339
,, Dorothy, 27, 48, 215
,, Elizabeth, 56, 229, 328
,, Ellen, 45, 89, 189, 197, 280, 313
,, Francis, 18, 34, 38, 39,* 43,* 45, 56, 76, 79, 152, 159, 180, 183, 207, 215, 217, 220, 236,* 246, 251, 255, 304, c. of 304, w. of 313
,, James, 218
,, Jane, 211, 255
,, John, 31, 41, 44, 46, 47, 48, 51, 56,* 59,* 63,* 74, 79, 89,* 129, 131, 132, 135, 137, 139, 155, 159, 162, 180, 186, 187, 210, 211, 213, 218,* 220, 229, 255, 272,* 280, 283, 296, 312,* d. of 323, 339
,, Katherine, 207, 218, 236, 312
,, Margaret, 34, 337, 352, 359
,, Richard, 10,* 18, 27, 31, 35,* 43,* 46, 51, 74, 76, 89, 108, 118, 213, 227, 230, 236, 247,* 278, 283, w. of 312, c. of 330, d. of 331, 344
,, Simon, 227
,, Susan, 246, 251
,, Thomas, 38, 89, 162, 165, 255, 261, 267, 272, 278, 308
,, William, 41, 296
Meakinsonn [see Makinson]
Medcalfe [Meatcalffe], Esther, 200
,, James, 185
Medcrofte, Medicroft, Medocroft, Medowcroft [see Meadowcroft]

Mekinsonn [see Makinson]
Melladew [Mellidew, Milladen],
,, Katherine, 260
,, Thomas, 260, 270,* c. of 340
Meller, Anthony, 57
,, George, 184
,, Thomas, 57
Mercroft, Mercrofte [see Marcroft]
Mere, Susan, 355
Michell, Ann, 355
Migley, John, 346
Milladen [see Melladew]
Millington, George, 249
,, Richard, 249
Mills [Milles, Mils], Dorothy, 269
,, Edmund, 269, c. of 319, 363
,, Edward, 249
,, Isabel, 295
,, James, 206, w. of 345, 351
,, John, 249
,, Ralph, 198
,, Sarah, 206
Milne [see Mylne]
Milner [Millner], Margaret, 309
,, Susan, 244
,, Thomas, 244, 309, 357
Milnes [Millnes, Milns, Mylnes],
,, Abraham, 56
,, Alice, 208
,, Ann, 250
,, Charles, 367
,, Edmund, 250
,, Edward, 256, 262
,, Elizabeth, 231
,, Isabel, 362
,, James, 73,* 208, 231, 252,* 272
,, Jane, 262
,, John, 264
,, Mary, 256, 272
,, Ralph, 56
,, William, c. of 324
Modes [see Maude]
Modesley, Modesleye [see Maudsley]
Molyneux [Mollenix, Mollynix, Mulenex, Mullenax, Mullinex],
,, John, 39,* 229, 230, 255,* c. of 311, c. of 324, c. of 330, 357
,, Mary, 230
,, Richard, 229
,, Robert, 135
Monckes [Munckes], Edmund, 39*
,, Grace, 183
,, Katherine, 351
Moreleye, Jane, 41
,, Nicholas, 41, 131
Morrey [see Murrey]

INDEX OF NAMES.   417

Vol. 1.—C. . pp. 1— 90 inclusive. Vol. 2.—C. . pp. 205— 280 inclusive.
  B. . ,, 91—168 ,,   B. . ,, 281—350 ,,
  W. . ,, 169—204 ,,   W. . ,, 351—412 ,,

Morris [Moris, Morresse, Morrice],
,, Alice, 206
,, Elizabeth, 33
,, Ellen, 145*
,, James, 26, 177
,, John, 206
,, Mary, 47
,, Peter, 26
,, Richard, 47
,, Robert, 363
,, Thomas, 33
,, William, 207*
Moser, Thomas, 176
Mounforte, Margerie, 298
Mulenex, Mullenex, Mullenax, Mullinex [see Molyneux]
Munckes [see Monckes]
Murrey [Morrey, Morry], Alice, 247
,, Ann, 227
,, Dorothy, 234
,, Elizabeth, 224
,, Francis, 231
,, George, 224, 227, 234, 238
,, Mr., 224, 227, 231, 234, 238, 247, 319
,, Rachel, 238, 346
Mylne, Isabel, 42
,, Jane, 42, 192
,, Richard, 113, 131,* 139

N

NABB [Nab, Nabbe, Nabe, Nabes],
,, Abraham, 13, 222, 229,* 237, 240, 245, 305, c. of 313, c. of 325, w. of 326, 330, 353
,, Alice, 23, 68, 228, 229, 239, 243, 274, 355, 371
,, Ann, 4, 229, 238, 259
,, Annis, 307
,, Anthony, 283, 286
,, Dorothy, 74, 298
,, Edmund, 239
,, Elizabeth, 3, 16,* 30, 64, 74, 192, 198, 225, 241, 245, 246, 251, 297, 305, 372
,, Ellen, 247
,, Ellis, 274
,, Francis, 3, 302
,, Isabel, 32, 55, 60, 210, 286, 289, 299, 324, 368
,, James, 26, 36, 42, 70, 154, 216, 261, 306
,, Jane, 23, 42, 85, 229, 239, 252, 259, 296, 302, 354
,, John, 16, 21, 26,* 30, 33, 36, 41, 47, 59, 75, 94, 117, 121, 129,

Nabb, John, continued—
    228, 243, 247,* 276, 286, 287, 295, 299, 319, 326*
,, Joseph, 23, 32, 46, 60, 70, 119, 176, 289, 302, 332, w. of 332
,, Joshua, 128, 205
,, Katherine, 46, 233, 302
,, Lawrence, 47, 57, 64, 70, 79,* 154, 190, 205, 240, 254,* 259, 276, 282, 289, 365
,, Margaret, 31, 33, 41, 196, 241, 261, 274, 280, 302, 309, 366
,, Mary, 8, 70, 252, 369
,, Oliver, 8, 13, 18, 23, 30,* 36, 68, 222, 235, 243,* 246, 251, 252, 259, 283, 293, c. of 317, w. of 318, c. of 323, c. of 341, 356
,, Ollynell [sic], 228
,, Richard, 26, 59, 262, 273, c. of 345, 370
,, Robert 36, 55, 68, 76, 85, 210, 216, 228,* 238, 243, 287, 291, 295, 296, 297, 298, c. of d. of 338, 345, w. of 349
,, Roger, 4, 16, 288, w. of 328
,, Sarah, 268
,, Susan, 259, 305
,, Thomas, 21, 76, 101, 157, 192, 225, 229, 233, 239, 243, 252, 258,* 259, 262, 268, 274, 280, 295, c. of 308, 309, c. of 314, 360
,, William, 18, 31, 45,* 57, 75, 92, 143, 179, 235, 237, 273, 283, 302, c. of 310, 328,* w. of 334
Naden [Nadane, Nadden],
,, Alexander, 42, 57, 66, 80, 123, 140, 153, 170, 174, 185, 281, 293, c. of 299
,, Alice, 211
,, Ann, 281
,, Cicelee, 57
,, David, 11,* 80, 110, 122, 133, 165, 202, 211, 216,* 222, 225, 232, 240, 298, c. of 316
,, Elizabeth, 33*
,, Genet, 105
,, James, 240
,, Jane, 42, 197, 293
,, John, 225
,, Jony, 198
,, Mary, 57, 222, 232, 298
,, Richard, 114
,, Robert, 66, 153
Nayler, Edward, 96
Nescio Cognomen, Isabel, 9

Vol. 1.—C. . pp. 1— 90 inclusive. Vol. 2.—C. . pp. 205—280 inclusive.
 B. . ,, 91—168 ,,   B. . ,, 281—350 ,,
 W. . ,, 169—204 ,, W. . ,, 351—372 ,,

Nescio Cognomen, John, 8
  ,, Richard, 8
  ,, Roger, 9
Newall [Newalle], Katherine, 23
  ,, Robert, 23, 112, 175
Newport, Edward, 266
  ,, Mary 266
Newton, Susan, 366
Neeld, Alice, 372
Nighell [see Nihill]
Nightgale, John, c. of 340
Nihill [Nighell], Ellen, 177
  ,, James, 276
  ,, Jonathan, 276
Noble [probably Nab], Elizabeth, 354
No Surname, Abraham, 164, 252
  ,, Anne, 242
  ,, Dorothy, 49
  ,, Edmund, 212, 250*
  ,, Edward, 256
  ,, Elizabeth, 50, 250, 356,* 368
  ,, Ellen, 49, 249
  ,, Henry, 255*
  ,, Isabel, 9, 250, 357, 359
  ,, James, 13, 213
  ,, John, 8, 164, 215,* 267
  ,, Jonathan, 249
  ,, Lawrence, 44
  ,, Margaret, 44, 360
  ,, Mary, 13
  ,, Matthew, 249
  ,, N. X. N., 314
  ,, Richard, 8, 372
  ,, Robert, 7
  ,, Roger, 9, 68,* 321
  ,, Thomas, 213, 249
  ,, William, 155, 250
Noris, Margaret, 354
Nuttall [Nuttale, Nuttall, Nutall,
    Nutalle, Nuttal, Nuttales,
    Nuttalgh],
  ,, Abiath, 39
  ,, Abraham, 182, 241, 273
  ,, Adam, 12, 20, 27, 37, 125,* 126, 172
  ,, Alice, 1, 13, 34, 53, 57, 64, 84, 85, 144, 161, 163, 165, 180, 186, 189, 206,* 209, 216, 221, 233, 259, 272, 277, 285, 296, 305, 315, 333, 368
  ,, Ann, 12, 23, 48, 57, 97, 148, 159, 164, 178, 212, 252, 268, 278, 297, 306, 357, 367
  ,, Bridget, 311
  ,, Cester, 248
  ,, Charles, 19, 21, 24, 28, 37, 38, 58,* 65, 78, 88,* 109, 112,

Nuttall, Charles, *continued*—
    129, 141, 152, 153, 155, 162, 200, 209, 212, 215,* 217,* 219, 230, 267, 270,* 274, 278, 290, 293, 302,* 316, 341, c. of 341, 354
  ,, Christopher, 80, 110, 121, 128, 130, 186, 290, 305, w. of 315
  ,, Dorothy, 2, 52, 69, 150, 234, 270, 276, 300, 351
  ,, Edmund, 12, 21, 27, 28, 37, 44, 57, 90, 98,* 145,* 170, 277
  ,, Edward, 30, 152, 166, 202, 302
  ,, Elizabeth, 8, 37, 38, 41, 52, 65, 71, 147, 158, 185, 190, 207, 231,* 285, 294, 302, 333, 353, 357, 372
  ,, Ellen, 20, 67, 207, 221, 234, 240, 243, 286, 310, 312, 324, 333
  ,, Esther, 15, 53, 225, 251, 278, 313, 331
  ,, Francis, 26, 28, 33, 62, 80, 103, 104, 114, 137,* 159, 160, 178, 228,* 240, 243, 244, 249, 253,* 257, 258, 265, 272, 273, 276, 291, 311, c. of 324, 328, 363
  ,, George, 2, 9,* 18, 77, 78,* 84, 97,* 105, 129, 165, 168. 198, 206, 210, 213, 217, 218,* 223, 229, 236, 241, 245, 251, 285, 287,* 302, 3 chn. of 315, 327,* 343, 352
  ,, Grace, 64, 200, 296
  ,, Henry, 1, 11, 28,* 37, 48, 59, 72, 80, 89, 95, 102, 104, 127, 129, 165, 198, 210, 213, 215, 220, 225, 233, 237, 240, 243, 244, 251, 253, 259, 264,* 271, 273, 277, 283, 293, 295, 298, c. of 300, c. of 312,* 317, c. of 317, w. of 329,* 336, c. of 349
  ,, Isaac, 241
  ,, Isabel, 208, 268, 274, 286, 371
  ,, Jacob, 241
  ,, James, 8, 24, 37, 39, 51, 58, 65, 140, 141, 153, 155, 214, 229, 254, 289, 346
  ,, Jane, 2, 145, 199, 222, 236, 271, 287,* 343
  ,, Jeffrey, 74, 153, 194, 330
  ,, Jennet, 63, 157, 160
  ,, John, 23, 37, 53, 54, 64, 77, 82, 100, 109, 111, 113, 114, 144, 155, 157, 170, 189, 193, 206,* 215,* 220, 223, 240, 253, 270, 277, 279,* 287, 305, 310, c of 349, 371

INDEX OF NAMES.

Vol. 1.—C. . . pp. 1— 90 inclusive. Vol. 2.—C. . . pp. 205—280 inclusive.
B. . „ 91—168 „ B. . „ 281—350 „
W. . „ 169—204 „ W. . „ 351—372 „

Nuttall, Kamuell, 51
„ Katherine, 33, 42, 192, 206, 225, 235, 258, 304, 370
„ Lawrence, 87, 135, 152
„ Letisse, 298
„ Lydia, 44, 230, 354
„ Margaret, 20, 89, 237, 257, 289, 290, 295, 328, 362
„ Martha, 59, 160
„ Martin, 12, 237, 283
„ Mary, 20, 21, 28, 31, 41, 63, 78, 79, 82, 162, 166, 189, 204, 209, 210, 223, 226, 231, 238, 241, 243, 244,* 247, 249, 295, 347, 352, 364
„ Matthew, 6, 20, 23, 31, 40,* 64, 115, 135, 231, 234, 300, 310, c. of 312, w. of 323
„ Michael, 121, 143
„ Nathan, 24, 259, 268, c. of 325, c. of 327, c. of 338, 364
„ N.X.N., 362
„ Peter, 54, 121
„ Priscilla, 62, 295
„ Radcliffe, Ratcliffe, 251
„ Ralph, 8, 65, 77, 82,* 87,* 93, 96, 97, 102, 157,* 161, 175,* 206, 207, 212,* 213, 215, 225, 234, 238, 241, 245, 248,* 268, 277, 286, 293, 296, w. of 311, c. of 318, 319, w. of 327, w. of 329, 341, 353
„ Richard, 7, 11, 15, 18, 19, 21,* 24, 28,* 34, 40,* 44, 53, 71,* 77, 78, 87, 90, 101, 115, 116, 123, 127, 129, 130, 132, 134, 143, 146, 147, 158, 160, 164, 167, 177,* 201, 209, 210,* 214, 215,* 216, 217,* 218,* 219, 221, 222,* 223,* 225, 231,* 235, 237, 243, 245, 252, 258, 259, 267, 271, 287,* 290,* 294, 300, 301,* c. of 304, c. of 307, c. of 308, c. of 309,* 310, 311, c. of 313, w. of 314, 315, w. of 316, c. 320, c. of 323, 331, 332, 354, 367
„ Roger, 27, 52, 57,* 69, 82, 106, 109, 123, 127, 135, 207, 275, 285, 296, 297, c. of 301
„ Rosymund, 191
„ Samuel, 8, 247, 273, c. of 289, c. of 291, 292, c. of 326, 346, c. of 346, 352
„ Sarah, 127, 223
„ Sisely, 243
„ Susan, 82, 86, 129, 225, 266

Nuttall, Thomas, 2, 6, 7, 12,* 13, 20, 21, 23, 27, 28, 29,* 30, 33, 37, 41,* 42, 44,* 52, 54,* 57, 63, 67, 72, 73,* 74, 76,* 78, 79, 80, 86, 90,* 116, 117, 123,* 128, 135, 136, 137,* 142,* 144, 145, 151, 153, 160, 161, 163, 170, 171, 177,* 182, 188, 195, 201, 208, 209,* 210, 213, 215, 221, 222, 225,* 226, 229,* 241,* 245, 248, 254,* 260,* 265, 266, 271, 275, 277, 278, 283,* 285, 286, 287, 296, 297,* 304, 306, c. of 313, 317, 322, c. of 323, 324, 327, 333, w. of 334, 336, 347, 349, 358, 362, 363, 365
„ William, 85, 258, 297, 344

O

Ogden, Alice, 263
„ Ann, 111
„ Dorothy, 263
„ Edmund, 128
„ Edward, 263, 267, c. of 336, 348
„ Gilbert, 263
„ Jane, 199
„ Margaret, 112
„ Martha, 53
„ Richard, 53
„ Robert, 41, 137
„ Roger, 41, 92, 122
„ Thomas, 267
„ William, 284
Oldham [Oldame, Ouldham],
„ Elizabeth, 38
„ George, c. of 324
„ John, 20,* 38, 175
„ Robert, 289
Openhard [Probably Oxenhard],
„ Anthony, 203
Openshaw [Openshawe, Openshay],
„ Alice, 154
„ Ann, 71, 111
„ Ellen, 15, 352
„ George, 254
„ James, 15, 31, 71, 79, 89, 154, 167,* 209,* 217, 234, 254, 257, 262, c. of 304, c. of 326,* 333
„ John, 31, 79, 169, 254, 257, 262, 267
„ Mary, 60, 89, 234
„ Simon, 60
„ Susan, 267
„ Thomas, 217

Vol. 1.—C. . pp. 1— 90 inclusive. Vol. 2.—C. . pp. 205—280 inclusive.
B. . ,, 91—168 ,, B. . ,, 281—350 ,,
W. . ,, 169—204 ,, W. . ,, 351—372 ,,

Ored [see Orred]
Orell [see Orrell]
Ormerod [Armoroid, Ormerode, Ormeroid, Ormeroyd, Ormorod, Ormroyd],
,, Alice, 277, 355, 371
,, Elizabeth, 271, 368
,, John, 263, 266, 271, 277, w. of 332
,, Margaret, 353
,, Oliver, 266
,, Richard, 158, 263
Orpe, Joan, 370
,, Thomas, 345
Orred [Ored, Oredd], Giles, 358
,, John, 171, 205, 297
,, Joseph, 205, 214, 297
,, Joshua, 80, 199, 290
,, Margaret, 80, 372
,, William, 214, 290
Orrell [Orell], Ann, 363
,, Jane, 355
,, Mr., 339
,, Richard, 344
,, William, 330, 339
Oswood, George, 232
,, Mary, 232
Oaldham [see Oldham]
Overall [Ouerall],
,, Alice, 191, 243, 247, 366
,, Ann, 89
,, Elizabeth, 271
,, Ellen, 218, 271
,, James, 116, 234, 264, 332
,, John, 35, 229,* 242, 247
,, Jonie, 108
,, Margaret, 85, 354
,, Mary, 209, 371
,, Richard, 16,* 25, 35, 85, 89, 130, 172, 209, 218, 223,* 225,* 233, 234, 243, 251, 264, 302,* c. of 323, 332
,, Susan, 251
,, William, 25, 108, 227,* 233, 242, c. of 312, 323,* 325, w. of 348, 350, 357, 359

P

PACOCKE, Pacoke, Pakok, Peacoke [see Peacock]
Parcivall, Parcyvall, Parsenall, Parsinall, Parseval, Parsevall, Parsival, Parsivall [see Percival]
Parker, Ann, 146
,, Elizabeth, 103

Parker, James, 162
Parkin, Jane, 365
Partington [Parkkington], Alice, 232
,, Arthur, 221, 228, 232, 236, 241, 246,* 297, c. of 303, c. of 307, 355
,, Edward, 96, 228, 236, 299, 322
,, Elizabeth, 241
,, Isabel, 221, 297, 322, 356
,, James, 120
,, Jone, 311
,, Margaret, 195
,, Margerie, 191
,, Roger, 97
Pasmond, Grace, 306
Pate [Pates, Pats], Ann, 278
,, Jane, 273
,, John, 192, 232, 273, 278, 349
,, Richard, 232
Paule, Pawell [see also Powell],
,, John, 147, 188
Pawna, Richard, 132
Peacock [Pacocke, Pacoke, Pakok, Peacocke, Peacoke, Pecock],
,, Ann, 188, 333
,, Elizabeth, 246
,, Ellen, 68, 148
,, George, 327
,, Isaac, 46
,, James, 46, 57,* 76, 131, 179, 209, 291, 292, 293, 296*
,, John, 315
,, Jony, 292
,, Katherine, 291
,, Mary, 360
,, Ralph, 59
,, Richard, 68, 148, 246, c. of 316, s. of 344
,, Thomas, 59, 76, 191, 209, 291, 293
Peake, John, 179
Peche, Robert, 11*
Pecock [see Peacock]
Pendlebury [Pendleburie],
,, Alice, 57, 288
,, Ann, 30, 227
,, Edmund, 48
,, Elizabeth, 38, 191
,, Francis, 22, 218,* 221, 227, 293*
,, Henry, w. of 332
,, Jane, 221
,, John, 22, 175, 288
,, Margaret, 299
,, Ralph, 30, 38, 48, 57, 133, 138, 140
,, Susan, 363
,, William, w. of 328

Vol. 1.—C. . pp. 1— 90 inclusive. Vol. 2.—C. . pp. 205—480 inclusive.
B. . ,, 91—168 ,,   B. . ,, 281—350 ,,
W. . ,, 169—204 ,,   W. . ,, 351—372 ,,

Pendleton [Pendlton], Arthur, 69
,, Francis, 69, 236
,, Henry, 353
,, Imyn, 236
Penley, John, 263
,, Susan, 263
Pens [Penns], Alice, 366
,, Elizabeth, 236, 361
,, Emmine, 252
,, Francis, 240, 252, c. of 313
,, George, 236
,, Richard, 240
Percival [Parcivall, Parcyvall,
   Parseuall, Parseval,
   Parsevall, Parsinall,
   Parsivall, Percivall,
   Percyvall, Percyvalle,
   Persevall, Persivall],
,, Abraham, 29, 35, 46, 134, 178,
     c. of 307
,, Alice, 12, 35, 46, 165, 281
,, Ann, 24, 148, 163, 185, 307, 360
,, Edmund, 24, 35,* 47, 66, 75, 84,
     140,* 146, 163,* 173, 193,
     286, 328, w. of 341
,, Elizabeth, 29, 47, 236,* 286
,, Giles, 66, 146, 148
,, Jeromia, 84, 163
,, Katherine, 35, 75, 179, 369
,, Margaret, 25, 136, 196
,, Richard, 12, 25, 35, 114, 115,
     120, 121, 281, 302, 307
Pickup [Piccop, Piccope, Pickope,
   Pickopp, Pikop],
,, Elizabeth, 204, 355
,, Elnor, 354
,, James, 197, 354
,, Jane, 177
,, John, 353
,, Lawrence, 339
Pierson, George, 190
Pikop [see Pickup]
Pilinge [see Pilling]
Pilking [? Pilkington], Ann, 354
Pilkington [Pilkingto, Pilkingtone,
   Pilkingtonne, Pilkinton,
   Pilkintonn],
,, Adam, 95
,, Alice, 228, 277, 306, 308, 352,
     359
,, Ann, 147, 184, 228, 237, 238,
     256, 281, 355, 365
,, Annice, 322
,, Charles, 230, 371
,, Edmund, 32, 70, 96, 102, 111,
     116, 119, 128, 132, 161, 181,
     213, 218, 236, 237, 241, 254,

Pilkington, Edmund, continued—
   259,* 283, 300, 306, c. of 306,
   308, 326, e. of 326
,, Edward, 165, 213, 226, 236, 273,
     c. of 313, 321, 367
,, Elizabeth, 63, 209, 255, 273, 308
,, Ellen, 281, 234, 336
,, Francis, 187, 208,* 217, 284,
     289, 354, 367, 368
,, Henry, 196, 210, 232, 260,* c. of
     300, 322
,, James, 140, 173, 273, 278
,, Jennet, 289
,, Joan, 369
,, John, 12, 142, 167, 235
,, Margaret, 87, 95, 154, 192, 202,
     226, 371
,, Mary, 87, 156, 210, 218, 222,
     232, 254, 348, 363
,, Ralph, 33, 94, 107, 185, 217, 297,
     308
,, Richard, 154, 230, 235, 251, 256,
     261, 278, 322, inf. of 349, 357
,, Roger, 87, 160, 200, 217, 277,
     w. of 341, 370
,, Sarah, 259
,, Thomas, 12, 33, 63, 70, 79,* 87,
     101, 108, 109, 156, 172, 209,
     217, 222, 228, 238, 241, 251,
     255, 259, 265,* 273, c. of 306,
     w. of 325, 330, 333, 336,* 337,
     365
,, William, 147, 261
Pilling [Pilinge, Pillinge], Alice, 352
,, Annes, 203
,, Edmund, 173, 197, 367
,, Elizabeth, 368
,, Jane, 351
,, John, 204, 355, 371
,, Mary, 371
Platt, George, 235
,, Jenet, 235
Pleasington, Jane, 355
Pollard [Pollarde], Alice, 16
,, Ann, 369
,, William, 16
Poole, John, 218
,, Robert, 218
Pott [Potto], Elizabeth, 370
,, Thomas, w. of 347
,, William, 206
Powell [(?) Paule, Pawell],
,, John, 147, 188, 283
,, Katherine, 283
,, Roger, 141
Prescott [Prascot, Prescod, Prescot],
,, Alice, 353

T

Vol. 1.—C.   . pp.   1— 90 inclusive. *Vol. 2.—C.   . pp. 205—280 inclusive.*
       B.   . ,,   91—168   ,,   *B.   . ,, 281—350   ,,*
       W.   . ,, 169—204   ,,   *W.   . ,, 351—372   ,,*

Prescott, Francis, 238
  ,, George, 245
  ,, Henry, w. of 330, 361
  ,, Jane, 250, 354
  ,, Rachel, 241
  ,, Richard, 238, 241, 245, 250, c. of 313, c. of 318, 322, c. of 324, w. of 344
Proctor, Francis (f.), 359

R

RADCLIFFE [Ratcliffe],
  ,, Alice, 25, 193, 352*
  ,, Ann, 185
  ,, Edward, 27, 226*
  ,, Henry, 58*
  ,, Jane, 53, 311
  ,, Margaret, 306
  ,, Richard, 48, 53, 133, 137, 187
  ,, Robert, 25, 48, c. of 328
  ,, William, 27
Radley [Radelley], Ellen, 354
  ,, Isabel, 362
Rainer [see Rayner]
Ramsbottom [Ramsbotham, Ramsbothome, Rombsebothom, Romsbotham, Romsbothom, Romsbothome, Romsbothum, Romsbotom, Romsbottom, Romsebothom],
  ,, Alice, 61, 211, 261, 283, 286, 291, 331, 348, 351, 372
  ,, Anne, 42, 49, 165, 177, 187, 207, 239, 265, 317, 351
  ,, Andrew, 231
  ,, Arthur, 249
  ,, Awdry, 211
  ,, Charles, 177, 229, 246, 254, 260, w. of 316, c. of 327, c. of 334, 338, 360
  ,, Dorothy, 237, 244
  ,, Edmund, 91, 120, 124, 291
  ,, Edward, 34, 45, 106, 174, 287
  ,, Elizabeth, 13, 34, 177,* 184, 242, 256, 257, 294, 338, 365
  ,, Ellen, 76, 91, 109, 334
  ,, Geffray, 91
  ,, George, 148, 286
  ,, Grace, 248
  ,, Henry, 84, 124, 184, 248, 254, 337, 341
  ,, James, 17,* 25,* 34, 49,* 97, 99, 109, 213, 253,* 256, 315, w. of 315
  ,, Jennet, 338

Ramsbottom, Jeremy, 5, 34
  ,, John, 5, 9,* 10, 13, 15, 30, 49, 61, 76,* 111, 159, 160, 170, 171, 189, 203, 211, 214, 215, 219, 227, 232, 246, 251,* 255, 257, 265, 268,* 270, 275, 291, 297, 311, w. of 312, w. of 329, s. of 329, 338, 347, c. of 349, 362
  ,, Judith, 15
  ,, Katherine, 81, 205, 223, 236, 287, 311, 353
  ,, Margery, 289
  ,, Martha, 284
  ,, Mary, 275
  ,, Mr., 255
  ,, Nathaniel, 255
  ,, Oliver, 368
  ,, Peter, 81, 88, 138, 145, 148, 151, 157, 163, 166, 190, 211, 231, inf. of 284, 289, 300, w. of 326, 331
  ,, Ratcliffe, 311
  ,, Richard, 30, 45, 58,* 67, 76, 84, 88, 94, 97, 100,* 105, 108, 150, 160, 165, 189, 207, 213, 214, 215,* 219, 223, 224, 227, 232, 237, 239, 242, 244, 245,* 246,* 248,* 249, 253,* 255, 261, 270, 283, c. of 289, 291, c. of 310, 311, c. of 313, c. of 319, w. of 329, 333, s. of 334, 335, s. of 341, 344, c. of 344, inf. of 346, w. of 350, 352, 358, 362
  ,, Thomas, 67, 260, 268
  ,, William, 10, 42, 121,* 194, 202, 205, 215, 223,* 224, 229, 236, 251, 255, 284, 287, w. of 313, s. of 327, s. of 329
Ramsden [Rambsdenn, Ramsdenn, Romsden],
  ,, Charles, 62, 143
  ,, Elizabeth, 277
  ,, John, 46,* 62, 69, 128, 143, 185, 277
  ,, Margaret, 69
Ransom [Ransome, Ranson], Ann, 242
  ,, Bernard, 269
  ,, Elizabeth, 271
  ,, George, 261
  ,, Isaac, 271
  ,, John, 242, 255*, 261, 269
Ratcliffe [see Radcliffe]
Rathbone [Rathboane, Rathborne, Rawborne, Rothbone],
  ,, Abel, 212

INDEX OF NAMES.

Vol. 1.—C. . pp. 1—90 inclusive. Vol. 2.—C. . pp. 205—280 inclusive.
B. . ,, 91—168 ,,   B. . ,, 281—350 ,,
W. . ,, 169—204 ,,   W. . ,, 351—372 ,,

Rathbone, Grace, 164
,, Joab, 220, 304
,, Mr., 164, 212
,, William, 220, 304
Raunseley, Susan, 188
Rawborne [see Rathbone]
Rawson [Rauson, Roesun, Rowsone],
,, Edward, 275
,, Ellen, 275
,, Isaac, c. of 342
,, John, 247,* c. of 324
Rawstorne [Rasthorne, Rastorne,
    Rausthorn, Rausthorne,
    Raustorne, Rawscorne,
    Rawschorne, Rawshorne,
    Rawshtorn, Rawsthorn,
    Rawsthorne, Rawstorn,
    Roshorne, Rostawrne,
    Rostherne, Rosthorn,
    Rosthorne, Rostorn,
    Rostorne, Rostron, Rostrone,
    Rostronn, Rostronne,
    Roustorne, Rowstron],
,, Adam, 109, 346, 356, 365
,, Alice, 5, 56, 87, 95, 177, 194,
    266, 281, 285, 353, 362, 364
,, Alse, 351
,, Ann, 63, 84, 98, 166, 194, 240,
    265, 268, 279, 314, 325, 353,
    370
,, Edward, 16, 27, 135, 209, 216,
    225, 245,* 256,* 259, 262,
    266, 277, 304, 317, 321, c. of
    329, 331, 340, 353, 364, 365*
,, Elizabeth, 23, 27, 181, 190, 194,
    206, 212, 223, 258, 259, 263,
    270, 301, 319, 332, 337, 340,
    353, 354, 357, 370
,, Ellen, 158,* 221, 233, 297, 365,
    367
,, George, 159, 160
,, Gennet, 302
,, Henry, 39, 50, 57, 71, 106, 107,
    108, 198, 214, 279, w. of 335
,, Isabel, 86
,, James, 225, 264, 272, 277, 302
,, Jane, 262, 288
,, Joan (Jony), 73, 196, 292, 367
,, John, 42, 64, 71,* 76, 79, 84,
    132, 135, 137, 185, 196, 211,
    219, 221, 234, 249, 259, 263,
    268, 272, 279, 285, 288, 297,
    330, 340*, w. of 347, w. of 349,
    352, 367,* 371
,, Jonathan, 249
,, Katherine, 51, 205, 253, 269, 354
,, Lawrence, 27, 42, 109,* 127, 269,
    277, 314, w. of 316

Rawstorne, Margaret, 57, 144, 183,
    215, 219, 220, 296, 308, 340,
    358
,, Mary, 71, 166, 211, 253, 259,
    270, 279, 280, 339
,, Mr., 109, 253, 256, 269, 277,
    296, 335, 340, 342, 349, 364
,, Mrs., 113, 328
,, Nicholas, 205, 263,* 270, 332,
    c. of 334, 345, w. of 348, 368
,, N.X.N., 362
,, Oliver, 309
,, Peter, 227, 230, 249, 308, 332
,, Rachel, 277
,, Ralph, 159, 352
,, Richard, 5, 16, 23, 26, 51, 59,
    65, 79, 86, 95,* 96, 104, 114,
    131, 148, 158, 166, 178, 192,
    205, 206, 209, 210, 211,* 214,*
    215, 216, 219, 220, 223, 234,
    240, 253, 258,* 263,* 264,
    270, 274, 287, 296, 297, 298,
    301, c. of 302, 308, 319, c. of
    330, w. of 331, 331, 336, 337,
    339, c. of 339, 352, 366
,, Robert, c. of 343
,, Sarah, 5. 95
,, Susan, 214
,, Thomas, 27, 39, 59, 65, 115, 141,
    183, 274, 280, 281, 288, c. of
    312, 339, w. of 350, 351, 353
,, Thurstan, 44, 50, 64, 95, 125,
    144, 146, 156, 179, 207, 230,
    233, 284, 288, c. of 307, 308,
    321
,, William, 44, 56, 63, 66,* 73,
    76, 87, 126, 137, 139, 163,*
    166, 182, 205, 207, 210,* 212,
    219, 227, 249, 258, 265, 284,
    285, 286, 292, c. of 298, 318,
    342, w. 344, 349, 351
Ray, James, w. of 344
Rayner [Rainer], James, 204
,, Jennet, 196
,, John, 67
,, Margaret, 67
Reade [Read, Reads], Andrew, 264
,, Ann, 255, 267
,, Edward, 264, 267, 269, 276*
,, James, 250, 258, w. of 329, 362
,, John, 265, 269
,, Mary, 258
,, Richard, 264
,, Robert, 250, 255, 265, c. of 324,*
    c. of 339, w. of 340
,, Thomas, 264
Redferne [Redffearne], James, 61

Vol. 1.—C. . *pp.* 1— 90 *inclusive.* *Vol. 2.—C.* . *pp.* 205—280 *inclusive.*
B. . ,, 91—168 ,, *B.* . ,, 281—350 ,,
W. . ,, 169—204 ,, *W.* . ,, 351—372 ,,

Redferne, John, 61
,, Mary, 369
Redforthe, Jonye, 32
,, Robert, 32
Redgate [Ridgate], Alice, 100
,, Elizabeth, 194, 301
,, William, 331
Redgate als Rothwell,
,, William, c. of 329
Redman, Elizabeth, 348
,, Mary, 351
,, Richard, 141, 142, 165
Rey, Elizabeth, 244
,, John, 243, c. of 317 [? Key]
,, Richard, 243, 244
Reydes [Reyds], Katherin, 314
,, Thomas, 142
Ridgate [see Redgate]
Ridgle [see Wrigley]
Ridings [see Rydings]
Rife [Rifi, ? Ryves], William, inf. of 349 371
Rigby [Rigbie, Rigbye, Wrigbey],
,, Adam, 188, 290*
,, Ann, 209
,, Edmund, 262
,, Elizabeth, 290
,, James, 81
,, John, 81
,, Mr., 331
,, Mrs., 348
,, Ratcliffe, c. of 338
,, Roger, 262
,, Thomas, 209*
Rigley [see Wrigley]
Riley [Roiley, Roileye, Roylaie, Royle, Royley, Royleye, Ryley],
,, Ann, 253
,, Elizabeth, 193, 286
,, Henry, 140
,, Isabel, 334
,, Jeffrey, w. of 334, c. of 349, 371
,, John, 52, 253, 265, c. of 322, c. of 334, 369
,, Oliver, 28, 52, 115, 122, 131, 188, 286, 298
,, Robert, 23*
,, Susan, 265
,, Thomas, 28
,, William, 112
Risheton, Rishton [see Rushton]
Roades [see Rodes]
Roberts [Robertes],
,, Elizabeth, 41
,, James, 41, 127
,, John, 184

Robinson [Robbinsonn, Robynson, Robynsonn, Rombinson],
,, Alice, 269
,, Ann, 366
,, Arthur, 20
,, Elizabeth, 93
,, Jennet, 242
,, John, 6,* 145, 215, 224, 242
,, Martha, 215
,, Miles, 93
,, Peter, 224
,, Richard, 269
,, Roger, 175
,, Thomas, 30
Rockley, Robert, 326
Rodes [Roads, Roades, Roodes],
,, Alice, 88, 369
,, John, 88, 202, 294
,, Katherine, 356
Roe [see Wroe]
Roesun [see Rawson]
Rogerson, Roger, 362
Roide [see Roydes]
Roiley [see Riley]
Rombinson [see Robinson]
Romsbotham, Romsbottom [see Ramsbottom]
Romsden [see Ramsden]
Roodes [see Rodes]
Roscow [Rosco, Roske],
,, Elizabeth, 207
,, Ellen, 30
,, Richard, 207, c. of 321
,, Thomas, 30
Roshorne, Rostorne, Rostrone [see Rawstorne]
Rothbone [see Rathbone]
Rothell [see Rothwell]
Rothmale [? Rothwell], Margaret, 149
,, Thomas, 149
Rothwell [Rothell, Rothewell, Rothowell, Rothwall, Rothwel, Rothwelle]
,, Abraham, 69, 95, 108, 153, 291, 306
,, Adam, 116, 352
,, Agnes, 147
,, Alice, 31, 62, 120, 144, 165, 184,* 201, 236, 240, 291, 304, 362, 370
,, Amos, 124
,, Ann, 32, 62, 90, 186, 188, 189, 202, 208, 242, 255, 319, 347, 352, 353
,, Annett, 354
,, Dionisse, 371
,, Dorothy, 26, 28, 56, 195, 206

INDEX OF NAMES.

Vol. 1.—C. . pp. 1— 90 inclusive. Vol. 2.—C. . pp. 205—280 inclusive.
„ B. . „ 91—168 „ „ B. . „ 281—350 „
„ W. . „ 169—204 „ „ W. . „ 351—372 „

Rothwell, Edmund, 56, 66, 124, 134, 150, 184, 236, 251,* c. of 327, 359
„ Edward, 49, 67, 77, 152, 223, 225, 229, 235, 242, 247,* 255, 267, 275, 289, 304,* 305, 368
„ Elizabeth, 31, 33, 66, 69, 71, 86, 97, 98, 145, 157, 194, 282, 286, 304, 314, 320, 338, 360, 361
„ Ellen, 186, 266, 304, 364
„ Ellis, 2, 106, 123, 304
„ Francis, 83, 246
„ George, 37, 132
„ Giles, 4, 19,* 25, 37, 56, 58, 67, 77, 86, 103, 116, 118, 152, 166, 169, 191, 208, 214,* 221, 245, 259, 298, w. of 301, 316, w. of 340, 347
„ Grace, 124, 298
„ Henry, 163, 217, 227, 306, 335, 356
„ Isabel, 26, 52, 54, 81, 223, 357
„ James, 1, 43, 81, 86, 87, 90, 102, 157, 194, 213, 217, 232, 235, 245, 263, 274, 290, 292, 302, c. of 339, 342, w. of 342, 353
„ Jane, 4, 16, 40, 196, 206, 232, 267, 294, c. of 339
„ Jennet, 15, 315
„ John, 27, 33,* 43, 52, 63,* 75, 89, 98, 105, 110, 120, 153, 175, 177, 224, 267, 291, 292, 301, 302, 304
„ Katherine, 180
„ Lettis, 303
„ Margaret, 153, 155, 217, 231, 241, 267
„ Mary, 67, 213, 225, 274, 290, 304
„ Mr., 257, 337
„ N.X.N., 83
„ Peter, 15, 29, 82, 89, 116, 127, 136, 164, 202, 216,* 260, 277,* 371
„ Ralphe, 29, 224
„ Richard, 1, 2, 16, 22, 27, 32, 33, 54, 62,* 71, 72, 74,* 82, 87, 90, 93, 96, 97,* 104, 112, 114, 115, 117, 119, 131, 136, 137, 144, 162, 163, 165, 173, 178, 189, 206, 217, 221, 229, 263, 275, 283, inf. of 289, 291, 294,* 298,* 301, c. of 302, c. of 304, 306, c. of 307,* 331, 366, 371
„ Robert, 25, 86, 201, 345
„ Susan, 22
„ Thomas, 49, 56, 58, 67, 72, 75,

Rothwell, Thomas, continued—
90, 96, 134, 138, 153, 155, 183, 188, 198, 225, 227, 231, 240, 241, 246, 259, 292, 304, 306, w. of 311, 324, 327, 333, d. of 334, 352, 360, 368
„ William, 28, 40, 62,* 127, 131, 183, 186, 233,* 253, 256, 257, 258, 260, 261, 263, 266,* 325, 327, c. of 329, 330, 332, 334, 336, 337, 365, 366, 367,* 368,* 369
Rothwell, als Redgate,
„ William, w. of 329
Roustorne [see Rawstorne]
Rowsone [see Rawson]
Rowstron [see Rawstorne]
Roydes [Roide, Royd, Royde],
„ Alice, 161, 226
„ Emar, 206
„ Isaac, 73, 81, 90, 211, 218, 226, 233, 352
„ John, 52, 161, 188, 206, 285
„ Joseph, 52
„ Margaret, 233
„ Martha, 90
„ Mary, 73, 285
„ Nathan, 81
„ Richard, 58,* 218
„ Sarah, 211, 371
Royle, Royley [see Riley]
Rude, Marie, 358
Rushe, Margaret, 146
„ Richard, 146, 148
Rushton [Risheton, Rishton, Rushtonn, Rysheton].
„ Alice, 55, 368
„ Cester, 248
„ Dorothy, 216
„ Elizabeth, 335, 340
„ Grace, 142
„ James, 329, 368
„ Jane, 248, 362, 365
„ Jeremy, 162
„ John, 238
„ Margaret, 55, 199
„ Mr., 176
„ Ralph, 206, 282
„ Richard, 247
„ Roger, 225, 231
„ Thomas, 216, 225, 231, 238, 247, inf. of 287, c. of 307, 352
„ William, 204, 206, 247,* 282, d. of 330
Ryder, John, 95
Rydings [Ridinges, Ridings, Rydinge, Rydeinge, Rydeings, Rydinges],

Vol. 1.—C. . pp. 1— 90 inclusive. Vol. 2.—C. . pp. 205—280 inclusive.
      B. . ,, 91—168   ,,   B. . ,, 281—350   ,,
      W. . ,, 169—204   ,,   W. . ,, 351—372   ,,

Rydings, Ann, 189, 277, 322
,, Dorothy, 59
,, Francis, 226
,, Grace, 86
,, James, 47, 118, 291, 292
,, John, 13, 18, 46, 274, 369
,, Katherine, 185
,, Margaret, 201
,, Martha, 242, 275
,, Mary, 218, 366
,, Peter, 142, 194, 303
,, Richard, 13, 18, 42,* 46, 47, 59, 78,* 177, 186
,, Robert, 85,* 218, 226, 242, 275, 277, w. of 316, 369
,, Susan, 200
,, Thomas, 86, 274
Ryley [see Riley]
Rysheton [see Rushton]
Ryves [see also Rife], Robert, 36*

S

SAGAR [Sagare, Sager], John, 213, 237
,, Mary, 229
,, Robert, 345
,, Stephen, 213, 229, 237, c. of 289, 315, 352
Sale [Saile, Sall, Salle, Sayle],
,, Alice, 10, 277, 281, 301
,, Andrew, 23,* 113, c. of 304, c. of 307, 328, 338, 354
,, Ann, 336
,, James, 22, 263, 274
,, John, 17, 208, 372
,, Katherine, 233, 369
,, Margaret, 38, 53
,, Martha, 234
,, Mary, 233, 240, 338
,, Michael, 164, 208, 300, c. of 301, 336
,, Peter, 255*
,, Richard, 6
,, Robert, 53, 136
,, Samuel, 6, 10, 17, 22, 38, 56, 234, 240, 253, 263, 281, 301
,, Susan, 253
,, Thomas, 56, 274, 277
Sanderson [Saunderson], Ellis, 190
,, James, 169
,, John, 200
Sandes, Ellen, 370
,, Katherine, 87
,, William, 87
Saundiforth, Humphrey, 369
Saxon [Saxonn], Ann, 143
,, Francis, 366

Saxon, Thomas, 143
Sayle [see Sale]
Schofeeld, Schofeild, Schofeild, Schofeld [see Scholfelde]
Scholes [Sckoles Scole, Scoles, Scowles, Skoles],
,, Adam, c. of 321, 322, w. of 334
,, Alice, 42
,, Ann, 30, 302, 322
,, Edmund, 49
,, Francis, 197
,, George, 20, 30, 42, 137, 175
,, James, 361
,, Jane, 356
,, John, 225*
,, Joseph, 78
,, Margaret, 3, 67
,, Mary, 199
,, Ralph, 273
,, Samuel, 49, 78, 178
,, Susan, 273
,, Thomas, 20, 162
,, William, s. of 340, 342, w. of 344
Scholfelde [Scoafeild, Scoafield, Schofeeld, Schofeild, Schofeld, Scholefeild, Scholefeld, Scofeild, Scofeilde, Scofielde, Scofilld, Scofeld, Scolefeild, Scolefeld, Scolefield, Scofeild, Scofield, Scofelde, Scolfeld, Scolfelde, Scoufild, Scovlefeld, Scowfild, Skofeild, Skofeld, Skolefeild, Skolefeld, Skolefelde, Skolfeild, Skolfeld],
,, Adam, 326, 355
,, Alexander, 269
,, Alice, 26, 30, 71, 72, 159, 183, 185, 208,* 262, 293, 300
,, Ann, 21, 51, 62, 92, 154, 233, 258, 275, 309, 315, 321,* 360, 368
,, Arthur, 125, 176, 209, 213,* 219, 225, 231, 249, 305, 320
,, Dorothy, 231
,, Edmund, 250, 309
,, Edward, 217, 228, 258, 293
,, Elizabeth, 11, 26, 52, 61, 178, 198, 201, 250, 313, 321, 355
,, Ellen, 80, 315
,, Ellis, 14, 58, 95, 310
,, Esther, 224, 232
,, Francis, 219,* 226, 232, 250
,, Grace, 58, 275, 368
,, Henry, 111, 159

INDEX OF NAMES.

Vol. 1.—C. . pp. 1— 90 inclusive. Vol. 2.—C. . pp. 205—280 inclusive.
B. . ,, 91—168 ,,   B. . ,, 281—350 ,,
W. . ,, 169—204 ,,   W. . ,, 351—372 ,,

Scholfelde, James, 35, 42, 52,* 62, 72, 82, 107, 110, 113, 155, 157, 181, 204, 207, 210, 215,* 217, 218, 219, 220, 224, 225,* 231,* 233,* 272, 276, 283, 291,* 293, 300, c. of 308, w. of 312, 313, c. of 316, 345. 354
,, Jane, 14, 42, 52, 195, 210
,, Jeremy, 326
,, John, 41, 139, 186, 209, 321, w. of 330, 346, 355
,, Judith, 190, 371
,, Katherine, 65, 366
,, Margaret, 192, 363
,, Mary, 28, 43, 219, 220, 225, 226, 233, 248, 250, 259, 305, 320, 365, 371
,, Mr., 276
,, Peter, 248
,, Richard, 11, 30, 35, 51, 52, 101, 111, 154
,, Robert, 21, 28, 43, 65, 101, 103, 116, 218, 223, 228, 235, 243,* 248,* 249, 259, 262, 269, 272, 303, w. of 326, 354, 367
,, Roger, 305
,, Samuel, 207, 219, 283
,, Susan, 369
,, Thomas, 31,* 41, 61, 71, 80, 82, 171, 180, 187, 223, 235, 287, 303, w. of 343
,, William, 293
Scole, Scoles [see Scholes]
Scott, Francis, 249
,, Thomas, 249
Scowles [see Scholes]
Seddon [Seadon, Sedden, Seddenn, Seden, Sedon, Sedonne],
,, Alice, 31, 34, 39, 53, 148, 158, 164, 208, 232, 239, 284
,, Andrew, 63
,, Ann, 35, 40, 53, 55, 165, 212, 267, 297
,, Dorothy, 32, 59, 70, 86, 157
,, Edmund, 24, 29, 34, 42,* 49, 58, 60, 62, 70,* 81, 148, 149,* 153, 165,* 177, 208, 211, 212, 222, 232, 239, 254, 284, w. of 312, w. of 322, 338, 345, 347, 351, 360, 361
,, Edward, 254
,, Elizabeth, 43, 49, 58, 61, 78, 165, 166, 188, 248, 249, 289, 306, 308, 348, 365
,, Ellen, 34, 69, 108, 151, 164, 369
,, Genit, 70
,, George, 258

Seddon, Grace, 236
,, Henry, 248, 292
,, Hugh, 59, 74, 85, 149, 157, 191, 208,* 214, 222, 297, 306, 329
,, Isabel, 222, 347
,, James, 214
,, Jane, 48, 56, 292
,, Joan (Jonie), 40, 48, 157
,, John, 29, 60, 74, 149, 223, 241, 244, 253, 254,* 336, 338, 349
,, Katherine, 370
,, Margaret, 38, 62, 149, 339
,, Margerie, 162
,, Mary, 45, 69, 70, 106, 152, 192, 254, 262, 362
,, Oliver, 24, 60, 117, 149, 159, 180, w. of 311, 369
,, Peter, 29, 37,* 45, 56, 78, 179, 206, 241, 248, 261, c. of 325, c. of 331, 331, w. of 336, c. of 337, inf. of 349
,, Ralph, 53, 71, 244, 249,* 253, 258, 262, 267, 271,* 336, c. of 347,* w. of 348, 362, 368
,, Richard, 15,* 24,* 32,* 35, 39, 40, 48, 55, 58, 69, 71, 74, 76, 85, 86, 102, 109, 121, 123, 125, 127, 146, 151, 152, 160, 164, 165, 176, 178, 182, 211, 226, 236, 244,* c. of 289, 290, 297, 347, 359
,, Robert, 38,* 76, 117, 157, 164, 165, 282, 301, 351
,, Roger, 29, 31, 32, 34, 38, 43, 48, 53,* 58, 61, 63, 70,* 74, 80, 81, 88,* 120, 137, 140, 158, 166,* 168, 180, 181, 188, 219,* 223, 226, 232, 238,* 244, 248, 254, 289, 292,* c. of 312, w. of 317, c. of 318, 323, w. of 330, 348, 351, 354
,, Sarah, 211
,, Thomas, 80, 168, 187, 206, 211, 222, 232, 249, 297, 371
,, William, 261
Seedall [see Siddall]
Setle, Jennet, 355
Shakeshaft, Alice, 275
,, John, 275, 277,* c. of 349
Shakleton, Abraham, 65, 81
,, Jane, 81
,, Mary, 65
Sharoke [see Skarrocke]
Sharpe [Sharp], Elizabeth, 149, 291
,, Ellen, 30
,, Francis, 48
,, John, 30, 40, 48, 130, 140, 149
,, Richard, 40

Vol. 1.—C. . pp. 1— 90 inclusive. Vol. 2.—C. . pp. 205—280 inclusive.
B. . ,, 91—168 ,, B. . ,, 281—350 ,,
W. . ,, 169—204 ,, W. . ,, 351—372 ,,

Sharpe, Robert, 291
Sharples, Alice, 193
,, Genet, 122
,, John, 187
Sharphouse [Sharphous, Sharpos, Sharpus],
,, Alice, 206
,, Ann, 206
,, Ellen, 79
,, James, 48
,, John, 48, 79, 139, 203*
,, Jony, 282
,, Richard, 132
,, William, 160, 200
Sharrocke [Sharoke], Margery, 288
,, Mary, 56
,, William, 56, 288, 360
Shaw [Shawe, Shawes],
,, Alice, 188, 333
,, Ann, 13, 299, 368
,, D. w. of 317
,, Dorothy, 27, 320
,, Elizabeth, 5, 95, 209
,, Ellen, 222, 351, 370
,, Francis, 5, 13, 95, 170
,, Jane, 182, 215, 316
,, Jo: 105
,, John, 171, 215, 222, 257, 299, c. of 310, 332, 337, 352, 357
,, Jone, 257
,, Joshua, 271, 276, 370
,, Lamberte, 304
,, Lawrence, 282
,, Leonard, 10, 94
,, Margaret, 94, 161, 276
,, Mary, 202, 260, 271, 276, 282
,, Mr., 105
,, Mrs., 105
,, Oliver, 94, 123, 128, 134
,, Peter, 10, 139
,, Richard, 76, 138, 201, 209, 282, c. of 292, 339
,, Robert, 189
,, Samuel, 76, 260, 276,* 333, c. of 334, 367, 370
,, Simon, 161
,, Thomas, 14
,, William, 27, 176
Shephen, Ellen, 282
,, John, 282
Shepherd [Sheaphard, Sheapharl, Shepard, Sheparde, Shepeherd, Shepeard, Sheperd, Sheperde, Shepert, Shephard, Shepheard, Shepherde, Sheppard, Sheppeard, Shiperd, Shipherd, Shipord],

Shepherd, Alice, 39, 294
,, Andrew, 63, 236, 286
,, Ann, 193, 241, 250, 255
,, Anthony, 196, 333
,, Elizabeth, 81, 244, 258, 342
,, Ellen, 2, 89, 241, 286, 369
,, Grace, 202
,, James, 67,* 77, 127, 141, 211,* 241, 246, 264, w. of 322*
,, Jane, 24
,, John, 75, 217, 260, 306
,, Jonathan, 235
,, Jony, 247, 297
,, Joshua, 73
,, Katherine, 127
,, Margaret, 102
,, Mary, 71, 75, 81, 150, 191, 211, 250
,, Peter, 242, 249
,, Ralph, 2, 54, 77, 92, 107, 134, 203, 210, 218,* 227, inf. of 282, 294*
,, Robert, 39, 49,* 52,* 54, 63,* 64, 71, 73, 81, 89, 94, 112, 143, 144, 150, 187, 190, 193, 194, 210, 211, 217, 227, 229, 235, 236, 241, 242, 244, 246, 247, 249, 250,* 255, 258, 260, 264, 271,* inf. of 287, 287, 297, c. of 318,* c. of 321,* c. of 326, w. of 334, 342, c. of 348, 352, 357, 370
,, Susan, 229
,, Thomas, 24, 210
Shippobotham [Sheepobothum, Shiplebothom, Shipobo, Shipobotham, Shipobothem, Shipobothom, Shipobothome, Shippobotha, Shippobothome, Shippobothum, Shippowbotham, Shippowbothame, Shippowbothome, Shypobothom],
,, Alice, 187, 260
,, Ann, 182, 334
,, Dorothy, 190, 273, 280
,, Edmund, 265
,, Elizabeth, 48, 100
,, Ellen, 162
,, Francis, 42, 63, 120, 150, 203
,, George, 18, 107, w. of 315
,, Henry, 18, 47,* 54, 92, 133, 142, 145,* 146, 187

INDEX OF NAMES.

Vol. 1.—C. . pp. 1— 90 inclusive. Vol. 2.—C. . pp. 205—280 inclusive.
B. . „ 91—168 „ B. . „ 281—350 „
W. . „ 169—204 „ W. . „ 351—372 „

Shippobotham, Isabel, 182
„ James, 188, 338
„ John, 54, 62, 162, 255, 260, 263, 265, 273, 280, 286, c. of 335
„ Katherine, 54
„ Margaret, 146
„ Mary, 202
„ Peter, 62, 131, 204, w. of 329
„ Richard, 42, 48, 54, 63, 80, 111, 130, 150, 154, 158, 196, 209, 283, 296, 315
„ Thomas, 80, 263, 266,* c. of 334
„ William, 209, 296
Shornley, Edmund, 295
Shorrock [Shorocke, Shorrok],
„ Jennet, 195
„ William, 143
Shriglay, Elizabeth, 36
„ Ellen, 36
Shruyde, Abraham, 215
„ Mary, 215
Shuttleworth [Shuttllworth],
„ Gennet, 352
„ James, 239, c. of 314
„ Jane, 239
Shypobothom [see Shippobotham]
Sickes, John, 359
Siddall [Seedall, Sidall, Sydall, Syddall, Sydell],
„ Alice, 13, 353
„ Edmund, 182
„ Edward, 40
„ Elizabeth, 66, 111
„ Ellen, 40, 256
„ Ellinor, 359
„ James, 206, 219, 293
„ Jane, 35
„ John, 35, 40, 46, 127, 180
„ Katherine, 157
„ Richard, 13, 46, 56,* 71,* 112, 157, 172, 188, 206, 219, 256, 293, 298, w. of 290, c. of 328, 366
„ Roger, 66
„ Thomas, 40
Simon, Simond, Simones [see Symons]
Singleton, Alice, 239
„ John, 239
„ Margaret, 202
Skarington, Richard, 83
„ William, 83
Skofeild, Skofeld, Skolefeild [see Scholfelde]
Skoles [see Scholes]
Skolfeld [see Scholfelde]
Slade [Slad],
„ Edmund, 109, 160, 275, 279, w. of 311

Slade, Edward, 360
„ Susan, 275
„ Thomas, 279
Sladen, Edmund, 13
„ George, 13, 103
Slake [? Slack], Edmund, 269*
Slate, Edmund, 334, 369
„ Ellen, 334
Slater [Slayter], John, 24,* 142
Smethurst [Smethehurst, Smetherst, Smetherste, Smetheurst, Smethrst, Smethurste, Smeythurst, Smithehurst, Smitherst, Smitherste, Smithirst, Smithurst],
„ Adam, 199
„ Alice, 14, 26, 64, 79, 88, 90, 147, 159, 185, 188, 221, 240, 252, 264, 366, 367
„ Ann, 52, 65, 70, 80, 84, 88, 176, 182, 193, 200, 217, 227,* 237, 250, 265, 266, 275, 299, 305, 307, 312, 337, 363, 364, 368
„ Arthur, 3, 28, 32, 73,* 164, 197, 212, 215, 222,* 229, 240,* 245, 250,* 251, 258, 265, 297, 327, 335, w. of 350, 353, 355, 357, 363, 364*
„ Bartholomew, 3, 36, 122, 182, 205, 212, 219, 224, 230, 237,* 248,* 320, w. of 329, 335, 340
„ Christopher, 14, 73, 112, 116, 120,* 147, 199, 227, 235, 299, c. of 313, 335, 356
„ Daniel, 2, 140
„ Dorothy, 50
„ Edmund, 13, 26, 43, 47,* 53, 58, 81, 103, 113, 123, 129, 133, 160, 179, 185, 205, 230, 305, 330
„ Elizabeth, 47, 58, 61, 62, 73, 144, 177, 241, 245, 259, 287, 306, 333, 352, 353
„ Ellen, 19, 34, 73, 81, 212, 227, 258, 273, 280, 296, 305, 369
„ Ellinor, 200
„ Francis, 45
„ Grace, 41, 194
„ Hannah, 217
„ Henry, 58, 139, 145, 147, 279
„ Isabel, 46, 62, 156, 203, 219, 335, 340
„ James, 24, 34, 40,* 64, 70, 73, 81, 82, 107, 141, 158, 177, 193, 211, 214, 219, 227, 258, 260, 265, 267, 309, 372
„ Jane, 27, 72, 147, 152, 176, 180, 283, 302, 305

U

Vol. 1.—C. . pp. 1— 90 inclusive. Vol. 2.—C. . pp. 205—280 inclusive.
　　　B. . ,, 91—168　　,,　　　　　　B. . ,, 281—350　　,,
　　　W. . ,, 169—204　　,,　　　　　　W. . ,, 351—372　　,,

Smethurst, Jennet, 160
　,, John, 59, 64, 206, 218, 223,* 231, 239, 246, 250,* 251, 252, 260, 265, 267, 273, c. of 303, c. of 336, 353
　,, Jonathan, 224
　,, Jony, 158, 355
　,, Katherine, 41, 43, 189, 343, 357
　,, Lawrence, 9, 13, 27, 32, 50, 65, 81, 100, 106, 119, 125, 172, 181, 235, 299, 302, w. of 346, 358
　,, Margaret, 9, 164, 299, 304
　,, Mary, 43, 55, 61, 66, 197, 205, 213, 231, 235, 267, 280, 317, 318, 329, 333,* 366, 370
　,, Oliver, 82
　,, Peter, 47, 148, 220, 239, 305
　,, Ralph, 24, 273, 333, 363, 364, 370
　,, Richard, 3, 6, 9,* 19, 28, 41, 52, 53,* 62, 64, 72, 80, 90, 106, 120, 121, 124, 140, 141, 152, 156, 171, 189, 205,* 214, 215, 221, 227, 229, 231,* 237, 245, 251, 252,* 257, 261, 267, 283, 287, 289, 305, w. of 318,* c. of 320, c. of 339, 341
　,, Robert, 41, 46, 53, 59, 62, 66, 73, 81, 187, 206, 213, 214, 219, 240, 245, 251, 252, 259, 264, c. of 298, c. of 299, 302, 306, c. of 320, 333, c. of 350,* 361, 364
　,, Roger, 2, 6, 18, 55, 64,* 79, 84, 97,* 106, 140, 159, 192, 210, 214,* 241, 287, 305, c. of 310, 333
　,, Samuel, 215, 261
　,, Susan, 210, 214, 287
　,, Theophilus, 230, 340
　,, Thomas, 6,* 18, 24,* 32, 45, 58, 62,* 145, 175, 211, 212, 215, 220, 222,* 227,* 230, 235, 239, 240,* 244,* 246, 249,* 250,* 252, 257, 258, 266, 273, 275, 279, 285, 299, c. of 307, c. of 315, c. of 316, w. of 324, 330, w. of 350, 355, 357,* 361
　,, Thurstan, 218
　,, William, 43, 239
Smith [Smithe, Smyth, Smythe],
　,, Alice, 104, 350, 372
　,, Ann, 81, 291, 354
　,, Dorathy, 67, 253
　,, Elizabeth, 75, 275, 296, 365, 371
　,, Ellen, 195
　,, Esther, 343

Smith, George, 8, 98, 238
　,, Henry, 76, 155, 198, 365
　,, Isabel, 98
　,, Israel, 83, 162
　,, James, 102, 151, 158, 207, 217, 277
　,, Jane, 7 60,* 152, 294, 365
　,, John, 7, 8, 36, 42, 50,* 60, 66, 67, 74, 81, 82, 87, 111, 112, 133, 150, 156, 173, 182, 193, 214,* 237, 238, 275, 288,* 290, 291, 296, 303, c. of 305, 334, 362
　,, Katherine, 78, 188
　,, Margaret, 36, 83, 162, 221, 264, 303
　,, Mary, 50, 60, 152, 211, 221, 232, 301, 318, 369
　,, Mr., 221
　,, Owen, 173
　,, Peter, 42, 232, 237, 246, 253, 264, 268,* c. of 325, w. of 329, c. of 336
　,, Priscilla, 80
　,, Richard, 197, 217, 272
　,, Robert, 82, 94, 129
　,, Samuel, 50, 246
　,, Sarah, 7, 74, 76, 155, 156
　,, Thomas, 66, 75, 78, 87, 150, 160, 207, 211, 221, 300, 301, w. of 301, 341, 351, 356
　,, William, 7, 76,* 80, 119, 123, 130, 165, 272, 277, w. of 343, c. of 348, w. of 350, 370
Smithehurst [see Smethurst]
Smither, Ellis, 21
　,, Thomas, 21
Smitherst, Smitherste, Smithurst [see Smethurst]
Smoolt [Smoult], Alice, 258
　,, Edmund, 251, 258
　,, Thomas, 251
Smyth, Smythe [see Smith]
Soar, Marie, 124
Sotte [see Stott]
Stackehouse [Stackhouse], James, 62, 63, 64, 143, 193, 194
　,, Susan, 62
Stancfeild [see Stansfield]
Standly, Mr., 328
Stanneringe [Staneringe]
　,, Abraham, 23, 163, 197
　,, Edmund, 23
Stanford, Alice, 372*
Stansfield [Stancfeild, Standfeild, Stanfeild],
　,, Lawrence, 307

INDEX OF NAMES. 431

Vol. 1.—C. . *pp.* 1— 90 *inclusive.* Vol. 2.—C. . *pp.* 205—280 *inclusive.*
    B. . ,, 91—168 ,,   B. . ,, 281—350 ,,
    W. . ,, 169—204 ,,   W. . ,, 351—372 ,,

Stansfield, Robert, 254, c. of 334
,, Thomas, 254
Starkie, Richard, 62, 144
,, Thomas, 62, 144, 148, 192
Staulman, Gennit, 197
Steele [Steile, Stele, Stile],
,, Alice, 77, 370
,, Ann, 151
,, Elizabeth, 43, 121, 286
,, James, 61, 121, 164, 285
,, Margaret, 34, 183
,, Owen, 93
,, Richard, 34, 43, 61, 77, 164, 286, 324
Steven, John, 134, 139
Stile [see Steele]
Stith, Elizabeth, 370
Stock [Stocke, Stoke], Ann, 203
,, James, 246, 260, 261,* 267,* 338, 367
,, John, 246
,, Mary, 260
,, Sarah, 338
,, Susan, 362
Stones [Stons, Stonnes], Alice, 52, 262
,, Allen, 356
,, Bartholomew, 209, 258, 262, 268,* 274, 280, 366
,, Daniel, c. of 291, 346
,, Elizabeth, 64
,, Ellen, 34, 43
,, Ellis, 34, 41, 49, 58, 69, 158
,, James, 43, 52, 55, 59, 64, 130, 142, 164, 185
,, Jane, 280
,, Jonie, 41, 179, 311
,, Mary, 69
,, Oliver, 59
,, Richard, 58, 258, 326
,, Robert, 55
,, Samuel, 156*
,, Thomas, 274
,, Wynifride, 49
Stopporte, Isabel, 57
,, Peter, 57, 191
Stott [Stot, Stote, Stotes, Stotte],
,, Abraham, 363
,, Ann, 248, 250
,, Arthur, 50
,, Francis, 28,* 42, 50, 62, 113, 143, 233, 240,* 248, 250, 266, w. of 342, w. of 348
,, James, 211, 238, 274,* 363, 370
,, Jane, 36
,, Jeremy, 207
,, John, 42, 86,* 203, 211, 224,* 231, 248, 265, 293,* 294, c. of

Stott, John, *continued*—
318, 321, 322, w. of 330, w. of 348, 355
,, Jonathan, 234
,, Joseah, 367
,, Margaret, 369
,, Mary, 233, 238, 248, 294
,, Ralph, 265
,, Robert, 62
,, Sarah, 266
,, Thomas, 231, 250,* c. of 312,* 322
,, William, 36, 207, 234, c. of 291, c. of 304, c. of 307, w. of 331, 345
Stranguishe, Ann, 82, 161
,, Robert, 82, 161
Street [Streete], George, 277*
,, John, 26, 236
,, Joseph, 372
,, Mary, 26, 236
,, Richard, 4, 5,* 129*
Strenge, Alice, 363
Strenger [see Stringer]
Strikeland, Alice, 192
Stringer [Strenger],
,, Abraham, 220, 226, 229, 292, c. of 308, 308, 353
,, Alice, 220
,, Jane, 178
,, Mary, 226, 292
,, Richard, 229, 281
Sturdicar, Richard, w. of 321, 359
Styne, Ellen, 187
Suell, Jane, 309
Sutcliffe [Sutley, Sutliffe, Suttcliffe, Suttliffe],
,, Adam, 231, 344
,, Alice, 336
,, Dorothy, 253
,, John, 239
,, Matthew, 231, 239, 253, 263, 336, c. of 339, c. of 344, 357
,, Richard, 263
Sydall, Syddall, Sydell [see Siddall]
Symons [Simon, Simond, Simones, Symon, Symond, Symonde, Symonds, Symones, Symonus],
,, Alice, 18, 28, 39, 351
,, Ann, 280
,, Edward, 28, 39, 46, 55, 63, 69, 77, 121, 128, 144, 158, 215, 220, 291, 343, w. of 348
,, Ellen, 77, 365
,, James, 13, 28, 215, 291
,, Katherine, 29, 69, 197, 363

Vol. 1.—C. . pp. 1— 90 inclusive. Vol. 2.—C. . pp. 205—280 inclusive.
　　　B. . ,, 91—168 ,,　　　　　　B. . ,, 281—350 ,,
　　　W. . ,, 169—204 ,,　　　　　　W. . ,, 351—372 ,,

Symons, Margaret, 34, 46, 355
　,, Mary, 220
　,, Richard, 2,* 6,* 13, 18, 21, 28,*
　　　40, 63, 77, 92,* 110, 118, 126,
　　　144, 184, 280, 317, w. of 340,
　　　w. of 350, 371
　,, Robert, 21
　,, Thomas, 13, 29, 34, 55, 103, 121,
　　　327, w. of 347
Sympson [Symson], Dorothy, 70, 184
　,, George, 50
　,, John, 50
　,, William, 70
Sythe, Peter, c. of 309

T

TABERNACLE [Tabernacke],
　,, John, 264,* 269,* 368
Taelior, Tailor [see Taylor]
Tattersall [Tatersall], Ann, 256
　,, Ellen, 153
　,, Henry, 256
　,, Jacob, 186
　,, John, 179, 366
　,, Lawrence, 353
　,, Mary, 113
　,, Richard, 153*
　,, Sarah, 179
　,, Susan, 185
Taylor [Taelior, Tailer, Tailere,
　　　Tailier, Tailor, Tayleor,
　　　Tayler, Taylere, Taylior,
　　　Taylore, Tealior, Teallior,
　　　Telior],
　,, Abraham, 218, 232, 237,* 293
　,, Adam, 12, 31, 108, 293
　,, Agnes, 296
　,, Alice, 3, 32, 34, 44, 180, 202,
　　　220, 225, 235, 288, 306, 351,
　　　368
　,, Ann, 39,* 197, 217,* 272, 278,
　　　323, 334
　,, Arthur, 45, 56, 65, 85, 139, 142,
　　　156, 159, 186, 243, 326, 341
　,, Constance, 21, 286
　,, Dorothy, 65, 88, 218, 278, 293
　,, Edmund, 5, 95
　,, Edward, 258, 353
　,, Edythe, 31
　,, Elizabeth, 12, 45, 76, 180, 183,
　　　210, 270, 288,* 292, 293, 295,
　　　323, 355
　,, Ellen, 41, 56, 186, 262, 319, 362
　,, Ellis, 36,* 298
　,, Elsabell, 223
　,, Francis, 9, 34, 37, 40, 48, 99,
　　　126, 178, 302, w. of 315

Taylor, Genet, 187, 363
　,, Grace, 199, 272, 353, 367
　,, Henry, 231, 272, 369, 370
　,, Hugh, 276, 279
　,, Isabel, 57, 95, 161, 190, 243, 354
　,, James, 57, 174, 232,* 234, 245,*
　　　262, 274, w. of 319, c. of 344,
　　　356, 361
　,, Jane, 32,* 85, 197, 203, 232, 247,
　　　276, 286, 296, 297, 364
　,, Jeffrey, 272, 278, 292, 323, w. of
　　　331
　,, John, 3, 7, 21, 40, 48, 76, 79,
　　　85, 88, 102, 104, 111, 113,
　　　118, 121, 133, 198,* 210, 220,
　　　226,* 227, 235, 240, 241, 243,
　　　262, 265, 271, 272, 276,* 279,
　　　286, 298, c. of 301, 304, 306,
　　　c. of 318, 342, 355, 369, 370
　,, Jonathan, 256
　,, Joseph, c. of 345, 366
　,, Joshua, 13, 102, 270, 274
　,, Katherine, 7, 95, 279
　,, Lawrence, 79, 101, 107, 128, 180,
　　　184, 195, 268,* 278, c. of 301,
　　　c. of 302, c. of 306, 370
　,, Lettice, 204
　,, Margaret, 13, 330, 366
　,, Margerie, 161
　,, Martha, 70, 198, 361
　,, Mary, 47, 227, 272, 279, 357,
　　　361, 371
　,, Michael, 165
　,, Oliver, 258, 363, 367
　,, Peter, 41, 146, 295, w. of 341,
　　　344
　,, Priscilla, 355
　,, Richard, 9, 39, 41, 47, 57, 65,
　　　66,* 70, 78,* 81,* 84,* 88,*
　　　110, 140, 146,* 153, 165, 196,*
　　　197, 208,* 223, 231, 236, 240,*
　　　254,* 262,* 276,* c. of 310,
　　　318, 333,* w. of 343, 343,* inf.
　　　of 350, 364, 371
　,, Robert, 32,* 37, 120, 133, 139,
　　　170, 181, 225, 234, 243, 274,
　　　c. of 323, 353, 356, 359, 366
　,, Roger, 52, 56, 183, 185, 236, 241,
　　　247, 256, 262, 271, 274, 279,
　　　356
　,, Samuel, 32, 44, 52, 56, 71, 212
　,, Sarah, 166, 201
　,, Sher [?], 236
　,, Sibbill, 369
　,, Susan, 39, 182, 196, 208,* 212,
　　　240, 279, 367
　,, Thomas, 5, 12,* 71, 95, 105, 106,*
　　　184, 239,* 270

INDEX OF NAMES. 433

Vol. 1.—C. . pp. 1— 90 inclusive. Vol. 2.—C. . pp. 465—480 inclusive.
     B. . ,, 91—108 ,,   B. . ,, 281—350 ,,
     W. . ,, 109—204 ,,   W. . ,, 351—372 ,,

Taylor, William, 36,* 41, 57, 65, 85, 110, 159, 161, 175, 183, 197, 265, 270, 276, 297, w. of 343, c. of 346, 368
Tealior, Telior [see Taylor]
Tennant [Tenant, Tennante],
,, Ann, 291
,, Thomas, inf. of 288, 291, 352
Thirnough, Ann, 368
Thornes, Thomas, 9, 291
Thornley [Thorneley, Thornly],
,, Ellen, 67, 276
,, Jeremy, 371
,, Richard, 67, 272, 290, w. of 350
,, William, 43,* 272, 276, 369
Thorneton, Ellen, 359
Thorpe, Ann, 193
Tilsey, Anthony, 202
,, Bridget, 153
Tilsley [see Tyldesley]
Tomlinson [Tominson, Tomlynson, Tumlinson],
,, Abel, 73, 196, 303, 324, 367
,, Ann, 73, 303
,, Dorothy, 38
,, George, 359
,, James, 324
,, Joseph, 371
,, Robert, 38
Tomson [Tompson], Christopher, 67
,, Frances, 177
,, Peter, 67
Tong [Tonge, Tunge], Alice, 269
,, John, 58
,, Mary, 371
,, Robert, 269
,, Thomas, 58, 361
Tootell [Toothill, Tootell, Totell, Tottell, Toutell, Tutel, Tutell, Tuttall, Tuttell],
,, Alice, 76, 157, 218
,, Ann, 70, 366
,, Ellen, 307
,, Francis, 210
,, James, 75, 85,* 197, 209, 210, 294
,, John, 216, 219, 223, 293
,, Jony, 146, 346
,, Katherine, 278
,, Peter, 70, 75, 76, 81, 88,* 157, 196, 209, 216, 219, 223, 228, 293, c. of 307,* 307, 346
,, Richard, 81, 83,* 110, 201, 205, 218, 278, 280,* c. of 298, 371
,, Sara, 205
,, Thomas, 228
Top, John, 148

Topping, John, 255
,, Thomas, 255
Towne, James, 18-
Townley, Barnard, 360
Townsend, Mary, 236
,, Samuel, 236
Tumlinson [see Tomlinson]
Tunge [see Tong]
Tunstall, Barnard, 145
Turnaghe [see also Turner], John, 101
Turner, Turnor [see also Turnaghe],
,, Alice, 78, 143, 147
,, Ann, 70, 219, 229, 286, 297
,, Edmund, 81, 216, 299, c. of 299
,, Elizabeth, 59, 81, 212, 295
,, Ellis, 89
,, Esther, 354
,, George, 248
,, James, 238, 266, 357
,, John, 54, 70, 81, 89, 101, 200, 212, 216, 217, 219, 277, 295, 298
,, Lawrence, 89, 92, 272, 277, c. of 349
,, Margerie, 301
,, Richard, 266
,, Robert, 81, 300
,, Thomas, 54, 59, 70,* 78, 89, 139, 143, 191, 210,* 217, 229, 238, 248, 272, 286, 297, 298
Tutel, Tutell, Tuttall, Tuttell [see Tootell]
Twyste, Wife, 125
Tyldesley [Tilsley, Tyldisleye, Tyldysley],
,, Elizabeth, 258
,, Henry, 22
,, John, 266
,, Ralph, 22, 112, 118, 124, 176
,, Thomas, 258, 266
Tytterton, Owyn, 174

U

Unsworth [Undsworth, Unseworth, Unsworthe, Vnsewoorth, Vnseworth, Vnseworthe, Vnsworth, Vnsworthe],
,, Alice, 5, 10, 50, 78, 124, 151, 212, 252, 291, 355
,, Ann, 8, 32, 85, 241, 244, 250, 298, 313, 353, 360, 367
,, Annes, 151
,, Charles, 79, 240, c. of 314, 361
,, Christopher, 80
,, Deborah, 178, 266
,, Dorothy, 54, 359

Vol. 1.—C. . pp. 1— 90 inclusive. Vol. 2.—C. . pp. 205—280 inclusive.
B. . ,, 91—108 ,, B. . ,, 281—350 ,,
W. . ,, 109—204 ,, W. . ,, 351—372 ,,

Unsworth, Edmund, 91, 140
,, Edward, 2, 226, 237, 258
,, Elizabeth, 27, 55, 163, 225, 248, 258, 267, 305, 354
,, Ellen, 155, 194, 292
,, Ellis, 67, 239, 246, 371, 372
,, Francis, 8
,, George, 2, 8, 103, 141, 155, 158, 218,* 221, 226, 232, 239, 244, 250, c. of 312, w. of 346, 354
,, Giles, 91, 233,* 237, 244,* 250, 259, 267, 357
,, Isabel, 32
,, James, 38, 92, 99, 221, 245
,, Jane, 271
,, Joan, 42, 57, 153, 257, 365
,, John, 37, 43, 45, 48, 50, 59, 67,* 72, 78, 80,* 110, 123, 124, 128, 131, 151, 163, 184, 185, 207, 239, 277, 287, 291, 298, 323
,, Joseph, 64*
,, Katherine, 240
,, Margaret, 55, 72
,, Margerie, 186
,, Mary, 15, 224, 232, 239, 259, 322, 370
,, Peter, 43
,, Ralph, 85, 201, 206, 214, 225, 233, 241, 245, 252, c. of 307, 322, c. of 326, w. of 330, w. of 347, 369
,, Ratcliffe, 45
,, Richard, 10, 14, 18, 37, 54, 103, 109, 110, 133, 145, 151, 153, 179, 182, 207, 212, 214, 233, 246, 248, 260,* 266, 271, 277, 322, 350, c. of 350, 363
,, Robert, 83, 112, 125, 139
,, Roger, 18, 27, 36, 38, 48, 57, 68,* 78, 83, 122, 157, 206, 224, 250, 257, 322, c. of 330, 330, 341, 350, 355
,, Samuel, 5, 8, 15, 42, 80, 108, 109, 134, 153, 164, 184, c. of 298
,, Sarah, 285
,, Susan, 14
,, Thomas, 121, 160, 179, 285, 286
,, William, 78, 157, 288, w. of 309
Usherwood, Usherwoode, Ushwood [see Isherwood]

V

VESYE [Veysy], Elizabeth, 78, 157
,, Richard, 78, 157
Vsherwood [see Isherwood]
Vnsworth [see Unsworth]

W

WADDINGTON [Wadington, Waddingtonn],
,, Ann, 186, 198
,, Edward, 41
,, Elizabeth, 41, 57, 319
,, Ellen, 337
,, John, 11, 107, 109, 170
,, Margaret, 183
,, Margerie, 310
,, Mary, 11
,, Richard, 57
Wade, Alice, 19
,, Henry, 19
,, Susan, 183
Wadington [see Waddington]
Wadsworth [Wadseworth, Wadseworthe],
,, Margaret, 74, 154
,, William, 74, 154, 197
Walch [see also Welche], John, 361
Walkden [Walkeden], Ellen, 252
,, John, 252
,, Nicholas, 354
Walker [Waulker], Alice, 257
,, Elizabeth, 20, 356
,, Jane, 28, 165, 186
,, John, 4, 213, 217, 293
,, Katherine, 272, 346
,, Mary, 72, 213, 272
,, Richard, 13, 209, 273
,, Roger, 333
,, Susan, 230, 279
,, Thomas, 4, 13, 20, 28, 72, 120, 134, 209, 217, 230, 257, 273, 279, 293
Walles [Waules], Anthony, 199, w. of 346, 371
,, George, 271
,, Susan, 271
Wallworke [Wallwarke, Walwark, Walwarke, Walwork, Walworke, Walworth, Walworthe, Waulworke, Wauwarke],
,, Ann, 67, 144, 364
,, Dorothy, 251
,, Elizabeth, 199, 272, 338, 370
,, Francis, 144, 290, c. of 304
,, Isabel, 182
,, James, 160, 216, 238, 272, 277, 338, 341, 357, 370
,, John, 67, 75,* 85, 99, 106, 208, 216, 223, 230, 251, 277, 308, 338, 364
,, Margaret, 160, 193, 197, 230

INDEX OF NAMES. 435

Vol. 1.—C. . pp. 1— 90 inclusive. Vol. 2.—C. . pp. 205—280 inclusive.
B. . ,, 91—168 ,, B. . ,, 281—350 ,,
W. . ,, 169—204 ,, W. . ,, 351—372 ,,

Wallworke, Martha, 230, 308
,, Mary, 230, 308
,, Peter, 208, 318
,, Richard, 85, 330
,, Robert, 238, 360
,, Sarah, 223
,, Susan, 338
Walmer [Wolmer],
,, Deborah, 237
,, Esther, 244
,, Thomas, 237, 244
Walmersley [Walmersleye],
,, Elizabeth, 45
,, James, 45, 130, 185, 228
,, John, 228
,, William, 228
Walshaw [Walshawe, Washaw],
,, Elizabeth, 335
,, Peter, 295
Walten, Thomas, 266*
Walworthe [see Wallworke]
Warburton [Warbarton, Warbartonn, Warberton, Warbertone, Warborton, Warbuton],
,, Adam, w. of 311
,, Alice, 42, 47, 49, 189, 231, 259, 268
,, Ann, 6, 84, 141, 177, 231, 288, 289, 295
,, Deborah, 247, 308
,, Dorothy, 263
,, Edmund, 35
,, Elizabeth, 17, 38, 52, 149, 216, 244, 275
,, Ellen, 275
,, Esther, 258
,, Francis, 42, 51, 52, 59, 65, 75, 80, 141, 183, 192, 206, 260, 289,* 291, 326, w. of 326, c. of 326, 332, 354
,, George, 2, 28, 48, 74, 93, 149, 153, 269, 281, 295, 309
,, Henry, 47
,, Isabel, 245
,, Jacob, 216
,, James, 153, 190, 196, 234, 262, c. of 310,* 321, d. of 324
,, Jane, 255
,, Jennet, 156
,, John, 2, 49, 59,* 75, 84, 89,* 93, 209, 216,* 217,* 228, 236, 241, 247, 248,* 252, 253,* 254, 263, 275, 280, c. of 290, 293, 308, c. of 309, inf. of 311, w. of 325, c. of 334, w. of 343, 350, 359, 363
,, Judith, 209, 228, 308

Warburton, Katherine, 65, 277
,, Margaret, 59, 153, 271, 273, 289
,, Mary, 55, 75, 188, 237, 246, 263, 355
,, Peter, 280
,, Richard, 217, 293
,, Robert, 91, 156, 165, 167, 234, 252, 257,* 263, 272
,, Susan, 80, 197, 332
,, Thomas, 6, 17, 28, 32,* 35, 38, 48, 51, 55,* 59, 74, 75, 77,* 89, 119, 120, 132, 134, 137, 138,* 153, 178, 191, 206, 231, 234, 237, 241, 244, 245, 246, 248, 250,* 254, 255, 258, 259, 262, 264.* 268, 269, 272, 273, 275, 277,* 281, 289, 308, 320, c. of 327, w. of 328, c. of 346, 350, 358, 361, 362
,, William, 102, 113, 236, 248, 250, 260, 271
Wardle [Wardeles], Francis, 53, 75*
,, James, 85
,, John, 53, 85, 210, 219, inf. of 282, 328, 351
,, Jonathan, 219, 372
,, Mary, 210
Wardleworth [Wardleworthe],
,, Alice, 236
,, Ann, 161
,, Elizabeth, 337
,, Jane, 24,* 178
,, John, 95, 236, 360
,, Richard, 9, 95
,, Robert, 91, 96, 161
,, William, 9, 96, 110, 119, 316, 354
Wardley, Ellen, 295
,, Francis, 153,* 295
Warwicke, Jane, 32*
Washaw [see Walshaw]
Waterhouse [Waterhowse, Waterouse],
,, Jeremy, 194
,, Margaret, 356
,, Sarah, 203
Watmough [Watmonghe],
,, Hugh, 68, 71, 73, 77, 78, 89, 150, 158, 161, 201, 210, 220, 287, 298, 352 353
,, Isabel, 89
,, John, 64
,, Joshua, 77
,, Mr., 64, 220, 298
,, Susanna, 220
,, Timothy, 73
Watson, N.X.N., 212

Vol. 1.—C. . pp. 1— 90 inclusive. Vol. 2.—C. . pp. 205—280 inclusive.
   B. . ,,   91—168   ,,   B. . ,, 281—350   ,,
   W. . ,, 109—204   ,,   W. . ,, 351—373   ,,

Watson, Richard, 212
Waules [see Walles]
Waulker [see Walker]
Waulworke, Wauwarke,
   [see Wallworke]
Wawan, Edith, 202
Welche [see also Walch], Ann, 204
,, Ellen, 100
,, Margaret, 288
,, Richard, 160, 285
Werrall [Wirrall], Ann, 16
,, Elizabeth, 8
,, John, 8
,, Margaret, 9
,, Owen, 16
,, Richard, 9
West, Henry, 350
Westonn [Weston], Margaret, 286
,, Thomas, 174, 286, 292
Wharledale, George, 355
Wharmby [Wharmbie, Wharnby,
   Wharneby],
,, Elizabeth, 252
,, Ellen, 247
,, John, 256
,, Thomas, 242,* 247, 252, 256,
   c. of 327, c. of 329
Wherrocks [see Horrocks]
Whetehead, Whetheade,
   [see Whitehead]
Whitaker [Whitakar, Whiticar,
   Whiticor, Whitikar,
   Whitiker, Whittacar,
   Whittacre, Whittaker,
   Whitticar, Withiteker],
,, Alice, 107, 200, 264, 269, 305
,, Ann, 76, 229, 247, 272, 279, 336
,, Anthonie, 282
,, Arthur, 13, 59, 110, 152, 176,
   232, 239, 324, w. of 327, 347
,, Edmund, 70, 85, 142, 229, 237,
   247, 341, w. of 342
,, Elizabeth, 23, 156, 237, 335
,, Ellin, 266
,, Francis, 90, 211, 262, 272, 279,
   336, c. of 339, 368
,, Hugh, 140
,, Isabel, 150
,, James, 58, 80, 109, 151, 160, 218,
   256, 260, 262, 264, 267,* 275,
   276,* 279,* 333, 335, 368
,, Jane, 17, 75, 105, 159, 262,* 351
,, Jennet, 366
,, John, 101, 142, 156, 233,* 260,
   265, 266
,, Margaret, 44, 51, 128, 274, 371
,, Mary, 233, 264, 370

Whitaker, Rauffe, 10, 17, 37, 43, 51,
   59, 76, 85, 131, 149, 171, 188,
   265, 335, 367
,, Richard, 133
,, Robert, 10, 44, 49,* 58, 63,* 70,
   75, 82, 90, 107, 130, 146, 149,
   151, 163, 184, 200, 215,* 233,
   239, 268,* 269, 274, 305, c. of
   309, w. of 314, w. of 323, 336,
   343, 360, 363, 369
,, Sarah, 275
,, Thomas, 13, 152, 256
,, William, 23, 37, 43, 80, 82, 145,
   149, 159, 160, 161, 163, 211,
   218, 232, 282, c. of 309, 333,
   334, w. of 338, 351
Whitehead [Whetehead, Whetheade,
   Whiteheade, Whithead,
   Whitheade, Whitbeades,
   Whithed, Whitihead,
   Whitthead, Whytcheade,
   Whythead, Whytheade,
   Witthead],
,, Abraham, 236
,, Alice, 2, 88, 146, 251, 259, 278,
   283, 359, 371
,, Ann, 33, 67, 84, 125, 176, 191,
   239, 247, 312, 357
,, Edward, 271
,, Elizabeth, 19, 44, 59, 179, 180,
   223, 232, 270, 303, 336, 364
,, George, 118, 261, 265
,, Henry, 37, 76, 85, 252
,, Isabel, 203, 205, 335, 366
,, James, 71, 93, 152, 219, 234
,, Jane, 190, 355
,, John, 7, 75, 77, 81, 84, 147, 150,*
   194, 206, 209, 213,* 215,*
   219,* 223, 224,* 232, 236, 239,
   246, 251, 252, 253, 259, 265,
   271, 273, 278, 283, 285, c. of
   291, 308, 312, 322, 334, w. of
   343
,, Katherine, 20, 96, 189, 303
,, Lawrence, 135, 176
,, Margaret, 50, 70, 182,* 219, 271,
   342
,, Margery, 57, 283
,, Martha, 214
,, Mary, 50, 75, 112, 206, 246, 251,
   267, 278, 322, 351, 368
,, Richard, 17, 55, 62,* 70, 71, 77,
   88, 138, 152, 196, 211, 219,*
   252, 283, 308, 309, c. of 313,
   314
,, Robert, 50, 59, 67, 76, 85, 214
,, Sarah, 253

INDEX OF NAMES.

Vol. 1.—C. . pp. 1— 90 inclusive. Vol. 2.—C. . pp. 205—280 inclusive.
B. . „ 91—168 „ B. . „ 281—350 „
W. . „ 169—204 „ W. . „ 351—372 „

Whitehead, Susan, 251, 303
„ Thomas, 2, 7, 8,* 11, 15, 17, 19, 20, 24,* 29, 33, 37, 44, 50, 55, 57, 70,* 81, 96, 97, 101, 108, 110, 116, 118, 130, 134, 135, 146, 150, 172, 177, 179, 205, 209, 211, 234, 238,* 242,* 247, 250,* 252, 261, 263,* 267, 270, 271, 273, 278, 293, 302, 303, 314, w. of 315, 318, c. of w. of 323, 335
Whitfeld, Richard, 197
Whiticar, Whitikar [see Whitaker]
Whitley [see also Whittle],
„ Elizabeth, 364
„ John, 283, 360
„ Margaret, 283
„ Samuel, 180
Whittaker [see Whitaker]
Whittle, Whitle, Whittell, Witell [see also Whitley],
„ Alice, 367
„ Elizabeth, 151
„ Ellen, 31
„ James, 360
„ Margery, 256
„ Mary, 57
„ Rauffe, 57, 139
„ Thomas, 256, c. of 327
„ William, 31, 125, 151, 159
Whitworth [Whitworthe],
„ Alexander, 122
„ Alice, 192
„ Ann, 360
„ Edmund, 9
„ Elizabeth, 155, 203
„ James, 297
„ Jane, 297
„ John, 155
„ Katherine, 180
„ Robert, 198
„ William, 9
Whorockes, Whorrockes [see Horrockes]
Whythead [see Whitehead]
Wigan [Wigen, Wiggan, Wiggin, Wigin, Wigon],
„ Alice, 208, 284
„ Ann, 214, 225
„ Dorothy, 51, 70
„ Elizabeth, 56
„ Henry, 51
„ James, 244
„ Jane, 296
„ Jennet, 265, 296
„ John, 56, 68,* 80, 190, 208, 214, 218, 251, 284, c. of 290, 294, 296,* 323

Wigan, Margaret, 278
„ Matthew, 251, 323
„ Mary, 218, 272, 293
„ Oliver, 53, 153, 190, 289
„ Richard, 80, 212,* 225, 233,* 244, 251, 265, 272, 278, 293, c. of 294, s. of 318, 323,* w. of 332, c. of 339, c. of 340, c. of 345
„ Roger, 53
„ Thomas, 45,* 70, 95
Wiggins [see Wigan], Elizabeth, 194
Wignall [Wignol, Wignolle],
„ Dorothy, 274
„ Giles, 67, 71, 151, 194
„ John, 67
„ Margaret, 151
„ Mary, 71
„ Richard, 274
Wigon [see Wigan]
Wild [Wilde, Weld, Wylde],
„ Abraham, 43, 246
„ Ann, 12, 17, 86, 194, 228, 271
„ Edmund, 67, 75,* 86, 216
„ Fardinando, 304
„ Isabel, 10, 183
„ James, 107, 265
„ Jane, 27, 216, 330
„ Jennet, 246
„ John, 10, 14, 108, 221, 228, 259, 314
„ Laurence, 60
„ Margaret, 67
„ Margerie, 183
„ Martha, 355
„ Mary, 221, 317
„ Richard, 43, 51,* 60, 178, 184, 259, 265, 271, 367
„ Roger, 12, 17, 27, 116, 117, 118
„ Samuel, 362
„ Sarah, 14
Wilkinson [Wilkingson, Wilkingsonn, Wilkinsun],
„ Abraham, 228
„ Edmund, 15
„ Jane, 238
„ John, 15
„ Richard, 212
„ Thomas, 53, 212, 228, 238, c. of 303, c. of 304, 342, w. of 316, 353
„ William, 53
Williams, Margaret, 215
„ Thomas, 215
Williamson [Willyamson],
„ Clemence, 353
„ Margaret, 47

v

Vol. 1.—C. . pp. 1— 90 inclusive. Vol. 2.—C. . pp. 205—280 inclusive.
       B. . „ 91—168   „   B. . „ 281—350   „
       W. . „ 169—204   „   W. . „ 351—372   „

Williamson, William, 47, 137
Wilson [Willsonne, Wilsone,
       Wilsonn, Wilsonne],
  „   Alice, 70, 149
  „   Ann, 45, 155, 259, 305
  „   Annis, 357
  „   Elizabeth, 223
  „   James, 38, 90, 201, 223, 239,
        247,* 251,* 259, 266, c. of
        303, c. of 307, 360
  „   John, 27, 90, 266
  „   Margaret, 311, 371
  „   Mary, 56
  „   Priscilla, 293
  „   Richard, 27,* 30,* 38, 45, 56,
        70, 115,* 137, 146, 149, 154,
        155, 178
  „   Robert, 294
  „   Thomas, 110, 239
  „   William, 359, 364
Winell, Margaret, 356
Winkley, Margaret, 337
Winterberow, Oliver, 363
Wirrall [see Werrall]
Withington, John, w. of 320
Withitcker [see Whitaker]
Witthead [see Whitehead]
Woasencroft [see Wolstencrofte]
Wod, Wode [see Wood]
Wodford, Alice, 198
Wolfenden [Wofenden, Wofendine,
       Woffendale, Woofenden,
       Woolfenden, Wowfenden],
  „   Adame, 170, 291
  „   Ann, 6, 39*
  „   Ellen, 34, 191, 248
  „   Ellis, 158
  „   Francis, 94, 247, 256, 345
  „   Isabel, 143
  „   Jane, 15, 82, 229, 306
  „   John, 4, 229, 232,* 247, 248, 335,
        c. of 349, w. of 349, 358,
        369
  „   Katherine, 41
  „   Margery, 291
  „   Mary, 345
  „   Peter, 6, 34, 41, 82, 126, 200
  „   Raulfe, 15
  „   Richard, 116
  „   Roger, 256
  „   Silvestris, 311
  „   Thomas, 4, 17, 25,* 143, 275,
        305, 306, 335
  „   Walter, 17, 275
Wolmer [see Walmer]
Wolsenam, Wolsenham, Wolsnam
       [see Wolstenholme]

Wolstencrofte [Woasencroft,
       Wolsencrofte, Woolsencrofte,
       Wosencroft, Wosencrofte,
       Wostencrofte],
  „   Elizabeth, 70, 150
  „   Henry, 247
  „   Isabel, 155
  „   John, 2, 106, 150
  „   Katherine, 192
  „   Ralph, 2, 10,* 19,* 155, 247, 298
  „   Roger, 70
Wolstenholme [Wolsenam,
       Wolsenham, Wolsenhame,
       Wolsnam, Wolsenholme,
       Woolsenham, Woolsenholme,
       Woolsncham,
       Woolstenholme, Woosnam,
       Wosenam, Wosnam,
       Wosname, Wosneham,
       Woulsonham].
  „   Abel, 64, 87, 207, 213, 218, 223,
        226, 234, 241
  „   Ann, 302, 349
  „   Dorothy, 181
  „   Edward, 213
  „   Ellen, 87, 243
  „   Emyn, 285
  „   Francis, 6, 218, 285
  „   Gabriel, 205, 286
  „   Henry, 223
  „   Imn, 220
  „   Isabel, 226
  „   James, 185, 220, 353
  „   Jane, 368
  „   Joan, 234, 294
  „   John, 129, 174, 185
  „   Katherine, 228, 231, 298
  „   Martha, 353
  „   Mary, 73, 152, 159
  „   Matthew, 6, 84, 221, 228, 231,
        239, 243, c. of 307, 331, 349
  „   Michael, 64, 84, 159, 205, 214,*
        235,* inf. of 286, c. of 301
  „   Peter, 239
  „   Richard, 148, c. of 304, 314
  „   Robert, 73, 152, 241
  „   Thomas, 207, 221, 294, 298
Wood [Wod, Wode, Woode, Woods],
  „   Abraham, 80, 252,* 254, 270,
        327, w. of 331, 341
  „   Alice, 9, 13, 55, 58,* 69, 87, 94,
        128, 152, 160, 232, 244, 250,
        270, 272, 284, 288, 314, 353,
        362
  „   Andrew, 56, 70, 80, 87, 133, 160
  „   Ann, 32, 70, 157, 192, 209, 215,
        232,* 239, 266, 372

INDEX OF NAMES.

Vol. 1.—C. . pp. 1— 90 inclusive. Vol. 2.—C. . pp. 205—280 inclusive.
B. . ,, 91—168 ,, B. . ,, 281—350 ,,
W. . ,, 169—204 ,, W. . ,, 351—372 ,,

Wood, Dorothy, 25, 32, 35, 157, 166, 222, 231, 359
,, Edmund, 207
,, Elizabeth, 8, 9, 22, 55, 74, 83, 86, 155, 162, 164, 167, 205, 214, 219, 233, 259, 270,* 278, 304, 318, 364, 367, 368*
,, Ellen, 36, 47, 79, 268, 355, 365
,, Francis, 5, 9, 23, 32, 49, 55, 58, 65, 69, 70, 79, 80,* 121, 128, 146, 163, 192, 205, 212, 221, 234, 283, w. of 300, c. of 304, 335
,, George, 233, 241, 245, 279,* c. of 321, 344
,, Grace, 258, 368
,, Henry, 2, 11, 48, 84, 92, 212, 218,* 224, 238, 252, 306, 318
,, Isabel, 5, 23, 360
,, James, 5, 52, 65, 72, 83, 94, 166, 207, 224, 275, 298, w. of 326
,, Jane, 5, 35, 94, 191, 234, 238, 255, 333, 345, 363
,, John, 13, 22, 25, 35,* 36, 39, 49, 55, 65, 68,* 75,* 76, 83,* 84, 87, 127, 139, 140,* 157,* 158, 162,* 188, 190, 207, 210, 213, 215, 217, 221, 222, 259,* 263, 266, 270, 272, 274,* 275, 278, inf. of 285, 295, 322, c. of 347, 347, 363
,, Jonas, 279, 371
,, Katherine, 47, 316
,, Margaret, 23, 224, 275, 305, 356
,, Mary, 2, 13, 75, 212, 224, 239, 241, 262, 275, 278, 344
,, Matthew, 5, 83, 164, 217, 219, 224, 288, 298, 303, 353
,, Rauffe, 13, 87,* 103, 105, 109, 166, 232, 278, c. of 346
,, Richard, 14, 22,* 52, 53,* 56, 58,* 61, 70, 72, 87,* 100,* 103, 125, 126, 147, 155, 156, 158, 166, 189, 201, 207, 209, 217, 224, 232,* 238,* 240, 244, 245, 250, 252, 271, 278, 283, 284, 285, 293, 298,* 299, 305, w. of 316, w. of 319, c. of 325,* 325, 355
,, Robert, 233, 240*
,, Roger, 111, 113, 131, c. of 304, 359
,, Samuel, 310
,, Susan, 184
,, Thomas, 5,* 6,* 9, 11, 14, 15, 23, 25, 26, 31,* 33,* 39, 47, 48, 58, 61, 65, 74, 75, 86, 87,

Wood, Thomas, continued—
109,* 114, 129, 144, 146, 164, 170, 176, 178, 195, 210, 212, 213,* 214, 217, 225,* 228,* 231, 232,* 233, 238,* 239,* 240, 245,* 252,* 254, 255, 258, 259, 262, 263, 266,* 268, 270, 271, 275,* 278, 279, c. of 290, 291, 301, 306, 309, w. of 312, 313, c. of 313,* c. of 319, w. of 319,* c. of 323, w. of 325, 327, w. of 331, d. of 331, 335,* 345, 353,* 356, 358, 360, 368
,, William, 5, 8, 15, 25, 32, 76, 113, 123, 126,* 167, 307
Woofenden, Woolfenden [see Wolfenden]
Woolner [? Wolmer],
,, Abraham, 246, 251
,, Esther, 244
,, John, 221
,, Mary, 225
,, Susanna, 231
,, Thomas, 221, 225, 231, 244, 246, 251, 341
Woolsencrofte [see Wolstencrofte]
Woolsenham, Woolsenholme, Woolstenholme, Woolsencham [see Wolstenholme]
Woosnam [see Wolstenholme]
Wormald [Wormall, Wormill, Wormold]
,, Elizabeth, 200
,, John, 84, 200, 206,* 286, c. of 300,* 300
,, Mary, 84
,, N.X.N., 296
,, Thomas, 121
Worrall, Margaret, 309
Worsley [Worseley, Worseleye, Worsle],
,, Alexander, 331
,, John, 211
,, Lawrence, 10, 24*
,, Richard, c. of 314, w. of 317, c. of 318, w. of 325
,, Thomas, 10, 211
Worthington [Worthinton] Jane, 368
,, Margaret, 200
Wosenam [see Wolstenholme]
Wosencroft Wostencrofte, [see Wolstencrofte]
Wosnam, Wosname, Wosncham, Woulsonham [see Wolstenholme]
Wowfenden [see Wolfenden]
Wrennoughe, Thomas, 8*

Vol. 1.—C. . pp. 1— 90 inclusive. Vol. 2.—C. . pp. 205—280 inclusive.
    B. . ,, 91—168 ,,   B. . ,, 281—350 ,,
    W. . ,, 169—204 ,,   W. . ,, 351—372 ,,

Wrigbey [see Rigby]
Wright, John, 139
Wrigley [Ridgle, Rigley, Wriglaie, Wriglay, Wriglaye],
  ,, Abraham, 17, 277
  ,, Ann, 3, 12, 45
  ,, Dorothy, 7, 289
  ,, Edmund, 8, 117, 214, 228, 353
  ,, Ellen, 286
  ,, Henry, 5, 6,* 29, 60, 96, 104, 118, 130, 160, 247, 291, 323
  ,, Hughe, 29
  ,, James, 8, 68, 84, 219, 249, 294, 354
  ,, John, 3, 8, 12, 17, 45, 50, 59,* 60, 68, 71,* 84, 108, 109, 151, 207, 228, 240,* 247, 249, 282,* 286, 288, 289,* 291, c. of 312, 323, 359, 362
  ,, Jonie, 5, 96
  ,, Margaret, 288
  ,, Martha, 214, 311
  ,, Mary, 50, 219, 294, 357
  ,, Ratcliffe, 277
  ,, Roger, 7, 8
  ,, Susan, 207
  ,, William, 151
Wroe [Roe], Alice, 3

Wroe, Ambrose, 125
  ,, Katherine, 63
  ,, Richard, 3
  ,, Robert, 63
Wyld, Wylde [see Wild]

Y

YATES [Yate, Yatte, Yeat, Yeate],
  ,, Alice, 72, 86, 152, 167
  ,, Elizabeth, 241, 280
  ,, Ellen, 207, 262
  ,, Elly [? Ellen], 284
  ,, Henry, 176
  ,, John, 35, 195, 228, 234,* 241, 246, 254, 262, 270, 280, c. of 316, c. of 340
  ,, Lawrence, 348, c, of 348
  ,, Mary, 65, 270
  ,, Richard, 246, 360
  ,, Samuel, 77
  ,, Susan, 254
  ,, William, 35, 58,* 65, 72, 77, 86, 114, 118, 124, 128, 131, 132, 152, 167, 175, 207, 228, 284,* w. of 340
Ysherwoode, Yssherwoode, [see Isherwood]

II.

Index Locorum.

Vol. 1.—C. . pp. 1— 90 inclusive. Vol. 2.—C. . pp. 205—280 inclusive.
B. . ,, 91—168 ,, B. . ,, 281—350 ,,
W. . ,, 169—204 ,, W. . ,, 351—372 ,,

[All the names except those in *Italics* are within Bury Parish.]

A

AEDENF [see Edenfield]
Affeside [Affesyde, Affiside, Aphiside],
 ,, 270, 276, 282
Ainsworth [Ainesworthe, Ains: Ainse,
  Ainseworthe, Ainsw,
  Ainsworthe, Answorth,
  Ayns, Aynsw: Aynsworth,
  Ensworth],
 ,, 65, 73, 79, 151, 159, 205, 211,*
   214, 245, 249, 268, 274, 279,*
   287, 301, 318,* 321,* 322,
   346, 349
Akrington, 296
Alas, 84
All, 87
Aphiside [see Affeside]
Ashenbothome, 281
Ashton-under-Lyne
  [Ashton-vnder-line],
 ,, 212
Ashwood, 244
Ashworth [Ash : Ashw : Ashworthe],
 ,, 67,* 72, 79,* 85, 88, 149, 154,
   211, 245, 246, 253, 261,* 270,*
   276, 288,* 318, 334, 341, 344
Aynsworth [see Ainsworth]

B

BALEHOLTE [Balehoult, Ye Ballholt],
 ,, 303, 343, 345, 350*
Baliden, 323
Balldenstone [Ballderstone,
  Bauderstone, Baudinstone],
 ,, 245, 256, 327
Ballholt Ye [see Baleholte]

Bamford [Baf., Bam., Bamf., Bamfo,
  Bamfor, Bamforde, Bamfort,
  Bamforte, Bamforth,
  Bamforthe, Bamfurth],
 ,, 46, 65, 70, 71,* 73,* 75, 78, 79, 81,
   82, 86, 88, 94,* 95,* 96, 109,
   146, 149, 151,* 152, 156, 158,
   159, 161,* 162, 195, 198,*
   200, 201, 202,* 203,* 206,
   207, 209, 210, 211, 213, 215,
   217, 220, 221, 222, 223,* 225,*
   226,* 227,* 228, 229,* 230,
   232,* 235,* 237, 242, 243,
   245, 247, 248,* 249,* 250,
   256,* 269, 273, 276, 281,*
   284, 287, 289, 291, 292, 293,
   294, 296, 297,* 299, 300,*
   303,* 305,* 306,* 307,* 308,*
   311,* 312, 313, 314, 316,*
   317, 319, 320,* 321,* 323,
   324, 325,* 326, 327, 330, 342,
   343, 344,* 345, 351,* 352,*
   353,* 354, 355,* 370
Bank Lane [Banke Lane, Bancklaine,
  Banclaine, Banklan, Bank L.],
 ,, 100, 211, 218, 237, 243, 303,*
   347, 348
Barnbrook [Barnbrooke], 279, 350
Barwick, 261
Bass lone, 242
Bawden [Bawds], 209, 286
Benley [Benle], 84, 319*
Bent, 46, 140, 147, 209, 214
Bentelee [Benteley, Benteley Lum,
  Bentlee, Bentleigh,
  Benteliye, Bentiley, Bentl,
  Bentlye],
 ,, 145, 156, 160, 271, 275, 276, 281,
   283, 290, 306, 308,* 330, 339

Vol. 1.—C. . pp. 1—90 inclusive. Vol. 2.—C. . pp. 205—280 inclusive.
 B. . ,, 91—168 ,, B. . ,, 281—350 ,,
 W. . ,, 169—204 ,, W. . ,, 351—372 ,,

Bentille Lum [Bentileigh Lum, Bentlum],
 ,, 78, 209, 343
Berchey, Berch Heay, Berch Hey, [see Birch Hey]
Berie [see Bury]
Berkhill, Berkill, Berkle [see Birtle]
Bevis, 341
Bir, 85
Birch [? Birch Hey], 157,* 213, 214, 251, 285, 291, 352
Birch Hey [Berchey, Berch Heay, Berch Hey, Birchehey, Birchey, Burch hey],
 ,, 22, 64, 70, 93, 113, 137, 144, 152, 156, 157, 201, 220, 225, 228,* 231,* 236,* 237,* 238,* 239, 240, 241,* 244, 246, 248,* 250, 272, 274,* 277, 280, 283, 285, 290, 295, 298,* 299,* 300, 309, 311, 312,* 315, 317,* 319,* 320, 323, 324, 327, 328, 330, 333, 342, 346, 351
Birchen Boure [Birchen Bowre], 316
Birchill [see Birtle]
Birdhole [Birdh: Bridhole, Bridhoole],
 ,, 82, 105, 156, 160, 200, 210, 232, 246, 274, 282, 342
Birkhill [see also Birtle], 215, 273, 276, 278,* 279, 341, 344*
Birtle [Bercle, Berkhill, Berkill, Berkle, Bertle, Bircell, Birchill, Birckhill, Birckle, Bircle, Birk, Birkhill, Birkill, Birkle, Birklee, Burkle]
 [see also Birkhill],
 ,, 22, 65, 70, 71, 72, 73, 75, 76, 79, 81, 83,* 84,* 87, 89, 110, 146,* 147, 149, 152, 154, 155, 157, 158,* 160, 162, 165, 166, 202, 203, 207,* 208,* 210, 212,* 213, 215, 216, 220,* 225, 230, 245, 246,* 254, 268, 273, 276, 278,* 279, 282, 283, 287, 288, 292,* 305,* 318, 323, 326,* 328, 335, 338, 344,* 345, 346,* 347, 350,* 352
Blackbrook Bridge [Blakebrook Bridge],
 ,, 273, 344
Blackholt [Blackhoulte, Blaucholte, Blakeholt], 212, 226, 305, 315, 318
Blackroade, 370
Blackworth Brig, 345
Blakeburne [Blaigburne, Blakeborne],
 ,, 195, 360, 363

Blak Toms, 74
Blakeholt [see Blackholt]
Boden, 162,* 286, 291
Bodingstone [Bodenston, Bodingestone], 21, 33, 82, 92
Bol : 156, 351
Bold, 217
Bolton [Bol : Bolt. Boulton], 206,* 224, 231, 310, 351, 352,* 353, 354, 355
Bolton Parish [Bolto. Boull, Boulton], 7, 30,* 33, 64, 67, 70, 79, 83, 150, 152, 159, 161, 164, 188, 195, 196, 199, 200, 243, 274, 304,* 309, 355,* 356, 357, 358, 359, 360, 361,* 364, 365,* 366,* 367
Booth [Boothe, Both], 70, 209, 239, 241, 244, 251, 263, 271, 315, 343
Borows [see Burrs]
Bouth Hall [Bothehaule, Bothhaule, Bouthall],
 ,, 152, 196, 229, 235, 351
Brad, 74
Brandlesome [Band, Br : Bradso, Brand, Brandl : Brandle, Brandlesa, Brandlesam, Brandlesham, Brandlesom, Brandlesome, Brandlso, Brandlsom, Brandlsome, Brands, Brundle],
 ,, 71, 80, 86, 89, 90,* 95, 153, 161, 162, 166, 167, 195, 196, 206, 224, 235, 247, 282,* 289, 290,* 309, 310,* 324, 335
Brandwood Edge, 198
Breighmet [Breighmit], 274
Bridge [The Bridge, Ye Bridge], 62, 98, 101, 145, 218, 222, 239, 244, 247, 255, 259, 262, 297, 324, 333, 334
Bridhole [see Bird Hole]
Bridge Hall [Bridg Hall, Bridge Hawle, Bridghale, Bridghall, Bridg Haule, Brigehall],
 ,, 145, 153, 167, 200, 225, 228, 234, 318, 345, 349, 350,* 371
Broad oake [Broadocke, Broadoke, Brodocke, Brodoke, Broody oke],
 ,, 149, 154, 197, 227, 231, 237, 245, 261, 290, 296, 305, 318, 320, 339, 341,* 342
Brodcar [Brodc, Brodcare, Brodecarre],
 ,, 82, 88, 162, 168, 207

INDEX OF PLACES.

Vol. 1.—C. . pp. 1— 90 inclusive. Vol. 2.—C. . pp. 205—280 inclusive.
     B. . ,, 91—168 ,,   B. . ,, 281—350 ,,
     W. . ,, 169—204 ,,   W. . ,, 351—372 ,,

Brodocke, Brodoke [see Broadoake]
Brok [Broke], 88, 289
Bronley Parish [see Burnley Parish]
Brood, 84
Brookesmouth, 345
Brookshaw [Broks, Brokshaw, Brokshawe, Brookeshawe, Bruckeshe, Bruckshawe, Bruks],
  ,, 62, 68, 72, 80, 152, 241, 283, 285, 318, 326
Brookhouse [Brookehouse], 346
Broughton, 197
Brownhill, 344
Bruckshawe [see Brookshaw]
Brundle [see Brandlesome]
Brunley Parish [see Burnley Parish]
Buckden [Buck: Buckd., Bukden],
  ,, 86, 159, 216, 221, 274, 291, 346,* 354
Burkle [see Birtle]
[Burnley] Parish [Bronley, Brunley],
  ,, 173, 360
Burrs [Burrowes, Borows, Bourh, Buros, Burros, Burroughs, Burrows, Burss],
  ,, 82, 94, 156, 217, 220, 241, 243, 252, 273, 286, 318
Bury [B: Berie, Bir, Birrie, Bu: Bur: Burie, Burih, Buriha, Burye],
  ,, 14, 18, 24, 26, 29, 32, 34, 36, 40, 44,* 47, 51, 54, 55, 56, 59, 63, 64,* 65,* 66,* 67,* 68,* 69,* 70,* 71,* 72,* 73,* 74,* 75,* 76,* 77,* 78,* 79,* 80,* 81,* 82,* 83,* 84,* 85,* 86,* 87,* 88,* 89,* 90,* 114, 116, 119, 126, 129, 132, 134, 138, 139, 141, 144,* 145,* 146, 147,* 148,* 149,* 150,* 151,* 152,* 153,* 154,* 155,* 156,* 157,* 158,* 160,* 161,* 162,* 163,* 164,* 165,* 166,* 167,* 168,* 178, 179, 181, 182, 184, 186, 187, 189, 191, 192, 195,* 196,* 197,* 198,* 199,* 200, 201,* 202,* 203, 204, 205,* 206,* 207,* 208,* 209,* 210,* 211,* 212,* 213,* 214,* 215,* 216,* 217,* 218,* 219,* 220,* 221,* 222,* 223,* 224,* 225,* 226,* 227,* 228,* 229, 230,* 231,* 232,* 233,* 234,* 235,* 236,* 237,* 238,* 239,* 240,* 241,* 242,* 243,* 244,* 245,* 246,* 247,* 248, 249,* 250,* 251,*

Bury, *continued*—
252, 253,* 254,* 256,* 257,* 259,* 262, 263, 265,* 266, 267, 268,* 269,* 270,* 271,* 272,* 273,* 274,* 275,* 276,* 277,* 278,* 279,* 280,* 281,* 282,* 283,* 284,* 285,* 286,* 287,* 288,* 289,* 290,* 291,* 292,* 293,* 294,* 295,* 296,* 297,* 298,* 299,* 300,* 301,* 302,* 303,* 304,* 305,* 306,* 307,* 308,* 309,* 310,* 311,* 312,* 313,* 314,* 315,* 316,* 317,* 318,* 319,* 320,* 321,* 322,* 323,* 324,* 325,* 326,* 327,* 328, 332, 335,* 336,* 337,* 339, 340,* 341,* 342,* 343,* 344,* 345,* 346,* 347,* 348,* 349,* 351,* 352,* 353,* 354,* 355,* 356,* 357, 362,* 370*
Bury Bridge [Bury Brige], 63, 163, 273, 343, 344
Bury Hamlet [B. H., Bu: Ham:, Burihame, Burihamel, Buri Hamell, Burieh, Burie Ha, Burie Hamell, Buriham, Buryha:, Bury Hamel, Bury Hamell],
  ,, 69, 74, 82,* 92, 93, 156, 161, 220, 221,* 222,* 224, 225,* 226,* 227,* 228,* 229, 230,* 231,* 232,* 233,* 234,* 235,* 236, 237,* 238,* 239,* 240,* 241,* 242,* 243,* 244,* 245,* 246, 268, 272, 277, 279, 280, 282, 284, 289, 291, 295, 296, 298,* 299,* 300,* 301,* 303,* 304,* 305,* 306,* 307,* 308,* 309,* 310,* 311, 312,* 313,* 314,* 315,* 316,* 317,* 318,* 319,* 337, 338,* 341, 342, 349, 350
Bury Lane, 85, 114, 241, 274, 315, 341,* 343,* 344, 345
Bury More, 73
Bury More Syde [Bury Mooreside],
  ,, 159, 344
Bury More Yate, 93, 167
Bury Parish, 223, 243,* 246, 248, 355, 356,* 357,* 358,* 359,* 360,* 361,* 362,* 363,* 364,* 365,* 366,* 367,* 369,* 370, 371
Butchy Lane, 343
Byrome [Byra], 230, 245

C

CARE, 309
Castle [Casle], 322

BURY PARISH REGISTERS.

Vol. 1.—C. . pp. 1— 90 inclusive. Vol. 2.—C. . pp. 205—280 inclusive.
     B. . ,, 91—168 ,,   B. . ,, 281—350 ,,
     W. . ,, 169—204 ,,   W. . ,, 351—372 ,,

Castle Hill [Caslehill], 211, 277, 344, 350
Cathole [Cath:, Cathoole, Catt], 78, 86, 215, 242, 280
Cawthorne Parish, 365
Chadderton, 263
Chamber [Chambers], 228, 252, 288, 306, 343, 371
Chaterton [see Chatterton]
Chaterton Hey, 346
Chatterton [Chaterton, Chatton], 161, 237, 297, 300, 306,* 308, 354
Chesham [Ch:, Ches:, Chesa, Chesam, Chesem, Chesh:, Chesom, Chesha, Chess, Chessome, Chesum],
  ,, 63, 66, 67, 71,* 73, 77, 80, 81, 82, 86, 87, 88, 90, 92, 143, 145, 146,* 150, 162, 200, 209, 211,* 217, 221, 227, 236, 240, 241,* 242, 243, 244, 246,* 249, 250,* 270, 288, 297, 306, 311, 312, 318,* 322,* 327, 342, 344, 346, 348
Chorley, 281
Church Par., 43
Cisely Hough, 73
Cleg, 344
Clithero [Clitharall, Clitherall, Clitherow],
  ,, 194, 199, 351, 353,* 355, 356,* 357
Cobbas [Cobas, Cobb, Cobhouse, Cobhowse, Kobbas],
  ,, 71, 84, 130, 149, 152, 204, 213, 219, 224, 234, 241, 256, 274, 280, 316, 346
Cockey [Cockeye, Cockhey, Cokehey, Cokey, Cokhey, Cookhey],
  ,, 77, 78, 94, 95, 135, 156, 163, 205,* 267, 271, 272, 276, 278, 282, 292, 355
Colpits, 79
Cowap, 197, 203, 204, 352*
Croelum [see Crowlum]
Croitshlawe [Croch, Crochlawe, Croichlaw, Croichley, Croislawe, Croithlaw, Croitsh, Croshlawe, Crotchlow, Croth, Croychl:, Croytchlaw, Croythlow],
  ,, 81, 130, 144, 148, 155,* 156, 160, 207, 208, 216, 235, 282, 289, 327, 351, 355
Croshall [Crossehall], 211, 215
Crosley, 147
Crowlum [Croelum, Crowelum, Crow lome],

Crowlum, 93, 287, 290, 317
Croych, Croytchlaw, Croythlow, [see Croitshlawe]

D

DEAN Bank [Deanbanke, Deanebancke, Deanebanke],
  ,, 213, 278, 342
Deane [Ye Deane], 338, 358, 362
Dry Gap [Driegapp, Drigape, Drygapp],
  ,, 96, 128, 254, 280, 304, 306, 316, 318, 328

E

Eccles [Ecles], 197, 352, 362
Edenfield [Aedenf, Ed: Ede: Edef: Eden, Edenf., Edenfeild, Edenfeilde, Edenfel, Edenfeld, Edenfelde, Edf:, Eten: Etenfeild, Etenfeilde, Etenfeld, Etenfelde, Ettenfield, Etenfild, Etonf., Etonfeild],
  ,, 87, 94,* 110, 144, 146, 149, 155, 157, 159,* 160, 161,* 162, 166,* 167, 168, 187, 196, 197, 198, 200,* 201, 202, 204,* 208, 213, 215, 220, 222, 224, 228, 229,* 231, 249,* 261, 272, 279, 282, 284, 287,* 288,* 291,* 292, 295, 296,* 301,* 302,* 305,* 306,* 307, 308,* 309, 310,* 311, 312, 313, 316, 322, 323, 330,* 351, 352,* 354,* 355*
Edge, The, 342
Edgeworth, 65
Elton [El: Ellton, Elltonn, Elt: Eltonn, Eltton, Elttonn],
  ,, 62, 63,* 65, 66,* 68,* 69, 70,* 71,* 72,* 74, 75,* 76, 77, 79,* 80,* 81,* 82, 83,* 84,* 86,* 87,* 88,* 89, 90, 130, 144, 146, 148, 149, 150,* 151,* 152, 153,* 154,* 155, 156, 158,* 160, 161, 162,* 163,* 164, 165, 195, 200, 201,* 203, 204, 205, 206,* 207, 209,* 210, 211,* 212, 213,* 214,* 216,* 217, 219,* 220,* 221,* 222,* 223* 224,* 225,* 226,* 227,* 228,* 229,* 230, 231,* 232, 233,* 234,* 235,* 237,* 238,* 239,* 240,* 241, 242,* 243,* 244, 245,* 246, 247, 250,*

Vol. 1.—C.	pp. 1— 90 inclusive.	Vol. 2.—C.	pp. 205—280 inclusive.
B.	,, 91—168 ,,	B.	,, 281—350 ,,
W.	,, 169—204 ,,	W.	,, 351—372 ,,

Elton, continued—
   251,* 255, 266,* 268,* 269,*
   271,* 272, 274,* 277,* 279,*
   280, 281, 283, 284, 286, 287,*
   289, 290, 292,* 293, 294,*
   295,* 296,* 297,* 298,* 299,
   300,* 301,* 302,* 303,* 304,*
   306,* 307,* 308,* 309,* 313,*
   314,* 315,* 316,* 317,* 318,
   320, 322, 323, 325,* 326,*
   328, 330, 333, 337, 340,* 341,
   342, 343,* 344,* 345,* 350,*
   351, 352,* 353,* 354,* 355*
Elton Fold, 276
Elton Car [Elton Karre], 111, 347
Ensworth [see Ainsworth]
Ernswoorrth [? Ainsworth], 316
Etenfeild, Etenfeld, Etonf., Etonfeild
   [see Edenfield]
Eues, The, 62, 153, 306*
Eues in Tottington, 281

F

FACID [Fac, Facide, Faside], 226, 230,
   247, 250, 261, 321, 323
Fear, Fearnes, Fearns [see Ferns]
Feelds, Feilds [see Fieldes]
Ferne Yard, 92
Fern gore [Fearnegore, Fearngore,
   Ferngor],
 ,, 71, 82, 148, 276, 300
Ferns [Fear, Fearnes, Fearns, Fernes],
 ,, 76, 87, 93, 160, 201, 207, 209,
   282, 332, 338
Fieldes, The [Feelds, Feilds,
   Ye feilds],
 ,, 161, 242, 247, 267, 273
Fishpool, 339
Fol, 283
Folcote [see Foulcote]
Foulcote [Folcote, Foulc, Foulcoats,
   Foulcot, Foulcots, Foulcote,
   Foulecote, Fowcoate,
   Fowle],
 ,, 66, 73, 75, 77, 88, 89, 98, 150, 153,
   159, 162, 167, 203, 284*
Foultes [Foult], 285, 330

G

GALLENRODE [see Gollingrod]
Gigge, 338
Gindles [Gindlee, Gyndles], 57, 245,
   255, 261, 278, 325, 342, 344
Glorybutts [Gloributts], 278, 315,
   342,* 343

Gollingrod [Gallenrode, Golenrode,
   Golingroyd, Golinroad,
   Golinrod, Golinrode, Goll:,
   Golling, Collinr, Gollinroad,
   Gollinrode],
 ,, 77, 84, 165, 168, 198, 213, 223,
   229, 241, 245, 315, 327, 343,
   347
Goodin, 347
Goosford [Gooseford, Gooseforth,
   Goseford, Goseforde,
   Goscfore, Gosforthe,
   Gouseforth, Gouseforthe,
   Gowseford],
 ,, 74, 75, 93,* 225,* 228, 230, 234,
   241, 276, 277, 280, 281, 288,
   306,* 307,* 326,* 332, 339,
   342, 343, 348, 354
Goosford Loane, 195
Greenhill [Grinhill], 242, 286, 309, 347
Grenes, 217
Grenmosse, 354
Gret Leuer [Great Lever], 191
Grinhill [see Greenhill]
Gristelhurste [Girslehurst, Grisl:
   Grislchurst, Grislehurste,
   Grisles, Gristhurste,
   Gristlehirst, Gristles,
   Gristlhurst, Gristlhurste,
   Grizzlehurst],
 ,, 64, 69, 77, 82, 88, 104, 127, 230,
   282, 295, 296, 308, 317, 325,*
   339, 343, 351
Gristlehurst Moore Yate, 342

H

HAGG, Ye [Hag, Hagge], 64, 283, 320
Halhill, 146
Halifax [Hallifax], 341, 342*
Harden Clough, 341
Hartlee [Hartlie], 158, 166, 216, 222,
   224, 227, 233, 292, 294, 304,
   320
Harwood, 156
Haslam [Has., Hasl., Hasle, Haslom],
 ,, 64, 84, 157, 203, 205, 291, 294,
   355
Haslam Hey [Haslom Hay,
   Haslam Heye,
   Hasleome Heigh,
   Haslom Hey,
   Haslome Hey,
   Hassellom Heay,
   Hasslome Hey],
 ,, 63, 82, 137, 150, 158, 191, 214,
   217, 236, 239, 240, 241, 243,*

W

Vol. 1.—C. . pp. 1— 90 inclusive. Vol. 2.—C. . pp. 205—280 inclusive.
B. . „ 91—168 „ B. . „ 281—350 „
W. . „ 169—204 „ W. . „ 351—372 „

Haslam Hey, *continued*—
    244, 245, 248,* 255, 273, 280, 286, 311,* 312,* 314, 317, 320, 339, 341, 343,* 346, 347,* 348

Haslingden [Hasl: Haslenden, Haslynden, Hasselingden],
  „ 160, 161, 195, 203, 205, 239, 351, 352, 353, 354, 355,* 366

Haugshawe [? Haukshaw], 232
Haughshaw Layne, 310
Haukshaw [Hauk, Haukshawe, Hawk: Hawsh],
  „ 98, 158,* 163, 209, 284, 297, 325, 328, 354

Hay: [see Hey:]
He; [? Heap or Heywood], 214, 321
Hawkshaw Lane, 341
Heap [Heape, Heapp, Heaupp, Hepe],
  „ 53, 64, 65,* 67, 68, 69, 70,* 71, 72,* 73, 77, 78,* 80,* 81,* 84,* 85, 86, 87,* 90, 92,* 93, 94, 96, 145,* 147, 148, 149, 150, 151, 157, 159, 160,* 161, 163, 165, 166, 197,* 199, 201, 205, 206, 207, 208, 211,* 213,* 214,* 215, 217, 220,* 221, 222,* 223, 224, 225, 226, 227,* 228,* 229, 232,* 233, 234, 235,* 236,* 237,* 239, 240,* 241, 242, 243,* 244, 245,* 246, 248, 249,* 250, 251,* 253, 259, 267, 271,* 272, 273, 274, 276, 279, 280,* 282, 284,* 286, 287, 290,* 293,* 295,* 297, 299,* 300, 302,* 306,* 307,* 309,* 310, 312, 313,* 314,* 315,* 316,* 317,* 318, 319,* 322, 338, 342, 343,* 345,* 347,* 350,* 351,* 353, 354

Heath, 217
Heathy, 208
Heathy Hill [Heathie Hill, Hethill, Hethy Hill],
  „ 65, 83, 157, 215, 291, 295

Hewood, Hewoode, Hewwood [see Heywood]
Hey, Hay, Heiye [? Heywood], 68, 83, 164, 205, 206, 207, 208, 214,* 216,* 217,* 219, 270, 291, 293

Hey Head [Heyheade], 275, 288, 348
Hey-opp, 63*
Heywood [Haywood, He:, Hea:, Heaw, Heawood, Hew:, Hewed, Hewo, Hewood, Hewoode, Howw: Hewwood,

Heywood, *continued*—
  Hey:, Heyw:, Heywod, Heywode, Heywoode],
  „ 65, 67, 70, 71, 75, 76, 78, 81,* 82, 83, 84, 85,* 86,* 87, 88, 89, 92,* 93, 94, 95,* 99, 104, 113, 145, 146, 147,* 148,* 149,* 151, 153, 154, 155, 157,* 160, 163,* 164, 165,* 167,* 168, 196,* 197, 199, 202, 203, 205, 206,* 207,* 209, 211, 212,* 214, 217, 218, 221,* 223,* 224,* 225, 226, 227, 228, 229, 230, 231,* 232,* 233,* 234,* 235,* 236, 237,* 238,* 239,* 240,* 241, 243,* 244,* 245, 246,* 247,* 248,* 249,* 250,* 251, 253, 255, 256, 267, 270,* 271, 273, 274,* 275, 276, 282,* 283, 284, 285, 286, 288, 289,* 291,* 292,* 293,* 294,* 295, 299, 301, 303,* 304,* 307, 309, 310,* 311,* 312,* 313,* 314,* 318, 319, 320,* 321,* 322, 325,* 326, 332, 341,* 342,* 343, 344,* 345,* 349, 350,* 351, 353, 355

Hoiles, 95
Holcome [Hocome, Hol, Hole, Holcoe, Holcom, Holcu, Holcum, Holkom, Holl, Hollcom, Hollcome, Houco, Houcom, Houl, Houlcombe, Houlcom, Houlcome, Houlcum, Houlkom, Howlcom],
  „ 62,* 63,* 65, 66,* 67,* 68,* 69,* 71,* 72,* 73,* 74,* 75,* 76,* 78,* 79,* 80,* 81,* 82, 83,* 84,* 85,* 86, 87,* 88,* 89, 90,* 92, 93, 94,* 95, 96,* 112, 143,* 144,* 145, 146, 147,* 148,* 149, 150, 151,* 152, 153,* 154,* 155,* 156,* 157,* 158,* 159,* 160,* 161,* 162,* 163, 164,* 165,* 166,* 167,* 195, 196,* 197,* 198,* 200, 201, 202,* 203,* 204,* 205,* 206,* 207,* 208,* 209,* 210, 211,* 212,* 213, 214, 215,* 216, 217,* 218, 219,* 220,* 221,* 222,* 223,* 224,* 225,* 226,* 227,* 228,* 229,* 230,* 231,* 232,* 233,* 234,* 235,* 236,* 237,* 238,* 239,* 240,* 241,* 242, 243,* 244,* 245,* 246,* 247, 248,* 249,* 250,* 251,* 252,* 259, 261,* 266,* 267,* 268,*

INDEX OF PLACES.

Vol. 1.—C. . pp. 1— 90 *inclusive.* *Vol. 2.—C.* . pp. 205—280 *inclusive.*
  B. . ,, 91—108 ,,   *B.* . ,, 281—350 ,,
  W. . ,, 109—204 ,,   *W.* . ,, 351—372 ,,

Holcome, *continued*—
    269,* 270,* 271,* 272,* 273,*
    274,* 275, 276,* 277,* 278,*
    280, 281,* 282,* 283,* 284,*
    285, 286, 287,* 288,* 289,*
    290,* 291,* 292,* 293, 294,*
    295,* 296,* 297,* 298,* 299,*
    300,* 301,* 302,* 303,* 304,*
    305,* 306,* 307,* 308,* 309,*
    310,* 311,* 312,* 313,* 314,*
    315,* 316,* 317,* 318,* 319,*
    320,* 321,* 322,* 323,* 324,*
    325,* 326,* 327,* 328,* 329,
    330, 331, 337,* 338,* 340,*
    341,* 342,* 343,* 344, 345,*
    346,* 347,* 348,* 349, 350,*
    351,* 352, 353,* 354,* 355,
    370
Holcome Hey [Holcom Hey], 254, 343
Holcom Hill, 196
Holecom Lane, 159
Holchouse [Holchowse], 290, 324,* 325, 345, 349
Holling, 332
Hollingreave [Holingreaue, Holingreve, Hollingreaue, Hollyngreave, Hollyngereue]
  ,, 73, 94, 126, 127, 159, 200, 242, 255, 265, 271, 316, 344, 347
Horncliffe [Horncliffe], 312, 322, 342
Houlcom, Houlkom [see Holcome]
Houghe [Hough], 22, 76, 166, 209, 216, 254, 269, 307, 348
Househey, 162
Huntley [Hūtl: Huntly], 155, 165, 267, 278

Huthersfeld pish, 298

I

IDUS, 115

K

KARRE, 111
Kobbas [see Cobbas]

L

LANE, 258
Lees, 75, 81,* 204,* 211, 212, 341
Lees Leach, 339, 341
Leach, 341
Leaygh, Parish of, 357
Leigh [Lee, Leeye, Leighe],
  ,, 151, 217, 330, 371

Lemands Hill [Leemons Hill], 276, 345
Lenches, 204, 355
Littlebridge [Litlebridge], 229, 302
Littlewood [Litlewood, Litlewoode, Litlwood, Littlwood],
  ,, 65, 95, 226, 228, 238, 242, 247, 256, 261, 277, 278, 279,* 294, 305, 316, 343, 346, 347
Lomax [Lomas, Lommas], 95, 206, 230,* 231, 243, 278,* 307, 308, 319, 330, 344,* 346
Lome [see Lum]
Low, 277, 342
Lum [Lome, Lume, The Lume, Ye Lume],
  ,, 165, 211, 245, 297, 298, 317, 325, 328
Lum car [Lumcare], 96, 113, 310

M

Manchester [Manchastar, Manc^r],
  ,, 82, 227, 231, 236, 305, 352, 354, 356, 360,* 362, 363
Marland, 202, 348
Middleton Parish [Midd, Middelton, Mide:, Midelton, Mideltonn, Midl, Midle, Midleton, Midletone, Midletonne, Midletonn, Midlt, Midlton, Midltone, Midltonn, Mildltorn, Myd, Mydelton, Mydleton],
  ,, 14, 15, 16, 21, 22, 31, 35, 42,* 43, 44, 45, 47, 57, 59, 63, 65, 66, 67,* 68, 69,* 72, 78, 85, 86, 87, 108, 110, 113, 129, 137, 140, 148, 149, 159, 195,* 196, 197,* 199, 200, 214,* 215,* 216, 217,* 219, 220, 221,* 222,* 223,* 224, 225,* 226,* 227,* 228, 229, 230,* 231,* 232,* 233,* 234,* 235,* 236,* 237,* 238,* 239,* 240,* 241,* 242, 243, 244,* 248,* 251, 253,* 268,* 269,* 270, 271,* 272, 273,* 289,* 290, 293, 294, 295, 296, 297, 298,* 299,* 302, 303, 309, 310,* 311,* 312, 313,* 314,* 315,* 317, 343, 352, 354,* 355,* 356,* 357, 358,* 359, 361,* 362,* 363,* 364, 365, 366,* 369, 370
Milkinthrop, 145
Millhous, 275
Moorhole [Moorehole], 253

Vol. 1.—C. . pp. 1— 90 inclusive. Vol. 2.—C. . pp. 205—280 inclusive.
B. . „ 91—168 „   B. . „ 281—350 „
W. . „ 169—204 „   W. . „ 351—372 „

Moorside [Mooersd, Mooreside, Moreside],
„ 271,* 272,* 273, 277,* 338, 340, 341, 342,* 346, 347*
Moor Yate [Moore Yate, Moreyate],
„ 272, 326, 341,* 342,* 350*
Mosse, 81, 167, 222, 255, 290, 291
Musbury [Mus., Musb., Musburie],
„ 99, 110, 147, 152, 195, 197, 198, 202, 203, 298, 303, 351, 353,* 355
Myd, Mydelton, *Mydleton* [see Midleton Parish]

N

NEWHALL, 335
Newhouse, 331
Nook [Nooke], 254
Nuttall [Nuttalg], 62, 167, 306, 313
Nuttall Lane, 285

O

OLLERBOTHOME [Ollerbothom], 309
Ouldham, 353, 362, 370
Owll, 328

P

PADDOCK LEACH [Padock Leach],
„ 342, 347
Pilkin : 351
Pilsworth [Pils], 63, 208, 278
Prestwich Parish [Pres., Presswhich, Prestwiche, Prestwick, Prestwitch, Prestwitche, Prestwithe, P'stwch],
„ 22, 64, 66, 67, 75, 82, 140, 196, 197,* 200, 202,* 220, 235, 239, 256, 271, 295, 303, 351,* 352, 353,* 356, 357, 358,* 359,* 360, 361,* 362,* 363, 367, 369, 370,* 371

R.

Radcliffe [Rade, Radel, Radclife, Rate, Ratcl, Ratcliff, Ratcliffe, Ratlife, Ratliffe, Rattell, Rattlife],
„ 10, 44, 67, 79, 154, 155, 181, 199, 202,* 204, 206, 215,* 220, 222, 226, 234, 241, 266, 271, 272, 273, 279, 297, 304, 351, 354, 356, 357, 360, 363, 364,* 365, 366, 370, 371

Rainshore, 342
Ramsbottom [Ram, Ramsb, Ramsbothom, Rombs, Romsbotham, Romsbothom],
„ 71, 242, 248, 261, 319, 341, 344
Ratcliff [Ratcliffe, Ratlife, Ratliffe], [see Radcliffe]
Rattell, 71
Rattlife [see Radcliffe]
Ravenshore, 204
Redgate Milne, 90
Rediso, 250
Redivales [Readiuales, Red, Redd, Reddiuls, Reddivells, Redds, Reds, Reddnols, Redi, Rediu, Rediuall, Rediuals, Rediualls, Rediuels, Rediuells, Redinols, Rediv, Redivall, Redivalles, Redivals, Redivalls, Redivers, Rediwels, Reds, Rednalls],
„ 66, 68, 72, 73,* 77, 78, 79,* 80, 81, 82,* 83, 86, 89,* 93,* 108, 143, 146, 147, 148, 150, 151, 152, 154, 155, 157, 158, 164, 167, 197,* 206,* 207, 208, 209, 210, 212, 213, 214,* 215, 216,* 217, 222,* 223,* 225,* 226, 227,* 228,* 230, 231, 232, 233,* 234, 235,* 237,* 239,* 240, 241, 242,* 243,* 244, 245,* 246, 247, 248, 249, 250,* 252, 253,* 256, 266, 267, 268,* 270,* 274, 276, 280,* 284,* 285, 286, 287, 292, 293,* 294, 298,* 299,* 300, 301,* 302,* 303, 305,* 306,* 307,* 309,* 312,* 313,* 314,* 315,* 316, 317,* 319,* 320, 323, 327,* 339, 341, 342, 343,* 344, 347, 348, 351, 352, 354
Redlees, 270
Renford Feild, 242
Road Elt, 223
Rochdale [Rach, Rachdale, Rachdall, Ratch, Ratchd, Ratchdale, Ratchdaile, Ratchdall],
„ 21, 42, 51, 68, 129, 131, 158, 194, 197, 198,* 199, 202, 204, 271, 293, 296, 305, 343, 351, 352,* 353, 355, 357,* 358, 359, 361* 362,* 363,* 364,* 366,* 367,* 369, 372
Rosendall, 300,* 301
Rowley, 286, 347, 349
Royle, 96

INDEX OF PLACES.

Vol. 1.—C. . pp. 1— 90 inclusive. Vol. 2.—C. . pp. 205—280 inclusive.
     B. . ,, 91—168 ,,   B. . ,, 281—350 ,,
     W. . ,, 169—204 ,,   W. . ,, 351—372 ,,

Ruggil Stile [Rughill Steele], 274, 317

S

SATLEWORTHE, 234
Scout [Ye Scout, Scoute, Scowte, Skoute, Skowte],
,, 67, 145, 147, 153, 217, 220, 229, 271, 282, 291,* 294, 295, 300, 303,* 305, 320, 340, 344, 348, 349, 350
Sedger Hey [Seger Hey], 65, 95, 111, 146
Seedfield, 83
Sheep Hey [Sheepehey, Shephey], 93, 94, 108, 211, 241, 281, 285, 310, 314, 320, 321,* 324, 328, 329, 350
Shippobotham [Ship., Shiplebothom, Shipob, Shipobotham],
,, 45, 63, 64, 144, 342, 350
Shuttleworth [Sh : Shut : Shutelworth, Shutl : Shutle, Shutlew, Shutlewort, Shutleworth, Shutleworthe, Shuttelworth, Shutt, Shuttl, Shuttle, Sutleworth, Sutleworthe, Sutlworth, Sutlworthe, Suttlewo, Suttleworthe, Suttlworthe],
,, 22, 62, 63, 66, 68, 71,* 74, 75,* 76, 80, 83, 84, 148,* 154,** 161, 162, 166, 195, 197, 199, 205, 206, 209,* 216, 224,* 228, 231, 232, 236,* 238, 243,* 245, 249,* 250, 251, 255, 268, 270, 271, 274, 288, 293, 296, 303, 306, 307, 313, 314, 315,* 316, 317,* 318, 320, 321, 322, 323, 324, 327,* 340, 341, 342,* 343, 345, 352
Shuttleworth Mylne, 92
Sillinhurst, 70, 343
Smithurst, 227
Smithy Yate [Smythie Yate], 325, 346
Standley Rake, 327
Stopford parish, 366
Stubbins [Stub: Stubb, Stubines],
,, 75, 80, 166, 196, 206, 277, 320
Sumerset [Somers, Somersett, Somerset],
,, 66, 76, 87, 166, 205, 286, 319, 325

T

TACKLEE, 252, 330
Tenter [Tenters, Tentores], 6, 220, 228, 279, 338, 346

The Edge in Tott, 295
The Lume [see Lum]
Titchroad [Ticheroade, Tichrod, Tichrode, Titchrode, Touchrode, Tuch, Tuchroad],
,, 214, 227, 252, 315, 331, 344, 350, 351, 355
Top, 130
Toproyle, 76, 113
Tottington [Tot: Toting, Totington, Tott, Tottenton, Totti, Tottin, Totting, Tottingeton, Tottingz, Tottingto, Tottingtonn],
,, 62, 63, 64,* 65, 67,* 68,* 69,* 70,* 71,* 72, 73,* 75,* 76,* 77, 79,* 80,* 81, 82,* 83,* 84,* 86, 87, 88, 89,* 90,* 92,* 93, 104, 137, 143, 144, 145,* 147,* 149,* 150, 151,* 152,* 154, 155, 156, 157,* 158,* 159,* 160,* 162,* 163,* 164,* 166,* 167,* 168, 195, 199, 200,* 201,* 202,* 203,* 205,* 206,* 207, 208,* 209, 210,* 211, 212,* 213,* 214,* 215,* 216,* 217, 218,* 220,* 221,* 222,* 223,* 224,* 225,* 226,* 227, 228,* 229,* 230,* 231,* 232,* 233,* 234,* 235,* 236,* 237,* 238,* 239,* 240,* 241,* 243,* 244, 245,* 248,* 249,* 250,* 251,* 252, 253, 266, 267, 269,* 270,* 271, 272, 273,* 274,* 275,* 276,* 277,* 278,* 279,* 280,* 281, 282,* 283,* 284, 285,* 286,* 287,* 288,* 289,* 290,* 291,* 292,* 293,* 294,* 295,* 296,* 297,* 298,* 299, 300,* 301,* 302,* 303,* 304,* 305,* 306,* 307,* 308,* 309,* 310,* 311,* 312,* 313,* 314,* 315,* 316,* 317,* 318,* 319, 322,* 325,* 326, 327, 328, 337,* 338,* 339, 341,* 342,* 344,* 345,* 346,* 347, 348,* 349,* 350,* 351,* 352, 353,* 354*
Touchrode [see Titchroad]
Towne, This, 245, 248,* 318,* 319,* 320
Trike, 150
Tuch, Tuchread [see Titchroad]
Turton, 337, 355

V

Vnsworth, 276

Vol. 1.—C.	pp. 1—90 inclusive.	Vol. 2.—C.	pp. 205—280 inclusive.
B.	„ 91—168 „	B.	„ 281—350 „
W.	„ 169—204 „	W.	„ 351—372 „

W

W : 209, 320
Walkf : 284
Walmersley [W: Wal: Walm, Wall.,
   Wallmer, Wallmerslay,
   Wallmersley, Wallmersly,
   Wallmesley, Wallmesleye,
   Walm., Walmer, Walmers,
   Walmershley, Walmersle,
   Walmersleey, Walmersly,
   Walmesey, Walmesl.,
   Walmesly, Walmesley,
   Walms, Walmsley,
   Walm'se, Walm'sley,
   Walmsly, Wamarsley,
   Wamersle, Wamerslee,
   Wamersley, Wamesley,
   Wamsl, Whamerslaye,
   Womersly],
  „ 63,* 64, 65, 66,* 68, 69,* 70,
   71,* 72,* 73, 75,* 76,* 78,
   79,* 80, 81,* 82,* 83, 84,*
   85,* 86, 87, 88,* 89,* 90,*
   92,* 93,* 143,* 145, 146, 147,
   148, 150,* 151,* 152, 154,*
   155,* 156, 157,* 158,* 159,
   161,* 162, 163,* 164,* 165,*
   166,* 167,* 195, 196, 198,
   199,* 200,* 201, 202, 203, 204,
   206, 207,* 208, 209, 210,* 211,*
   212,* 213,* 214, 215,* 216,*
   217, 218, 219, 220,* 221,* 222,*
   223,* 224,* 226,* 227, 228,*
   229,* 231,* 232,* 233,* 234,*
   235,* 236, 237,* 238, 239,*
   240,* 241,* 242,* 243,* 244,*
   245,* 246,* 247,* 248, 250,*
   251,* 252, 254, 267, 268,*
   269,* 270, 271,* 272,* 273,*
   274, 275,* 276, 277, 279,*
   281, 282, 283, 284,* 285, 286,*
   287, 288, 289,* 290, 291,* 292,*
   293,* 294, 296,* 297, 298,*
   299,* 300,* 301,* 302,* 303,*
   304,* 305,* 306,* 307,* 308,*
   309,* 310, 311,* 312,* 313,*
   314,* 315, 316,* 317,* 319,*
   320,* 321,* 322, 323, 324,
   326,* 330, 331,* 340,* 341,
   342,* 343,* 344, 345, 346,
   347, 348, 351,* 352,* 353,*
   354, 355*
Walshaw, 67

Walshaw Lane [Walsaw L.], 241,*
   274, 290,* 345, 346
Walton parish, 356
Washy Lane [Washe Lane], 236, 276,
   277, 311, 317,* 342
Water, 254
Whaley [Whaly], 362,* 365, 366
Wham, 150, 205, 251, 289, 290, 291,
   297, 299
Whamerslaye [see Walmersley]
Wharnetan, 345
White Car [Whitcar, Whitckar,
   Whitkar],
  „ 73, 107, 318, 322
Whitewall [Whitewal],
  „ 280, 336, 341, 343
Whitkar [see Whie Car]
Whitt: [? Whittle], 320
Whittle [Whitle], 158, 162, 202, 277,
   290, 291, 292, 326
Whitwale [Whittwall], 196, 274
Widdell [Widd, Widdall, Widdill,
   Widell, Widill, Wydell],
  „ 109, 162, 197, 210, 217, 223, 224,
   229,* 236, 242, 243, 245, 248,
   251, 261, 296, 305, 311, 314,
   320, 328, 339, 348
Wigan, 306
Winwicke, 261
Withins [Withens], 122, 134, 157
Woodgate Hill [Wodyate Hill,
   Woodyate Hill],
  „ 98, 205, 236, 277, 315,* 343,*
   348*
Womersly [see Walmersley]
Woodroad [Wodroad, Wodrod,
   Wodrode, Wodrood,
   Wooderode, Woodr:
   Woodroade, Woodrod,
   Woodrode, Woodrood],
  „ 49, 73, 84, 88, 130, 150, 151, 155,
   158, 159, 203, 209, 217, 223,
   229, 246, 248, 251, 254, 275,
   291, 310, 318, 326, 336
Woof: [Woolf, (?) Woolfold], 250, 253
Woolfold [Woofould, Woolf,
   Woollfould],
  „ 245, 274, 347
Wydell [see Widdell]
Wynd, 208

Y

Yorkshire, 343

III.

Index of Trades, Descriptions,
and various matters.

Vol. 1.—C. . pp. 1— 90 inclusive. Vol. 2.—C. . pp. 205—280 inclusive.
 B. . ,, 91—168 ,, B. . ,, 281—350 ,,
 W. . ,, 169—204 ,, W. . ,, 351—372 ,,

A

aliter, alias, 125, 144, 146, 148
Alte, Mr. commencement of curacy, 267
 ,, age of, 280
ancient professor, 153
anonimus, 212

B

bachelor of divinity, 139
Bamford great mortality, 320, 321
banns, 171
baptisms not at Bury, 242, Thomas Whitehead
baptism or burial out of place, 355, John Both
barn, woman dying in, 155
betrothed, 182
birth date of 278, Anne Brooke
borne of a barowe, 300
blacksmith, 350
boy [see also "poor"], 153
burial husband and wife, 337
burial or baptism out of place, 355, John Both
buried at, churches other than Bury, 155, 158, 160, 161
Bury school, gift to, 324
butcher, 96, 211, 295, 298

C

captain, 349
carrier, 149
cavallier, 344*
ch [church], 152
chancell, 310
chapel, 145,* 160, 161
child without christian or surname, 303
churchwarden, 26, 29, 36, 40, 44, 47, 51, 59, 63, 68, 114, 116, 122, 126, 129, 132, 141, 150, 158, 178, 179, 182, 184, 186, 192, 193, 194, 201, 334
clerk, 67, 71
clericus [clicu], 44, 45, 122, 129, 138, 178, 186, 191
cockle [? a place name], 161
collier, 71, 74, 76,* 77, 79, 80, 83, 88, 160, 201, 208, 212, 282, 352
cook, 67
cripple, 105, 121, 300
curate, 26, 29, 32, 36, 40, 44, 47, 51, 55, 59, 63, 64, 71, 78, 114, 116, 119, 126, 129, 132, 134, 138, 141, 143, 144, 158, 178, 179, 181, 182, 184, 186, 187, 189, 191, 192, 193, 194, 201, 236, 239, 242,* 253, 256, 257, 258, 260, 261, 263, 266,* 311, 325, 327, 330, 332, 334, 336, 365, 367,* 368,* 369

D

d [debitum], 150, 151, 155
de eadem, 94
Dikar, The, of Holcome 296,
drowned, 158, 281*

E

e [ecclesia], 149 to 168
Easter day, 72
Elder the, 342
eodem die, 193
esquire, 64, 143, 161, 206, 218, 224, 247, 266, 296
exiled from Halifax, 342

F

famous, 161
fees given, 143
Festo Bartholomei, 215
filius [filia], passim
filiolus, 148*
fitter, 297
found dead, 306,* 308

```
Vol. 1.—C.  .  pp.   1— 90 inclusive.   Vol. 2.—C.  .   pp. 205—280 inclusive.
         B.  .   „   91—168       „              B.  .   „  281—350       „
         W.  .   „  169—204       „              W.  .   „  351—372       „
```

G

g [? given], 149 to 168
gemelli [gemini], 69, 87, 88, 149, 157,
    208, 209, 215, 216,* 261, 263,
    279, 280
generosus, 62, 71, 129
gentleman [gent], 227, 235, 255, 264,
    309, 310, 323, 344
given, 144,* 149
glazier, 84
godly man, a very, 312, 342, 350
grandfathers name given as well as
    father, 210
gto, 144
gracious woman, 339

I

illegitime, 199
infans, 146,* 151
infant, passim
Irish traveler, child of, 338

J

Jinnie used as christian name, 298
Johns of George, a child of, 301
joiner, 163
jugulatus [see murdered], 327, 350
junior, 4, 54, 208, 209, 241, 255, 268,
    288, 300, 314, 339, 340,* 350

L

licence, 199
licensed without banns, 171
lieutenant, 285, 289
limer, 166
longevity, 337

M

M [Mortuary], 143 to 163
Madame, 335
Maid [see "poor"], 139
"maried I know not wheare" 351
maried by William Rausthorne, 351
mark, passim
married by, 187
master in arts, 345
minister, 255, 276, 278, 329, 338, 340,
    343, 347, 349, 350
mortuary, 143 to 163
Mr., 7, 8, 10, 14, 15, 27, 53, 64, 90,
    92, 94, 95, 102, 107, 109, 114,
    127, 136, 139,* 143, 155, 158,

Mr., *continued*—
    160, 164, 167, 176, 220, 221,
    224, 227,* 230, 231, 234,* 238,
    242, 245, 247, 253,* 254,
    255, 256, 257, 260, 263, 264,
    265, 266, 267, 269, 276, 277,
    282, 283, 289, 296,* 298, 308,
    309, 310, 313, 317, 319, 320,
    321, 323, 324,* 325,* 327,
    328, 331, 333, 335, 337, 338,
    339,* 340, 342,* 343,* 350,*
    364,* 367, 369, 372
Mrs., 95, 104, 105, 113, 323, 325, 328,
    348, 344* 364*
murdered "jugulatus," 327, 350

N

name, passim
nescio cognomen, 8, 9
nil, 144
north, 145, 160
not paid, 144

O

occisus, 147
old, 105, 106, 113, 191
old maid, 147
old man, 296
one, 98, 105, 110*
one of the Howarths, 299
"ould," 300
out of book, 197
over [ou'], 98

P

p [parish] passim
p [per] passim
paied [paid], 248
painful preacher, 160
parson [pso], 10, 64, 105, 224, 227,
    231, 247, 298, 219
parsonage house, 342
pastor, 280
pd [paid], 151 to 168, 248
peregrinus [pegin], 71
pious woman, 350
poor boy, 162
poor child, 300, 301, 306
poore criple, 300
poor folks, 108
poor lame man, 145
poor lame woman, 145
poor maid, 144, 148
poor passenger, 149, 150, 165

INDEX OF TRADES, Etc.

Vol. 1.—C. . pp. 1—90 inclusive. Vol. 2.—C. . pp. 205—280 inclusive.
B. . ,, 91—168 ,, B. . ,, 281—350 ,,
W. . ,, 169—204 ,, W. . ,, 351—372 ,,

poor woman, 94, 95,* 98, 149, 150, 155, 161, 162
posthumus, 276
preacher [p'acher], 160, 164
professor [pfessor], 153
,, a very zealous, 343
,, ancient, 350

R

rector, 68, 71, 73, 77, 78, 89, 150, 158, 201, 234, 238
reputed father, 28
Roger of Holcom, 321

S

said, 11, 98, 134
saxton, 341
school [see Bury school]
senior, 94, 207, 211, 242, 270, 271, 278, 339, 340
servant woman, 328
sher [? meaning], 236
shoemaker, 110
since Easter, 144
since my account, 143*
sine baptismo, 146
single woman, 151, 160
smith, 159, 161
south, 145
sojourning at Heywood, 341, 342
sojourning at ye parsonage house, 342
soldier, 343, 344,* 350
soldier murdered, 350
spinster, 152
spuria, 152
spurius [spurious], 156, 161, 212, 252
stabbed, 344
stranger, 12, 145, 344
supposed, 20, 36, 99
surgeon, 102, 136

surnames used as Christian names, 251 (Ratcliffe), 277 (Ratcliffe), 311 (Ratcliffe), 338 (Ratcliffe), 360 (Ashton)

T

tailor, 69, 337
templum, 145*
teste me, 158, 161, 201
three children buried, 315
trike, 150
triplets, 230, 241, 246 (here described as "twins")
twinles, 247
twins, 89, 166, 206, 207, 212, 244, 246, 264,* 266,* 268, 273, 275, 316*

U

uxor [vx'] passim

V

vicar, 338, 372
vicarage Halifax, 341, 342
vidua, passim
vulgo, 148

W

waller, 201
wanderer, 150, 281
widow passim
woman cripple, 105
wrong priest, 349

Y

younger, youngest, 33, 37, 41, 95, 108, 117, 344
young man, 148
youth of great promise, 345

Episcopal Transcripts.

CHRISTENINGS.

PAGE OF THIS VOL.	DATE.	BURY REGISTER.	EPISCOPAL TRANSCRIPT.
210	31 Jan	Richear son	Mary d.
,,	21 March	Benson	ffenton
211	23 April	Awdry	Alice
,,	26 ,,	Seddon	Holte
212	2 October	Mary	Thomas
,,	5 Nov'	Easter	Sarah
213	20 February	Hames	Hamer
214	8 May		Alice d. of Thomas Nuttall
,,	2 July		Henry s. of Abraham Cowpe Smyth
,,	11 August	(1st entry of this date) Smethurst after last entry	Richard s. of Edmond Leach
216	25 March		Ellen d. of Matthew Bury
217	16 May	(3rd entry of this date) John son	Jane d.
219	27 Jan		B. Anne d. of Willm Heald & Ellen Oldham
,,	28 Feb	Brearley	Bury
220	21 April	before this date...	. . s. of John Croston of Elton 25 March . s. of Richard Dauemporte 25 March . s. of Josephe Holte 25 March . s. of Edmond Turner 25 March . d. of Matthew Bury 25 March James s. of Edmonde Wilde 1 April James s. of Richard ffletcher 1 April James s. of James Lomax 1 April Dorothy d. of Thomas Rushton 1 April Peter s. of Peter Cloughe 2 April Edmund s. of James Hauworthe & Ann Besweeke 3 April

EPISCOPAL TRANSCRIPTS.

Page of this vol.	Date.	Bury Register.	Episcopal Transcript.
220	21 April	before this date ...	Richard s. of John Bageley & Isabell Heald of Redivalles 7 April
			Ann d. of John Holte 8 April
			. . s. of Robert Nab 8 April
			. . d. of Richard Nuttall 8 April
			. d. of Richard Allens 15 April
			. s. of James Holte 15 April
			. William Healde 15 April
			. s. of Roger Pilkington 15 April

[These entries are incomplete through the parchment being torn away].

220	21 April	Imn ...	Eme daughter
,,	5 May	Cropper ...	Cowper
,,	9 June	James ...	John
,,	27 ,,	after this date ...	Ann d. of James Kaye
,,	11 August	Hugh Watmoughe	Parson of Bury [in margin]
,,	,, ,,	...	Richard son of Xpofer Cunliff
221	3 Octob	Ellen d. of ...	Ellen & Jane d.
,,	6 ,,	Howorthe ...	Holte
,,	3 November	Asheworthe ...	Leach
,,	26 January	after this date ...	Ann d. of Thomas Walker 2 February
,,	13 March	Isabell ...	Elizabeth
223	25 Aprill	Road Elt ...	Wood Road
224	29 July	Brandlsō ...	Elton
,,	12 September	Sutlworthe	Walmersley
,,	12 Dec'	Tott ...	Crouchlowe
,,	23 Jan	Widdell ...	Elton
,,	,, ,,	Boulton ...	Wal
225	6 Feb	Roger son ...	Richard son
,,	,, ,,	Burie ...	Heap
,,	6 March	(6th entry of this date) Elton ...	Holcombe
,,	24 April	Broomle of Heape	Broome of Burie
,,	1 May	Scole ...	Stotte
226	26 ,,	Tottington ...	Hol
,,	23 June	after 3rd entry of this date ...	Raphe son of James Lyvsey of Heape 23 June
,,	4 Sept	Lawrance ...	Ellis
,,	18 ,,	Tottington	Hol
227	30 Nov	Martyne ...	Richard
,,	5 March	Midlto ...	Broadcocke

Page of this Vol.	Date.	Bury Register.	Episcopal Transcript.
228	19 March	Suttlworthe	Wal
229	20 August	little Bridge	Buriham
,,	,, ,,	Holcom	Moss
,,	1 November	Buriha	Chesham
230	9 December	daughters	twins
,,	14 Januarij	Facid	Wal
,,	28 ,,	(5th entry of this date) Holcome	Elton
,,	18 Februarij	(9th entry of this date) Tott	Bury
231	18 March	after Mr.	George
,,	24 April	Burihamell	Heape
,,	29 ,,	Buriha	Rochdale
232	1 July	Thomas Wood	Richard Wood
,,	24 September	Oswood	Wood
,,	30 ,,	Francis son	Francis dau'
233	11 November	Isherworthe	Isherwood
,,	24 Februarij	Richard	Thomas
234	6 March	after Butterfield	of Bolton
,,	23 ,,	Tottington	Holcome
,,	20 April	Satleworthe	Shuttleworth
,,	11 Maij	Gosforthe	Whamersley
,,	1 Julij	Jonas	James
235	10 Auguste	Hunte	Hoult
,,	,, ,,	Brandlesome gent	Gristlehurst Esq
236	28 December	Furnas	Fournaca
242	27 March	after Bamford	Gent
243	3 July	(2nd entry) N.X.N.	Anne
,,	7 August	(2nd entry) after Jane	d. of Roger *
,,	14 ,,	Rey	Kaye
,,	,, ,,	Ane	Alice
,,	11 September	Kary	Bury
244	22 January	Raph	Richard
,,	29 ,,	Mary	Grace
,,	26 February	Rey	Kaye
,,	4 March	Ashwood	Ashworthe
245	7 October	Elizabeth	Marie
,,	18 November	Roger	Richard
246	23 December	Warburton	Barlow
,,	10 February	Birkle	Bury
,,	24 ,,	Cowp	Hopwood
,,	3 March	Ashworth	Hawarth
247	28 July	Jonie	Jane

* An attempt to erase these three words has been made, but they are perfectly legible.

EPISCOPAL TRANSCRIPTS.

457

PAGE OF THIS VOL.	DATE.	BURY REGISTER.	EPISCOPAL TRANSCRIPT.
248	22 Sept	after this date ...	Elin d. of William Hitchinson 13 Oct
			John s. of Jerime Ensworth
			Hen s. of Ralfe Bridge
			John s. of Thomas Turner 27 Oct
			Alice d. of Samuel Macon
			Thomas s. of William Kay
			John s. of Thomas Whamerbie
			John s. of Thomas Warburton 3 Nov
			Thom s. of John Brooke
			Rich s. of Jam Yate 17 Nov'
			John s. of John Bridge
			Sarah d. of John Greenall 1 Dec'
			Asher s. of Thomas Woulmer
			Alice d. of James Hartlie 5 Jan
			John s. of John Stott
			John s. of James Romsbothame
			Ginet d. of George Heworth 9 March
			Richard s. of Giles Vnsworth
249	6 April	after Holt	of Holcom
,,	13 ,,	after Lomax ...	of Tott
,,	,, ,,	Tott	Holc
,,	,, ,,	after 3rd entry of this date ...	Marie d. of John Warberton de Tott 13 April
,,	14 May ...	after Thomas ...	Warberton de Holc
,,	25 ,, ...	after Rostron ...	de Holc
,,	,, ,, ...	after 4th entry of this date ...	Elizabeth d. of Roger Seddon 1 June
250	June	(3rd entry from top) after Bentlie	of Haslomhey
,,	,,	(4th entry from top) after Holt	of Haslomhey
,,	13 Julie ...	of Redivalls ...	de Burie
,,	20 ,, ...	after Hamer ...	de Walmsley
,,	27 ,, ...	after Millnes ...	de Burie
,,	10 August ...	after Johnes ...	of Heape
,,	,, ,, ...	after Edm	Holt de Edenfeild
,,	17 ,, ...	after Willm ...	Holt de Holc
,,	,, ,, ...	(blank) of Houl...	Willm Booth de Holc
,,	31 ,, ...	after Greenhalghe	of Tott
,,	2 November	after Brook ...	de Burie
,,	16 ,, ...	after Hopwood ...	of Asheworth

Page of this vol.	Date.	Bury Register.	Episcopal Transcript.
251	1 March	after Ainsworth...	de Tott
,,	,, ,,	after Wilson	de Tott
252	13 September	Henry	James
255	2 October	Martincroft	Marcroft
,,	9 ,,	James Holt	John Holt
,,	30 ,,	no surname	Lion
,,	8 January	Matorcroft	Maircroft
256	3 April	after Rausthorne	Gentl
257	27 Aug	Mr. Rothwell Curat	Mr. William Rothwell Clef
258	24 Dec^r	Francis	Francis
260	21 Oct	(3rd entry) John	James
263	26 Jany	(3rd entry) Edward	Edmund
266	21 Maij	(2nd entry) Bidd	Bridd
,,	,, ,,	after Hardman	of Bury
,,	3 June	Barlow	Holt
,,	22 ,,	Walten	Walker
,,	9 Sept	Grenne	Greenehalgh

BURIALS.

281	23 April	Cowap	Cowpe
,,	16 May	Ellis son	Elizab daug.
291	6 December	Ric	Edmond
292	20 May	James	Thomas
293	27 August	N.X.N.	Elizabeth
294	10 Feb	Cooperes	Cropp
295	24 Dec^r	Ellis	Richard
296	10 Jan	The Dikar of Holcome	omitted
,,	,, ,,		Richard Rothwell
,,	30 ,,	dau.	wife
302	3 April	Josephe	John
,,	,, ,,	Walmersley	Tottington
,,	11 ,,	Litle Bridge	Heap
,,	5 June	The wife	Alice the wife
303	26 Julij	after Bamford	Gent
,,	6 Nouember	Banclaine	Wal
,,	12 ,,	Hurle	Hunt
,,	21 ,,	Tottington	Holcombe
,,	23 December	Tott	Hol
304	29 Marche	James	John
305	3 Julij	Flom	Elton
,,	8 August	Ann Wilson of Holcome	Ann wife of John Wilson
,,	21 ,,	Burie	Holcome
,,	24 October	dau.	wife

EPISCOPAL TRANSCRIPTS.

PAGE OF THIS VOL.	DATE.	BURY REGISTER.	EPISCOPAL TRANSCRIPT.
306	10 April	Greane	Greave
,,	12 ,,	Chatterton	Etenfield
307	28 June	Houghe	Wal
,,	24 Julij	Tottingtō	Hol
,,	13 Auguste	Burie	Red
,,	16 October	Etenfeild	Suttleworth
308	12 December	Bentilee	Wal
,,	,, ,,	Fletcher	Haslam
309	3 Julij	Grinhill	Walmersley
,,	28 ,,	after Brandlsome	Esquire
,,	31 ,,	after Elisabethe...	wife
,,	13 Auguste	The wiffe	Ann the wiffe
,,	17 November	Isherwood	Isherworthe
,,	,, ,,	Tottington	Holcome
,,	29 Januarij	Ollerbothom	Etenfeild
310	10 March	after Buriham	Gentleman
,,	23 ,,	Lumcare	Holcome
,,	16 June	Haughshaw layne	Tottington
,,	23 July	Brandlesom	Cristlehurst
311	7 January	Jone	Jane
,,	26 February	Jone	Jane
,,	4 March	Washy lane	Tottington
316	3 October	Buys	Bury
317	27 Dec⁺	Washe	Walshey
,,	2 January	Washe	Walshey
,,	15 ,,	Reys	Keys
319	14 April	Benle	Berckle
,,	26 ,,	Benle	Berckle
320	22 Sept	after this date	A Child of John Barlow of this town 24 Sep
			The wif of Lenard Gest of this hamell 28 Sep
			A Child of James Gests of this ham 30 Sep
			The wif of Cersto Smethurst 6 Oct
			George Vnsworth of this hamell 12 Oct
			The wife of John Wilde of Heape 16 Oct
			Roge Kaye of Horneclife 19 Oct
			A child of Jarvise Greenhalghe of Tot 21 Oct
			Richard Holt of Holcome 23 Oct
			John Lomas of Berch hey 24 Oct
			A child of Ann Holilese 26 Oct

Page of this vol.	Date.	Bury Register.	Episcopal Transcript.
320	22 Sept	after this date ...	A child of Richard Hithinsonne 26 Oct
			Richard Nuttall of Holcom 29 Oct
			The wif Richard Nuttall of Houlcome 7 Nov
			George Warbertonn 27 Nov
			Alice Warbertonn 3 Dec
			James Crompton of Heywood 14 Dec
			The wife of Henery Crosle 30 Dec
			Richard Seddon 1 Jan:
			Saraw Bath of this hamell 5 Jan
			The wife of Henery Cunlife
			Rafe Wousencroft 14 Jan
			The wife of Thomas Bridge 18 Jan
			A child of Peter Lomax 21 Jan
			Oliuer Booth 24 Jan
			The wife of Hadocke 26 Jan
			John Kaye of Wamersle 30 Jan
			John Hamer of Wamersle
			Eliz Didgle 2 Feb
,,	6 Feb	after this date ...	A child of Thomas Booth of Holl 9 Feb
			Cater Kay of Wamersle 17 Feb
			Frances Kay of Wamersle 20 Feb
			A child of John Nabb 22 Feb
			Mary Taylor 29 Feb
			Henry Prescod 12 Mch
			Caterine Blawclo 21 Mch
,,	26 April	... Ric Holt	vxor of Ric Holt
,,	9 June	... Longworth ...	Howarth
321	4 July	... He:	Holc
,,	3 Nov^r	... G^r	Gryme
,,	9 ,,	... after this entry ...	vxor of Jeremie Barlowe
,,	31 Dec^r	... after Barlow ...	de Holcom
,,	14 Jany	... after Stott ...	de Heywood
,,	16 ,,	... after Rostron ...	de Summerseat
,,	18 ,,	... after Jackson ...	de Burie
322	4 Feby	... after Royley ...	of Burie
,,	7 ,,	... after Kaie	of Burie
,,	17 , ,,	... after Fenton ...	of Burie
,,	,, ,,	... after this date ...	Raph Nuttall de Tottington
,,	2 March	... after Shepherd ...	de Chesham

EPISCOPAL TRANSCRIPTS. 461

PAGE OF THIS VOL.	DATE.	BURY REGISTER.	EPISCOPAL TRANSCRIPT.
322	2 March	after this date ...	A child of James Jackson de Burie 5 March
,,	7 ,,	after Kaie	de Elton
,,	10 ,,	Leach	Reade de Redivalls
,,	12 ,, ...	Heald	de Burie
323	26 August ...	Tayler	Sayle [?]
326	13 Dec' ...	Walm	Rainforfeild
328	12 Sept ...	Coptill	Coxhill
329	26 Jany ...	child	William
,,	10 Febr ...	Lawrance Haslom	Lawrance Haslom
331	3 November	after Rigby ...	of Whittle
332	29 Jany	John	Robert
,,	27 August ...	(2nd entry) Elizabeth ...	Elizabeth
333	25 Nov'	Peter son	Peter son
337	16 Aug	after last entry ...	A child of Thomas Turton de Bury
,,	18 Sept	after Kay ...	de Bury
,,	18 Nov'	Mary	Mary

WEDDINGS.

351	9 June ...	George Mane [?]	George Manne
352	31 April ...	James Greaue ...	James Greave
,,	8 Nov' ...	Cowap	Cowpe
354	3 June ...	Rausthorne ...	Nuttall
,,	3 Sept ...	Noble [? Nab] ...	Noble
,,	13 Nov' ...	Hamer ...	Haworth
,,	15 ,, ...	Pilking ...	Pillinge
356	14 September	no surname	Bouthe
,,	21 November	no surname	Cronkeshawe
357	22 May ...	Jane Kaie ...	Jane Bcuthe
359	4 November	no surname	Rothwell
,,	15 Aprill ...	Fogge ...	Fox
,,	22 June ...	Casson ...	Mason
,,	24 ,, ...	Sickes ...	Stock
360	19 November	Bromley ...	Burnley
,,	16 February	no surname	Kaie
362	23 April ...	Rachdale pish ...	both of this pish
,,	31 Jany ...	Lees	Gee
363	14 Aug ...	Orell	Orwell
,,	15 Sept ...	(4th entry of this date) Margret	Alice
,,	,, ,,	after 3rd entry of this date ...	Robert Hamer of Rachdale pish Jone Howworth of this pish 26 Dec

Y

Page of this vol.	Date	Bury Register.	Episcopal Transcript.
			John Kay & Mary Didgle both of this pish 9 Feb
			John Bar . . . & Mary Pilkington both of this parish 25 Feb
			James Crompton of Boulton & Eliz: Holt of tnis pish 5 Mch
,,	29 April	Bellett	Pallet
364	17 Oct	after Telior ...	de parish of Halsall
,,	15 Dec^r	after this date ...	Robte Horrobine & Marie Nuttall
,,	7 Jany	after this date ...	Roger Nuttall & Margaret Graue 7 Feby
366	26 May	Coup	Coup
368	25 July	no surname ...	Robinson
,,		at end of year 1639	Thomas Barlow ⎫ John Booth ⎪ George Howorth ⎬ Churchwardens Hennry Hardman ⎪ Arthur Kaie ⎪ Francis Shipobothom ⎭
369		at end of year 1641	William Alte Minister

Index to Episcopal Transcripts.

I.

CHRISTIAN NAMES AND SURNAMES.

A

AINSWORTH, Jeremy, 457
,, John, 457
Allen, N.X.N., 455
,, Richard, 455
Alt, William, 462

B

BAGULEY, John, 455
,, Richard, 455
Bannister, Mary, 454
Bar . ., John, 462
Barlow, Jeremy, w. of 460
,, John, c. of 459
,, Mary, 456
,, Thomas, 456, 462
Bath [? Booth], Sarah, 460
Beswicke, Ann, 454
,, Edmund, 454
Bird, Marie, 458
,, Thomas, 458
Blacklow, Catherine, 460
Booth, Alice, 456, 458
,, Elizabeth, 461
,, Francis, 458
,, Grace, 456
,, Jane, 461
,, John, 462
,, Oliver, 460
,, Roger, 456
,, Thomas, c. of 460
,, William, 457
Bridge, Henry, 457
,, John, 457*
,, Ralph, 457
,, Thomas, w. of 460
Brooke, John, 457
,, Thomas, 457
Broome, John, 455
,, Humphrey, 455
Bury, Ellen, 454
,, James, 458
,, Katherine, 456
,, Mary, 454
,, Matthew, 454*
,, N.X.N., 454

Bury, Richard, 454
,, Robert, 456
,, William, c. of 459

C

CLOUGH, Peter, 454*
Cowpe, Abraham, 454
,, Henry, 454
,, John, 458
,, Margaret, 462
,, Peter, 454
Cowper, John, 455*
Coxhill, Robert, c. of 454
Crompton, James, 460, 462
,, Jane, 454
Cronshaw, Elizabeth, 461
Cropper, James, c. of 458
Crossley, Henry, w. of 460
Croston, James, 456
,, John, 454
,, N.X.N., 454
Cunliffe, Christopher, 455
,, Henry, w. of 460
,, Richard, 455

D

DAVENPORT, N.X.N., 454
,, Richard, 454
Diggle, Elizabeth, 460
,, Mary 462

E

ELTON, Susan, 458

F

FENTON, James, 454
,, Edmund, 454
Fletcher, Elizabeth, 458
,, James, 454
,, Richard, 454
,, Thomas, 456
Fox, Alice, 461

G

Gee, Mary, 461
Geste, Jas., c. of 459
,, Leonard, w. of 459
Greave, Margaret, 462
,, James, 461
,, John, 459
Greenhalgh, Dorothy, 458
,, Ellen, 458
,, John, 457
,, Gervase, c. of 459
,, Sarah, 457
Grime, Richard, w. of 460

H

Haddock, N.X.N., w. of 460
Hamer, Ann, 459
,, Jane, 454
,, John, 454, 460
,, Robert, 461
Hardman, Henry, 462
Hartley, Alice, 457
,, James, 457
Haslam, Lawrence, c. of 459, 461
,, Richard, 458
Haworth, Edmund, 454
,, Elizabeth, 461
,, Ellis, 455
,, George, 456, 457, 462
,, James, 454
,, Jennet, 456, 457
,, Joan, 461
,, John, c. of 460
Heald, Ann, 454
,, Isabel, 455
,, N.X.N., 455
,, Richard, 455
,, William, 454, 455
Heaton, Ann, 456
Heywood, Thomas, 454
Holliley, Ann, c. of 459
Holt, Ann, 455
,, Edmund, 454, 457, 458
,, Elizabeth, 457, 462
,, James, 455
,, John, 455,* 458*
,, Joseph, 454
,, Mary, 455, 461
,, N.X.N., 454, 455
,, Oliver, 456
,, Richard, 456, 459, w. of 460
,, Robert, 455, 458
,, Sarah, 454
,, William, 457, 458
Hopwood, Richard, 455
,, Susan, 456*
Horobin, Robert, 462
Hull, Alice, 461

Hunt, Elizabeth, 458
,, Margaret, 458
Hutchinson, Ellen, 457
,, Richard, c. of 460
,, William, 457

J

Jackson, James, c. of 461

K

Kay, Ann, 455
,, Arthur, 462
,, Catherine, 460
,, Elizabeth, 455, 456
,, Francis, 460
,, James, 455
,, John, 456, c. of 459, 460, 462
,, Margaret, 461
,, Richard, 455, 456*
,, Roger, 459
,, Thomas, 457, 458
,, William, 457

L

Law, Sarah, 454
Leach, Edmund, 454, 458
,, Elizabeth, 455
,, Leonard, 455
,, Richard, 454
Lion, Henry, 458*
Livsey, James, 455
,, Ralph, 455
Lomax, James, 454*
,, John, 459
,, Peter, c. of 460

M

Makin, Alice, 457
,, Samuel, 457
Manne, George, 461
Marcroft, Mary, 458
,, Robert, 458
Mason, Ellen, 461
Murrey, George, 456

N

Nabb, John, 458, c. of 460
,, Marie, 456
,, N.X.N., 455
,, Robert, 455
Noble, Elizabeth, 461
Nuttall, Alice, 454
,, Marie, 456, 462
,, N.X.N., 455
,, Ralph, 460

Nuttall, Richard, 455, 460, w. of 460, 461
" Roger, 462
" Thomas, 454

O

OLDHAM, Ann, 454
" Ellen, 454
Ormerod, Robert, 461
Orwell, Ann, 461

P

PALLET, John, 462
Partington, Jane, 459
Pilkington, Mary, 462
" N.X.N., 455
" Roger, 455
Pilling, Ann, 461
Prescott, Henry, 460

R

RAWSTORNE, Ellen, 455
" Jane, 455
Reade, Robert, c. of 461
Robinson, Elizabeth, 462
Romsbotham, Alice, 454
" James, 457
" John, 457
Rothwell, Isabell, 461
" Mr., 458
" Richard, 458
" William, 458, 461
Rushton, Dorothy, 454
" Thomas, 454

S

SALE, Elizabeth, 461
Seddon, Elizabeth, 457
" Richard, 456, 460
" Roger, 457
Shepherd, Jane, 456
Shippobotham, Francis, 462
Smethurst, Christopher, w. of 459
Smith, Robert, 454
" Roger, 454

Stock, John, 461
Stones, Jane, 459
Stott, John, 455,* 457*

T

TAYLOR, Mary, 460
Turner, Edmund, 454
" John, 457
" N.X.N., 454
" Thomas, 457
Turton, Thomas, c. of 461

U

UNSWORTH, George, 459
" Giles, 457
" Richard, 457

W

WALKER, Ann, 455
" Thomas, 455, 458*
Warburton, Alice, 460
" George, 460
" John, 457*
" Jonathan, 457
" Marie, 457
" Thomas, 457*
Wharmby, John, 457
" Thomas, 457
Whittaker, James, 458*
Wilde, Edmund, 454
" James, 454
" John, w. of 459
Wilson, Ann, 458
" John, 458
Wood, Marie, 456
" Richard, 456
Woolner, Asher, 457
" Thomas, 457
Wolstencrofte, Ralph, 460
Wolstenholme, Eme, 455

Y

YATES, James, 457
" Richard, 457

Index to Episcopal Transcripts.

II.
PLACES.

[All the names except those in *Italics* are within Bury Parish.]

A

Ashworth, 456, 457

B

BIRCH HEY, 459
Birtle, 459*
Bolton, 456, 462
Broad Oake, 455
Burnley, 461
Bury, 455,* 456,* 457,* 458, 459, 460,* 461,* 462*
Bury Hamlet, 456, 459,* 460
Bury Parish, 461,* 462*

C

CHESHAM, 456, 460
Croitshlawe, 455

E

EDENFIELD, 457, 459*
Elton, 454, 455,* 456, 461

G

GRISTLEHURSTE, 456, 459

H

Halsall Parish, 462
Haslam Hey, 457*

Heap, 455,* 456, 457, 458, 459
Heywood, 460*
Holcome, 455,* 456, 457,* 458,* 459,* 460*
Horncliffe, 459

M

MOSSE, 456

R

RAINFORFEILD, 461
Redivales, 455, 459, 461
Rochdale, 456
Rochdale Parish, 461

S

SHUTTLEWORTH, 456, 459
Summerseat, 460

T

TOTTINGTON, 457,* 458,* 459,* 460
Town, This, 459

W

WALMERSLEY, 455,* 456,* 457, 458, 459,* 460*
Walshey, 459*
Whittle, 461
Woodroad, 455

III.
DESCRIPTIONS, ETC.

C

CHURCHWARDEN, 462
Clericus, 458

E

ESQUIRE, 456, 459

G

GENTLEMAN, 456, 458,* 459

M

MINISTER, 462

P

PARSON of BURY, 455

T

TWINS, 456

Errata.

Page 211, 16 May, (2nd entry), *for* 'Banklam' *read* 'Banklane.'
,, 215, 7 Jan (2nd entry), *for* 'Whitchad' *read* 'Whitehead.'
,, 219, 3 March (2nd entry), *for* 'Fancis' *read* 'Francis.'
,, 237, 29 March, *for* 'Fo. 28' *read* 'Fo. 82.'
,, 245, 10 June (2nd entry), *for* 'Emersome' *read* 'Emersone.'
,, 246, 28 January, *for* 'Margeris' *read* 'Margerie.'
,, 257, 21 July, *for* 'Jarnice' *read* 'Jaruice.'
,, 272, 2 Dec^r *for* 'Rolt' *read* 'Robt.'
,, 282, 6 Dec^r *for* 'Shephen' *read* 'Stephen.'
    [Therefore in Index at "Steven, John," insert p. 282, also insert Steven, Ellen, p. 282 and delete "Shephen, Ellen and John," on p. 428 of Index.]
,, 311, 29 January, Ellen Medowcroft.
    [This page-number 311 is omitted against Ellen Medowcroft's name in Index.]
,, 313, 8 August, *for* 'Walmelsrey' *read* 'Walmersley.'
,, 324, 2 February, *for* 'dedid' *read* 'dedit.'
,, 338, 8 March, *for* 'Naabs' *read* 'Nabbs.'
,, 343, 7 Feby. *for* 'Dumster' *read* 'Dunster.'
,, 354 24 May, James Holt.
    [This page-number 354 is omitted against James Holt's name in Index.]
,, 363, 15 Sept (4th entry), *for* 'Bockome' *read* 'Beckome.'
,, 367, 30 Jany, Margaret (Scoles) Scholes.
    [After this entry on p. 426 of Index delete Nos. 3, 67, and insert p. 367.]
,, 369, December (3rd entry), *for* 'Chadwich' *read* 'Chadwicke.'
,, 371, top of page, *for* '1644-1646' *read* '1644-1645.'
,, 372, top of page, *for* '1649' *read* '1646.'

www.ingramcontent.com/pod-product-compliance
Lightning Source LLC
Chambersburg PA
CBHW032002230426
43672CB00010B/2246